THE PRESIDENCY IN
THE COURTS

Da Capo Press Reprints in

AMERICAN CONSTITUTIONAL AND LEGAL HISTORY

GENERAL EDITOR: LEONARD W. LEVY

Claremont Graduate School

THE PRESIDENCY IN
THE COURTS

By

Glendon A. Schubert, Jr.

DA CAPO PRESS • NEW YORK • 1973

Library of Congress Cataloging in Publication Data

Schubert, Glendon A
  The Presidency in the courts.

  (American constitutional and legal history)
  1. Executive power—United States. 2. Judicial
review—United States. I. Title.
[KF5050.S35   1973]   342'.73'062   72-8122
ISBN 0-306-70529-X

This Da Capo Press edition of
The Presidency in the Courts
is an unabridged republication of the
first edition published in Minneapolis
in 1957. It is reprinted by special
arrangement with the University of
Minnesota Press.

Published by Da Capo Press, Inc.
A Subsidiary of Plenum Publishing Corporation
227 West 17th Street, New York, New York 10011

Manufactured in the United States of America

The Presidency in the Courts

THE PRESIDENCY IN
THE COURTS

Glendon A. Schubert, Jr.

UNIVERSITY OF MINNESOTA PRESS, Minneapolis

To Betty

Preface

SINCE this book has been worked on and worked over for almost a decade, there have been a number of persons from whose advice and encouragement I have benefited at various stages of preparation. Helpful suggestions bearing on the substance of the study have come from Professor Spencer Parratt of Syracuse University; my erstwhile colleagues, Professors Foster Sherwood, Thomas Jenkin, and Russell Fitzgibbon, all of the Department of Political Science of the University of California at Los Angeles; Professor David Fellman of the University of Wisconsin; Professor Earl Latham of Amherst College; and Professor C. Herman Pritchett of the University of Chicago. I have profited much from discussions about the book with former Dean Paul H. Appleby of the Maxwell School of Syracuse University, the late Mr. Justice Robert H. Jackson, and Mr. Lyman Windolph of Lancaster, Pennsylvania.

My former colleague, Professor Nelson Francis of the Department of English of Franklin and Marshall College, generously consented to read through an earlier draft of the manuscript; although his comments and suggestions regarding matters of style may not have succeeded in making the work readable, they certainly have made it less prolix than were my pristine endeavors. Several of my present or former graduate students have helped to prepare the manuscript for publication, including Mr. George Kantrowitz of the University of Pittsburgh, Miss Margaret Fuller of Michigan State University, and

M. Augustine Nguyen-Thai of Saigon, Viet-Nam. The Table of Cases was done by Miss Paula Irving of Michigan State University. The final draft of the manuscript was typed through the courtesy of the Department of Political Science of Michigan State University, by the competent hands of Miss Barbara Guthrie.

My wife, Betty Harris Schubert, has indulged this insatiable enterprise for many years; her patience and faith have been a constant source of encouragement.

If such friends and helpmates have not enjoyed complete success in their efforts to dissuade me from committing iniquities in the pages that follow, surely they should be absolved from responsibility for such shortcomings as may have escaped them.

GLENDON A. SCHUBERT, JR.

East Lansing, Michigan
November 30, 1956

Table of Contents

ix

Table of Contents

Appendixes

The Presidency in the Courts

CHAPTER

1

Introduction

EVERY schoolboy knows that democracy in the United States is dedicated to the proposition that the President wields executive power, the Congress has legislative power, and the judiciary, judicial power.[1] This work is a study in the powers of the Presidency, as seen through the eyes of the courts. Its purpose is not to describe what the President can do and does, but rather what the judges *say* he can do. It is, therefore, primarily an analysis of judicial behavior, even though its unifying theme is executive behavior. It is based on an examination of traditional materials by orthodox methods of legal analysis, although these materials are combined under political rather than legal concepts to support specific findings and generalizations that are new.

It is a study of both constitutional and administrative law in the area where the overlap of these two differently defined branches of public law is greatest. An examination of any casebook in either subject reveals the startling fact that the law of the presidency appears fragmentary and brief, as though the gloss of sixteen decades had added little to the patently economical language of the Constitution itself. In spite of the light that beats upon the Throne — and it certainly shines upon our Chief Executive as well — it may be said without too much exaggeration that the judicial formulation of the institutional role of the President is the Dark Continent of our public law. Certainly, this seeming neglect is not a reflection of the relative significance of the subject. Not only the fate of the United States, but the fate of Western civilization will hang in the balance of the American President's exercise of his official powers during the next decade.

Those powers are unquestionably great. The possibility of their abuse needs no demonstration here; neither need we comb history to verify the assumption that totalitarian regimes may come to power by lawful means: yesterday's example of such modern dictators as Mussolini, Hitler, and Huey Long should suffice. On the other hand, there can be little doubt that the people of the United States respect, above all other public officers, their judges — or at least those judges who sit on appellate courts; and most of the time[2] their veneration for the Supreme Court of the United States, is akin to the worship of the Constitution itself. They undoubtedly expect that, should the occasion ever arise, the Supreme Court would uphold the majesty of the law against the pretensions of a usurper. History warns us, however, that this assumption may be false: in every major constitutional crisis between the executive and the judiciary, the President has emerged the victor.[3] The Supreme Court has itself admitted its own ultimate weakness on more than one occasion, as Mr. Justice Jackson reminded us not too long ago in a dissenting opinion where he said:

I would not lead people to rely on this Court for a review that seems to me wholly delusive. . . . If the people ever let command of the war power fall into irresponsible and unscrupulous hands, the courts wield no power equal to its restraint. The chief restraint upon those who command the physical forces of the country, in the future as in the past, must be their responsibility to the political judgments of their contemporaries and to the moral judgments of history.[4]

To admit this much is hardly to deny the importance of the courts in the operation of the American system of governance. The large question remains whether the courts can and do exercise any effective check upon a President who will submit to their authority. If it should be true that in practice the courts fail to exercise such a check, the cause of constitutional democracy may be better served by discarding myths which inhibit the creation of alternative and more realistic approaches to the problem of executive responsibility. The purpose of this study is to provide a partial answer to this fundamental question, by means of a systematic and comprehensive analysis of the opinions and decisions of the courts themselves. No previously published study has undertaken this task.

Introduction

There are obvious limitations inherent in this approach, but certain compensating advantages. It is primarily concerned with presidential legislation and adjudication: presidential proclamations, executive orders, administrative directives and instructions, and the formal approval of regulations, orders, and decisions of subordinate officers that are written or printed in form and to which the President has affixed his signature. It is concerned with these only when someone has challenged the authority of the presidential action before a court of record which has in turn handed down a formal decision, usually accompanied by a written opinion, that has been reported by either an official or a commercial publisher. It therefore cuts across many of the substantive areas of presidential power which may or may not be implemented and reviewed in this manner. A major presidential foreign policy radio address, for instance, is not within its scope; neither is a direct verbal order, a suggestion carried by a presidential administrative assistant, a gesture or remark at a news conference or a Cabinet meeting, or even such a formal and written presidential act as the approval or veto of a legislative act. The rationale for excluding the latter is that it is essentially a facet of a different constitutional question: judicial review of congressional legislation and the legislative process. As to the others, all of these and many other forms may be effective vehicles for carrying the "presidential will" (or the power of the bureaucracy), but there is some justification for the present selection: the implementation of executive power through the form of the executive ordinance has a very long history[5] and it leaves a public record which can be introduced as evidence in a court of law. In addition, the ordinance usually states a rule of more or less general application and has sanctions associated with it so that it partakes of the nature of legislation as we customarily use that term.

Some difficulty arises from the fact that the traditional forms of presidential legislation, the executive order and proclamation, never have been used consistently according to any rational standards of subject matter or purpose. Many Presidents, even since the turn of the present century, have used them quite interchangeably; and the courts have been equally loose in their own terminology, calling what were in fact proclamations "executive orders," and vice versa. Somewhat greater standardization was brought about by the Federal Register Act of 1935,[6] but about all that can be said is that, in general, proclamations have been used for action in the realm of foreign affairs, for ceremonial purposes, and when required by some older statutes as a device for giving public notice and a more widespread distribution to administrative legislation;[7] while executive orders have been preferred where the impact of the ordinance was considered to be primarily internal to the executive branch.

The unique status of the American President, the immunities that attach to his person alone, the direct sources of constitutional power that exist for none of his subordinates, his commanding position as the political leader of the nation, his direct powers in the process of statutory legislation, his power to appoint the judges who are called upon to review his action — all these factors clearly differentiate the President from any other officer in the executive branch of the national government. Therefore the most exhaustive analysis of judicial review of administrative legislation and adjudication may tell us very little about the status of the Chief Executive in the eyes of the courts. The Constitution itself gives the President many powers directly affecting the process of statutory legislation. He periodically recommends legislation; he calls Congress into session to consider urgent business; and his power to withhold his assent to bills is equivalent, even in quantitative terms, to the votes of 289 representatives and 63 senators. It is the President who makes treaties, and since custom has eliminated the rendering of formal senatorial advice, he is certainly the senior partner in this particular legislative function. And all of this is apart from the legislative power inherent in his status as the Commander in Chief, the Chief of State, the Chief Administrator, and a political leader who as the only officer of the national government chosen by a national electorate can claim with some justification to represent most closely the interests of the nation as a whole.

But what has been mentioned so far is the least part of the President's legislative power. Most of his legislative power is delegated to him by Congress itself, and it took almost a century and a half for the Supreme Court to find an instance in which Congress had attempted to delegate the "essence" of its legislative power to the President. Even here, only a very brief flurry of happy hunting occurred in the spring of 1935; since then, the Court has discovered no additional instances of this evil, although the Congress has kept right on delegating whatever it is that Congress delegates to the President, and on a scale during the past two decades that dwarfs the New Deal by comparison. The reason for both the expansion in delegation and the retirement of the Court from the field of battle is hardly obscure: the only feasible way that we thus far have discovered for the national government to carry out a large number of new and complex functions in a short period of time is to place them in the hands of the President.

It goes without saying that the preceding discussion concerning "the President" implies the institution of the Presidency, and not merely the individual incumbent of the office. Since our President is the counterpart of both King and Prime Minister, the distinction drawn in the United Kingdom between the powers of the King and the powers of the Crown does not afford a very exact analogy. On the other hand, it is certainly true that only a small fraction of the powers he legally possesses can be personally exercised by the President. Many of the decisions that he does make personally are of great importance; many others are *pro forma* or of slight importance. Much of his power is expressly subdelegated to subordinates; much of his power, while remaining in his hands in legal theory, is in fact exercised by subordinates, official and unofficial. Our purpose here is not to trace out the legal implications of these relationships,[8] although two general rules followed by the courts should be stated: (1) the judiciary assumes that the executive officers who report to the President act in his name and that their actions are, in law, equivalent to his own action;[9] and (2) the personal acts of the President are not subject to prospective judicial control, although the "ministerial" acts of even his principal subordinates, including members of his Cabinet, may be. The President is never considered in modern judicial practice to be, personally, an indispensable party to a case, because the effect of making him so would be to render the court impotent to resolve the issues in the case before it. Although many of the cases which follow are concerned with personal action on the part of the Chief Executive, in the majority of instances — and notwithstanding the patent legal fiction to the contrary — the phrase "the President" functions in fact as a legal vessel to hold the highly complex and multifarious administrative relationships characteristic of the functioning of the Executive Office of the President in contemporary practice.

It is noteworthy that the problem of constitutionality, as it applies to presidential legislation and orders, is significantly different from the corresponding matter of judicial review of statutes. By definition, a statute can be held unconstitutional only if it is held to be in conflict with some provision, explicit or inferred, of the Constitution. Executive legislation must, of course, meet the test of constitutionality; but it may also be *ultra vires* if it is found to conflict with a statute, joint resolution, or treaty.[10] A related question that is not easily resolved relates to the effect and importance to be attributed to statements of courts which are directly in point but patently *obiter dicta* (or "obiter dissertation," as Jefferson said of John Marshall's opinion in *Marbury v. Madison*). Since the dictum of an earlier case, particularly if the decision was by an appellate court, subsequently may be cited as a controlling precedent, or at least as a controlling principle, it certainly cannot be completely disregarded. Much of our public law has been created by judges who took advantage of what appeared to be propitious opportunities to rule upon questions not raised by the facts, and sometimes not even raised by the parties,[11] in the cases before them, but which were nevertheless of large public interest and considerable contemporary importance. This study attempts to point out the more obvious instances where a ruling or quotation appears to be of this nature; but the writer also has tried to keep in mind the unabashed admonition of a federal district judge who recently took occasion to observe that "in the last analysis the Judges of the Supreme Court are the final arbiters as to what is or is not dicta in a previous opinion."[12]

Perhaps it should also be explicitly pointed out that all the opinions quoted from and cases cited in the text are not of equal authority and "precedent value." Of course, it is not to be assumed that a decision of the Surrogate's Court of New York County has the same value as an authoritative precedent as a decision of the Supreme Court of the United States.[13] Many important questions of public law, however, never reach the Supreme Court of the United States. The Court did not, for instance, rule upon the highly frictional matter of the enforcement and amenability to judicial review of National War Labor Board orders during World War II.[14] Many other questions ruled upon by lower courts, both federal and state, are not in turn reviewed and ruled upon by the Supreme Court, even when an appeal is taken to the highest court. Sometimes there are no federal court decisions on points considered in state court cases. Moreover, where opinions of the same

Introduction

or coordinate courts are in conflict, the more recent decision is a more authoritative precedent. On the other hand, an undisturbed decision, even by a subordinate court, may be considered authoritative *because of* its age, especially as evidence to reinforce a claim of constitutional power accompanied by consistent executive practice and congressional acquiescence. Lower federal court decisions may also combine to create patterns of opinion which the Supreme Court is loath to disturb when it does reach a question which has received extensive consideration in the circuits. For all these reasons, the scope of this study is not limited to the pronouncements of the Supreme Court but, on the contrary, is premised on the assumption that a comprehensive analysis of the law in this area necessitates a comprehensive examination of judicial opinion. It is as myopic to study judicial review of the Presidency by looking only to the Supreme Court as it would be, for example, to study the administration of American foreign policy by examining only what is done by the President in that regard.

As a study in the exercise of presidential power, this work is subject to the limitations inherent in the judicial process itself: the treatment of the plenitude of executive authority is fragmentary and discontinuous. If it succeeds in throwing greater light upon a highly complex institutional relationship, it will have served its purpose.

What, then, does the record reveal? Do American courts exercise judicial review of the official acts of the President of the United States? Do they restrain Presidents from committing illegal and unconstitutional acts? How? And when? Let us turn to the reports, and see what the judges have done.

Notes

[1] The classic statement of this theory is found in the Massachusetts Constitution of 1780: "In the government of this commonwealth, the legislative department shall never exercise the executive and judicial powers, or either of them; the executive shall never exercise the legislative and judicial powers, or either of them; the judicial shall never exercise the legislative and executive powers, or either of them; to the end that it may be a government of laws and not of men."

[2] The Court currently is under attack by the southern interpositionists, including former Associate Justice James Byrnes, who charge that the Court acted "politically" and "usurped power" in deciding the *School Segregation* cases. Of course, this is true: the Supreme Court has been judicially legislating under the Fourteenth Amendment for almost ninety years. Thus far, however, the fine sense of timing and political sensitivity of the Court have been sufficient unto the day and the occasion. For a Court that is more liberal than either the President or the Congress, the rantings of a few vociferous reactionaries is all part of the day's work.

[3] To recall only a few of the better known instances, we have Andrew Jackson, who

is reputed to have remarked, "John Marshall has made his decision, now let him enforce it"; Abraham Lincoln, who ignored Roger Taney's opinion in the *Merryman* case; and Franklin Roosevelt, who replaced the elder of Nine Old Men with some younger ones. The recent decision in the *Steel Seizure* case — Youngstown Sheet and Tube v. Charles Sawyer, 343 U.S. 579 (1952) — is not an exception because there was no conflict between executive and judicial power, at least from the President's point of view; he explicitly offered in advance of the Court's decision to abide by it whatever it might be, and in fact he did so.

[4] Korematsu v. United States, 323 U.S. 214, 248 (1944).

[5] Marguerite Sieghart, *Government by Decree; A Comparative Study of the History of the Ordinance in English and French Law* (London: Stevens, 1950), Part I; and Glendon A. Schubert, Jr., "Judicial Review of Royal Proclamations and Orders-in-Council," *University of Toronto Law Journal* 9:99 (1951).

[6] In addition to the *Federal Register* and the *Code of Federal Regulations*, the *United States Code Congressional and Administrative News* (St. Paul: West Publishing Co.) has since 1942 published executive orders and presidential directives in addition to presidential proclamations. The *Statutes at Large*, on the other hand, include only the proclamations, and these in precisely the same manner as was done in Volume XI, which printed the laws of the 34th and 35th Congresses (1855–1859), and brought up to that date an incomplete list of presidential proclamations beginning with Washington's term. The numbered series of executive orders does not begin until Lincoln's incumbency; see James Hart's discussion on executive rule-making in the *Report of the President's Committee on Administrative Management* (Washington, D.C.: GPO, 1937).

[7] See, for example, the Migratory Bird Treaty Act of July 3, 1918, 40 *Stat.* 755, and Lansden v. Hart, 168 F. 2d 409 (1948), certiorari denied 335 U.S. 858 (1948).

[8] This has already been done in two recent articles; see Glendon A. Schubert, Jr., "Judicial Review of the Subdelegation of Presidential Power," *Journal of Politics*, 12:668–693 (November 1950), and "The Presidential Subdelegation Act of 1950," *Journal of Politics*, 13:647–674 (November 1951).

[9] See the first reference of the preceding footnote, pp. 685–686, and cases cited therein. There are a few cases to the contrary; two of these concerned the World War I Industries Board: United States v. McFarland, 15 F. 2d 823, 831 (1926), and United States v. Smith, 39 F. 2d 851, 858 (1930).

[10] Whether the additional yardsticks of international law and concurrent resolutions should be recognized is a matter of some current controversy. There are few cases in which conflict between executive legislation and international law has been directly in controversy; and none concerning concurrent resolutions. The answer in both instances would appear at this time to be clearly negative.

[11] See, for instance, Terminiello v. Chicago, 337 U.S. 1, 7 (1949).

[12] Ochikubo v. Bonesteel, 60 F. Supp. 916, 930 ftn. 28 (S.D.Cal.C.D., 1945).

[13] The hierarchy of descending authority is as follows: the Supreme Court of the United States, the federal courts of appeals, the federal district courts, state supreme courts, and inferior state courts.

[14] The leading case is Employers Group of Motor Freight Carriers v. N.W.L.B., 143 F. 2d 145 (C.A.D.C., 1944) Cf. one of the three leading cases on the President's removal power (the other two being Supreme Court decisions): Morgan v. Tennessee Valley Authority, 115 F. 2d 990 (6 C.C.A., 1940).

I

The Chief Administrator: Minions and Dominion

"The President's duty in general requires his superintendance of the administration; yet this duty cannot require of him to become the administrative officer of every department and bureau, or to perform in person the numerous details incident to such services which, nevertheless, he is, in a correct sense, by the Constitution and laws required and expected to perform." Williams v. United States, 1 Howard 290, 296 (1843)

"The President was in a position to know when the public interest required particular portions of the people's lands to be withdrawn from entry or location." United States v. Midwest Oil Co., 236 U.S. 459, 471 (1915)

2

Presidential Management of Public Personnel

The Executive Power of Appointment and Removal

MILITARY PERSONNEL

BEGINNING in the first year of Washington's first term as President, the scope and exercise of the presidential power of removal (as the principal legal basis for his control of the executive branch) has evoked tough, tenacious constitutional problems.[1] In the only instance in which a President of the United States has been impeached, the precise basis of the charges lay in executive-congressional conflict over this constitutional question, and that dispute was so serious that President Johnson was acquitted by the margin of a single vote. Other matters of particular contemporary significance to be examined in this chapter, such as civil servant loyalty, the presidential power of administrative direction, the function of intermediate-order systems, and the subdelegation of presidential power, all rest, explicitly or implicitly, on this ultimate sanction in the enforcement of presidential administrative authority.

Only on rare occasions has it been possible for dismissed officers and employees of the executive branch of the national government to challenge the authority of the President in the courts. Although many state courts will review the exercise of gubernatorial removal power (New York is a notable example), the law applicable to the President is almost completely statutory and administrative rather than case law. Moreover, cases dealing with administrative removal of civil service employees of the national government are rare, because Congress has made no statutory provision for direct review by the courts of the decisions of the Civil Service Commission (in cases that reach that agency on appeal).[2] Such decisions are likewise not subject to review by certiorari because they are of an administrative rather than a judicial nature — at least so say the courts. The employee has no right to his job. He can gain no vested interest in it. Having exhausted whatever administrative remedy may be open to him upon his removal, he normally encounters administrative finality.

For three decades following the Civil War, however, this distinction between "judicial" and "administrative" powers plagued the Supreme Court as it struggled unsuccessfully to establish a conceptual basis for expanding the scope of judicial review of administrative action to cover presidential removal of military personnel. Like imprisonment or loss in pay, dismissal from the armed services as the result of the decision of a court-martial approved by the President was considered the exercise of judicial discretion. Such a "judicial" decision was not subject to review by the regular civil courts, however, for historical reasons that will be discussed in Chapter 6. Dismissal as the result of a decision based on programmatic goals rather than as individual punishment for specific wrongdoing was looked upon as a quite different matter involving the exercise of administrative judgment. For a while, the courts considered themselves competent to review administrative removal of military personnel based upon "quasi-judicial" decisions.

The earliest case in which the Supreme Court discussed presidential removal of a military officer as an administrative matter concerned a disciplinary removal. First Lieutenant McElrath of the Marine Corps was summarily removed by order of the Secretary of the Navy while the Civil War was in progress,[3] and his successor was appointed and received a commission on July 13, 1866, the day on which President Johnson approved a statute limiting his power to remove military officers in time of peace.[4] McElrath subsequently was notified by the Secretary of the Navy that he had been dismissed because of a mistaken understanding of the facts; his dismissal was accordingly revoked and his resignation accepted as of July 10, 1873. Upon his application for pay from the time of his removal to that date, he was granted half-pay; but when he sued in the Court of Claims for full pay, he lost the amount already awarded to him on the counterclaim of the government. The Supreme Court dismissed his appeal on the ground that, since the President had the power to remove him summarily in time of war, the reasons for his removal, including the fact that they might have been based upon a misunderstanding of what actually had happened, were irrelevant, because the President's discretion could have been exercised irrespective of the facts.[5] His successor, moreover, had been legally appointed and could have been removed under the terms of the 1866 statute only after court-martial proceedings, which had not taken place. Since there was no vacancy to which McElrath could have been appointed in 1873, the order directing his reinstatement was illegal and void, and beyond the power of the President to issue:

The President, at the time he asked the advice and consent of the Senate to the appointment of Lieutenant Haycock in place of Lieutenant McElrath, had the power to dismiss the latter, summarily, from the service. That power, if not possessed by the President, in virtue of his constitutional relations to the army and navy (and as to that question we express no opinion), was given by an act of Congress approved July 17, 1862. . . .

[But] the orders which issued from the Navy Department under the signature of Secretary Robeson, in 1873 and 1874, even if issued by direction of the President, were inoperative for the purpose of reinstating [Lieut. McElrath] in his position as a first lieutenant in the Marine Corps. The position to which it was attempted to restore him had . . . been previously filled by constitutional appointment, and by the laws *then* in force the incumbent could neither be displaced nor dismissed, except "upon and in pursuance of the sentence of a courtmartial to that effect, or in commutation thereof."[6]

The nature of the limitation imposed by the act of 1866 was further examined the following year, when the Court decided that the statute was not intended to prohibit removal of a military officer by the device of appointing, with Senate confirmation, his successor. The actual problem facing the Court, however, was similar to that of the *McElrath* case: assuming the valid removal of the first officer and the valid appointment of his successor, and assuming that for a single position there can be only one incumbent officer *de jure* entitled to draw compensation from the government, must not a presidential order purporting to reinstate the first officer (either to active duty or for the purpose of compensation) be illegal? Again, the Court's answer was yes. The claimant here was a psychoneurotic post chaplain whose resignation had been accepted and to whose office a successor had been appointed. He changed his mind afterwards, however; and when a vacancy in the Chaplain's Corps was created about eight years later, President Hayes reappointed him, reciting in his executive order of September 28, 1878: "It appearing from the evidence . . . that Chaplain Blake was insane at the time he tendered his resignation, it is held that said resignation was and is void, and the acceptance thereof is set aside." Blake then sued in the Court of Claims for his salary for the period from the acceptance of his resignation in 1869 until his reappointment in 1878. He appealed an adverse decision there to the Supreme Court which also dismissed his claim, holding that the primary effect of the act of 1866 was to restrict the President's former power summarily to remove military officers without senatorial concurrence; but since Blake's removal was legal and the appointment of his successor was valid, Blake had no right to salary during the interval until his purported reappointment:

From the organization of the government, under the present Constitution, to the commencement of the recent war for the suppression of the rebellion, the power of the President, in the absence of statutory regulations, to dismiss from the service an officer of the army or navy, was not questioned in any adjudged case, or by any department of the government. . . .

Such was the established practice in the Executive Department, and such the recognized power of the President up to the passage of the Act of July 17, 1862 [which merely recognized the existing practice by delegating authority to the President to make removals for the good of the service].

Our conclusion is that there was no purpose, by the fifth section of the Act of July 13, 1866, to withdraw from the President the power, with the advice and consent of the Senate, to supersede an officer in the military or naval service by the appointment of some one in his place. If the power of the President and Senate, in this regard, could be constitutionally subjected to restrictions by statute (as to which we express no opinion), it is sufficient for the present case to say that Congress did not intend by that section to impose them. . . . There was . . . no intention to deny or restrict the power of the President, by and with the advice and concurrence of the Senate, to displace them by the appointment of others in their places.[7]

The executive order of September 28, 1878, was, therefore, illegal and void, and could not operate in such a way as to revoke Blake's former removal, or to appoint him, in the absence of senatorial concurrence, to any existing vacancy.

Presidential Management of Public Personnel

From the Court's point of view, neither the *McElrath* nor the *Blake* case limited the President's removal power, but they did limit his power of appointment in cases where the constitutional requirement of senatorial concurrence had not been met. From a practical point of view, the Court refused to sanction the payment of what it considered to be unjust claims against the government. In effect, however, the Court was applying the technical doctrine in judicial decision-making of *res judicata* to the President's action in these cases, viewing the exercise of presidential discretion in the original dismissals of both McElrath and Blake as *judicial* judgments.[8] Certainly, legislative power is not exhaustible;[9] Americans generally accept the contrary premise that varying political majorities should be able to change the decisions of their predecessors. Equally so, one of the fundamental justifications for creating administrative authorities and exercising administrative powers is to gain flexibility; and it is certainly now clear that *res judicata* does not usually apply to administrative adjudication.[10] There were also precedents, of which the *Legal Tender Cases* of a decade earlier[11] was the most recent, which would seem to indicate that, at least, the power *of the Supreme Court* to change its mind was not exhaustible.[12]

The conceptual basis of these decisions became explicit in the very next case to arise, a suit for a counterclaim by the government for the overpayment of a naval officer. President Grant had approved the findings of a retirement board, which ordered the retirement of one Burchard on furlough pay on October 26, 1874; but it was later decided that the causes of his incapacitation for active duty were incident to the service, and that he should be granted the higher rate of pay allowed to retired officers. Again, the Court reached the just decision by an awkward and devious route, holding that, although the original determination of President Grant was *res judicata* and not open to reconsideration by a different President at a later time, the consequences of the decision to relieve Burchard from the active list for physical incapacity remained discretionary to the extent that a retroactive change in his retirement status was permissible.[13]

Clarification of the semantic issues did not come for another quarter of a century. In the leading case, the petitioner was a psychoneurotic who contracted his illness in line of duty as the result of overwork in the Philippine Islands. By direction of the President he had been discharged by the Secretary of War under the provisions of the act of

17

October 1, 1890, instead of being retired on three-fourths pay for life; and he sued in the Supreme Court of the District of Columbia for a writ of certiorari to examine the legality of the proceedings of the military examination board that had recommended his discharge. The Court now held that the proceedings of these retirement boards were administrative rather than quasi-judicial in nature: they were concerned with increasing the efficiency of the service rather than with trying individuals for the violation of laws, and therefore their decisions were not subject to review in the civil courts by certiorari:

> To those in the military or naval service of the United States the military law is due process. The decision, therefore, of a military tribunal acting within the scope of its lawful powers cannot be reviewed or set aside by the courts . . . the decision is not final with the board, but must be reported with the proceedings to the President, and may be approved or disapproved by him. This is the only relief from the errors or the injustice that may be done by the board which is provided. The courts have no power to review. The courts are not the only instrumentalities of the government. They cannot command or regulate the Army.[14]

Certiorari could not be granted, in other words, because if it were the Court could not control the subsequent decision of the President.[15] Granting certiorari would amount to the review of an intermediate order, which might in any event be disapproved or disregarded by the President. The effect of this decision was to eliminate the original basis for distinction between military judgments of a "judicial" and an "administrative" nature: administrative judgments affecting military personnel were henceforth no more subject to review in the civil courts than the decisions of courts-martial; and the highest appellate tribunal, in either case, remained the President. This rule has been followed in the cases which have reached the Court during the ensuing four decades,[16] and the trend in more recent cases is to uphold the administrative power of removal of the civilian heads of the military departments on the basis of the President's constitutional authority as Commander in Chief.[17] Since the effective scope of presidential discretion seems now to be equally broad (and the power of judicial review correspondingly curtailed) in the case of military removals predicated upon either "judicial" or "administrative" decisions, it would appear that the distinction formerly drawn by the Supreme Court on this point is only too literally one without a difference.

Presidential Management of Public Personnel

THE CIVIL SERVICE

The status of civil officers and employees of the national government varies according to whether the office is subject to appointment by the President with the advice and consent of the Senate, to direct appointment by the President or one of his principal administrative subordinates, or to appointment under the classified civil service. Presidential appointees fall within or between the rules of two very well known decisions of the Supreme Court. The rule of the *Myers* case was that the President could remove without limitation all officers whom he appointed; an exception to this rule was created in the *Humphrey* case, where the Court decided that members of the independent regulatory commissions were the agents of Congress and not subject to the President's power of administrative direction.[18] Therefore, Congress could limit the President's power by requiring that he remove such a commissioner only in accordance with the terms of the statute creating his office, and subject to the possibility of challenge and review by the courts. But not all the basic statutes establishing regulatory commissions purport to limit the President's removal power. Thus all presidential appointees who are not subject to senatorial confirmation, and most of those who are, hold office at the pleasure of the President; those who sit on some of the eight or ten regulatory commissions — certainly fewer than fifty individuals all told — may contest their removal in the courts. There remain important constitutional questions for which there are no certain answers.[19]

Until June 6, 1956, the rule with respect to civil service employees was much more definite. The President was legally bound by neither the civil service rules and regulations — which he had to approve and promulgate in the first instance — nor statutory limitations.[20] Inherent in his status as the Chief Executive of the executive branch was the power to direct the activities of his subordinates, and ancillary to this was the power to remove for disciplinary *or other reasons*. Others beneath the President or the principal subordinates who functioned as his legal alter-ego might be bound by the rules and orders he made; but he was bound by neither his own orders nor those of his predecessors.

The extension of this principle to include the heads of the executive departments is well illustrated in a case involving a former President, at a time when he headed one of the principal executive departments. The plaintiff, a civil service clerk, wrote a derogatory article about

19

President Theodore Roosevelt which appeared under her by-line in a Washington newspaper. Taft, as Secretary of War and the woman's administrative superior, fired her because of the article, but denied that he had violated civil service rules in so doing. Two lower courts denied her petition for a writ of mandamus for reinstatement; and the Supreme Court dismissed the case for lack of jurisdiction, holding that the statutes then permitted a writ of error to issue only when (among other things) the validity of authority exercised under the United States was questioned, and it did not appear that such was involved in this case. Civil service rules and regulations, in other words, were not "laws of the United States" in the constitutional sense; and correspondingly, an employee whose claim of legal right was based upon them raised no question of constitutional right when he protested his discharge contrary to their provisions.

The relator did not, however, question the authority of the President or his representatives to dismiss her, if the required formalities had been complied with. What she claimed was that there were certain rules and regulations of the civil service which were not observed in the matter of her dismissal, and that, therefore, such dismissal was illegal.

But this contention did not draw in question the validity of an authority exercised under the United States, but the construction and application of regulations of the exercise of such authority.[21]

In addition to the President's constitutional power to remove civil servants, the Pendleton Act gave him additional statutory power to disregard the requirements of the act in specific instances: "Any necessary exceptions from said eight fundamental provisions of the rules shall be set forth in connection with such rules, and the reasons therefore shall be stated in the annual reports of the commission."[22]

By his Executive Order No. 7201 of September 26, 1935, President Franklin Roosevelt excepted the appointment of certain persons to the office of attorney for the Federal Communications Commission from the provisions of the civil service rules. A World War I veteran with 10-point preference sought a mandamus to require the Civil Service Commission to discharge the temporary appointees who had been given permanent appointments pursuant to the President's order, and, since he had headed the civil service register of eligibles for the positions open, to require his own appointment. Thus three questions were raised: (1) was the executive order valid? (2) could the President be forced to remove individuals whose appointment he had authorized? and (3) did the court have jurisdiction to grant the writ? The Court of Appeals for the District of Columbia held that Article 2, Section 2, of the Constitution was not relevant because the petitioner was not an "officer"—that is, the position to which he sought appointment was not an office in the constitutional sense, but employment; and in any event, the court decided, mandamus would not lie to try the title to the position:

From the fact — of which we take judicial notice — that various Presidents have from time to time issued executive orders pursuant to which designated persons were brought into the classified civil service without regard to the eight fundamental rules, we assume that these words [of the Pendleton Act] have been, in practice at least, construed to include the sort of action taken in the instant case . . . to say that the President, in whom the Constitution vests the executive authority, may not when he declares the public service demands it in a particular case [as Roosevelt explicitly did in Executive Order No. 7201], suspend a rule [i.e., 41 *Stat.* 37, 5 U.S.C.A. sec. 638] of the civil service — a practice which, as we have seen, has been indulged without challenge from time to time for half a century — would involve deciding a question which, in view of the uncertain language of the statute on the one hand and the established practice on the other, is by no means so free from doubt as to be controlled by mandamus.[23]

THE LOYALTY EXECUTIVE ORDERS

The question of civil servant loyalty, as well as the loyalty of citizens generally, has assumed the proportions of a major problem during the past fifteen years. A single precedent from World War II bears on this matter. Under the war service regulations issued by the Civil Service Commission, agency heads were required to remove, subject to appeal to the commission, any persons concerning whose loyalty there was basis for reasonable doubt. All wartime employees of the national government were supposed to be investigated by the F.B.I. under these same regulations, but the number of new appointees was so great and other demands placed upon the bureau were so extensive that there was usually a lag of at least six months (and frequently much longer) in completing even the cursory four-way record check. Morton Friedman, the chief of the classification division of the War Manpower Commission, had been placed in this war service position by conditional transfer subject to the routine loyalty-check.[24] When it was subsequently determined that he was an active member of an organization that the Attorney General had proscribed as a Communist-front group, the Civil Service Commission took steps to remove him. This action was ultimately successful, but in the meantime Friedman was afforded every possible procedural safeguard. His administrative appeal consumed several months during which he retained title to his job and continued to draw his salary; and after passing through various stages of the administrative hearing process, his case was passed upon by two lower federal courts and his petition was ruled upon by the Supreme Court of the United States. The Court of Appeals for the District of Columbia examined only the procedure under which Friedman had been dismissed, and held that since the United States has the right to prescribe the qualifications of its employees and to attach conditions to their employment, the war service regulations permitting removal where "reasonable doubt as to loyalty" existed were reasonable, proper, and within the scope of the authority of the Civil Service Commission:

We are not concerned here with the question as to whether Friedman was in fact disloyal. . . . In these circumstances the Commission's finding is conclusive. It is beyond our province, and it was beyond the province of the District Court, to review the finding of the Civil Service Commission.[25]

Four days after the Supreme Court refused to review the decision of the Court of Appeals in the *Friedman* case, President Truman issued his "loyalty order," Executive Order No. 9835 of March 21, 1947. It has been assumed that two factors were of primary significance in the timing of this order: (1) it was widely accepted that the Supreme Court's decision should be interpreted to mean that the removal of civil servants on grounds of disloyalty was not subject to judicial review; and (2) it was also assumed that the President issued his order to forestall the much more drastic action then contemplated by the Congress. The order directed the setting up of a series of agency and departmental boards, and a Civil Service Commission Loyalty Review Board, to consider the evidence in cases where the board determined that reasonable grounds for doubt as to the loyalty of any civil servant existed. A basic criterion of disloyalty was membership in or affiliation with any group or organization designated on a list compiled by the Attorney General and furnished to the Loyalty Review Board of the Civil Service Commission.

Presidential Management of Public Personnel

It took four years for cases challenging the loyalty order to reach the Supreme Court, and then only one inconclusive opinion was delivered; but in the meantime, a much larger number of cases were decided by the Court of Appeals for the District of Columbia, which, because of its location, exercised considerable influence upon this area of the law as time went on. There were two principal lines of attack upon the loyalty order: one followed the path of appeal by an individual from a decision by the Loyalty Review Board affirming his removal, and the other took the form of attempts by organizations to enjoin the Attorney General from designating them as subversive and placing them on his list of proscribed groups.

The first case to arise involved twenty-six employees of the Post Office Department who had received written notice of their proposed removal on the basis that reasonable grounds existed for the belief that each was disloyal to the United States. They petitioned the District Court for the District of Columbia for a declaratory judgment that Executive Order No. 9835 was unconstitutional, and for a permanent injunction against its enforcement. The trial court dismissed the suit, however, holding that it was bound by the decision in the *Friedman* case.[26] Although the hearing contemplated by the loyalty order did not satisfy the Fifth Amendment's requirement of due process, it was not necessary that it should do so because dismissals such as these were of an executive rather than a judicial or quasi-judicial nature; and the court refused to examine the record of the hearings in the case of the appellants, because the due process clause did not, in any event, apply to the employer-employee relationship between the government and its civil servants.[27]

Before this case reached the Court of Appeals, a similar appeal from a different decision of the district court already had been disposed of. The issues in this case were the same, although this appellant was not an employee protesting removal, but a former employee who appealed from a decision denying her reinstatement. This fact, in the eyes of the court, made her position even weaker, because her failure to gain appointment raised no question of procedural constitutional right. In a strong but divided (2–1) opinion, the court upheld the loyalty order as against charges that it violated the First, Fifth, and Sixth amendments, and that it was based on a discriminatory classification. The specificity of the charges on which the judgment of disloyalty was

23

based was wholly discretionary;[28] and since the power of removal was an incident to the presidential power of appointment, there was no *constitutional* bar to removals for purely political or partisan reasons.[29] The court did not do so in precise terms, but it might well have paraphrased *Reaves v. Ainsworth:*[30] To those in the civil service of the United States, executive law is due process. What it did say was that:

It is our clear opinion that the President, absent congressional restriction, may remove from Government service any person of whose loyalty he is not completely convinced. He may do so without assigning any reason and without giving the employee any explanatory notice. If, as a matter of policy, he chooses to give the employee a general description of the information which concerns him and to hear what the employee has to say, he does not thereby strip himself of any portion of his constitutional power to choose and to remove.[31]

The position of Judge Edgerton, who dissented vigorously, may be succinctly summarized in his own words: "Freedoms that may not be abridged by law may not be abridged by executive order."[32]

With the *Bailey* case as a precedent, the disposition that the Court of Appeals would make of *Washington v. Clark* was a foregone conclusion. There were, moreover, the intervening decisions of this court in the *Joint Anti-Fascist Refugee* and *International Workers* cases which are discussed below. The decision of the trial court was affirmed, and the additional allegation that the defendants were mostly Jews or Negroes, and were being discriminated against on the basis of race and religion, was overruled for lack of any evidence to countervene the government's affidavits.[33]

When these two cases reached the Supreme Court about a year later, the Court was equally divided, so the effect of its inability to come to a decision was to affirm the ruling of the Court of Appeals.[34] Of course, if the Court of Appeals decision had been that Executive Order No. 9835 was unconstitutional, the effect of the Supreme Court's indecision would have been to affirm that ruling, too. Some comfort may be taken from the fact that Justice Clark, had he participated, would most certainly have joined the faction upholding the loyalty order, but the fact clearly remains that with respect to this critical constitutional question, four justices of the highest Court thought that the President's order was unconstitutional, and the Court was so effectively polarized that it was unable to come to any decision in the matter. The Court has not yet ruled on the merits of the issue of the President's independent constitutional power to authorize the removal of civil servants who claim that such action violates their civil liberties.

The other approach to the problem of attacking the loyalty order in the courts proved to be the more fruitful, probably because other citizens than government employees were directly affected by the Attorney General's designation of private groups and organizations as subversive. Interestingly enough, the precedents that the Court of Appeals found persuasive in handling the legal issues involved in the Attorney General's power of designation were those from World War II relating to the orders and directives of the War Labor Board and the War Manpower Commission, agencies whose orders, it had been determined, were legally unenforceable except through the intervention of the President and the exercise of his powers: therefore, their decisions were only intermediate orders and a form of administrative advice to the President. The first case involved an attempt, by an organization that had been determined by the Attorney General to be a "Communist front" within the meaning of the loyalty order, to enjoin the Attorney General from continuing to list it as subversive. The basis for this petition lay in the argument that Executive Order No. 9835 and Section 9A of the Hatch Act,[35] on which it was in part based, were unconstitutional; but the court not only found that both the loyalty order and the statute were constitutional, but also held that the petition of the plaintiff did not present a justiciable controversy:

[The Attorney General's] letter to the [Loyalty Review] Board simply complies with the directions of the President in whose behalf he was acting. He has done for the President only that which the President could have done for himself. Had the President done so his action would have been within the realm of executive power, not subject to judicial review.[36]

Furthermore, neither the executive order nor the Attorney General's designation was a "law" in the sense necessary to present a justiciable controversy, but rather, both were, in this context, informational or advisory. However:

We do not doubt validity of the Executive Order. It is the President's duty to take care that the laws are faithfully executed. . . . It is his right and duty to protect and defend the government against subversive forces which may seek to change or destroy it by unconstitutional means. Vesting of the executive power in the President is essentially a grant of power to execute the laws. He cannot do so alone. He must have the aid of subordinates. Therefore, he must have the power to select others to act for him, under his direction, in executing the laws. . . . The Executive Order exhibits a proper effort by the President to carry out the provisions of Section 9A.

We do not doubt validity of the Attorney General's act. Had the President performed the task himself, his acts could not have been challenged legally. . . . The fact that they were done by the Attorney General, for and at the President's direction, does not change their essential character as acts of the President himself.[37]

Judge Edgerton again dissented, but he did not consider it necessary to decide the question of the constitutionality of the executive order, since he felt that the designation by the Attorney General was invalid because inconsistent with and beyond the terms of the executive order.[38]

The intermediate order theory was much more explicitly stated in the next case, which concerned a group that called itself a "fraternal insurance organization" and had been designated as subversive by the Attorney General. The nexus of the court's decision this time was that the executive order and the action of the Attorney General thereunder, unlike the action of the Federal Communications Commission in regulating private business, related to an internal administrative matter, and that designation was only an intermediate step in a program to ensure employee loyalty, and as such was unreviewable:

The President did no more than to prescribe conditions to govern executive agencies in the selection of their employees, and to instruct the Attorney General to advise them with respect thereto. To do so, within the limits of his constitutional and statutory authority, was the right and duty of the Chief Executive.

When the Attorney General designated I.W.O. as a subversive organization for the purposes of the Executive Order, he did no more than to advise the executive department in that respect, as he had been directed to do. If he was mistaken as to the true character of I.W.O., no court can cause him to change his conclusion. The correctness of administrative advice cannot be reviewed by the courts.[39]

Both the *Joint Anti-Fascist Refugee* and *International Workers* cases were consolidated for argument and, together with a third case,[40] were decided by the Supreme Court on the same day that its *per curiam* decision in the *Bailey* case was announced. Indicative of the confusion into which the Court was thrown by the issues raised in these cases is the fact that the eight participating justices wrote six different opinions.[41] All that the Court actually did, however, was to dispose of the case on a technicality, and remand it to the district court for further argument which might make possible a decision on the merits, as the latter was now defined by the Supreme Court. Since the Attorney General had demurred to the motion of the plaintiffs in the trial court in each case, he had taken the position that even if everything they alleged in their petitions — including, of course, strong protestations of their own loyalty[42] — were true, he could nevertheless, on the basis of any evidence or no evidence, include them on his list. The Court decided only that on this state of the pleadings, the Attorney General's action was arbitrary on its face, and beyond the scope of his power under the loyalty order.

Upon remand, after the lapse of another year, the trial court refused to accept the Attorney General's affidavit, which summarized parts of the data on which he relied and which he felt could be discussed without jeopardizing national security, as a substitute for evidence justifying his designation of the plaintiff organizations; but the court also denied plaintiff's request for a preliminary injunction *pendente lite*, on the ground that the plaintiffs already had sustained substantially all the injuries that would accrue to them as the result of designation.[43] Two more years passed, and the trial court then ruled on April 5, 1954, that the issues had become moot because of the intervening supercession of the Truman loyalty order by President Eisenhower's "security" order of April 27, 1953; so the complaints were dismissed. Both rulings of the trial court were appealed to the Court of Appeals for the District of Columbia, which affirmed the earlier opinion refusing the preliminary injunction, but reversed the later decision, holding that the case was not moot since the Attorney General's designations under the Truman order were expressly preserved under the Eisenhower order. The rules issued under the latter order provided an administrative "remedy" whereby affected organizations that did not wish to "acquiesce" in being listed were afforded ten days in which to protest their designation to the Attorney General. Although this time long since had elapsed and the plaintiffs had not requested an administrative hearing under the rules, the Court of Appeals decided that they should be given, on order of the district court, an opportunity to do so; and in the event that they should fail to "exhaust" this administrative remedy, the district court was then to dismiss the case.[44]

By this time (1954) seven years had elapsed, and the government, with the active cooperation of the judiciary, had managed effectively and successfully to forestall a timely decision on the merits of one of the most controversial and constitutionally dubious questions of the Cold War period.

The government was less successful in its attempts to extend the application of the Attorney General's list to affect the legal rights of private individuals as such — and as distinguished from the employment rights of federal civil servants and the claims of organizations to be free from defamation and designation. The Supreme Court refused to upset the decisions of a number of state courts which upheld the right of tenants in federally subsidized housing projects to refuse to sign certificates of nonmembership in proscribed organizations.[45] The municipal housing authorities had adopted regulations pursuant to the Gwinn Amendment,[46] requiring the eviction of tenants who would not sign the certificates. The state courts held the regulations to be unconstitutional and in conflict with the First and Fourteenth amendments as well as state statutory and constitutional provisions, although they avoided direct rulings on the constitutionality of the federal statute.[47] Similarly, a federal court of appeals ruled (2–1) that regulations issued by the commandant of the Coast Guard, on the basis of executive orders extending the security program to employment in the merchant marine, were in direct violation of the Fifth Amendment and unconstitutional.[48] But the decision enjoined only the administrative regulations, and it did not rule directly on the constitutionality of the underlying executive orders. The 1955–56 term ended without the government having made any attempt to appeal this case to the Supreme Court.

There appeared to remain only the possibility of attacking other aspects of the administrative practice under the executive orders. Although the constitutionality of Truman's loyalty order was assumed, the Court of Appeals for the District of Columbia did find that its requirements had been disregarded in one case.[49] The Loyalty Review Board's Memorandum No. 32, dated December 17, 1948, and addressed to all executive departments and agencies, stated that the removal of any employee found to be a member of a designated organization was "mandatory." Executive Order No. 9835 made the recommendations of the loyalty boards advisory, leaving it to the head of each agency to determine whether on all the evidence there were reasonable grounds for belief that an employee was disloyal to the government of the United States. The Court of Appeals decided that Memorandum No. 32 was *ultra vires* the executive order, and that the removal of the plaintiff on the admitted and exclusive basis of his membership in a proscribed organization was illegal. He was entitled to an independent determination on the personal judgment of the agency head, said the court, although the Attorney General's designation of an organization of which the plaintiff was a member was competent evidence to be considered by the agency head in coming to his decision. The government did not seek certiorari from the Supreme Court to review this case.

The Supreme Court did, however, come to a similar conclusion to that of the Court of Appeals of the District of Columbia when a case finally reached it for decision. The plaintiff here, it should be noted, was no ordinary tiller in the vineyards of the federal bureaucracy; he was a physician and professor in the Yale Medical School who had been employed for several years as a special consultant to the United States Public Health Service. At his several loyalty hearings, the distinguished defendant presented as character witnesses a former president of Yale University, a former dean of the Yale Medical School, and a federal circuit judge. A majority of the Court disposed of the case without reaching the constitutional issues, holding that the (by now, former) Loyalty Review Board's practice of post-auditing agency decisions on its own motion was illegal because the board's regulation which purported to authorize this was *ultra vires* Executive Order No. 9835 and "beyond the Board's delegated jurisdiction under the Order."[50] Moreover, the board's order removing Dr. Peters was illegal because such a decision could properly be made only by his agency head, Mrs. Hobby. Under the executive order the board's function was to *advise* responsible administrators, not to interpose its own judgment for theirs. The two dissenting judges (Reed and Burton) also found it unnecessary to reach the constitutional issues, but Black — in concurrence, of course — wanted it distinctly understood that:

I have grave doubt as to whether the Presidential Order has been authorized by any Act of Congress. That order and others associated with it embody a broad, far-reaching espionage program over government employees. These orders look more like legislation to me than properly authorized regulations to carry out a clear and explicit command of Congress. I also doubt that the Congress could delegate power to do what the President has attempted to do in the Executive Order under consideration here. And of course the Constitution does not confer lawmaking power on the President. *Youngstown Co. v. Sawyer* [343 U.S. 579, 584 (1952)].[51]

The *Peters* decision, which came on the final decision day of the 1954–55 term, dealt principally with dead issues. The Court could not grant Dr. Peters' request for reinstatement in his position, since his appointment had terminated a year and a half earlier while the case was in litigation. Moreover, the executive loyalty order had been superseded over two years previously by President Eisenhower's security order; and Executive Order No. 10450 appeared to be even more secure than the earlier order from effective challenge in the courts, since it was based directly on statutory authority in addition to the President's constitutional powers.

The statutory basis for the security order was the act of August 26, 1950, which provided that the heads of eleven designated agencies might, in their "absolute discretion and when deemed necessary in the interest of national security, suspend, without pay, any civilian officer or employee."[52] The President was expressly authorized to extend the application of the statute "to such other departments and agencies of the government" as he might, "from time to time, deem necessary in the interests of national security." Although President Truman did not choose to exercise this delegated power, President Eisenhower did so soon after he took office, and his Executive Order No. 10450 extended the act to include all civilian employees of the federal government. Like the loyalty order, the security order made membership in any organization on the Attorney General's list evidence of disloyalty, although the security order also broadened substantially the basis on which dismissal might be placed.[53]

One Cole, an inspector for the Food and Drug Administration, who admitted that he belonged to the Nature Friends of America (a proscribed group), challenged the security order as being *ultra vires* the enabling statute. Both the trial court and the Court of Appeals, however, thought that the President could doubtless justify his security order on the basis of his direct constitutional authority under the investiture and faithful execution clauses, although they found it unnecessary to reach such issues since, in their view, the executive order was perfectly compatible with the statute. And if there *were* conflict, it might well be that the executive order would prevail over the statute!

There is a line somewhere beyond which Congress cannot go in enacting prescriptions in respect to executive power over executive employees. It might be, for example, that if Congress required the hiring of executive personnel whose employment the President deemed not consistent with the national security, the enactment would be void. Congress has the power to make the laws and so can make laws concerning Government employ; but the President has the power, and so the responsibility, of carrying out all the laws, and Congress cannot impinge upon that power.[54]

Cole's veteran status was immaterial, since the 1950 statute had repealed employees' rights under the Civil Service and Veterans' Preference acts insofar as security removals were concerned. In the view of the majority of the Court of Appeals, such policy questions were political in nature and of no concern to courts, who would be concerned only if there were express disagreement between the President and the Congress. Judge Edgerton dissented.

Once again, the Supreme Court was asked to strike down the federal loyalty-security program. A decade had elapsed since the Court had denied certiorari in the *Friedman* case, and the Court had not yet found it necessary (or possible) to decide whether the loyalty-security program was constitutional. And when the Court disposed of Cole's case on the final decision day of the 1955–56 term, it defined the issue as being one of interpreting the will of Congress rather than a question of the correlative scope of the ultimate powers of the President and the Congress, and of individual rights under the Constitution. "The sole question for decision," said Mr. Justice Harlan for the majority, "is whether petitioner's discharge was authorized by the 1950 Act." The Court then proceeded to interpret the phrase "national security," as used in that statute, to refer only to "sensitive" jobs; and such jobs, indicated the Court, were most likely to be found in "sensitive" agencies whose functions were directly related to military and international affairs. The eleven agencies designated by Congress in the statute were all of this character, and the majority thought that Congress never had intended to authorize the President to declare the entire executive branch to be "sensitive," thus negating many other well-established congressional policies such as preferential procedural rights for veterans who were government employees.

31

Since the government had conceded that Cole "did not have access to Government secrets or classified material and was not in a position to influence policy against the interests of the Government," the conclusion to this syllogism was obvious: Executive Order No. 10450 was *ultra vires* the 1950 statute on which the President had relied for authority to issue his order. The symmetry of this logical apparatus did not quite succeed in obscuring the really critical issues, which Harlan sublimated in the concluding footnote at the very end of his opinion:

No contention is made that the Executive Order might be sustained under the President's executive power even though in violation of the Veterans' Preference Act. There is no basis for such an argument in any event, for it is clear from the face of the Executive Order that the President did not intend to override statutory limitations on the dismissal of employees, and promulgated the Order solely as an implementation of the 1950 Act. Thus sec. 6 of the Order purports to authorize dismissals only "in accordance with the said Act of August 26, 1950," and similar references are made in sec. 4, 5, and 7. This explicit limitation in the substantive provisions of the Order is of course not weakened by the inclusion of the "Constitution," as well as the 1950 and other Acts, in the omnibus list of authorities recited in the Preamble to the Order; it is from the Constitution that the President derives any authority to implement the 1950 Act at all. When the President expressly confines his action to the limits of statutory authority, the validity of the action must be determined solely by the congressional limitations which the President sought to respect, whatever might be the result were the President ever to assert his independent power against that of Congress.[55]

This contention was met head-on by three dissenters — Clark, Reed, and Minton — who argued:

The majority excuses its failure to pass on this question by saying that no contention was made that the President's Order might be sustained under his executive powers. We cannot agree. The Government specifically asserted that "if Congress had meant to prohibit the President from acting in this respect under [the Act] a serious question as to the validity of that enactment would arise." It devoted eight pages of its brief to this point. Furthermore the Court of Appeals noted that if it "thought the President's Order inconsistent with the Act, [it] would have to decide the constitutional question thus presented." As further justification the majority contends that the President acted here only under the directions of the Act. In answer we need quote only the enacting clause of the President's Order: "Now, therefore, by virtue of the authority vested in me by the Constitution and statutes

32

of the United States . . . and as President of the United States." In issuing the Order, the President invoked all of his powers, and since his Order is voided by the majority as not being in conformity with the Act, the question of the scope of his other constitutional or statutory powers is presented.[56]

Nor was this all. The dissent also accused the majority of indulging in the most high-handed kind of judicial legislation, substituting the policy predilections of a handful of judges for the composite political judgment of *both* Congress and the President:

The President believed that the national security required the extension of the coverage of the Act to all employees. That was his judgment, not ours. He was given that power, not us. By this action the Court so interprets the Act as to intrude itself into presidential policy making. This the Court should not do and especially here where the Congress has ratified the President's action. As required by the Act the Executive Order of extension was reported to the Congress and soon thereafter it came up for discussion and action in both the House and the Senate. It was the sense of the Congress at that time that the Order properly carried out the standards of the Act and was in all respects an expression of the congressional will. . . . In addition, Congress has made appropriations each subsequent year to the order for investigations, etc., under its provisions. This in itself "stands as confirmation and ratification of the action of the Chief Executive." *Fleming v. Mohawk Wrecking & Lumber Co.*, 331 U.S. 111, 116.[57]

The immediate implications of the decision were these: Cole was reinstated in his position; the White House acquiesced, which meant that the loyalty-security program would have to be revised again; and various congressional critics, linking this case with the *School Segregation* decision, fulminated against the Warren Court's proclivity for usurping political power. There was, however, no uproar in the press, such as there had been in anticipation of and in witness of the *Steel Seizure* decision. In fact, the only elements common to both decisions appeared to be that each had come on the eve of a presidential election campaign, each had denounced as illegal an executive order of the President, and in each a majority of the Court had ignored the Court's precedents and the facts in the case in order to reach the desired result, while the three most conservative members of the Court (at the times the decisions were announced) dissented. It certainly was remarkable that the Supreme Court had twice nullified presidential orders within a four-year span. One who was predisposed to ignore the bulk of our constitutional history and look only at these two recent cases might well argue that intimations of the unlikelihood of judicial review of presidential action, like reports of the demise of Mark Twain, are greatly exaggerated.

The Executive Power of Administrative Direction
THE EXECUTIVE "RULE-MAKING" POWER[58]

The first and still the leading case on the constitutional power of the President to issue rules and regulations for the government of the armed forces, in this instance flowing from his status as Commander in Chief of the Army and Navy, was decided in a unanimous opinion of the Supreme Court over a century ago, when it held:

The power of the executive to establish rules and regulations for the government of the army, is undoubted. . . . The power to establish rules implies, necessarily, the power to modify or repeal, or to create anew.

The secretary of war is the regular constitutional organ of the President for the administration of the military establishment of the nation; and rules and orders publicly promulgated through him must be received as the acts of the executive, and, as such, be binding upon all within the sphere of his legal and constitutional authority.[59]

A more recent decision of a lower federal court indicates that the passing of a century has brought about no change in the judicial recognition of the scope of the President's rule-making powers in this area:

Under Section 2, Article 2 of the Constitution, the President is made the Commander in Chief of the Army and the Navy of the United States. Under this section, as Commander in Chief, the President has the power to employ the Army and the Navy in a manner which he may deem most effectual. This includes the power to establish rules and regulations for the government of the Army and the Navy and such regulations made pursuant to the authority thus conferred upon the President, have the force of law.[60]

There are practically no cases directly challenging the President's undoubted power to promulgate rules and regulations for the government of the civil service, both incident to his constitutional power as the Chief Executive and by the explicit delegation of authority in the Pendleton Act. In an early decision arising under that legislation, a federal district court did venture the dictum that civil service regulations made by the Civil Service Commission and the President, and promulgated by the President, can in no way have the effect of modifying, altering, or changing the statutory law relative to the civil service.[61] At the same time, however, the court recognized that the President's rule-making power over civil servants, when not in conflict with statutory law, is plenary.[62]

Sixty years later, however, the Court of Appeals of the District of Columbia based the President's rule-making power over the civil service directly on the investiture and faithful execution clauses. From this major premise, the court readily deduced the proposition that a statutory provision delegating powers directly to a subordinate administrator must be accommodated to the President's constitutional power of administrative direction:

Cole seems to argue that, since the statute places the discretion in the "agency heads", the President had no power to issue an Order upon the subject. In the first place, this is an executive matter and, if Congress had meant to prohibit the President from acting in respect to it, a serious question as to the validity of its act would arise. As we have already said, the Constitution vests the executive power in the President. In the second place, Congress knew, or must be conclusively presumed to have known, that subordinate officers in the executive branch of the Government act under the direction of the President, and it must have had that fact in mind when it conferred discretion upon these agency heads in this statute. Such an understanding is implicit in the enactment. . . . The President surely has the right to lay down the lines within which his subordinates shall exercise discretions confided in them, and their operation within such lines is valid. . . .[63]

Although a sharp distinction may be made in theory between executive rule-making intended to have effect only upon internal administrative relationships and executive regulations which directly affect persons outside of the government (i.e., the "public"), it is of course true that orders of both types are frequently included within the same regulation just as the same lack of differentiation on this point is characteristic of statutes. Moreover, it may be difficult if not impossible in many instances to distinguish between the "internal" and "external" effects of any given order.[64] At the same time, the concept of the scope of "internal" in this context must frequently be broadened to include the judiciary and the Congress as well as the executive branch. An example of this is provided by President Truman's Executive Order No. 10290 of September 25, 1951, relating to agency classification of security information. On its face, the executive order was addressed only to the President's administrative subordinates in the executive branch, directing them to adopt certain common administrative procedures and practices in the release of information to persons outside the agency. In effect, however, the limitations on the accessibility of information have been felt by press, general public, courts, and legislature alike. Turning the other side of the coin, presidential regulations which appear to fall in the "external" category — and these will normally be addressed to the public at large, even though their predictable impact will be upon only a limited public, such, for instance, as those who control the management of railroads — will inevitably have considerable bearing upon the "internal" question of administrative relationships within an agency or among agencies.

A recent decision reveals a keen awareness, on the part of a trial judge, of such complexities inherent in the exercise of presidential rulemaking. The critical point of law in this case was the constitutionality of Executive Order No. 9786, made under Section 3 of the Lucas Act of August 7, 1946, which authorized the continuance in effect of the power of executive agencies to consider claims for relief from losses sustained by war contractors in cases where, in the judgment of the agency, "such action would facilitate the prosecution of the war." This power originally had been delegated to the President by the First War Powers Act, and it had been administratively determined that this statute had lapsed on V-J Day. Upholding the legality of the executive order, the court remarked:

As a continuance of the First War Powers Act, which empowered the President to authorize agencies and departments to modify contracts without consideration, it was only natural that the act of August 7, 1946, should confer broad authority on the President. *Delegation of rule making power to the President rather than to the heads of departments highlights the extent of the discretion delegated and the essentially legislative character of the power to issue regulations.* . . . [T]he President's regulations are integrated into the act and limit departmental, agency, and court allowance alike.[65]

DIRECTIVE ORDERS AND INSTRUCTIONS

Another form of the President's power of administrative direction is that of issuing orders and instructions to individual executive officers concerning the performance of their duties, including those prescribed by statutory law. Apparently the oldest decision of the Supreme Court in which such presidential instructions were challenged was the celebrated case of *Marbury v. Madison*, in which Chief Justice Marshall declared in *obiter dictum* that President Jefferson's order to Secretary of State Madison, to withhold delivery of the signed judicial commissions of appointment of Marbury and others, was "violative of a vested legal right."[66] Shortly thereafter, President Adams' instructions to the captains of public vessels of the United States, directing a somewhat more vigorous enforcement of the non-intercourse laws than had been prescribed by statute, were held invalid by the Court;[67] and in the Circuit Court of South Carolina, Justice William Johnson of the Supreme Court ruled that President Jefferson had no authority to control by his orders the discretion vested by statute in the collectors of the customs.[68]

The latter case decided that the President could not control the discretionary action of his subordinates; the next reaffirmed that he could not control their ministerial actions. Congress had authorized the solicitor of the Treasury Department to settle certain claims; the Postmaster General directed that payment should be withheld in part on some of them, and the Court held that such instructions, even if emanating from the President himself, were illegal and without authority of law:

The executive power is vested in a president; and as far as his powers are derived from the constitution, he is beyond the reach of any department, except in the mode prescribed by the constitution through the impeaching power.[69] But it by no means follows, that every officer in every branch of that department is under the exclusive direction of the President. Such a principle, we apprehend, is not and certainly cannot be claimed by the President. . . .

It was urged at the bar, that the postmaster-general was alone subject to the direction and control of the President, with respect to the execution of the duty imposed upon him by this law; and this right of the President is claimed, as growing out of the obligation imposed upon him by the constitution, to take care that the laws be faithfully executed. This is a doctrine that cannot receive the sanction of this court. It would be vesting in the President a dispensing power, which has no countenance for its support in any part of the constitution; and is asserting a principle, which, if carried out in its results, to all cases falling within it, would be clothing the President with a power entirely to control the legislation of congress, and paralyze the administration of justice.

To contend that the obligation imposed on the President to see the laws faithfully executed, implies a power to forbid their execution, is a novel construction of the constitution, and entirely inadmissable. But although the argument necessarily leads to such a result, we do not perceive from the case that any such power has been claimed by the President.[70]

It was almost exactly a century after the inauguration of the first President that the question whether the President could direct a civil officer to perform a duty not required by any statutory law was raised before the Supreme Court. This, too, is a familiar case: *In re Neagle*.[71] A majority of the Supreme Court upheld the validity of the President's order[72] on both constitutional and statutory grounds; but the dissenting justices, denying that Congress had enacted a specific and relevant statute, limited their discussion to the constitutional issue, and denied that a letter from the Attorney General — presumably authorized by the President — was a "law" within the meaning of the habeas corpus act, or that the President had either constitutional or prerogative sources of legislative power to justify his orders.

Whatever one may assume with respect to the personal objectivity of the justices sitting on the bench at the time, they must have felt an inescapable and particular interest in a set of circumstances that raised the fundamental question of the power of the federal courts to function in the face of the most brazen contempt and attempted intimidation imaginable; and the duty of judges to preserve the institution of which they are a part must have been strongly felt, apart from any consideration they may have given to the equity of the case and the obvious moral justification in favor of Neagle. In other words, the unique facts in this case were undoubtedly significant factors in shaping the form assumed by the law in this, the leading and almost only case on this point of constitutional law. Here the majority held:

The Constitution, section 3, article 2, declares that the President "shall take care that the laws be faithfully executed." . . . We cannot doubt the power of the President to take measures for the protection of a judge of one of the courts of the United States, who, while in the discharge of the duties of his office, is threatened with a personal attack which may probably result in his death, and we think it clear that where this protection is to be afforded through the civil power, the Department of Justice is the proper one to set in motion the necessary means of protection.[73]

Another aspect of the President's constitutional responsibility for the faithful execution of the laws is his power to direct the Attorney General to undertake criminal prosecutions in the name of the United States. Since it is widely accepted and certainly true that the prosecutory function is inherently discretionary in nature — it is patent that all the laws cannot be "enforced" with equal vigor all the time — this would appear to be one question concerning presidential power for which the answer is found in explicit and unmistakable terms in the Constitution. An example is a decision of the Court of Appeals of the District of Columbia, which upheld the power of the President to direct by his Executive Order No. 7163 that the Attorney General institute a suit in counterclaim against an alien corporation which had been paid fraudulently over $3,000,000 with the collusion of the former alien property custodian (who was, incidentally, convicted for his own part in the fraud).[74]

The older pre-Civil War cases mentioned above, together with a few lower court decisions of more recent vintage,[75] are inconsistent with the general fabric and pattern of the case law governing the relationship between the President and his principal administrative subordinates, and it is absolutely certain that they no longer correctly state the law. As the Supreme Court more recently and clearly recognized in the *Humphrey* case, the presidential removal power and his power of administrative direction are opposite sides of the same coin: if an officer is subject to the President's power of removal, he is also subject to his power of direction.[76] Whether the immediate source of the subordinate's particular responsibility lies in a statute, in an executive or some other presidential order, or in administrative regulations, is immaterial; nor does it matter whether the duty is "discretionary" or "ministerial." Since the presidential removal power over such an officer is unqualified, breach of presidential instructions may be punished by removal and the appointment of a more tractable successor, and the factors which will condition presidential action in such circumstances will be political rather than legal. Of course, a dilemma is theoretically posed when the courts decide that the subordinate's duty is "ministerial," because the subordinate may then be mandamused into the performance of the prescribed duty; to the extent that "ministerial" is a concept of no fixed or certain content, therefore, the President's subordinates are subject to the power of administrative direction of the judiciary. This is not a serious matter in practice, however, since there are apparently fewer than half a dozen cases in which mandamus has successfully lain to compel the performance of such duties. Where this has been attempted in the past, the courts have usually managed to find some other solution to the case, frequently discovering a defect in their own jurisdiction to act, as did Chief Justice Marshall in the first of these cases, *Marbury v. Madison.*

PRESIDENTIAL TRANSFER OF ADMINISTRATIVE POWERS

The President's power of administrative direction includes the power to transfer statutory duties vested in one subordinate to another. His power to transfer statutory duties originally vested in himself from one subordinate to another is unquestioned,[77] but much broader authority must underlie his power to direct the transfer of duties from a statutory agent to another agent of his own choosing.[78]

The earliest case in which the latter question appears to have been raised was *Gelston v. Hoyt,*[79] which will be discussed in Chapter 4; on that occasion the Court decided that President Madison's order was illegal. Exactly one hundred years passed before this question arose again. Congress had delegated to the Secretary of the Treasury the authority to lease certain unoccupied and unproductive islands in Alaska for the propagation of foxes, but President Theodore Roosevelt directed in his executive order of February 2, 1904, that the Secretary of Commerce and Labor should undertake this function. Rejecting the argument that this order was invalid because the President had attempted thereby to assume authority over the public domain which by the Constitution was expressly vested in Congress, the Ninth Circuit Court of Appeals ruled:

It has always been recognized that the President, as the head of the respective executive departments, in the absence of any inconsistent statutory provision, has authority to assign to the heads of the departments powers which are vested in the executive [branch].[80]

Only a few years later, the Teapot Dome scandal erupted. This is such a well-known story that only the essential and directly relevant facts will be sketched here. By his executive order of May 31, 1921, President Harding had committed certain lands containing naval petroleum reserves to the administration and control of the Secretary of the Interior "in consultation and cooperation with the Secretary of the Navy," although the act of June 4, 1920, had delegated this responsibility directly to the Secretary of the Navy alone. In direct defiance of the statutory mandate that the oil on these lands was to constitute a reserve for the fleet in time of war and to be withdrawn only for essential naval uses, Secretary of the Interior Albert B. Fall approved leases in the Teapot Dome reserves in Wyoming and in other reserve fields in California to his personal friends and prospective employers, who set up a fraudulent Canadian corporation which siphoned off a major share of the profits of this entrepreneurial venture. Part of these ill-gotten gains, in the form of cash and United States bonds, were returned to Secretary Fall as deposits in fugitive bank accounts in the name of his son-in-law. The exposé led to a series of cases which resulted in the executive order being held unconstitutional in the Ninth Circuit and constitutional in the Eighth Circuit; and yet the Supreme Court could find no reason for passing upon the validity of the executive order when it disposed of the appeals from both circuits.

The first decision, by a district court ruling upon the validity of the California leases, held them to be void on the alternative grounds that they had been procured through fraud, and that President Harding had no power to issue the executive order upon which the legal authority for this whole fiasco must have rested if it were to be upheld:

If the executive order of May 31, 1921, purports to confer upon the Secretary of the Interior the authority which Congress has lodged exclusively in the Secretary of the Navy, it is, in my opinion, void to that extent. The President in peace time could not even, under his powerful and extensive general executive authority, transfer from one member of his Cabinet to another member of his Cabinet powers and duties that had been conferred by the Congress on a specified Cabinet officer, that call for the exercise of discretion by the Cabinet officer from whom such power is attempted to be transferred. In so far as systematizing, co-ordinating, and facilitating the conduct of the executive departments of government are concerned the President could lawfully transfer duties between Cabinet officers; but the transfer attempted by the executive order of May 31, 1921, goes much further.[81]

In a related case involving the same defendant, the government sued for the cancellation of additional leases in Naval Petroleum Reserve No. 1 in California. In this case, the trial court ruled that the evidence did not establish fraud,[82] but it was reversed on this point by the Ninth Circuit Court of Appeals, which at this time went out of its way to rule on the constitutional question that it had avoided in the first *Pan-American* case:

The lower court held, and we believe, correctly, that "the . . . Executive Order of May 31, 1921, attempting to transfer the administration of the Naval Petroleum Reserves from the Secretary of the Navy to the Secretary of the Interior, was invalid."[83]

Although the opinion of the Court of Appeals is not very clear in this matter, it is apparent that the reference above was to the opinion of the trial court in the first *Pan-American* case, rather than to the opinion of the trial court in the instant proceeding.[84] The entire record of the first case was made, by stipulation, a part of the record in the second case. It should be noted that the same district court tried both cases, but different judges presided over the two trials. Since, however, the Ninth Circuit Court of Appeals did thus expressly decide that President Harding's executive order of May 31, 1921, was unconstitutional, and the Supreme Court refused to review the decision by certiorari, this latest expression of judicial opinion in this series of cases should probably be accepted as authoritative on the constitutional question. The fact remains that the Supreme Court has never faced the issue squarely.

In the meantime, the "Teapot Dome" case had already been decided. The trial court had found no fraud in the leases to the Wyoming oil lands, and had avoided a decision on the constitutional question.[85] But the court went on to hold that "the invalidity of the executive order . . . has been very largely eliminated from the case"[86] on the grounds that the counsel for the government had admitted that there was no evidence of fraud in the issuance of the executive order, and further that the President had the authority to issue it, and that the provisions of the executive order were immaterial to the validity of the lease, since the Secretary of the Navy had personally, or through his representatives, dominated the negotiations preceding the execution of the lease.[87] Although the Eighth Circuit Court of Appeals reversed because it found that the leases had been fraudulently obtained, it affirmed that part of the trial court's opinion which said there had been in fact no transfer of power effected by the executive order, remarking:

The President had no authority to transfer from the Secretary of the Navy to the Secretary of the Interior powers which Congress had provided should be exercised by the former. The validity of this executive order does not seem to have been seriously questioned in the presentation of the case to this court.[88]

The Supreme Court affirmed, and in its own statement of the facts noted:

The Assistant Secretary [of the Navy, Theodore Roosevelt, Jr.] told [Secretary of the Navy] Denby that he thought that the property [Naval Oil Reserve No. 3: "Teapot Dome"] should not be turned over to the Interior Department. Denby replied that the matter had been decided by the President [Harding], Fall and himself. Later the Assistant Secretary took to Denby a suggestion, prepared by him and his associates, for the amendment of the proposed order [requiring the consultation and cooperation of the Secretary of the Navy in regard to the change of general policy as to drilling or reserving lands located in a naval reserve.] . . . Fall agreed to the change, and the President signed [on May 31, 1921] the form of [the executive] order as amended.[89]

Nevertheless, the Supreme Court summarily avoided the constitutional question at the heart of this whole proceeding with the cryptic statement that "It is not necessary here to consider the validity or effect of the executive order."[90]

President Wilson's action in directing the Secretary of the Treasury to take over and operate the railroads, when the act of August 29, 1916, specified that he was "empowered through the Secretary of War to take possession and assume control of any system of transportation," was probably the most patently *ultra vires* transfer of authority made by a President in recent times; but no successful challenge to his proclamation was made before Congress enacted the Federal Control Act of March 21, 1918, which "expressly ratified the action of President Wilson in the appointment he had made."[91] A similar objection to President Franklin Roosevelt's Executive Order No. 9108, ordering the director of the Office of Defense Transportation (instead of the Secretary of War) to take over the Toledo, Peoria, and Western Railroad, was overruled on the ground that, although the executive order would have been illegal standing alone under the earlier 1916 statute, the broad discretion to transfer duties between officers of the executive branch contained in the First War Powers Act was sufficient authorization for the action taken. Moreover, the President's subsequent order of December 27, 1943, taking over all the railroads in the United States, did direct that possession be taken by the Secretary of War, in strict conformity with the World War I statute.[92]

Other transfers of duties brought about by executive orders under the authority of the First War Powers Act near the end of the period of active hostilities — and particularly during the period of reconversion after hostilities had ceased — resulted in some confusion in a few of the district courts[93] until the issues reached the Supreme Court for authoritative clarification in the spring of 1947. On December 12, 1946, after hostilities had ceased, the President issued his Executive Order

No. 9809, acting by virtue of the authority vested in him "by the Constitution" and by Title I of the First War Powers Act of 1941 and Title III of the Second War Powers Act of 1943, and s. 201(b) of Emergency Price Control Act of 1942 and s. 2 of the Stabilization Act of 1942, "and as President of the United States" and "for the purpose of further effectuating the transition from war to peace and in the interest of the internal management of the Government." This executive order created an Office of Temporary Controls in the Office of Emergency Management in the Executive Office of the President; transferred to it functions of the Office of War Mobilization and Reconversion, the Office of Economic Stabilization, the Office of Price Administration, and the Civilian Production Administration; and created the position of administrator of temporary controls, with a salary of $12,000 and no provision for senatorial confirmation "unless the Congress shall otherwise provide." Congress did not so provide, and President Truman appointed Philip B. Fleming as the administrator.

The Supreme Court upheld in unequivocal terms Executive Order No. 9809 and the subsequent administrative action taken pursuant to it. The only question that the Court avoided was that of the President's power to transfer functions from an officer whose appointment had necessitated Senate confirmation to one appointed by the President without such confirmation. The Court found it unnecessary to decide the question at this time, because Fleming had been previously appointed by the President and confirmed by the Senate to the position of federal works administrator, and he was therefore the incumbent of an office "existing by law," as required by the Emergency Price Control Act, at the time he was appointed as administrator of temporary controls. Therefore, reasoned the Court, it would be inconsistent with the broad scope of presidential authority under the First War Powers Act to hold that Fleming must be again confirmed before taking up his new duties; and in any event, Congress had approved the appointment in a recent appropriation bill.[94]

Although *Fleming v. Mohawk* proved to be conclusive in the resolution of the constitutional questions in this matter, attempts were made to challenge President Truman's subsequent action, in Executive Order No. 9842, transferring functions from the Office of Temporary Controls to other agencies when it was terminated on June 1, 1947, by Executive Order No. 9841. The former order, which directed the Attorney

General to prosecute in the name of the United States suits for violations of maximum price regulations covering commodities which had been (by then) removed from controls, was held to have been authorized by both the First War Powers Act and the Emergency Price Control Act;[95] and although a circuit court of appeals came to a directly opposite conclusion in a later case,[96] it was shortly and sharply reversed in an unanimous decision of the Supreme Court.[97]

Only one case, and that a very recent one, appears to have raised the question of the President's power to transfer among his subordinates subdelegated powers that flow from his own constitutional authority and status. Apparently the reason this question has not been raised before is that the President seldom exercised this authority until recent years and it has been generally assumed to be unimpeachable. In this case, a federal district court remarked:

I am not impressed by petitioner's argument that there was a change in the nature or power of the court merely because, prior to the effective date of the [Western Germany] Occupation Statute, the system of which it was a part operated under orders of the Department of the Army, but was afterwards carried on through the Department of State. It makes no difference through what agency he may act; the President is still commander-in-chief, and as such vested with power to continue the military government during the transition period between the cessation of hostilities and the treaty of peace. It is worthy of note that the Federal Constitution, from which the President's power as commander-in-chief is derived, makes no mention of separate departments of the government, nor does it limit him in the exercise of the powers which go with the office of military commander-in-chief.[98]

Although this decision deals with the exercise of power held to have been derived from the President's status as Commander in Chief, the *problem* discussed above is administrative, not peculiarly military; and there is no obvious reason why the same argument would not apply to any equivalent transfer among executive agencies of subdelegated fragments of what the Constitution calls "The executive Power."

EXECUTIVE REORGANIZATION PLANS

Closely related to but clearly distinguishable from the President's power to transfer specific powers from one executive officer to another is his statutory authority to carry out reorganization of the executive branch. The first of such statutes was the Overman Act of May 20, 1918, which delegated broad reorganizational powers to the President;

45

and an early attempt to challenge the transfer of the Coast Guard back to the Treasury Department from its wartime service under the Navy Department, by executive order of August 28, 1919, failed when a lower federal court upheld the President's action without question. Apart from the Overman Act, ample authority was contained in the act of January 28, 1915, which provided that "The Coast Guard, which shall constitute a part of the military forces of the United States and which shall operate under the Treasury Department in time of peace and operate as a part of the Navy, subject to the orders of the Secretary of the Navy, in time of war or when the President shall so direct"; and although the President's order specifically recited that he was acting under the Overman Act, the court found the latter source of power adequate by itself, holding that "A mere reading of the act shows that the President was clothed with the widest measure of discretion, so far as concerned 'matters relating to the conduct of the present war.'" [99]

Similar broad powers were delegated to the President during the depression, and in one form or another have become accepted as an important adjunct to his powers of administrative control and direction. It is also noteworthy that the President's reorganizational powers are now looked upon as a normal part of his peacetime authority, and not merely as a temporary expedient to meet an existing national emergency. The Reorganization Act of March 3, 1933, authorized the President to regroup, consolidate, transfer, or abolish any executive agency or agencies, subject to congressional veto by resolution of either House during a sixty-day period following the issuance of his order.[100] By his Executive Order No. 6166 of June 10, 1933, President Roosevelt integrated in the Department of Justice various legal functions heretofore scattered among the executive agencies. The effect of Section 5 of this executive order was to transfer from the Treasury Department to the Department of Justice the specific responsibility for defending before the courts and determining whether or not to appeal cases involving protests against classifications of goods made by the collectors of the customs; and the Court of Customs and Patent Appeals upheld both the executive order and the Reorganization Act, remarking: "No rights were vested in the collector or Secretary of the Treasury which might not be divested by executive order, when we once concede the validity of the enabling act under which the President acted." [101]

Another section of Executive Order No. 6166 abolished the United

States Shipping Board, and transferred its functions to the Secretary of Commerce.[102] This part of the executive order was based on both the act of March 3, 1933, and the reorganization provisions of the Economy Act of June 30, 1932, to which it was amendatory. Section 402 of the 1932 statute defined the executive agencies which the President might abolish or whose functions he might transfer as "any commission, board, bureau, division, service, or office in the executive branch of the government"; but Section 406 specifically withheld from the President the authority to abolish or transfer the functions of the Shipping Board. The 1933 statute, however, omitted the latter limitation, and added the phrase "independent establishments" to the enumeration of executive agencies subject to his reorganizational powers. As required by the 1932 statute, the President transmitted a copy of his executive order to the Congress, which adjourned a few days after having received it without taking any action upon it.

In 1937, the Supreme Court decided two cases, each of which sought to challenge the validity of the transfer of the Shipping Board. In the first of these, various constitutional questions were pressed upon the Court: that the executive order had automatically lapsed by the adjournment of Congress, since it had lain there for less than the required sixty days; that the order was unconstitutional because it attempted to transfer quasi-legislative and quasi-judicial powers from the Shipping Board to "an executive officer," thus "attempting to make the head of an executive department also a judicial officer and a legislative officer of the United States"; and that the order was unconstitutional because it contravened the due process clause, since the President had issued his order "without notice and hearing and failed in the order adequately to specify the grounds for his action." The Court, however, was able to avoid these constitutional issues on the ground that they were moot as to the appellant, since Congress had ratified the executive order by various appropriation acts as well as by Section 204 (a) of the Merchant Marine Act of 1936, and since the Maritime Commission created by that act had expressly continued in effect the orders of the Department of Commerce effective at the time it was created.[103] In the second case, decided a month later, the Court reviewed and followed its own recent precedent, except that it now felt compelled to consider the due process argument, because, unlike the order in the *Isbrandtsen-Moller* case which had "determined no rights and prescribed no duties," the rate order here "is of a different sort." The question of the validity of the executive order was still considered immaterial, since there was no doubt of the power of Congress to abolish the Shipping Board and transfer its functions to the Secretary, or of the power of Congress to approve and ratify a presidential order to the same effect.[104] Although both these decisions of the Court have been frequently cited during the past twenty years, no subsequent cases appear to have questioned the President's powers of reorganization.

INTERMEDIATE ORDERS

A much more formal organizational relationship between the President and an administrative officer or agency has been frequently created by statutes in a twofold attempt to "canalize" or guide the discretion of the President while at the same time ensuring the continuous exercise, at least in a formal sense, of his power of administrative direction over a given class of decisions. In such systems of sublegislation or administrative adjudication, the advice of the administrative subordinate assumes the form of intermediate orders which are subject to the review and approval of the President. Several examples of this relationship will be discussed in subsequent chapters. Some of those in which the intermediate orders were considered to be legislative include the following: recommendations of changes in rates of customs duties by the Tariff Commission, N.R.A. codes, Civil Service Commission regulations, Army and Navy regulations, regulations of the Veterans Administration, and certain of the acts of the legislatures and governors of territorial governments such as Hawaii and Alaska.[105] Intermediate orders of a "judicial" nature would include orders of the Civil Aeronautics Board affecting foreign carriers or foreign air routes, orders of the War Labor Board and War Manpower Commission during World War II, and reports of fact-finding boards appointed by the President in cases of "national emergency" strikes, under the Labor-Management Relations Act of 1947. Difficult to classify under either the "legislative" or "judicial" concepts is a third type, which might be termed executive or managerial. An instance of this type was provided by Sections 202 and 203 (a) of the National Industrial Recovery Act of 1933, which conditioned presidential approval of the construction of dams for flood control and other purposes upon the express prior authorization of Congress or, in the alternative, the recommendation of the chief of Army Engineers.[106]

Presidential Management of Public Personnel

The common characteristics of all the intermediate orders above may be reduced to two fundamentals: (1) the intermediate orders create no rights and confer no duties, having no binding effect because they are viewed in law as a form of administrative advice to the President; and (2) they are never, as such, subject to judicial review. There are two other characteristics which are frequently, but not universally, true of intermediate-order systems: (1) they extend the President's power of administrative direction over administrative agencies, such as the Civil Aeronautics Board and the Tariff Commission, where presumptively it would not reach in the absence of explicit statutory exceptions to the general rule; and (2) the effect of formally institutionalizing the administrative decision-making process in this way is to make this kind of administrative order, when final, immune, or at least less subject to judicial review than other orders of the same agencies and officers, because the effect of presidential approval of their intermediate orders is to interpose the peculiar breadth and "delicacy" of discretion usually attributed to presidential action by the courts. In addition, subjecting presidential action to review involves special procedural problems, which are either less pressing or else not involved in the application of judicial review to the "final" orders of the administrative agencies themselves.

Although a number of Supreme Court decisions support these generalizations, it cannot be said that the Court has as yet faced squarely the constitutional issues implicit in this pattern of administrative relationship and sublegislative process.[107] Moreover, the leading decision by a lower federal court occurred in time of war and related to a wartime agency; and the administrative situation here also varied in another respect: National War Labor Board orders were not subject to express presidential approval before issuance, but their major sanction was the threat of presidential action to seize industrial facilities. Holding that orders of the National War Labor Board were not subject to judicial review, the Court of Appeals of the District of Columbia said:

The Board's order is not reviewable.
It is clear and undisputed that no statute authorizes review of the War Labor Board's order. . . .
The Board's directive order in this case was expressly issued by virtue of the powers vested in the Board by the two Executive Orders which we have cited, 9017 and 9250. . . . Executive Order 9370, issued

49

August 16, 1943, which authorizes the Director of Economic Stabilization, when the War Labor Board reports to him that its orders have not been complied with, to direct withdrawal of priorities and government contracts "in order to effectuate compliance," is irrelevant here. . . .

Appellants say in effect . . . that if they do not comply with the order the Board may notify the President of their noncompliance and the President may take possession of their plants and facilities. We have no occasion to decide whether in our opinion this is true. In some instances concerns which had failed to comply with Board orders have ultimately been taken over by Presidential orders. In other instances concerns which had not been the subject of any Board order have been taken over by Presidential orders. If it be true . . . that the President may ultimately take possession of their plants and facilities, that possibility is irrelevant not only because it is speculative but also because it is independent of the Board's order. Neither the broad constitutional power nor the broad statutory power of the President to take and use property in furtherance of the war effort depends upon any action of the War Labor Board. Any action of the Board would be informatory and "at most, advisory." Appellants' demand that we annul and enjoin the Board's order therefore amounts to a demand that we prevent the Board from giving the President advice which appellants contend would be erroneous. A court might as well be asked to prevent the Secretary of State or the Attorney General from giving alleged erroneous advice. The correctness of administrative advice cannot be reviewed by the courts. They have neither the necessary authority nor the necessary qualifications for such work.[108]

On the other hand, it may be just as important to note what are *not* considered to be intermediate orders. Two recent decisions of the Supreme Court afford some insight on this point. In the first, the Court held that the decision of the Attorney General to refuse to suspend the deportation of an alien under Section 19c of the Immigration Act of 1917 was "final" administratively, and although subject to possible modification within six months by concurrent resolution of the Congress, it was *not* an intermediate order and it was subject to judicial review; [109] C.A.B. recommendations to the President and the *Chicago and Southern Airlines* case were explicitly distinguished. In the other case, a majority of the Court, for widely divergent reasons, found that the designation and public listing, by the Attorney General, of a private organization as subversive raised constitutional questions of sufficient substance for a trial court to proceed to hear evidence on the merits of the issues.[110] It is also noteworthy that, in the latter case, the administrative advice was not given directly to the President for approval or action, but rather to another presidential agency, the Loyalty Review Board attached to the Civil Service Commission, which functioned, like the Attorney General himself in this respect, on the basis of and within the limits set by the President's executive order. No direct presidential action was called for, further distinguishing these orders of the Attorney General from the genus of intermediate order as described and defined here.

The Subdelegation of Presidential Power

The question of the power of the President to subdelegate his own powers, that is, to delegate to administrative subordinates powers that have been delegated to him by the Constitution or by statutes, is actually considered through the greater part of this study. Although presidential orders of a "judicial" nature do not characteristically entail the exercise of this power, those of a "legislative" nature usually do, and it is almost inherent in "executive" executive orders and directives that power is subdelegated to subordinates to act for the President. Only in rare instances has the President ever attempted *formally* to subdelegate his constitutional powers — such as the making of foreign policy — but administrative necessity and the limits to the capacities of the individual human mind and body make it inevitable that even in this respect, only a fragment of the decisions and decisional processes necessarily involved in the carrying out of his constitutional responsibilities can entail personal action by the President. It is more useful for present purposes, however, to limit the concept of subdelegation to those formal acts, usually taking the form of executive orders, presidential proclamations, or presidential administrative directives, in which he explicitly delegates to specific subordinate officers powers that were delegated, in the first instance, to him. Almost without exception, the source of such delegation to the President will be statutory rather than constitutional; and except in time of *de facto* national emergency, the recipients of such subdelegated presidential powers will be officers whose status is clearly recognized as being within the "executive branch." Although the courts, since an early period and without significant exception, have recognized the implied constitutional power of the President to subdelegate his statutory powers on the pragmatic basis of sheer administrative necessity, the increasing tendency in recent years has been to include specific "subdelegation" clauses — not unlike specific "separability" clauses — in each individual statute that delegates substantial additional duties and responsibilities to the President. On the other hand, there has also been a tendency in recent legislation to include specific clauses prohibiting the subdelegation of certain presidential statutory powers. A temporary climax in the development of both these trends was reached, at the apparent solicitation of the President himself, in the enactment of the Presidential Subdelegation Act, approved by the President on August 8, 1950.[111]

In an early case, a justice of the Supreme Court pointed out that:

First, the power of the president under the first section of the law, to establish by his proclamation or other public acts, rules and regulations for apprehending, restraining, securing, and removing alien enemies, under the circumstances stated in that section, appears to me to be as unlimited as the legislature could make it. . . . the powers vested in him, necessarily conferred all the means of enforcing his orders; and since it would be absurd to suppose that the president could personally enforce his own decrees, it follows that he might direct others to do it . . . the authority of the marshall to carry into execution the regulations and orders of the president, is implied in the power conferred on the president to establish these regulations.[112]

The same idea was expressed by the Supreme Court as a whole when it said, a few years later:

The President's duty in general, requires his superintendence of the administration; yet this duty cannot require of him to become the administrative officer of every department and bureau, or to perform in person the numerous details incident to such services which, nevertheless, he is, in a correct sense, by the constitution and laws, required and expected to perform.[113]

In the post-Civil War period, emphasis was shifted from the *power* of the President to act through others to the assumption that he had exercised this power by directing his subordinates to undertake the actions which had, in fact, occurred:

[I]f the seizure was made by virtue of the act of Congress, as the information avers it was, it was necessarily caused to be made by the President, for only he was empowered by the act to cause it. Then the Attorney-General must have been the agent of the President to give instructions to the district attorney, and through him to the marshal. The language of the statute is, "it shall be the duty of the President to cause the seizure", etc. This implies that the seizure is to be made by the agents of the President. And a direction given by the Attorney-General to seize property liable to confiscation under the act of Congress must be regarded as a direction given by the President.[114]

The underlying basis in necessity of the implied constitutional power of the President to subdelegate to subordinates duties that have been expressly delegated to him by statute was first clearly stated by the Supreme Court a few years later, and the passing of time has brought about no significant change in the rule the Court formulated then:

There are, undoubtedly, official acts which the Constitution and laws require to be performed by the President personally, and the performance of which may not be delegated to heads of departments, or to other officers in the executive branch of the Government. It is equally true that, as to the vast multiplicity of matters involved in the administration of the executive business of the government, it is physically impossible for the President to give them his personal supervision. Of necessity he must, as to such matters, discharge his duty through the instrumentality or by the agency, of others.[115]

There have been very few exceptions to the rule. A characteristic example of the insignificance of such judicial sports is provided by one of a bizarre pair of cases that arose in lower courts in New York City following World War I, dealing with the somewhat exceptional matter of presidential discretion in the naturalization process. Although alien enemies were the petitioners here, the governing statute was based on the power of Congress "To establish an uniform rule of naturalization" rather than on the war power. The act of June 29, 1906, as amended by the act of May 9, 1918, provided that "the President of the United States may, *in his discretion*, upon investigation and report by the Department of Justice fully establishing the loyalty of any alien enemy not included in the foregoing exemption, except such alien enemy from the classification of alien enemy, and thereupon he shall have the privilege of applying for naturalization."[116] The President, by his executive order of November 26, 1918, excepted certain persons from the classification of alien enemy solely for the purpose of permitting them to apply for final naturalization papers. The Department of Justice then investigated the individuals who had applied to the President, and notified the Secretary of Labor directly of the results of the loyalty check. In the federal district court, Judge Learned Hand granted an application for naturalization of an Alsatian, assuming but not deciding the validity of the blanket declassifiation made by Wilson's executive order.[117] Less than two years later, however, the state Supreme Court for Kings County became hopelessly entangled in problems of presidential subdelegation of its own creation, denying the application for naturalization before it on the ground that the President personally had to weigh and decide upon the loyalty of each applicant! The court also decided that the President's function was "judicial" in nature.[118] The only relevant precedent, that established by Judge Hand in the neighboring federal district court only eighteen months previously, was not even mentioned in the opinion of Judge Benedict, which held Wilson's executive order to be unconstitutional:

> I think it is requisite under the statutory provision quoted that the President shall personally determine in each case whether the alien enemy shall be excepted from that classification. . . . Not only does the statute itself seem to contemplate personal action by the President upon the report of the Department of Justice, but the power is clearly of a judicial character, the execution of which cannot be delegated.
>
> In the present cases it appears, from the form of the certificates, that the cases of these applicants have never been brought to the personal attention of the President, and never acted upon by him, but that he has attempted by a general executive order, dated November 26, 1918, to delegate to the Department of Justice the function of passing upon the question of the loyalty of alien enemies who may desire to be naturalized, and of exercising the discretion with which the act in question vests him. This, I hold, he could not do under the act.[119]

A more recent decision of a circuit court of appeals indicates the extent to which modern judicial opinion has reached a position where it not only coincides with, but even anticipates in some respects, the general pattern of administrative practice in presidential subdelegation:

> [I]t is true that the section gives the President an unrestricted power to be exercised at his discretion and without any standard except that he shall act through "rules and regulations." The only objection to this which can be raised is that it disturbs the constitutional "separation of powers" . . . [which] is in the end a matter of degree anyway. . . . Nor does it matter that by Executive Order No. 9095 . . . the President in turn delegated his powers to the Custodian, authorizing him to "vest" in himself the property of a friendly alien when he determined that this was "necessary in the national interest." That was in effect the same condition on which the President's own power was conferred; and in the nature of things the President cannot personally exercise the least fraction of the manifold powers of every

description which are granted to him—more truly, which are imposed upon him. If he may not depute their exercise, they are sterile as stones.[120]

A similar and almost contemporaneous ruling was made by the Second Circuit Court of Appeals in a criminal prosecution of a defendant who had violated Regulation 28 of the solid fuels administrator for war by making excessive and illegal carload shipments of coal to a New York City dealer. The constitutionality of Executive Order No. 9332 of April 19, 1943, subdelegating presidential rationing authority to the solid fuels administrator for war, was directly challenged before and upheld by the court, which held:

We have already decided that the delegation of power to the President under the Second War Powers Act was lawful. . . . The subsequent delegation of power by the President to SFAW was equally so and the promulgation of Reg. 28 was, beyond any fair doubt, a proper exercise of that delegated power in form and scope.[121]

The critical and somewhat fugitive issue, at least from the point of view of recognition and consideration in the courts of the United States, of sub-subdelegation was squarely faced by the Court of Claims the following year. This case took the form of an action by a government contractor to recover from the government his increased labor costs resulting from a directive of May 1943 of the regional manpower director, making the forty-eight-hour week applicable to his area, thus forcing him to pay time and a half for all work in excess of forty hours. The directive, which was based on Executive Order No. 9301 of February 9, 1943, was issued after he had entered into his fixed-sum contract on March 9, 1943. Executive Order No. 9301 declared that, for the duration of the war, the minimum workweek for effective utilization of manpower was forty-eight hours, and "directed the departments and agencies of the Government to require their contractors to comply with that workweek and with the policies, directives, and regulations prescribed in accordance with the Executive Order. The Chairman of the War Manpower Commission was empowered to issue policies, directives, and regulations to carry out the order and effectuate its purposes." In accordance with War Manpower Regulation No. 3 of March 3, 1943, the regional manpower director of Region V, by directive of April 2, 1943, designated the area in which Piqua, Ohio, was located as an area subject to the forty-eight-hour workweek, effective May 1, 1943. The plaintiff was then notified to comply with Executive

Order No. 9301 and the War Manpower Commission's directives, and he did so. The court held:

The plaintiff urges that the directive applying Executive Order to the Piqua, Ohio, area was issued by the Regional Manpower Director of Region V, and not by the Chairman of the War Manpower Commission. It argues that the latter official had, himself, only a delegated authority and hence he could not further delegate it, as he did in his Regulations. The Executive Order was inclusive in its grant of authority, the territory to be covered was the whole of the country and its economy. We have no doubt that the Executive Order contemplated extensive redelegation to accomplish its purpose.[122]

When the Supreme Court decided *Ludecke v. Watkins* a few months later something of a cycle had been completed, because the Court was asked to pass upon the constitutionality of the same statute and was presented with the same substantive issues that Mr. Justice Washington had ruled upon a hundred and thirty-one years previously in *Lockington v. Smith*. Both the relevant administrative process and the judicial comprehension of that process had grown more complex and sophisticated in the interim, but the guiding principle of law remains unchanged:

The power with which Congress vested the President [in 1798] had to be executed by him through others. He provided for the removal of such enemy aliens as were "deemed by the Attorney General" to be dangerous. But such a finding, at the President's behest, was likewise not to be subjected to the scrutiny of the courts. For one thing, removal was contingent not upon a finding that in fact an alien was "dangerous." The President was careful to call for the removal of aliens "deemed by the Attorney General to be dangerous." *But the short answer is that the Attorney General was the President's voice and conscience.* A war power of the President not subject to judicial review is not transmuted into a judicially reviewable action because the President chooses to have that power exercised within narrower limits than Congress authorized.[123]

The courts have interposed no obstacles to presidential subdelegation or administrative sub-subdelegation of the President's constitutional or statutory powers. Congress has given both general and specific authorization for such practices, above and beyond the case law. The most cursory examination of recent and contemporary executive orders and administrative regulations reveals how widespread the formal devolution of legal authority has become. What is conspicuously absent in most of the statutory provisions, and utterly lacking in the judicial opinions, is any formulation of standards to guide presidential and administrative discretion in transferring decisional authority to centers of the executive hierarchy to which Congress has not delegated powers. Such standards are usually, but not always,[124] supplied in presidential and administrative instruments of subdelegation, for reasons of executive policy. But the point here is that the judiciary has given almost carte blanche to the Chief Executive in his practice of subdelegating — up, down, and across the hierarchies of the executive branch — without having developed corresponding limitations to assure the responsible exercise of such powers. Whatever may be the myths of the common lawyer,[125] the control of bureaucracy in this regard must fall back upon political restraints over the Chief Executive. In his control over the personnel of the executive branch of the national government, the President is subject to precious little check by the federal judiciary.

Notes

[1] For an excellent development of the political and legal theory relevant and supplementary to this chapter, see Nathan D. Grundstein, "Presidential Power, Administration and Administrative Law," *George Washington Law Review*, 18:285–326 (April 1950). See also James Hart, *Tenure of Office Under the Constitution* (Baltimore: Johns Hopkins, 1930).

[2] Except under Section 12(c) of the Hatch acts of 1939 and 1940, 53 *Stat.* 1147, as amended. As the Supreme Court noted in United Public Workers v. Mitchell, 330 U.S. 75. 93 (1947): "The act provides no administrative or statutory review for the order of the Civil Service Commission." See also Carr v. Gordon, 82 F. 373 (C.Ct.Ill.N.D., 1897).

[3] His commission was revoked because he allegedly jumped ship when his company was sailing for possible combat duty.

[4] The Army Appropriation Act of July 13, 1866, limited the President's power to remove military officers in time of peace to the execution of a court-martial sentence, or the commutation thereof.

[5] The act of July 17, 1862, 12 *Stat.* 596, c. 200, had delegated authority to the President to remove military officers for the good of the service.

[6] McElrath v. United States, 102 U.S. 426, 437–439 (1880). There was no evidence to indicate, of course, that either the President or the Secretary of the Navy had ever directed or intended that Lieutenant Haycock should be removed in order to restore McElrath to full-time active duty; the apparent intent had been to rectify what was accepted as an administrative mistake by granting retroactively partial restitution for the loss in pay suffered by McElrath. The Court's argument here must be interpreted as a rather clumsy rationale for denying the claimant any legal right to compensation during the period between his dismissal in 1862 and his purported resignation in 1873.

[7] Blake v. United States, 103 U.S. 227, 231, 233–234, 236–237 (1881). Cf. Mullan v. United States, 140 U.S. 240 (1891).

[8] A climax in this kind of thinking was reached by the Supreme Court in its opinion in Runkle v. United States, 122 U.S. 543, 557–558 (1887), where it held: "There can be no doubt that the President, in the exercise of his executive power under the Constitution, may act through the head of the appropriate executive department. . . . Here, however, the action required of the President is judicial in its character, not ad-

ministrative. As Commander-in-Chief of the Army he has been made by law the person whose duty it is to review the proceedings of courts martial in cases of this kind. This implies that he is himself to consider the proceedings laid before him and decide personally whether they ought to be carried into effect. Such a power he cannot delegate . . . his judgment, when pronounced, must be his own and not that of another. . . . Undoubtedly the President, in passing upon the sentence of a court-martial, and giving it the approval without which it cannot be executed, acts judicially."

[9] Except to the extent that state legislatures are limited by the contract clause. United States Constitution, Art. I, Sec. 10, Cl. 1.

[10] Jason v. Summerfield, 214 F. 2d 273, 276 (C.A.D.C., 1954), certiorari denied, 348 U.S. 840 (1954). Kenneth Davis argues to the contrary in his *Administrative Law* (St. Paul: West Publishing Co., 1951), p. 565.

[11] Knox v. Lee, 12 Wall. 457 (1871).

[12] It should be noted, however, that the Court changed its mind on the *issue*; the judgment in the original case remained, of course, final.

[13] United States v. Burchard, 125 U.S. 176, 179–180 (1888).

[14] Reaves v. Ainsworth, 219 U.S. 296, 304, 306 (1911).

[15] For the very reason that the judiciary could not control the administrative decision after an appeal was taken to the President, the Court of Appeals of the District of Columbia ruled that mandamus *would* lie to cause an Army review board to remove from the file of a retired officer certain papers (which the court considered to be inadmissible under an act of Congress) before proceeding to a rehearing in his case. Chambers v. Robertson, 183 F. 2d 144, 147 (C.A.D.C., 1950). The Supreme Court disregarded the question of whether judicial review was possible, and reversed on the ground that the papers were properly admitted for consideration. Robertson v. Chambers, 341 U.S. 37 (1951).

[16] Ed. Denby, Secretary of the Navy v. Berry, 263 U.S. 29, 38 (1923).

[17] Nordmann v. Woodring, 28 F. Supp. 573, 574, 575 (W.D.Okla., 1939); Seltzer v. United States, 98 Ct. Cl. 554, 559–562 (1943).

[18] Myers v. United States, 272 U.S. 52 (1926); Rathbun v. United States, 295 U.S. 602 (1935). See also Porter v. Coble, 246 F. 244 (8 C.C.A., 1917); Shurtleff v. United States, 189 U.S. 311 (1903); and Parsons v. United States, 167 U.S. 324 (1897).

[19] The Civil Aeronautics Board, for instance, is clearly under the direct administrative control of the President for certain purposes, as discussed in Chapter 4. Both the Maritime Board and the Civil Service Commission are subject to the President's reorganizational powers, and the recent changes that were made in their status was in each case expressly intended to facilitate presidential administrative direction. The board of governors of the federal reserve system has important managerial as well as regulatory responsibilities: cf. the President's power to remove the chairman of the board of directors of a government corporation, Morgan v. Tennessee Valley Authority, 115 F. 2d 990 (6 C.C.A., 1940). Is the presidential removal power unqualified with respect to the members of these boards?

[20] An exception to this generalization is provided by the language recently used by the Court of Appeals of the District of Columbia, which ruled that Executive Order No. 10463 of June 25, 1953, should not be construed to authorize the summary administrative removal, without regard to the removal procedures of the Lloyd-LaFollette Act, of an attorney with competitive status who was appointed to his position *before* it was transferred to Schedule A. "Neither the formula of 'excepting' the kind of position a person holds," said the court, "nor any other formula, can obviate the requirement of the Lloyd-LaFollette Act that 'No person in the classified civil service of the United States shall be removed . . . therefrom' without notice and reasons given in writing. The power of Congress thus to limit the President's otherwise plenary control over appointments and removals is clear." Roth v. Brownell, 215 F. 2d 500, 502 (1954); certiorari denied, 348 U.S. 863 (1954).

Presidential Management of Public Personnel

[21] United States *ex rel* Rebecca J. Taylor v. William H. Taft, Secretary of War, 203 U.S. 461, 464 (1906).

[22] Civil Service Act of 1883, Section 2, 5 U.S.C.A. Sec. 633.

[23] United States *ex rel* Crow v. Mitchell, 89 F. 2d 805, 807, 809 (C.A.D.C., 1937). Cf. Elder v. Brannan, 341 U.S. 277 (1951). Another unsuccessful attempt, this time on the part of the Congress, to coerce the President's removal power was made in 1943 when a rider to an appropriation bill directed that no part of the monies made available therein should be used to pay, after a named date, any part of the salaries of three stipulated individuals who had been stigmatized as "un-American" by the notorious Dies Committee. The President did not remove them, and the officers concerned sued for their salaries in the Court of Claims, alleging the unconstitutionality of that part of the statute which directed the withholding of their salaries. The Supreme Court, in Lovett v. United States, 328 U.S. 303 (1946), held an act of Congress invalid for the second time in ten years, and decided that the action of the Congress here involved was a bill of attainder within the meaning of the Constitution, and therefore unconstitutional. The act was without much doubt unconstitutional for the additional reason that it represented an attempted encroachment upon the discretion of the Chief Executive, but the Court did not reach this ground in its decision.

[24] His previous position was in an exempt peacetime agency to which the regulations did not apply.

[25] Friedman v. Schwellenbach, 159 F. 2d 22, 25 (C.A.D.C., December 16, 1946); affirming 65 F. Supp. 254 (D.Ct.D.C., April 1, 1946); certiorari denied by the Supreme Court, 330 U.S. 838 (March 17, 1947).

[26] Washington v. Clark, 84 F. Supp. 964, 965–967 (June 28, 1949).

[27] See Arch Dotson, "The Emerging Doctrine of Privilege in Public Employment," *Public Administration Review*, 15: 77–88 (1955).

[28] ". . . in giving to suspected employees the measures of protection afforded by his Executive Order the President was not acting from necessity." Bailey v. Richardson, 182 F. 2d 46, 54 (1950).

[29] "In blunt terms, the President can discriminate [in making appointments] for political reasons [unless limited by Congress]." *Ibid.*, 63.

[30] 219 U.S. 296 (1911).

[31] Bailey v. Richardson, 182 F. 2d 46, 65 (1950).

[32] *Ibid.*, 73.

[33] Washington v. McGrath, 182 F. 2d 375 (April 17, 1950). Attorney General Clark, the defendant in the lower court, had been elevated in the meantime to the Supreme Court, so his successor in office was substituted in his place as defendant before this court and the Supreme Court.

[34] Bailey v. Richardson, 341 U.S. 918 (April 30, 1951); Washington v. McGrath, 341 U.S. 923 (May 7, 1951). Justice Clark was disqualified because he had been the official in charge of the loyalty investigations in both cases and the defendant in one. The apparent division among the rest of the Court was Black, Douglas, Frankfurter, and Jackson for reversal; and Burton, Minton, Reed, and Vinson for affirmance. See Nathaniel L. Nathanson, "Central Issues of American Administrative Law," *American Political Science Review*, 45: 383 (June 1951), on the inference of the Court's division in these cases; and for a general discussion of these and the cases immediately following in the text, see *ibid.*, 378–383.

[35] The act of August 2, 1939, U.S.C.A. Sec. 118j.

[36] Joint Anti-Fascist Refugee Committee v. Clark, 177 F. 2d 79, 82 (1949). Compare Barsky v. United States, 167 F. 2d 241 (1948), also a decision of the Court of Appeals for the District of Columbia and relating to an investigation of the Joint Anti-Fascist Refugee Committee by the House Committee on Un-American Activities.

[37] *Ibid.*, 84.

[38] *Ibid.*, 89–90.

[39] International Workers Order v. McGrath, 182 F. 2d 368, 371 (1950).

[40] National Council of American-Soviet Friendship, Inc. v. McGrath, dismissed *per curiam* (unreported) by the Court of Appeals for the District of Columbia on the authority of its previous decision in the *Joint Anti-Fascist Refugee Committee* case. See 341 U.S. 123, 132 (1951).

[41] Burton announced the decision of the Court in an opinion in which Douglas joined, although Douglas also wrote a separate concurring opinion; separate concurring opinions were also delivered by Justices Black, Frankfurter, and Jackson. The only point these justices appeared to agree upon was that the petitioners presented a justiciable claim. Justice Reed was joined by Chief Justice Vinson and Minton in a single dissenting opinion. Clark did not participate.

[42] The complaint of the Joint Anti-Fascist Refugee Committee did not contain an express denial that the organization was within any of the six classifications named in Part III, s. 3, of Executive Order No. 9835, although it did allege various grounds on which the executive order and the Attorney General's action were unconstitutional, and that it was suffering irreparable loss and that no adequate remedy was available to it except through the equity powers of the district court. In the *National Council* and *International Workers Order* cases, the complaints specifically alleged that the organizations were completely loyal, and denied that they had ever in any way engaged in any activity or conduct which would bring them within any of the classifications of disloyalty based on the executive order. Joint Anti-Fascist Refugee Committee v. McGrath, 341 U.S. 123, 132, 133, 134 ftn. 9 (April 30, 1951).

[43] Joint Anti-Fascist Refugee Committee v. McGrath, 104 F. Supp. 567 (April 23, 1952).

[44] Joint Anti-Fascist Refugee Committee v. Brownell, 215 F. 2d 870 (August 5, 1954). A similar result was reached by the same court a year later in National Lawyers Guild v. Brownell, 225 F. 2d 552 (C.A.D.C., July 14, 1955), certiorari denied, 351 U.S. 927 (May 17, 1956).

[45] Lawson v. Housing Authority of Milwaukee, 70 N.W. 2d (Wis.) 605 (June 1, 1955), certiorari denied, 350 U.S. 882 (November 7, 1955); and Housing Authority of Los Angeles v. Cordova, 279 P. 2d (California Superior Court, Appellate Department, Los Angeles County) 215 (1955), certiorari denied, 350 U.S. 696 (February 27, 1956). Accord: Chicago Housing Authority v. Blackman, 122 N.E. 2d (Ill.) 522 (1954); Peters v. New York City Housing Authority, 128 N.Y.S. 2d (New York Supreme Court, Special Term Kings County) 244 (1953), modified and affirmed by the Appellate Division, Second Department, 128 N.Y.S. 2d 712 (1954), and reversed, on other grounds than those relevant here, in 307 N.Y. (Court of Appeals) 519 (1954), and 148 N.Y.S. 2d (Appellate Division, 2D Department) 859 (1955). The Illinois and New York cases were not appealed to the Supreme Court of the United States.

[46] The Gwinn Amendment, a rider to the Independent Offices Appropriations Act of 1953 (approved July 5, 1952), 66 *Stat.* 403, provided that no housing unit constructed with federal funds shall be occupied by a person who is a member of an organization designated as subversive by the Attorney General.

[47] The Municipal Court of Appeals of the District of Columbia upheld the constitutionality of the Gwinn Amendment in Rudder v. United States, 105 A. 2d 741, 745 (1954). The New York trial court originally held both the Gwinn Amendment and the resolution of the housing authority to be in violation of the Fifth Amendment and therefore unconstitutional, but the Appellate Division reversed the ruling on the constitutionality of the federal statute and ultimately rested its decision on the same grounds as had the courts of the other states. Peters v. New York City Housing Authority, 128 N.Y.S. 2d 224, 241, 712 (1953), and 147 N.Y.S. 2d 859 (1955).

[48] Parker v. Lester, 227 F. 2d 708 (9 C.C.A., October 26, 1955).

[49] Kutcher v. Gray, 199 F. 2d 783 (1952).

[50] Peters v. Hobby, 349 U.S. 331, 338 (June 6, 1955).

[51] *Ibid.*, 350.

Presidential Management of Public Personnel

[52] 64 *Stat.* 476, 5 U.S.C.A. Sec. 22–1.

[53] The standard of the Truman Loyalty Order No. 9835 of March 21, 1947, had been "that, on all the evidence, reasonable grounds exist for belief that" an employee was disloyal. This was amended by Executive Order No. 10241 of April 28, 1951, so that "reasonable doubt" as to an employee's loyalty became the standard; this was the same standard that had been used for the World War II loyalty program. Executive Order No. 10450 of April 27, 1953, eliminated these negative standards, and made it the duty of agency heads to remove any employee whose continued employment was not "clearly consistent with the interests of the national security."

[54] Cole v. Young, 226 F. 2d 337, 340 (1955), affirming 125 F. Supp. 284, 286 (1955).

[55] Cole v. Young, 351 U.S. 536, 557 ftn. 20 (June 11, 1956). It is noteworthy that the distinction drawn by the majority between "sensitive" and non-sensitive positions, particularly in the light of the government's admission that Cole was not in a position to influence policy-making, is precisely the distinction that the Court had refused to make a decade earlier in United States Public Workers v. Mitchell, 330 U.S. 75 (1947) (where the question was whether a workman in the mint could engage in partisan political activities).

[56] *Ibid.*, 568 ftn.

[57] *Ibid.*, 567–568.

[58] For a more general discussion of the theory of and literature on the subject, see Glendon A. Schubert, Jr., "The Executive Rule-Making Power: Hart and Comer Revisited," *Journal of Public Law*, 4:367–421 (Fall 1955).

[59] United States v. Eliason, 16 Peters 291, 301, 302 (1842).

[60] Nordmann v. Woodring, Secretary of War, 28 F. Supp. 573, 576 (W.D.Okla., 1939).

[61] There is still no clear pattern of opinion in the Supreme Court on the question of whether such executive regulations are "laws" in the constitutional sense. This was manifest in the confusion that engulfed the Court in its various expression of views in the *Joint Anti-Fascist Refugee Committee* case, where this point was a major jurisdictional issue.

[62] Fleming v. Stahl, 83 F. 940, 943 (W.D.Ark., 1897). See also Carr v. Gordon, 82 F. 373, 379 (C.Ct.N.D.Ill., 1897).

[63] Cole v. Young, 226 F. 2d 337, 340–341 (C.A.D.C., 1955), reversed by the Supreme Court on somewhat different grounds, 351 U.S. 536 (June 11, 1956).

[64] Note, however, that Congress has attempted to do precisely this by sec. 3(a) (3) of the Administrative Procedure Act of 1946, 60 *Stat.* 237, which requires administrative agencies to publish in the Federal Register all permanent rules and regulations that affect the public at large.

[65] Fogarty v. United States, 80 F. Supp. 90, 94–95 (D.Minn., 1948); affirmed on other grounds in 176 F. 2d 599 (8 C.C.A., 1949), and 340 U.S. 8 (1951). Italics supplied. With respect to the italicized words, it should be noted that an additional reason why Congress selected the President to exercise the broad rule-making powers delegated by the statute may well have been to secure *uniformity* in the regulations.

[66] 1 Cranch 137 (1803). The rationale was that although appointment is the discretionary act of the President, the delivery of a commission is the ministerial act of the Secretary of State; therefore, the President cannot authorize his subordinate to omit the performance of duties which are required by statutory law.

[67] Little v. Barreme, 2 Cranch 170 (1804).

[68] Gilchrist v. Collector, 10 Fed. Cas. 355 (1808), No. 5420. An excellent analysis of the implications of an unbridled presidential power of administrative direction is contained in Justice Johnson's appended letter to the press of August 26, 1808, in reply to United States Attorney Rodney's letter of January 15, 1808.

[69] What the Court must have meant here is this: beyond the reach of *prospective* control; he certainly is amenable to judgment in the courts and retaliation by the Congress after the fact. This general rule applies alike to constitutional and statutory powers of the President.

[70] Therefore, the essay above is a dictum. Kendall v. Stokes, 12 Peters 524, 610, 612–613 (1838).

[71] Cunningham v. Neagle [In re Neagle], 135 U.S. 1, 63, 67 (1890).

[72] The President's instructions took the form of a letter dated May 27, 1889, from Attorney General W. H. Miller to United States Marshal J. C. Franks at San Francisco, directing him to provide a personal bodyguard for elderly Supreme Court Justice Stephen Field while he was riding circuit in the execution of his official duties. One Terry — a California judge — had made open threats against Field's life, and Terry was attempting to carry out his threats at the time he was shot and killed by Field's bodyguard, Deputy Marshal Neagle.

[73] This would seem to imply that the President might have acted alternatively through his constitutional powers as Commander in Chief and have ordered the use of federal troops as a bodyguard for Justice Field. Compare, however, the older case of Gelston v. Hoyt, 3 Wheat. 246 (1818).

[74] Cummings v. Société Suisse pour Valeurs de Métaux, 85 F. 2d 287 (1936).

[75] Campbell v. Chase National Bank of the City of New York, 5 F. Supp. 156 (S.D. N.Y., 1933); British-American Tobacco Co. v. Federal Reserve Bank of New York, 104 F. 2d 652, 654 (2 C.C.A., 1939); United States v. West Virginia Power Co., 33 F. Supp. 756 (S.D.W.Va. at Bluefield, 1940) and 39 F. Supp. 540 (S.D.W.Va. at Bluefield, 1941), reversed in 122 F. 2d 733 (4 C.C.A., 1941) and certiorari denied at 314 U.S. 683; but see also 91 F. 2d 611 (4 C.C.A., 1937).

[76] Affirmation of this statement, by indirection, is provided by a more recent decision of the Supreme Court which is premised on the principle that in the absence of explicit statutory authority, the President's power of administrative direction does not extend, even in time of war, to control of the decisions of the independent regulatory commissions. Jersey City v. United States, 54 F. Supp. 315, 319 (D.N.J., 1944); reversed in Interstate Commerce Commission v. Jersey City, 322 U.S. 503, 506, 517 ftn. 5, 520, 523–524 (1944). This is an excellent example of an inter-agency case, because the real parties to this dispute were the Office of Price Administration and the Interstate Commerce Commission.

[77] See United States ex rel Knauff v. Shaughnessy, 338 U.S. 537, 544 (1950).

[78] See Glendon A. Schubert, Jr., "The Presidential Subdelegation Act of 1950," Journal of Politics, 13:661 (November 1951). Cf. the dictum in United States v. Bussoz, 218 F. 2d 683, 686 (9 C.A., 1955), certiorari denied, 350 U.S. 824 (1955).

[79] 3 Wheat. 248 (1818).

[80] Whelpley v. Grosvold, 249 F. 812, 815 (1918).

[81] United States v. Pan-American Petroleum Co., 6 F. 2d 43, 87–88 (S.D.Cal.N.D., May 28, 1925). The Ninth Circuit Court of Appeals and the Supreme Court both affirmed this decision on appeal, but relied only on the ground of fraud and neither approved nor disapproved of that part of the trial court's opinion quoted above. Pan-American Petroleum Co. v. United States, 9 F. 2d 761 (January 4, 1926), and 273 U.S. 456 (February 28, 1927). In a parallel case, the question of the constitutionality of the executive order was also argued, but was not ruled upon by the Ninth Circuit Court of Appeals which held this point to be immaterial, since there was no question of fraud in the case, the Secretary of the Navy had in fact approved the lease in controversy, the lease was in the public interest, and Congress had ratified both the lease and the executive order by various appropriation acts in 1921, 1922, and 1923. United States v. Belridge Oil Co., 13 F. 2d 562 (July 12, 1926), certiorari denied, 273 U.S. 733 (November 29, 1926).

[82] United States v. Pan-American Petroleum Co., 45 F. 2d 821 (S.D.Cal.C.D., November 10, 1930).

[83] United States v. Pan-American Petroleum Co., 55 F. 2d 753, 769 (1932). Certiorari denied by the Supreme Court, 287 U.S. 612 (October 10, 1932).

[84] The closest reference that can be found in the trial court's opinion in this proceed-

Presidential Management of Public Personnel

ing appears among the recitations of facts (as distinguished from the rulings of law), in which the district court stated: "On May 31, 1921, the President issued an executive order putting the matter of leasing of lands within the Naval Reserves in charge of the Secretary of the Interior, the order making special reference to the act of February 20, 1920. This order was held to be invalid [by the district court itself, only] in the first Pan-American Case [United States v. Pan-American Petroleum Co., 6 F. 2d 43 (1925)]." United States v. Pan-American Petroleum Co., 45 F. 2d 821, 824 (S.D.Cal.C.D., 1930).

[85] United States v. Mammoth Oil Co., 5 F. 2d 330, 332 (D.Wyo., June 19, 1925).

[86] *Ibid.*, 344.

[87] The latter point was directly contradicted by the evidence and the subsequent findings of the Circuit Court of Appeals and the Supreme Court.

[88] United States v. Mammoth Oil Co., 14 F. 2d 705, 716 (September 28, 1926).

[89] Mammoth Oil Co. v. United States, 275 U.S. 13, 38 (October 10, 1927).

[90] It is ironic to note that Roosevelt's amendment to the executive order, an apparently sincere attempt to safeguard the interests of the Congress, the Navy, and the public in this matter, not only failed to prevent the subsequent fraudulent commercial exploitation of the fleet's oil, but became the legal peg on which the Supreme Court was enabled to exonerate the President of any responsibility for what had been done.

[91] Toledo, Peoria & Western Railroad v. Stover, 60 F. Supp. 587, 592 (S.D.Ill.N.D., 1945).

[92] *Ibid.*, 593, 595–596.

[93] Wartime Executive Orders had been upheld in California Lima Bean Growers Ass'n v. Bowles, 150 F. 2d 964, 967 (Emergency C. A., August 14, 1945); and Troy Laundry Co. v. Wirtz, 155 F. 2d 53, 57 (9 C.C.A., 1946), c.d. 329 U.S. 723 (1946). The President's Executive Order No. 9809 was ruled invalid in Porter v. Ryan, 69 F. Supp. 446 (D.Ore., January 8, 1947); Porter v. Wilson, 69 F. Supp. 447 (D.Ore., January 25, 1947); and Porter v. Hirahara, 69 F. Supp. 441 (D. Hawaii, January 29, 1947), which was reversed in United States v. Hirahara, 164 F. 2d 157 (9 C.C.A., October 31, 1947), following the intervening decision of the Supreme Court in Fleming v. Mohawk, *infra.* Executive Order No. 9809 was upheld in Porter v. Anderson Motor Co., 71 F. Supp. 857 (D.Md., February 28, 1947); Bowles v. Ell–Carr Co., 71 F. Supp. 482 (S.D.N.Y., March 19, 1947); Porter v. Bowers, 70 F. Supp. 751 (W.D.Mo.W.D., March 20, 1947); Porter v. American Distilling Co., 71 F. Supp. 483 (S.D.N.Y., April 9, 1947).

[94] Fleming v. Mohawk Wrecking and Lumber Co., 331 U.S. 111, 114–118 (April 28, 1947).

[95] Porter v. Stegar, 74 F. Supp. 109, 113 (D.Md., July 22, 1947).

[96] United States v. Allied Oil Corp., 183 F. 2d 453 (7 C.C.A., 1950).

[97] United States v. Allied Oil Co., 341 U.S. 1, 3–5 (April 9, 1951).

[98] Madsen v. Kinsella, 93 F. Supp. 319, 324 (S.D.W.Va., 1950); affirmed, 188 F. 2d 272 (4 C.C.A., 1951), and 343 U.S. 341 (1952).

[99] United States *ex rel* Bryant v. Houston, 273 F. 915, 918 (2 C.C.A., 1921).

[100] 47 *Stat.* 1518.

[101] United States v. Paramount Publix Corp., 73 F. 2d 103, 105 (1934).

[102] These functions were subsequently transferred from the Secretary of Commerce to the Maritime Commission, following its creation pursuant to the act of 1936; and they were later transferred back to the Department of Commerce by President Truman's Reorganization Plan No. 21 of 1950, effective May 24, 1950.

[103] Isbrandtsen-Moller Co. v. United States, 300 U.S. 139, 147–149 (February 1, 1937). Section 204(a) referred to the functions of the former Shipping Board as "now vested in the Department of Commerce pursuant to section 12 of the President's Executive Order No. 6166," and in turn transferred them to the new Maritime Commission.

[104] Swayne & Hoyt v. United States, 300 U.S. 297, 300–303 (March 1, 1937).

[105] Many other such actions have raised no challenges to presidential authority, such as the provision of the Curtis Act of June 28, 1898, 30 *Stat.* 495, which delegated the

power of "legislation" to certain Indian tribes subject to the approval of the President, with enforcement of such ordinances a responsibility of the Secretary of the Interior. See Morris v. Hitchcock, 194 U.S. 384, 393 (1904).

[106] See United States v. West Virginia Power Co., 39 F. Supp. 540 (S.D.W.Va. at Bluefield, 1941); 122 F. 2d 733 (4 C.C.A., 1941); certiorari denied, 314 U.S. 683 (1941).

[107] It might be argued that two of these decisions, relating to the Tariff Commission and the Civil Aeronautics Board respectively, were colored by the circumstance that they fell within the area of foreign commerce, and were therefore affected, even in this respect, by the peculiar constitutional pre-eminence of the President in this domain: see United States v. Bush & Co., 310 U.S. 371 (1940), and Chicago and Southern Air Lines v. Waterman S.S. Co., 333 U.S. 103 (1948), and Chapter 5. In the other principal case decided by the Supreme Court, the relevant discussion concerning the intermediate order characteristics of N.R.A. codes is found in the dissenting opinion of Justice Cardozo: see Panama Refining Co. v. Ryan, 293 U.S. 388 (1935).

[108] Employers Group of Motor Freight Carriers, Inc. v. N.W.L.B., 143 F. 2d 145, 146, 148, 150, 151 (1944). The fact that the board was created by executive order rather than by statute is not a distinguishing factor, because the board was given express statutory recognition and status by Section 7 of the War Labor Disputes (Smith-Connally) Act of June 25, 1943, 57 *Stat.* 163, 166; the sanction of presidential seizure was authorized by Section 3 of the same statute. Cf. Zimmer-Thomson Corp. v. National Labor Relations Board, 60 F. Supp. 84 (S.D.N.Y., 1945), which expressly follows the *Employers' Group* decision, and holds that a certification order by the N.L.R.B. is informative only, and not subject to judicial review until a cease and desist order based on the certification is issued by the board.

See also a decision of the Ninth Circuit Court of Appeals affirming a district court decision ordering compliance with an administrative subpoena of the enforcement division of the Tenth Regional War Labor Board of the National War Labor Board, which was investigating to see if wages paid by the appellant exceeded those established by the regulations of the President under the Emergency Price Control Act of 1942. "The order [of the Economic Stabilization Director and approved by the President, 7 Fed. Reg. 8748, 8750] made the [War Labor] Board's determination of under or overpayments *final* in the exercise of any of the price fixing administrative functions of the President and in calculating any revenue law deductions." Troy Laundry Co. v. Wirtz, 155 F. 2d 53, 55–56 (1946), certiorari denied 329 U.S. 723 (1946). Italics supplied.

[109] McGrath v. Kristensen, 340 U.S. 162, 168 (December 11, 1950).

[110] Joint Anti-Fascist Refugee Committee v. McGrath, 341 U.S. 123 (April 30, 1951).

[111] Public Law 673, 81st Cong., 2d sess., repealed and reenacted as Chapter 4 of Title 3 of the *United States Code* by the act of October 31, 1951, 65 *Stat.* 713. The extant literature may be found in the following articles (and references cited therein): C. Dwight Waldo and William Pincus, "The Statutory Obligations of the President: Executive Necessity and Administrative Burden," *Public Administration Review*, 6:339–347, especially Part III (Autumn 1946); Nathan Grundstein, "Presidential Subdelegation of Administrative Authority in Wartime, "*George Washington Law Review*, 15:247–283 (April 1947), and 16:301–341, 478–507 (April, June 1948); Glendon A. Schubert, Jr., "Judicial Review of the Subdelegation of Presidential Power," *Journal of Politics*, 12: 668–693 (November 1950), and "The Presidential Subdelegation Act of 1950," *Journal of Politics*, 13:647–674 (November 1951); and Eli E. Nobleman, "The Delegation of Presidential Functions: Constitutional and Legal Aspects," *Annals of the American Academy of Political and Social Science*, 307:34–43 (September 1956). For examples of presidential subdelegation under the act of 1950, see Executive Order No. 10621, July 6, 1955, "Delegation of Certain Functions of the President to the Secretary of Defense," and other executive orders which are reprinted following Section 301 of Title 3 of the *United States Code*.

[112] Lockington v. Smith, 15 Fed. Cas. 758, 760 (C.Ct.Pa., 1817), No. 8448.

[113] Williams v. United States, 1 Howard 290, 297 (1843).

Presidential Management of Public Personnel

[114] United States v. Clarke, 20 Wall. 92, 109 (1874).

[115] McElrath v. United States, 102 U.S. 426, 436 (1880). Compare with Runkle v. United States, 122 U.S. 543, 556 (1887), holding that the President could not subdelegate "judicial" powers vested in him by statute. The *Runkle* decision was overruled *sub silentio* almost immediately by the Court's decisions in United States v. Fletcher, 148 U.S. 84, 91 (1893); and the rule of the *Runkle* decision has never been applied by the Court in a subsequent case. See, for instance, Sima v. United States, 119 Ct. Cl. 405 (1951).

[116] The exemption applied to those who had already applied for naturalization. Italics supplied.

[117] *In re* Pfleiger, 254 F. 511 (S.D.N.Y., 1918).

[118] The foreshadowing of the equally impossible standard set by the United States Supreme Court for the Secretary of Agriculture in Morgan v. United States, 298 U.S. 468 (1936) is apparent. One is tempted to ask: if Congress had made the same exception by statute — as it unquestionably might have done in lieu of delegating such a responsibility to the President — would such an act of Congress have been a "judicial" act?

[119] *In re* Schuster 182 N.Y.S. 357, 359–360 (1920). Neither of these conflicting decisions was appealed, but there is little question that the *Pfleiger* case, which upheld the administrative and executive practice, should have and would have been the one to prevail, if they had reached the Supreme Court.

[120] Silesian-American Corp. v. Markham, 156 F. 2d 793, 796 (2 C.C.A., 1947); affirmed in Silesian-American Corp. v. Clark, 332 U.S. 469 (1947). Compare: LaPorte v. Bitker, 55 F. Supp. 882 (E.D.Wis., 1944), upholding presidential subdelegation and administrative sub-subdelegation to a local hearing officer of the O.P.A. of the power to issue rationing suspension orders; affirmed and distinguished from the Morgan case (Morgan v. United States, 298 U.S. 468 (1936)) in 145 F. 2d 445 (1944) by the Seventh Circuit Court of Appeals, where the question of administrative sub-subdelegation was pressed because the suspension order was issued by the administrative superior of the hearing officer who took evidence and made the initial findings of fact in the case.

See also United States *ex rel* Hack v. Clark, 159 F. 2d 552 (1947), also a decision of the Seventh Circuit Court of Appeals, upholding the power of the President to subdelegate to the Attorney General the President's statutory duty of determining whether an enemy alien was dangerous to the public peace and safety of the United States.

[121] United States v. Peach Mountain Coal Mining Co., 161 F. 2d 476, 477 (1947).

[122] Alger-Rau, Inc. v. United States, 75 F. Supp. 246, 247 (Ct.Cl., January 5, 1948). See also Grundstein, *loc. cit.*, 16:312; Shreveport Engraving Co. v. United States, 143 F. 2d 222 (5 C.C.A., 1944); and United States v. Bareno, 50 F. Supp. 520, 527 (D.Md., 1943).

[123] Ludecke v. Watkins, 335 U.S. 160, 165–166 (June 21, 1948). Italics supplied. The analogy of the italicized words to the historic relationship of the Lord Chancellor, who was "Keeper of the King's Conscience," to the English sovereign is, of course, obvious. See also the closely related decision of the Supreme Court in United States *ex rel* Knauff v. Shaughnessy, 338 U.S. 537, 543 (January 16, 1950), where it was held: "Thus the decision to admit or to exclude an alien may be lawfully placed with the President, who may in turn delegate the carrying out of this function to a responsible executive officer of the sovereign [sic], such as the Attorney General. The action of the executive officer under such authority is final and conclusive."

[124] United States v. Bareno, 50 F. Supp. 520 (1943).

[125] See, for example, Bernard Schwartz, *American Administrative Law* (London: Pitman, 1950), and also his *French Administrative Law and the Common-Law World* (New York: New York University Press, 1954), Chapter 1.

Presidential Management of the Public Domain

Military Reservations

THE closing of the frontier in the continental United States is usually dated at approximately 1890. The end of the frontier also marked the denouement in the development of what used to be an important area of presidential power; apart from its historical significance, the strand of public law which relates to presidential control of the public lands merits attention today because it contains the formulation of a prerogative theory of presidential power that is not found, to any marked degree, in association with other presidential action of domestic impact in peacetime.

As in his exercise of managerial powers over the officers, employees, and agencies of the executive branch of the national government, part of the President's authority to function as general manager of the public lands has derived directly from his constitutional status as Chief Executive, and part has come from statutory delegation. In addition, however, Presidents have acted from time to time under an undefined and undelegated power inherent in the nature of the office of the Presidency: the power to act in the name of the public welfare as the only officer of the national government chosen by a national electorate,[1] and particularly with respect to the conservation of national resources which belong to the people collectively.[2]

The principal form which this exercise of power has taken has been the reservation of parts of the public domain for public purposes, to prevent their falling into the hands of individuals, corporations, and land companies who would otherwise have been entitled, under existing legislation, to pre-empt, purchase, or otherwise gain title to them. The three most important purposes for which Presidents have made reservations have been for military posts, for the conservation of natural resources, and for the resettlement of the displaced persons who held the original title to much of the area that is now the United States.

A series of decisions of the Supreme Court during the middle decades of the nineteenth century laid down the basic principles that presidential action under statutory authority need not be personal, but could be taken for the President by a subordinate administrative officer; that reservations might be made without specific statutory authorization; and that any doubts concerning the legality of a presidential reservation were completely resolved by congressional ratification. In the first of these decisions, the Court held:

[I]n the act of 1830, all lands are exempted from premption which are reserved from sale by order of the President. Now although the immediate agent in requiring this reservation was the secretary of war, yet we feel justified in presuming that it was done by the approbation and direction of the President. The President speaks and acts through the heads of the several departments in relation to subjects which appertain to their respective duties . . . we consider the act of the war department in requiring this reservation to be made, as being in legal contemplation the act of the President; and, consequently, that the reservation thus made was in legal effect, reservation made by order of the President, within the terms of the act of congress.[3]

Another early case involved a suit by the government for the cancellation on the grounds of fraud or mistake, of a patent on lands which had been reserved from sale by the President in 1830 for the creation of Camp Leavenworth, Kansas. Declaring the patent to be void, the Supreme Court found that the land in controversy was within the limits of a reservation made by the President for military purposes, and that this reservation was valid in spite of the fact that there was no specific statute authorizing the President's action.[4] The same question was raised again a few years later, when it was argued that a presidential military reservation was illegal because the lands in question were part of an incorporated city, and not a part of the public domain; and that even if they were public lands, the President could not reserve them from sale without specific statutory authority. Having decided that the reservation included only public lands, and that the plaintiff had no standing to challenge the President's authority to reserve them from sale as long as the title remained in the United States, the Court nevertheless took the occasion to remark:

[F]rom an early period in the history of the government it has been the practice of the President to order, from time to time, as the exigencies of the public service required, parcels of land belonging to the United States to be reserved from sale and set apart for public uses.

The authority of the President in this respect is recognized in numerous acts of Congress. . . . The provisions in the acts of 1830 and 1841 show very clearly that by "competent authority," is meant the authority of the President, and officers acting under his direction.

The action of the President in making the reservations in question was [in any event] indirectly approved by the legislation of Congress in appropriating moneys for the construction of fortifications and other public works upon them.[5]

Two general trends in legislation were to delegate to the President more authority to make reservations, and to specify in greater detail how he was to exercise it. Thus, the acts of September 27, 1850, and February 14, 1853, authorized the President to reserve from settlement public lands in Oregon, to comprise (1) not over 640 acres at any one place for military reservations, and (2) not over 20 acres for other necessary public uses, including lighthouse reservations.[6] By his executive order of September 11, 1854, President Pierce directed the reservation of a lighthouse area by marking on a map the general area of Port Oxford, Oregon. No subsequent action was taken by the President personally to demark a more specific location and surveyed boundaries for the lighthouse reservation. Three decades later, the Circuit Court for the District of Oregon upheld the claim of a settler under land patents subsequently issued, holding that, although the military authorities had converted for temporary use some lands which included the claimant's, no lighthouse reservation had ever been made as a matter of law, because the Presidential order only *authorized* such a reservation to be made:

Besides, it was not in the power of the president to establish or declare a reservation for light-house purposes upon land already reserved for military or other purposes. . . . So soon as Tichenor became a settler upon this land under the donation act [of 1850] there was no longer any power in the president to appropriate it for any purpose. It had thereby become private property, and could only be taken for public uses by authority of congress acting under the right of eminent domain, and upon making just compensation therefore.[7]

In a second case decided by the same court at the same time, this *de facto* military reservation was held to be insufficient to defeat the title of a private claimant because it failed to comply with other specific requirements of the statutes.[8]

A closely related question was resolved by the Supreme Court of Oregon a few years later. President Pierce made a reservation from public lands in Oregon through Secretary of War Jefferson Davis, whose order of May 18, 1854, specifically contemplated the settlement of private claims to lands taken for the reservation. A military camp came into existence and operated on the land for several years. On April 2, 1872, when the need for a military post at this location no longer existed, the lands of the reservation were sold to the growing town of Dallas City for five dollars an acre. One Bigelow filed on November 2, 1853, a claim to land subsequently included within the reservation; and his claim was ultimately confirmed by a patent issued May 5, 1881. By this time, of course, the land he claimed and had patented had been sold to the city by the United States. The principal question, therefore, was whether a valid military reservation, which included the land in controversy, had been made on or before November 2, 1853, when Bigelow filed his claim. Concluding that no such reservation ever had been made under the authority of the President, the state court added:

[I]f his settlement were lawful under the [donation] act, his claim could not be rightfully encroached upon by the secretary of war or the President. . . . The settlement, and compliance with the law authorizing it, secured to Bigelow and his grantees a vested right in the claim notified upon, of which they cannot be deprived by the exercise of any power of the government, for any purpose, without payment of just compensation.[9]

It is noteworthy that none of these cases was appealed to the Supreme Court of the United States, which almost certainly would have had to reverse the decisions on the basis of its own earlier precedents. It is also true that *Wilcox v. Jackson* and *Grisar v. McDowell* have been cited and followed many times during the past century; but these Oregon decisions have never, apparently, been persuasive in the decision of any other reported cases. Their value as an authoritative interpretation of the scope of presidential power in this regard is therefore very slight.

The frontier had moved on to Alaska by the turn of the century, and the next case to arise was decided, appropriately, by the First Division of the District Court for Alaska. Officers of the United States Navy had occupied and constructed buildings on certain parts of the public lands when the townsite of Juneau, Alaska, was laid out. Their action was approved by a letter to the Secretary of the Navy. The civil authorities were subsequently permitted to occupy the buildings, but the Navy retained the right to repossess if necessary for naval purposes. Did this constitute a military reservation, and if so, under what authority was it made? The court held that the acts of the Secretary of the Navy in reserving parts of the public domain are, in legal effect, the acts of the President. Therefore, a portion of the public lands in Alaska set apart by order of the Secretary of the Navy and used by that department for public purposes connected with naval affairs constituted a valid reservation by the President.[10]

The events in a case decided by the Supreme Court of Florida in the same year go back to a much earlier period. The defendant introduced in evidence a certified copy from the United States Land Office of an order of the President dated February 9, 1842, directing the commissioner of the Land Office to cause reservations of certain lands on Amelia Island to be made for military purposes. A patent, also issued by the Land Office, was held null and void under collateral attack, on the ground that its issuance was illegal because the land in question had already been reserved for military purposes at the time the patent was issued, and therefore the land was not subject to pre-emption. This state court noted: "It is well settled that the President of the United States, by executive order, could reserve a part of the public domain for a specific lawful purpose, such as a military reservation."[11]

At about the same time, the Supreme Court of the United States upheld another appropriation of public lands in Florida for a military reservation, denying the pre-emption claim of an individual. The facts here, which are stated adequately in the Court's opinion below, go back to an even earlier time when Florida itself was the frontier:

The plaintiffs are the sole descendents . . . of Robert J. Hackley, who . . . in November, 1823 . . . settled upon and cultivated the tract in controversy. At that time the surrounding country was a dense wilderness and he was the only settler. He erected on the tract a substantial dwelling and other buildings. In 1824 Colonel Brooke, with a detachment of United States troops, was sent to this portion of Florida, located a camp . . . on this tract, dispossessed Hackley, and took possession of the house and land so occupied and cultivated by him. The Secretary of the Interior . . . found that this action was taken by order of the War Department.[12] . . . [On] December 10, 1830 . . . by an executive order of the President the Fort Brooke military reservation was established. . . .

Prior to [the Florida Pre-emption Act of April 22, 1826, 4 *Stat.* 154] he [i.e., Hackley] was wrongfully in possession of the tract, and could have been summarily removed by order of the President. . . . His dispossession was by authority of law. It was done in the exercise of the power vested in the President as Commander-in-Chief of the Army, the order of the War Department being presumed to be that of the President. The occupation . . . was rightful, being an occupation of property of the government by direction of the proper officer. . . .

The judgement of the War Department, whose action is presumed to be the action of the President, was that, having reference to the Florida Indians, who were about to be removed to that vicinity, it was important to have a military post established. . . . It was until the post was abandoned an appropriation of the land for military purposes.[13]

There is only one recent decision that bears upon this point. The United States claimed that, during the emergency of World War II, the Navy Department was entitled to the free use and occupancy of a tract of land in Puerto Rico under a reserve clause in a 999-year lease granted by the Navy Department on July 15, 1921, to one Lieutenant Commander Baker, U.S.N. (retired). A real estate company sought compensation for the use of the land, and asserted that the reserved right of free use was in effect extinguished or released by a presidential proclamation of August 26, 1929, which transferred to the people of Puerto Rico all right, title, and interest of the United States in a part of the military reservation of San Juan known as the San Geronimo tract, and in which Baker's lands were included. The authority for the proclamation was Section 7 of the Organic Act for Puerto Rico.[14] The opinion of the First Circuit Court of Appeals is notable as being one of the relatively few expressions of judicial sentiment which frankly recognizes the fact that a question of *public law* is being decided:

In our opinion it is beside the point to try to fit the reserved right into one of the traditional categories of property law, either under the system of the common law or of the civil law. We are dealing here with a right reserved in the Baker lease pursuant to the explicit command of Congress, which has plenary legislative power in the premises.[15]

The court went on to decide that neither the Congress, in the Organic Act, nor the President, by his proclamation, had had any intention of extinguishing the reserved rights of the Navy.

Presidential Conservation of Natural Resources

EXECUTIVE ORDERS IN AID OF PROPOSED LEGISLATION

The Ordinance of 1787 had reserved to the United States rights to one third of the lead mines in the Northwest Territory. An act of Congress adopted in 1807 reserved from sale all lead mines in the Indiana territory, but the President was authorized to lease, for a term not exceeding five years, any lead mine that had been or might thereafter be discovered in that territory. Later, the United States sued on the bond of a presidential licensee to collect royalty ore which, as a condition of the license, was supposed to have been turned over to the superintendent of United States mines.[16] The President's power, under the statute, to make such a contract in the form of a conditional license was upheld by the Supreme Court.[17]

However, a directly contrary conclusion was reached three years later by the first Supreme Court of the Territory of Iowa, when the equivalent question with respect to Iowa was raised under the same statute. An important fact to recall when assessing the significance of this decision is that the question of the right to work the lead mines in Iowa was at this time a major political issue in the territory: the last great Indian War with Black Hawk had ended in 1832, and a wave of frontiersmen had rushed into the territory during the ensuing decade to mine and farm, in direct violation of the act of 1807. In a case that began as an action of forcible entry and detainer before a justice of the peace, the territorial Supreme Court was asked to decide whether the President had any authority to authorize the granting of leases to any lead mines "on the west side of the Mississippi River." The court decided that the President had neither constitutional nor statutory power to do so, since the President could act only under statutory powers and the act of March 3, 1807, was construed to apply only to the former territories (by then, states) carved out of the Northwest Territory. The fact that Congress had enacted statutes on the subject was considered to be proof that the President had no inherent power as general superintendent of the public domain, because if he had, congressional action would have been unnecessary:

It has been urged, that the president is vested with the power in question, in consequence of the general supervision of the public lands with which he is by law entrusted. Such a power, however, should have a more substantial basis. It is not a branch of prerogative. It should not result from implication . . . no power of this nature can exist independent of an unequivocal statute. . . . We . . . conclude that there is no law to authorize the leasing of lead mines within this territory.[18]

The new state of Iowa also figured in one of the most interesting series of cases in the evolution of our constitutional and administrative law.[19] The legal category of executive power to make reservations *in aid of proposed* legislation emerged from these cases; but doubts of both the wisdom and the constitutionality of the action taken troubled the administrations of half a dozen Presidents over the span of two decades.

An act of Congress of September 4, 1841, gave parcels of the public lands to the (then) western states, including organized territories such as Iowa upon their admission to statehood, subject to such reservations as might subsequently be made by statute or by proclamation of the President. A later statute of August 8, 1846, made a supplementary grant to the new state of Iowa of alternate sections along the banks of the Des Moines River, a tributary of the Missouri, for sale to private settlers to raise funds for improving the navigability of the river. During the five-year period between these two statutes, the President had directed the Land Office to reserve from public sale these lands bordering the Des Moines, in anticipation of the statute which was in fact adopted in 1846. The Des Moines, which ran almost due north and south, could not be made navigable beyond what was called the Raccoon Fork, although the main tributary extended to the river's source near the northern border of the state. The Land Office, however, continued to reserve from public sale the lands to the north of the Raccoon Fork until Congress finally acted to resolve the question of whether or not these lands had been included in the grant to the state in 1846. Further complications and conflicting claims were introduced by an intervening grant of Congress to a railroad, whose right-of-way passed from east to west across the upper Des Moines above Raccoon Fork.

73

In the first of this series of cases, the Supreme Court decided that the grant to the state in 1846 did not include public lands bordering the upper Des Moines, because the river could not be improved for navigation north of Raccoon Fork, and this was the condition and the purpose of the federal grant-in-aid.[20] Almost immediately, however, Congress "overruled" the Supreme Court by a joint resolution of March 2, 1861, and an act of July 12, 1862, which confirmed the state's title to the lands above the fork. In the next of these cases to come before it, the Court was asked to decide whether the reservations of the Land Office along the upper Des Moines were valid. In view of its holding in the *Dubuque* case, the Court could not hold that the reservations were based on the act of 1846; therefore, if they were to be upheld, some other source of authority had to be found. The Court's decision was that the reservations were valid, *because they were made in aid of the proposed legislation of 1861 and 1862*:

It has been argued that these lands had not been reserved by competent authority, and hence that the reservation was nugatory. As we have seen, they were reserved from sale for the special purpose of aiding in the improvement of the Des Moines river — first, by the Secretary of the Treasury [on June 16, 1849], when the Land Department was under his supervision and control, and again by the Secretary of the Interior [on April 6, 1850], after the establishment of this department, to which the duties were assigned, and afterwards continued by this department under instructions from the President and cabinet. Besides, if this power was not competent, which we think it was ever since the establishment of the Land Department, and which has been exercised down to the present time, the grant of 8th August, 1846, carried along with it, by necessary implication, not only the power, but the duty, of the Land Office to reserve from sale the lands embraced in the grant. . . . The serious conflict of opinion among the public authorities [as to whether the lands were under the jurisdiction of the Federal Government or the State] made it the duty of the land officers to withhold the sales and reserve them to the United States till it was ultimately disposed of.[21]

The form taken by the directives creating the reservations had been that of orders signed by the commissioner of the Land Office. The act of 1841, however, explicitly had authorized such reservations to be made either by act of Congress or by "Proclamation of the President of the United States." Was such an administrative order a presidential proclamation within the meaning of the statute? Any literal construction of the statute obviously demanded a negative answer; but in an exceptionally liberal opinion, the Supreme Court decided:

If the President himself had signed the order in this case, and sent it to the registers and receivers who were to act under it, as notice to them of what they were to do in respect to the sales of the public lands, we cannot doubt that the lands would have been reserved by proclamation within the meaning of the statute. Such being the case, it follows necessarily from the decision in *Wilcox* v. *Jackson* that such an order sent out from the appropriate executive department in the regular course of business is the legal equivalent of the President's own order to the same effect. It was, therefore, as we think, such a proclamation by the President reserving the lands from sale as was contemplated by the act.[22]

Before Congress had taken any action to permit pre-emption of the public lands on the islands off the southwest coast of Alaska, a commercial salmon packer had established a factory on Afognak Island. When Congress did grant this privilege by an act of March 3, 1891, it expressly reserved by Section 14 of that statute "any lands belonging to the United States . . . which shall be selected by the United States Commission of Fish and Fisheries on the island of Kodiak and Afognak for the purpose of establishing fish-culture stations." Shortly thereafter, the President issued his proclamation of December 24, 1892, reserving the whole of Afognak Island for the purpose of establishing such a fish-culture station on it, and warning all persons to remove themselves from the island. When the packing company refused to leave voluntarily, it was ejected, and it filed suit in the Court of Claims for the value of the improvements it had constructed on the land and for the damages it had suffered through the loss of profits as the result of its expulsion. That court found no merit in its contentions; and when the case reached the Supreme Court on appeal, the Court without hesitation upheld the public right rather than the private privilege.[23]

The most fundamental constitutional question raised by the public land cases, however, was whether the President could create reservations *in the absence* of any statutory authority. Although this had been the unbroken presidential and administrative practice for almost a century, a lower federal court ventured a dictum to the effect that "The truth is . . . that the President . . . cannot reserve any public lands from sale except when authorized by some treaty, law, or authorization by Congress." [24] Another federal court decided, however, that any such question respecting reservations made in aid of anticipated legislation was conclusively laid to rest by the adoption of such legislation and its ratification of such reservations:

[I]f the withdrawal, when made [by order of the Secretary of the Interior] in 1908, was a nullity for want of authority, such authority was expressly conferred upon the President by Act of June 25, 1910 [36 Stat. 847]. And the continuous recognition and maintenance of the withdrawal by the departments administering the public domain as the representatives of the President, and presumably by his direction, in legal effect rendered it valid by renewal or ratification on and after the date of said act, even as though then expressly renewed or made.[25]

It was not until the following year, long after the opportunity for the President to exercise powers of reservation on any extensive scale had passed, that the Supreme Court faced the question of his constitutional power to make reservations independent of a governing statutory policy. There was little likelihood that this decision would have any marked effect upon the actions of future Presidents because the economically valuable public lands in continental United States had been largely disposed of by this time, and Congress had delegated express authority to the President to make withdrawal orders in the recent act of June 25, 1910. The particular lands included in the withdrawal order in this case were of considerable value, both economic and political, as the subsequent development of events revealed, for they included the celebrated Teapot Dome oil reserves with which the Court was so conspicuously concerned, in another context, a decade later.

On September 27, 1909, the Secretary of the Interior promulgated, by direction of the President, "Temporary Petroleum Withdrawal Order No. 5." [26] When he received explicit statutory authority to make withdrawal orders of this type under the act of June 25, 1910, the President personally issued on July 2, 1910, an "Order of Withdrawal. Petroleum Reserve No. 8," which explicitly ratified the administrative order of September 27, 1909. As a test case, an oil corporation filed suit to challenge the constitutionality of President Taft's executive order; and the Eighth Circuit Court of Appeals ultimately certified six questions for the decision of the Supreme Court:

1. Prior to the act of 1910, did the President (or the Secretary of the Interior) have power to withdraw oil lands from private entry for the purpose of aiding prospective legislation?

2. Did Withdrawal Order #5 amend the Act of 1897, in effect, so as to prevent entry on lands withdrawn by persons authorized to enter lands under the Act of 1897?

3. Is the purpose motivating Withdrawal Order #5 relevant or material?

4. If (3) is (yes), must the purpose be expressly stated in the order itself?

5. If (4) is (no), must the purposes be alleged by the government, or will the court take judicial notice thereof?

6. If the stated purposes are insufficient to sustain validity, should additional purpose(s) be presumed to exist in the absence of proof to the contrary?

Largely ignoring these somewhat obviously slanted queries, the Supreme Court, in an opinion by Justice Lamar in which Chief Justice White and Justices Holmes, Hughes, and Pitney joined, delivered what is probably the most sympathetic essay in support of executive power ever given by the United States Supreme Court. It is supremely ironic that Theodore Roosevelt's Stewardship Theory,[27] so severely criticized by William Howard Taft,[28] should have received its greatest judicial sanction in a case in which the chief protagonist was none other than President Taft. Moreover, the decision was made by a majority of five which included four of Taft's own appointees to the Court, with only the ultraconservative Willis Van Devanter, of his appointees still on the bench, dissenting.[29] The ostensible basis for the Court's decision here was the premise that "silence means consent," or more specifically, that the failure of Congress to protest what might have been considered executive usurpation must be accepted as a tacit delegation of the power in question to the President. In the alternative, the Court found justification for the President's action, not in any specific clause of the Constitution, but rather in the nature of the office of the Presidency. The underlying basis for the decision, however, lay in the premise that the acquisition of public lands, like the status of public employment, raised only questions of privilege, and not questions of legal right. The Court's opinion is quoted at some length, because it affords the best and most complete exposition of the presidential role as general manager of the public domain to be found anywhere in the decisions of the American judiciary:

On the part of the Government it is urged that the President, as Commander-in-Chief of the Army and Navy, had power to make the order for the purpose of retaining and preserving a source of supply of fuel for the Navy, instead of allowing the oil land to be taken up for a nominal sum, the Government being then obliged to purchase at a great cost what it had previously owned. It is argued that the President, charged with the care of the public domain, could, by virtue of the executive power vested in him by the Constitution (art. 2, sec. 1), and also in conformity with the tacit consent of Congress, withdraw, in the public interest, any public land from entry or location by private parties.

The Appellees, on the other hand, insist that there is no dispensing power in the Executive and that he could not suspend a statute or withdraw from entry or location any land which Congress had affirmatively declared should be free and open to acquisition by citizens of the United States. They further insist that the withdrawal order is absolutely void since it appears on its face to be a mere attempt to suspend a statute — supposed to be unwise, — in order to allow Congress to pass another more in accordance with what the Executive thought to be in the public interest.

We need not consider whether, as an original question, the President could have withdrawn from private acquisition what Congress had made free and open to occupation and purchase. . . . For the President's proclamation of September 27, 1909,[30] is by no means the first instance in which the Executive, by a special order, has withdrawn lands which Congress, by general statute, had thrown open to acquisition by citizens . . . he has, during the past 80 years, without express statutory authority — but under the claim of power to do so — made a multitude of Executive Orders which operated to withdraw public land that would otherwise have been open to private acquisition . . . prior to the year 1910 there had been issued

   99 Executive Orders establishing or enlarging Indian Reservations;
   109 Executive Orders establishing or enlarging Military Reservations and setting apart land for water, timber, fuel, hay, signal stations, target ranges and rights of way for use in connection with Military Reservations;
   44 Executive Orders establishing bird reserves.

. . . it is to be specially noted that there was no act of Congress providing for Bird Reserves or for these Indian Reservations. . . .

In making such orders, which were thus useful to the public, no private interest was injured. For prior to the initiation of some right given by law the citizen had no enforceable interest in the public statute and no private right in land which was the property of the people. The President was in a position to know when the public interest required particular portions of the people's lands to be withdrawn from entry or location. . . .

This right of the President to make reservations — and thus withdraw land from private acquisition — was expressly recognized in

Presidential Management of the Public Domain

Grisar v. *McDowell* . . . [And] Secretary [of the Interior] Teller [said] in 1881: "That the power resides in the Executive from an early period in the history of the country to make reservations has never been denied either legislatively or judicially, but on the contrary had been recognized." . . . in determining the meaning of a statute or the existence of a power, weight shall be given to the usage itself — even when the validity of the practice is the subject of investigation.[31]

It is true, said the Court, that the President cannot by his own course of action create a power, but:

the long-continued practice, known to and acquiesced in by Congress, would raise a presumption that the withdrawals had been made in pursuance of its consent or of a recognized administrative power of the Executive in the management of the public lands. This is particularly true in view of the fact that the land is property of the United States, and that the land laws are not of a legislative character in the highest sense of the term (art. 4, sec. 3), "but savor somewhat of mere rules prescribed by an owner of property for its disposal." . . . The power of the Executive, as agent in charge, to retain that property from sale need not necessarily be expressed in writing. . . .

For it must be borne in mind that Congress not only has a legislative power over the public domain, but it also exercises the powers of the proprietor therein. . . .

[T]he validity of withdrawal orders, in aid of legislation, has been expressly recognized in a series of cases involving a number of such orders, made between 1850 and 1862 [citing the *Des Moines River* cases].

. . . The officer of the Land Department, in his answer . . . shows that there have been a large number of withdrawals made for good but for nonstatutory reasons. He shows that these 92 orders had been made by virtue of a long-continued practice and under claim of a right to take such action in the public interest "as exigencies might demand. . . . " Congress with notice of this practice and of this claim of authority, received the Report. Neither at that session nor afterwards did it ever repudiate the action taken or the power claimed. Its silence was acquiescence. Its acquiescence was equivalent to consent to continue the practice until the power was revoked by some subsequent action by Congress.[32]

The essential thesis of the dissenting opinion was that the refusal of the Congress, in enacting the 1910 statute, to provide the express ratification that the President had asked for, should be construed as evidence of disapproval of the presidential action:

In our opinion, the action of the Executive Department in this case, originating in the expressed view of a subordinate official of the Interior Department as to the desirability of a different system of public land disposal than that contained in the lawful enactments of Congress, did not justify the President in withdrawing this large body of land from the operation of the law and virtually suspending, as he necessarily did, the operation of that law, at least until a different view expressed by him could be considered by the Congress. This conclusion is reinforced in this particular instance by the refusal of Congress to ratify the action of the President, and the enactment of a new statute authorizing the disposition of the public lands by a method essentially different from that proposed by the Executive.[33]

A comparison of the majority and minority opinions in this case demonstrates the pitfalls and uncertainties inherent in the judicial process of making determinative and conclusive inferences from either congressional silence or congressional inaction.[34] Semantic considerations to one side, however, one salient fact emerges: the justices who comprised the majority in this decision accepted President Taft's identification of the public interest, and the justices who dissented could not accept it.[35] The statute of 1897 reflected the older national policies characteristic of an age which viewed the exploitation of the public domain as "opening up the country"; Taft's executive order was a product (however reluctant) of the new conservation movement, which held the center of public attention at this time.[36] But the determination of the locus of the public interest is essentially a political rather than a legal question. Therefore, the decision in the *Midwest Oil* case, like the decisions in many of the other leading cases in our public law, was in actuality based on political rather than legal criteria.

As might be expected, the cases which came up during the next two decades in which related questions were raised all followed in the wake of the *Midwest* decision, which was found in each case to be determinative, in principle, of the issues subsequently raised. The year following that of the *Midwest* decision, the Supreme Court reversed a lower court and upheld the power of the President to include within the Cascade Range Forest Reserve unsurveyed public lands, noting that the power to make permanent reservations included the power to make temporary withdrawals, that the order of the Secretary of the Interior must be regarded as the act of the President, and that "The disposition by the President, under the authority of Congress, was a disposition by Congress."[37] The Court considered itself bound to uphold the validity of a withdrawal order similar to the one involved in the *Midwest* case in a later decision where claimants, acting on legal advice to the effect that the President's order was unconstitutional, had established mining locations in direct defiance of the terms of the executive order. Mr. Justice Sutherland, who may have felt some occupational sympathy for corporation lawyers, announced the somewhat unusual legal principle that one who knowingly and deliberately breaks the law on the advice of "competent counsel" is morally justified in having done so.[38] The Court of Appeals for the District of Columbia decided that the President's withdrawal order of August 13, 1912, under the Pickett Act of June 25, 1910, in aid of a bill then before Congress proposing to include the withdrawn lands within a national forest reservation, was valid in spite of the fact that the bill failed of enactment. Since the court noted that in accordance with Section 1 of the statute, such a withdrawal order remained in effect and valid "until revoked by him or an act of Congress," it would appear that the specific denial of presidential power, contained elsewhere in the act of 1910, to create forest reserves in the Rocky Mountain and Pacific states, was in substantial measure nugatory, because the President could accomplish the same objective by issuing withdrawal orders in aid of proposed legislation that never materialized! This court also pushed the theory of the *Midwest* case to the logical limits never quite reached in the Supreme Court opinion, when it flatly declared that "The power of withdrawal is inherent in the President without the express authority of Congress."[39]

THE MODERN DOCTRINE: UNASSAILABLE EXECUTIVE DISCRETION

Just at the close of World War II, a federal district judge was asked to decide whether a proclamation of the President was consistent with the statute on which it was purportedly based. This judge upheld a presidential reservation by declaring that the question facing him was a *political* question; and in support of his decision, he cited two Supreme Court decisions dealing with the scope of presidential power in time of war and in the realm of foreign affairs.[40] In this case, however, the President was doing nothing remotely touching either of these constitutional facets of his power: he was in fact reserving some public land for conservation and recreational purposes; and even in form, he was merely reserving an object of antiquarian interest for the edification of tourists en route to and from Yellowstone National Park. But in the words of the court:

This case involves the Jackson Hole National Monument located in Teton County, Wyoming. . . . In its complaint the plaintiff asserts . . . that the segregated area, by virtue of the Proclamation over which the defendant threatens management and control, is outside the scope and purposes of the Antiquities Act under which the Proclamation was issued in that such area contains no objects of an historic or scientific interest required by the Act; that the Proclamation is void and of no effect in that it is not confined to the smallest area compatible with the proper care and management of a National Monument: that by said Proclamation an attempt has been made to substitute, through the Antiquities Act, a National Monument for a National Park, the creation of which is within the sole province of Congress, thereby becoming an evasion of the law governing the segregation of such areas. . . .

In short, this seems to be a controversy between the Legislative and the Executive Branches of the Government in which, under the evidence presented here, the Court cannot interfere. Undoubtedly great hardship and a substantial amount of injustice will be done to the State and her citizens if the Executive Department carries out its threatened program, but if the Congress presumes to delegate its inherent [sic] authority to Executive Departments which exercise acquisitive proclivities not actually intended, the burden is on the Congress to pass such remedial legislation as may obviate any injustice brought about as the power and control over and disposition of government lands inherently rests in its Legislative branch. What has been said with reference to the objects of historic and scientific interest applies equally to the discretion of the Executive in defining the area compatible with the proper care and management of the objects to be protected. . . .

Neither can the Court take any judicial interest in the motives which may have inspired the Proclamation described as an attempt to circumvent the Congressional intent and authority in connection with such lands.[41]

In spite of the fact that there were, in addition to the President and Congress, other obvious parties to this dispute such as the nominal parties (the state of Wyoming and the national government) and various sheep growers and lumber companies, on the one hand, and several bureaus in different departments of the national government on the other, the judge disposed of this case as though it raised no legal issues. But to anyone who has seen the 221,610-acre national park which passes under the name of Jackson Hole Monument, it bears no more resemblance to one of the rusting plaques at Gettysburg than does Pike's Peak to Capitol Hill.

No attempt was made to appeal the decision in *Wyoming v. Franke*, but the Supreme Court has shown no disposition of late to review the decisions of the lower federal courts relating to the control of natural resources by presidential regulations; it may be justifiable to infer from this that the Court regards this area of law as largely settled. Perhaps this helps to explain why over a generation elapsed, after the Supreme Court upheld the constitutionality of the Migratory Bird Treaty Act of 1918,[42] before a direct challenge was raised to any of the many presidential proclamations that had been issued annually under the statute. The proclamation at issue had temporarily enlarged the area surrounding a state game preserve which was closed to the taking of wild geese during the period of their annual flight to the south. The enlarged area included several private commercial hunting lodges. In successive decisions, the federal court of appeals sitting at Chicago ruled that there were no private rights in public fowls, any more than in public employment or in public lands: "[N]o person has any property right in live migratory birds and the withdrawal of the privilege of hunting such birds by Federal and State Governments does not deprive anyone of a property right because no such right exists."[43] When the case returned to it two years later, the court stated emphatically: "[W]e hold, as we did on the former appeal in this case . . . that Presidential Proclamation 2748 is valid, as representing a proper exercise of the unlimited and unreviewable discretion vested and reposed by the Act."[44]

A new dimension to public land reservation was added by the executive order challenged in another recent case. When the Secretary of the Interior's establishment of roadless areas, within the Quetico-Superior region of the Superior National Forest in northern Minnesota, no longer served to keep this wilderness canoe country undefiled by commercial exploitation, the President set apart an airspace reservation over the territory. This was the first attempt to implement the President's authority under Section 4 of the Air Commerce Act of 1926, "to provide by Executive order for the setting apart and the protection of airspace reservations in the United States for national defense *or other governmental purposes*, and, in addition, in the District of Columbia for public safety purposes,"[45] other than for national defense or for safety purposes in the District of Columbia. "An airspace reservation is literally just that: a reservation of all or part of the cubic space within vertical lines projected upward from specified geographical areas or boundaries, within which aircraft flights are restricted or prohibited."[46] The defendant resort owners, to whose camps wealthy sportsmen had been flown by a commercial aviation service, had had no quarrel with the roadless ban; the trial judge quoted one of the resort adveriesments as stating: " 'I pray the good Lord daily that my camp remain roadless. Doubtless you are aware of what auto highways mean to good fishing — Amen.' "[47] But the airspace reservation would, and was intended to, put them out of business. Nevertheless, the trial court decided that the executive order was only a reasonable extension of the road ban regulations, and within the authority delegated by Congress since the purpose was a valid and governmental one. " 'The airspace, apart from the immediate reaches above the land, is part of the public domain.' "[48] The federal court of appeals affirmed;[49] and an attempt to get the Supreme Court to reverse, on the theory that the executive order was unconstitutional because it took the petitioners' property without due process of law, failed when the Supreme Court declined to review the case.[50] Early in 1955, Canada imposed a similar airspace reservation over part of the Quetico Provincial Park on the Ontario side of the border.

The consequence of the withdrawal of the courts—and especially the Supreme Court — from the exercise of judicial review of the merits of administrative legislation in this area has been, in practice, the substitution of executive discretion. It is apparent, however, that this represents no very significant departure from trends that have been manifest throughout the past century.

Executive Order Indian Reservations

The third major object for which Presidents have reserved public lands from sale has been to provide new tribal homesites for the Red Men who had to be "resettled" after being dispossessed of their original homes and hunting grounds. This disseizin took place over the course of three centuries, but mostly during the middle decades of the nineteenth century. It was accomplished by the technologically and numerically superior whites through conquest and purchase, and was accorded legal sanctity in a series of contracts which were given, doubtless unnecessarily, the constitutional status of treaties.[51] The public lands of the people of the United States were largely comprised of the former holdings of the Indians, so it was altogether fitting and proper, as well as necessary, that minimal reservations from these vast areas should be made for their original proprietors. As the Supreme Court pointed out in its decision in the *Midwest Oil* case, the way in which this was usually accomplished was by an Executive Order Indian Reservation, based on the inherent powers of the Chief Executive as the general manager of the public domain rather than on specific delegation of authority in statute or treaty. There is no instance in which the courts have denied the power of the President to make such reservations. A possible explanation for this unanimity of acquiescence on the part of both Congress and courts, although one which does not characteristically find conscious verbalization in judicial opinions, lies in the close relationship that the exercise of this power bears to the President's constitutional pre-eminence in military affairs and the exercise of the treaty-making power.

Cases challenging the President's authority did not appear until the closing decades of the last century. In the first to arise, a federal district court held that the "Pyramid Lake Indian Reservation," created by President Grant's executive order of March 23, 1874, was "Indian country" within the meaning of acts of Congress forbidding trading without a license and selling liquor therein. Turning to the question of the validity of the order, the court remarked:

It is said . . . that there is no law of congress setting it apart or giving the president authority to do so. [Citing *Wolcott v. Des Moines Nav. & Ry. Co.*, upholding a presidential withdrawal order in aid of proposed legislation for natural resources development; and *Grisar v. McDowell*, affirming the validity of an executive order military reservation.]

No direct authority to the president to reserve lands and set them apart for public purposes is found in either case, but in each the president's authority is recognized by acts of congress which proceed upon the ground that he has it, and that the reservations so made are made by competent authority.[52]

In the first case to reach it, the Supreme Court upheld the power of Congress retroactively to delegate authority to the President to create a reservation, through ratification of his action:

[T]he White Mountain Indian Reservation was a legally constituted Indian reservation. True, when the Territory of Arizona was organized, on February 24, 1863 . . . there was no such reservation; and it was created in the first instance by order of the President, in 1871. Whatever doubts there might have been, if any, as to the validity of such executive order, are put at rest by the act of Congress of February 8, 1887 . . . the first clause of which is "That in all cases where any tribe or band of Indians has been, or shall hereafter be, located upon any reservation created for their own use, either by treaty stipulations or by virtue of an act of Congress or executive order setting apart the same for their use, the President of the United States be, and hereby is, authorized, whenever in his opinion any reservation, or any part thereof, of such Indians is advantageous for agricultural and grazing purposes, to cause said reservation, or any part thereof, to be surveyed, or resurveyed if necessary, and to allot the lands in said reservation in severalty to any Indian located thereon, in quantities, as follows."

The necessary effect of this legislative recognition was to confirm the executive order, and establish beyond challenge the Indian title to this reservation.[53]

On the other hand, the Court held that the President could not reserve for other purposes lands included within an Indian reservation created by an earlier treaty. This could be done by statute, but not by executive order. The use of the Chippewa fishing encampment at the falls of the St. Mary's River at Sault Ste. Marie in upper Michigan had been guaranteed to the Indians by the treaties of June 26, 1820, and March 24, 1836. An act of March 1, 1847, established the "Lake Superior land district" in Michigan, and provided for the sale of the non-mineral lands therein, excepting school sections and "such reservations as the President shall deem necessary for public uses." Part of the fishing encampment land was then reserved by an executive order of April 3, 1847, in aid of proposed legislation for the enlargement of military defenses and the construction of a ship canal. The legislation ultimately took the form of the act of August 26, 1852, granting to the state of Michigan the right of way and a donation of public lands for the construction of a ship canal around the falls of the St. Mary. The work on this canal was completed in 1855, and it cut right through the Indian reservation, dividing it into three parts; so the Chippewas signed another treaty, in 1855, releasing to the United States their fishing rights under the earlier treaty of 1820. But the Supreme Court held that the executive order was *ultra vires* the statute of March 1, 1847, and in direct conflict with the treaty of 1820 (and therefore invalid on that count also); the early treaty was abrogated by the statute of 1852, not by the executive order in anticipation of the statute.[54] This is the only decision which fails to uphold a temporary presidential withdrawal of public lands; and like the earlier decision of the Supreme Court of Iowa,[55] it would appear to have been overruled by the subsequent decision in the *Midwest Oil* case.[56] And although the Court failed to recognize this, it appears that even in this case the President was not acting independently, but was the agent of Congress (or the War Department) in a matter where treaty rights of Indians were being abrogated by a change in legislative policy.

The converse, however, does appear to hold true: public lands which have been reserved by the President in aid of a proposed Indian treaty are not subject to donation, and it must be presumed that Congress did not intend to include them in a later grant of lands to a railroad.[57] It would appear, then, that where direct conflict existed between an executive order and a statute or treaty, the courts would uphold the latter forms of legislation in which Congress shared directly; on the other hand, such conflict would not be presumed and would be avoided in interpretation, if possible. Where direct conflict did not exist, executive orders, treaties, and statutes were of equal weight and force, and functioned interchangeably for the purpose of creating reservations. Thus, as the Ninth Circuit Court of Appeals held during this same period around the turn of the century:

On the 9th day of April, 1872, an executive order was issued by President Grant, by which was set apart . . . the "Colville Indian Reservation." There can be no doubt of the power of the President to reserve those lands of the United States for the use of the Indians. The effect of that executive order was the same as would have been a treaty with the Indians for the same purpose.[58]

And with respect to a reservation for the Spokane Indians on unoccupied public lands in the state of Washington, created by the executive order of January 18, 1881, the same court added: "There can be no doubt that such a reservation by proclamation of the executive stands upon the same plane as a reservation made by treaty or act of Congress."[59]

A later decision of this court, which came years after the *Midwest Oil* case and expressly followed that decision of the Supreme Court, extended further the doctrine of the inherent power of executive reservation. Annette Island, lying off the southeast coast of Alaska, had been reserved by the act of Congress of March 3, 1891, and the President had later reserved the surrounding waters by his proclamation of April 28, 1916. In making this decision, the court turned significantly to the English cases and the historical scope of the royal prerogative in holding that the United States exercised all sovereignty over the territory of Alaska, and hence "in view of the powers of the king over lands flowed by the tide,"[60] held that the United States had complete control over Alaskan waters flowed by the tide which were within its maritime jurisdiction. Consequently, the President might, in view of his powers to reserve public lands, "carry out the purpose of an act of Congress" by reserving such waters; and in any event: "we can think of nothing more practical, under all the circumstances, than the reservation by the President of the waters immediately surrounding Annette Island for the use and benefit of these Indians.[61]

A number of cases have reached the Supreme Court during the past decade, generally on appeal from the Court of Claims, in which questions concerning the status and validity of Executive Order Indian Reservations have been raised. These more recent decisions have focused, quite naturally, not on the original power of the Presidents to make these reservations — this is now settled law — but rather on the question of who has power to amend or revoke the terms of such reservations. As we have seen, it was settled at the turn of the century that this could be done by statute or by treaty. Could this be done, however, by a subsequent executive order, or by state law, or by an administrative officer acting under subdelegated presidential and statutory powers?

The principle of res judicata, which from time to time has been suggested as applicable to other substantive areas of presidential action and has been uniformly rejected by the judiciary, was rejected again by the Supreme Court when it held that the creation of the Hoopa Valley Indian Reservation by President Grant in his executive order of June 23, 1876, did not exhaust presidential statutory authority to establish Indian reservations in California under the act of April 8, 1864. Such authority was of a continuing nature and was properly exercised by President Harrison in his executive order of October 16, 1891, extending the boundaries of the original reservation to include also the original Klamath River Reservation.[62]

On the other hand, no reservation was created by an act of Congress authorizing presidential reservations which were never, in fact, made.

Presidential Management of the Public Domain

Treaties of September 4 and 8, 1852, had authorized the President to make reservations of lands to which the Minnesota Sioux bands would be removed, and an act of 1863 directed the President to assign and set aside for the Sioux bands a tract of unoccupied land sufficient to enable him to assign to each member an allotment of acreage; but several Presidents failed to act under either the permissive powers of the treaty or the directive powers of the statute. Perhaps the chief reason why no action was taken was that the Sioux had gone on the warpath in 1862 and remained at war for several years.[63] In 1868, however, a treaty was made by the United States with the Sioux Nation, which was ratified by the Senate the following year, providing that a certain definite tract of public land was to be set apart for the absolute and undisturbed use and occupation of the Sioux tribes and bands. In addition to this treaty reservation, executive orders withdrawing public lands from settlement and sale, and temporarily adding to the reservation, were promulgated on January 11, 1875, March 16, 1875, May 20, 1875, and November 28, 1876. The primary purpose of these executive orders was to help in the control of liquor traffic with the Indians. These lands temporarily withdrawn were restored to the public domain by the subsequent executive orders of August 8, 1879 and March 20, 1884, which expressly revoked the earlier executive orders of 1875 and 1876.

Over half a century later, the descendents of these Indians sued under special enabling legislation, claiming that Presidents Hayes and Arthur, by their executive orders of 1879 and 1884, had taken the private lands of the Sioux for public use; and that this taking was illegal because the President had no power to confiscate private property in this manner. In the alternative, it was claimed that, if he had any such power, it was the power of eminent domain; and the Indians were thus entitled to the just compensation which they had not as yet received. This spurious argument was of course rejected by the Court of Claims, which upheld the validity of the executive orders, ruling:

There are three kinds of Indian reservations: those which have been created by treaties previous to 1871; those which have been created by acts of Congress since 1871; and those made by Executive Orders whereby the President has set apart public lands for the use of the Indians in order to keep them within a certain territory. By the act of June 30, 1919, the President was expressly prohibited from issuing Executive Orders creating reservations out of the public lands [except under statutory delegation of power].[64]

In reference to Executive Order reservations, there was no law under which the President acted, but it has been recognized that the President issued these Executive Orders setting aside these public lands for public use *under the right of the Executive to carry out the policy of preserving the public interest.* The fee of any interest in these lands was never in the Executive. . . .

In order to dispose of the public lands it is necessary for the Congress to take some action either by direct legislation or by conferring upon the President the power of the Congress so that he, acting as the agent of the Congress, can dispose of the lands. . . .

The President had no right to dispose of public lands under the Constitution. . . .[65]

The Supreme Court affirmed on appeal, noting:

It is significant that the executive department consistently indicated its understanding that the rights and interests which the Indians enjoyed in executive order reservations were different from and less than their rights and interests in treaty or statute reservations. . . .[66]

Perhaps the most striking proof of the belief shared by the Congress and the Executive that the Indians were not entitled to compensation upon the abolition of an executive order reservation is the very absence of compensatory payments in such situations. It was a common practice, during the period in which reservations were created by executive order, for the President simply to terminate the existence of a reservation by cancelling or revoking the order establishing it. That is to say, the procedure followed in the case before us was typical. No compensation was made, and neither the Government nor the Indians suggested that it was due.[67]

Although the President could not create any compensable right for the Indians in public lands that he had set aside for their use by executive order, nevertheless, the effect of creating such a reservation might be legally to extinguish their rights to lands they had formerly used and occupied, and they would be entitled to compensation for them. This was true in the instance of the executive order of November 8, 1855, issued without any statutory authority and for the purpose of temporarily withdrawing certain lands to which the Tillamook Indians still claimed title, in what was called the "Coast Reservation." The government proposed to settle several other groups of Indians on this reservation. A treaty negotiated with the Tillamook tribes and bands and signed on August 11, 1855, ceded to the United States lands substantially the same as those withdrawn by the executive order on the consideration that certain money payments would be made by the United States and a reservation for the Indians would be created out of the ceded lands. This treaty was submitted to the Senate in February 1857, but it was never ratified. Part of the land in controversy was withdrawn from the reservation and opened to public sale and entry by the executive order of December 21, 1865; and other Indian tribes not signatory to the unratified treaty were moved onto the Coast Reservation. Congress by act of March 3, 1875, ratified the executive orders of 1855 and 1865, and reduced further the size of the reservation by authorizing the removal of the Indians from part of the lands without their consent; by the simple expedient of throwing these lands open to immediate settlement, the coerced consent of the Indians was actually secured.

The petition of the claimants alleged "that by Executive Order of December 21, 1865, the defendant took away from said Indians without authority of law to their great damage said tract." The Court of Claims refused to accept this thesis, although it did find that since the Treaty of 1855 had never been ratified, the title of the Indian tribes who had signed the treaty and who had previously enjoyed beneficial use and occupancy of these lands was never legally extinguished — by the treaty. However, Congress could unquestionably have extinguished their legal title to the lands, although with an implied obligation to pay just compensation, and the court held that Congress had in fact done this by the act of 1875, which ratified the executive orders.[68] Therefore, reasoned the court, the effective date of the transfer of title from the Indians to the United States was the date of the first executive order — although that had been intended as a temporary withdrawal of lands that were not at the time the public lands of the United States, in aid of a pending treaty that was never ratified!

It is not easy to understand why, in the case of the *Sioux Tribe*, the President could not give title to the Indians by executive order, while, in the case of the *Alcea Band* just described, he could take it away from them by executive order. The explanation of the judiciary is, of course, that in the first case, Congress did not ratify the executive orders, while in the second case, Congress did ratify them. Therefore, it was *really* Congress who, some twenty years before the ratifying statute was passed, had created the reservation and taken title from the Indians.[69]

In another recent decision, the Supreme Court had occasion to reaffirm its ruling in the case of the *Sioux Tribes* that the President had no power to confer upon the Indians a compensable title to public lands by executive order. As in the earlier decision, nothing indicated that either of the Presidents directly involved had ever attempted to do so; rather, counsel for the descendants of the affected tribes sought to establish a claim against the government by arguing that the executive orders should be interpreted to have had such an effect. In this case, a treaty of 1868 had established the boundaries of the Ute Reservation in Colorado. Some white settlers tried to encroach on the more valuable part of the lands in the northern part of the reservation, the White River Valley, where the tribe was settled and the Indian agent and the government buildings were located. Afterwards one Miller knowingly and fraudulently surveyed a line fifteen miles south of the actual treaty boundary. This line was then accepted as the northern boundary of the reservation; and it had the effect, of course, of excluding the White River Valley from the reservation. Acting on the advice of the Secretary of the Interior, the President issued an executive order in 1875, setting aside additional territory to the north of the reservation, and purportedly including the White River Valley, to be withdrawn from sale and reserved for the use of the Ute Indians. A climax to the increasing encroachment of the white settlers was reached when a massacre took place in 1879; and as a punishment, Congress enacted in 1880 a statute which had the effect of removing the Utes from their lands. The lands were to be sold, with certain exceptions not material here, and the proceeds turned over to the Indians. The President then issued another executive order in 1882, restoring to the public domain the lands set aside by the earlier executive order of 1875.

Suit was brought by the claimants under a special jurisdictional act of 1938, which authorized the Court of Claims to render judgment and compensation for any lands *formerly belonging to the Indians* and taken by the United States without compensation. As it happened, the White River Valley lands, although purportedly covered by both executive orders, were not included in the court's disposition of this case; they were considered separately in a connected but independent suit before the Court of Claims. Presumably, there would be no question of the Indians' right to compensation for the White River Valley lands, because they were *in fact* a part of the lands covered by the treaty; and as to them, the executive order was, in retrospect, a nullity, except as it made them temporarily available to the Indians where otherwise they would not have been. The present case was concerned rather with the right of the Indians to compensation for the additional lands north of the true boundary, temporarily reserved for their use by the executive order of 1875, and restored to the public domain by the later executive order. The Supreme Court denied that claim.[70]

Although the rights of Indians settled on an Executive Order Indian Reservation were subject to such modifications and limitations as subsequent executive orders might bring about, a state has no power to interfere with or change rights conferred upon the Indians by executive order. It is true that in the recent case in which this rule was established the executive order was considered to have been issued under the authority of an earlier treaty; but the same rule would presumably apply in the case of an executive order based only on the inherent powers of the Chief Executive, under principles established in other substantive areas of the law where the equivalent question has been raised, such as in the case of executive agreements. In the instant case, the United States sued on behalf of the Quillehute Tribe of Indians to enjoin Milo Moore, director of fisheries of the state of Washington, from interfering in any manner with the Quillehute Indians in their free use of the waters of the Quillehute River and the tidelands of the Pacific Ocean bordering on the reservation, and to prevent the state from exercising jurisdiction over the Indians' fishing rights. The Quillehutes were a fish-eating tribe whose commercial fishing industry was almost their only means of livelihood, their lands being valuable for practically nothing else. Subjection to the licensing powers of the state would have been a severe if not a crippling blow to their economy. The federal district court granted an injunction without hesitation, holding that the rights of the Indians had become "fixed by the promulgation of the presidential proclamation of February 19, 1889."[71]

In its most recent decision in this area, the Supreme Court unanimously upheld the power of an administrative officer, acting under subdelegated presidential authority, to amend the boundaries established in an earlier Executive Order Indian Reservation. The Secretary of the Interior's Public Land Order No. 128 of May 22, 1943, established a temporary reservation including lands actually settled by Karluk Tribe Village on Kodiak Island, and also included 3000 feet of the adjoining coastal waters which constituted part of the best salmon fishing grounds in Alaska. The President's earlier Executive Order No. 8344 of February 10, 1940, which was thus modified, had withdrawn Kodiak and other islands lying off the coast of Alaska for classification and in aid of proposed legislation to the extent necessary to permit the designation as an Indian reservation of a described area. The Supreme Court decided:

In this case the significant part of No. 128 is that the Secretary included in the reservation by paragraph 2, adjacent tidelands and coastal waters along the entire shore line of the uplands that touched Shelikof Strait between Kodiak Island and the Alaska Peninsula. The authority of the Secretary to utilize presidential power in the designation of this reservation out of public lands in Alaska flows from a delegation to the Secretary of presidential power to withdraw or reserve public lands and revoke or modify prior reservations.[72] . . . The presidential power over reservations is made specific by the Act of June 25, 1910.[73] Another statutory provision, however, is the principal basis for Order 128. This is s. 2 of the Act of May 1, 1936, 49 Stat. 1250. . . .[74]

Taking into consideration the importance of the fisheries to the Alaska natives, the temporary character of the reservation, the Annette Islands case, the administrative determination, the purpose of Congress to assist the natives by the Alaska amendment to the Wheeler-Howard Act, we have concluded that the Secretary of the Interior was authorized to include the waters in the reservation.[75]

In a very real sense, the fact that administrative legislation has formally displaced executive orders as a vehicle for public land management is indicative of the extent to which the large and uncertain questions of constitutional power of a century ago are now foreclosed. The settlement and resettlement of the Red Man has become routine.

Notes

[1] The Vice President has certainly not been a relevant exception, at least not before the 1956 election.

[2] The Lockean definition of the prerogative in English public law is "power to act according to discretion for the public good, without the prescription of law and sometimes even against it . . . there is a latitude left to the executive power to do many things of choice which the laws do not prescribe." *Second Treatise on Government* (1690), sec. 160. See Glendon A. Schubert, Jr., "Judicial Review of Royal Proclamations and Orders-in-Council," *University of Toronto Law Journal*, 9:71–72, ftn. 7, 76–79 (1951).

[3] Wilcox v. Jackson, 13 Peters 498, 513 (1839).

[4] James C. Stone v. United States, 2 Wallace 535, 537 (1865).

[5] Grisar v. McDowell, 6 Wallace 363, 380–381 (1868).

[6] 9 *Stat.* 497 and 10 *Stat.* 158.

[7] United States v. Tichenor, 12 F. 415, 421, 423–424 (1882).

[8] United States v. McGraw, 12 F. 449, 453 (1882).

[9] Kelly v. Dallas City, 24 P. 449, 454 (1890). Kelly was Bigelow's grantee under the patent. The validity of Bigelow's claim and the patent had already been upheld in a collateral case decided by the federal circuit court for Oregon, Kelly v. Pike (apparently unreported). See 24 P. 449, 453.

[10] Behrends v. Goldsteen, 1 Alaska 518 (1902).

[11] Florida Town Improvement Co. v. Bigalsky, 33 So. 450, 451 (1902).

[12] War Department Order No. 70, signed by the Adjutant General, read: "Colonel Brooke . . . will proceed . . . to Tampa Bay, East Florida, where he will establish a military reservation. He will select a position with a view to the health [of his men] and in reference to the Florida Indians."

[13] Scott v. Carew, 196 U.S. 100, 101, 109, 114 (1905).

[14] 39 *Stat.* 954, 46 *Stat.* 3004.

[15] United States v. San Geronimo Development Co., 154 F. 2d 78, 85 (1946); certiorari denied, 329 U.S. 718 (1946). Compare, however, an earlier decision of this same court where, in Baldrich v. Barbour, 90 F. 2d 867, 871 (1937), the court had held that a proclamation of the President creating a forest reserve should "have, at least, the effect of a quitclaim deed . . . to establish a 'proper title' required by section 1858 of the Puerto Rican Civil Code."

[16] The license had been issued on September 1, 1834, by the Army officer in charge of the lead mines, who was under the direction of the President's delegate, the Secretary of War. It provided: "That the said party of the second part is hereby permitted, by and with the approbation of the President of the United States, to purchase and smelt lead ore at the United States' lead mines, on the Upper Mississippi, for the period of one year, from and after the date hereof, upon the following conditions, viz. . . . "

[17] United States v. Gratiot, 14 Peters 526, 537, 538, 539 (1840).

[18] Lorimier v. Lewis, 39 Am.D. 461, 462–463, 465 (1 Morris 253) (1843). This was a political decision which was not appealed to the Supreme Court of the United States; it would almost certainly have been reversed if it had been. As an exposition of the law, the territorial court's decision was wrong on both scores. Control over the mineral rights in the lands of the Crown most certainly was an element of the direct prerogative; compare the King's power to license mineral rights in *private* lands, The Case of the King's Prerogative in Saltpetre (1607) 12 Co.Rep. 12; 77 E.R. 1294. As to the inherent power of the President, see the subsequent decision of the Supreme Court in United States v. Midwest Oil Co., 236 U.S. 459 (1915).

[19] There were ten decisions of the Supreme Court comprising the *Des Moines River* cases, only three of which are of direct interest here. For a good historical summary of the preceding cases and events, see the last two of these decisions, Bullard v. Des Moines Valley and Fort Dodge R.R. Co., 122 U.S. 167 (1887), and United States v. Des Moines Navigation and R.R. Co., 142 U.S. 510 (1892).

[20] Dubuque & P. Ry. Co. v. Litchenfield, 23 How. 66 (1860).

[21] Wolcott v. Des Moines Navigation & R.R. Co., 5 Wall. 681, 688, 689 (1867).

[22] Wolsey v. Chapman, 101 U.S. 755, 770 (1880).

[23] Russian-American Packing Co. v. United States, 199 U.S. 570 (1905). President Theodore Roosevelt's proclamation of January 17, 1903, issued under authority of an act of July 1, 1902, and creating the "Luguillo Forest Reserve" in Puerto Rico and warning all persons not to occupy or use the lands thus reserved, was upheld by the First Circuit Court of Appeals on similar grounds in Baldrich v. Barbour, 90 F. 2d 867, 871 (1937).

[24] United States v. Blendauer, 122 F. 703, 707 (D.Mont., 1903). Upon appeal, however, the Ninth Circuit Court of Appeals reversed, and held that the reservation by the President was valid: 128 F. 910 (1904).

[25] United States v. Hodges, 218 F. 87, 88 (D.Mont., 1914).

[26] "In aid of proposed legislation affecting the use and disposition of the petroleum deposits on the public domain, all public lands in the accompanying lists are hereby

temporarily withdrawn from all forms of location, settlement, selection, filing, entry, or disposal under the mineral or nonmineral public-land laws. All locations or claims existing and valid on this date may proceed to entry in the usual manner after filing, investigation, and examination." Private entry on the lands thus withdrawn had been authorized by the act of February 11, 1897.

[27] Alpheus T. Mason, *Bureaucracy Convicts Itself* (New York: Viking, 1941), p. 26.

[28] William Howard Taft, *Our Chief Magistrate and His Powers* (New York: Columbia University Press, 1916), pp. 139–140, 144–145, and cf. Mr. Justice Jackson, concurring in Youngstown Sheet & Tube v. Sawyer, 343 U.S. 579, 635, ftn. 1.

[29] See Daniel S. McHargue, "President Taft's Appointments to the Supreme Court," *Journal of Politics*, 12:478–510 (August 1950).

[30] The rule of Wolsey v. Chapman, ftn. 22, *supra*, is implicit here: the President issued no proclamation on September 27, 1909; the Secretary of the Interior, however, did issue an administrative order under the direction of the President.

[31] United States v. Midwest Oil Co., 236 U.S. 459, 468–473 (1915).

[32] *Ibid.*, 474, 476, 481 (1915). The President's power was expressly so revoked, in part, by the act of June 30, 1919, sec. 27 of which provided that thereafter, "no public lands of the United States shall be withdrawn by Executive Order, proclamation, or otherwise, for or as an Indian reservation except by act of Congress."

[33] *Ibid.*, 511–512.

[34] A more recent and equally instructive example is provided by the majority and minority opinions of the Court in Girouard v. United States, 328 U.S. 61 (1946).

[35] The dissenting opinion clearly states that the minority would be quite willing to accept an executive withdrawal order, for which no prospective delegation of authority from Congress existed, provided it were for the purpose of creating an Indian or military reservation, *because this would be an acceptable identification of the public interest.*

[36] For a discussion of the mood of the times, see Alpheus T. Mason, *Bureaucracy Convicts Itself* (New York: Viking, 1941), especially pp. 21–23.

[37] United States v. Morrison, 240 U.S. 192, 212 (1916). Cf. Byron v. United States, 259 F. 371 (9 C.C.A., 1919); certiorari denied, 251 U.S. 556 (1920).

[38] "The defendants . . . took possession of the lands in violation of the withdrawal order, but they did so in the honest though mistaken, belief that the order was wholly without authority. Some of them had legal advice from competent counsel to that effect. It is common knowledge that the validity of the withdrawal order in question . . . was in grave doubt until the decision of this court in *United States v. Midwest Oil Co.* . . . Not only was a substantial opinion to be found among members of the profession that the order was invalid, but the decision here was by a divided court. In view of these circumstances, we think it fair to conclude that the mining locations of defendants . . . were in moral good faith, within the meaning of the Louisiana Code and decisions." Mason v. United States, 260 U.S. 545, 556 (1923).

[39] Shaw v. Work, 9 F. 2d 1014, 1015 (1925); certiorari denied, 270 U.S. 642 (1926). The orders of President Taft that were challenged in the *Midwest* case were still involved in litigation a quarter of a century after their promulgation, and on the authority of that Supreme Court decision were upheld by a federal district court in California in Bourdieu v. Pacific Western Oil Co., 8 F. Supp. 407, 408, 410 (S.D.Cal.N.D., 1934). The Supreme Court reversed at 299 U.S. 65 (1936), but on grounds that are irrelevant here.

[40] Dakota Central Telephone Co. v. So. Dakota, 250 U.S. 163 (1919) (presidential public utility rate-making under the war power); United States v. Bush & Co., 310 U.S. 371 (1940) (presidential tariff-making, in the field of foreign affairs).

[41] State of Wyoming v. Franke, 58 F. Supp. 890, 892, 896 (D.Wyo., 1945). Compare Cameron v. United States, 252 U.S. 450 (1920), upholding the presidential proclamation of January 11, 1908, on the grounds that the Grand Canyon was in fact an object of historic or scientific interest.

[42] Missouri v. Holland, 252 U.S. 416 (1920).

Presidential Management of the Public Domain

[43] Lansden v. Hart, 168 F. 2d 409, 412 (7 C.A., 1948); rehearing denied, 168 F. 2d 409 (1948); certiorari denied, 335 U.S. 858 (1948).

[44] Lansden v. Hart, 180 F. 2d 679, 683 (7 C.A., 1950); rehearing denied, 180 F. 2d 679 (1950); certiorari denied, 340 U.S. 824 (1950); and rehearing denied, 340 U.S. 894 (1950).

[45] 44 *Stat.* 570. Italics supplied.

[46] Russell P. Andrews, *Wilderness Sanctuary* (University, Ala.: Inter-University Case Program, No. 13, 1953), p. 1.

[47] United States v. Perko, 108 F. Supp. 315, 320 (Dist. Minnesota, 5th Div., 1952).

[48] *Ibid.*, 322, quoting from United States v. Causby, 328 U.S. 256, 266 (1946).

[49] Perko v. United States, 204 F. 2d 446 (8 C.A., 1953).

[50] Certiorari denied, Perko v. United States, 346 U.S. 832 (1953).

[51] See Paul I. Wellman, *Death on Horseback* (Philadelphia: Lippincott, 1947); and for an exceptionally perceptive and lucid exposition of the role of the Court of Claims and the Supreme Court in the legal post-mortem to this march of civilization, see the concurring opinion of Mr. Justice Jackson in Northwestern Bands of Shoshone Indians v. United States, 324 U.S. 335, 354–358 (1945).

[52] United States v. Leathers, 26 Fed. Cas. 897, 898 (D.Nev., 1879), No. 15,581. The court also decided that President Grant's order was valid in this case because it had been ratified by Congress. Decided by the same court the same day, and accord: United States v. Sturgeon, 27 Fed. Cas. 1357 (D.Nev., 1879), No. 16,413.

The Circuit Court for the District of Minnesota approved, in a dictum, the principle of executive reservation, noting: "An Indian reservation may be set aside by an act of Congress, by treaty, or by executive order. . . . " 43 Cases of Brandy, 14 F. 539 (1882).

[53] *In re* Wilson, 140 U.S. 575, 576, 577 (1891).

[54] Spalding v. Chandler, 160 U.S. 394 (1896).

[55] Lorimier v. Lewis, 39 Am.D. 461 (1843).

[56] 236 U.S. 459 (1915).

[57] United States v. Grand Rapids & Iowa R. Co., 154 F. 131, 135 (C.Ct., Mich., 1907), affirmed, 165 F. 297 (6 C.C.A., 1908).

[58] McFadden v. Mountain View Mining and Milling Co., 97 F. 670, 673 (1899); reversed on other grounds not relevant here, 180 U.S. 533 (1901). See, however, United States v. Pelican, 232 U.S. 442 (1914), in which the Supreme Court expressly upheld the validity of this executive order reservation.

[59] Gibson v. Anderson, 131 F. 39, 42 (9 C.C.A., 1904).

[60] Compare: United States v. California, 332 U.S. 19 (1947); see also United States v. Stotts, 49 F. 2d 619 (W.D.Wash.N.D., 1930), United States v. Moore, 62 F. Supp. 660 (W.D.Wash.S.D., 1945), and Hynes v. Grimes Packing Co., 337 U.S. 86 (1949), *infra.*

[61] Alaska Pacific Fisheries v. United States, 240 F. 274, 281 (9 C.C.A., 1917). Utilitarian or no, the fact remained that there was no statutory authority for the President's action. In an unanimous decision, the Supreme Court affirmed, but on other grounds, at 248 U.S. 78 (1918).

Compare with the later decision of the Supreme Court of Montana, also following the *Midwest Oil* and *Mason* decisions of the Supreme Court of the United States dealing with natural resources reservations, and holding: it appears to us to be clear that an executive order Indian reservation, within the meaning of sections 398a, 398b, and 398c [title 25, USCA], is one which owes its existence to an order made by the Chief Executive withdrawing the land within its boundaries from settlement or making other disposition of it under the public land laws of the United States *without any specific or general law enacted by Congress authorizing such withdrawal.*" Santa Rita Oil Co. v. Board of Equalization, 54 P. 2d 117, 122 (1936). Italics supplied.

[62] Donnelly v. United States, 228 U.S. 243 (1913).

[63] Sisseton and Wahpeton Bands of Sioux Indians v. United States, 58 Ct. Cl. 302 (1923); certiorari denied at 275 U.S. 528 (1927).

[64] In 1927, Congress provided that any further changes in the boundaries of executive order reservations should be made only by Congress. See Section 4, 44 *Stat.* 1347.

[65] Sioux Tribe of Indians v. United States, 94 Ct. Cl. 150, 170, 171 (1941). Italics supplied.

[66] See 34 *Opinions of the Attorney-General* 171, 176: " . . . the President has in fact, and in a number of instances, changed the boundaries of executive order Indian reservations by excluding lands therefrom, and the question of his authority to do so has not apparently come before the courts." (Quoted in a footnote in the case at 316 U.S. 317, 327.)

[67] Sioux Tribe of Indians v. United States, 316 U.S. 317, 327, 330 (1942).

[68] Alcea Band of Tillamooks v. United States, 59 F. Supp. 934, 958, 968 (1945).

[69] United States v. Alcea Band of Tillamooks, 329 U.S. 40, 43, 44, 54 (1946). It should also be noted that, as the Supreme Court pointed out, "By an act of 1894, Congress officially accepted and approved the reservation as it then existed, and thence forward did not take reservation lands without compensation." The claimants were prevented from suing the United States, under the doctrine of sovereign immunity, until Congress enacted in 1935 the special jurisdictional statute under which this suit was brought.

[70] Confederated Bands of Ute Indians v. United States, 330 U.S. 169, 176 (1947).

[71] United States v. Moore, 62 F. Supp. 660, 668 (W.D.Wash.S.D., 1945). Affirming, the Ninth Circuit Court of Appeals added: "In construing the sufficiency of the Presidential reservation as complying with the treaty provisions for a reservation 'sufficient for their wants,' that language is 'to be liberally construed, doubtful expressions being resolved in favor of the Indians.'" Moore v. United States, 157 F. 2d 760, 762 (1946); certiorari denied, 330 U.S. 827 (1947). Cf. United States v. Stotts, 49 F. 2d 619 (W.D. Wash.N.D., 1930), holding the boundaries fixed by executive order for the Lummi Indian Reservation conclusive as against the asserted power of the state of Washington to sell tidewater lands therein to private citizens.

[72] This executive order provided: "By virtue of the authority vested in me by the act of June 25, 1910, c. 421, 36 Stat. 847, and as President of the United States, I hereby authorize the Secretary of the Interior to sign all orders withdrawing or reserving public lands of the United States, and all orders revoking or modifying such orders."

[73] This statute provided: "That the President may, at any time in his discretion, temporarily withdraw from settlement, location, sale, or entry any of the public lands of the United States including the District of Alaska and reserve the same for water-power sites, irrigation, classification of lands, or other public purposes to be specified in the orders of withdrawals, and such withdrawals or reservations shall remain in force until revoked by him or by an Act of Congress."

[74] This statute extended to Alaska the benefits of the Wheeler-Howard Act of June 18, 1934, and provided for the designation of Indian reservations in Alaska by the Secretary of the Interior, including among other circumstances any other public lands which were actually occupied by Indians or Eskimos, providing his designation of the reservation should be approved by a majority secret vote in a referendum of the Indian or Eskimo tribe concerned.

[75] Hynes v. Grimes Packing Co., 337 U.S. 86, 89–91, 116 (1949).

II

The Chief of State: Sole Organ
of the Nation

"The President is the sole organ of the nation in its external relations, and its sole representative with foreign nations." John Marshall, speaking in the House of Representatives, March 7, 1800, *Annals,* 6th Cong., col. 613; and United States v. Curtiss-Wright Export Corp., 299 U.S. 304, 319 (1936)

"In substance and to a great extent in form, the action of the [Tariff] Commission and the President is but one stage of the legislative process. . . . And the judgment of the President on the facts, adduced in pursuance of the procedure prescribed by Congress, that a change of rate is necessary is no more subject to judicial review under this statutory scheme than if Congress itself had exercised that judgment." United States v. Bush & Co., 310 U.S. 371, 379–380 (1940)

"Presidential control [over overseas and foreign air transportation] is not limited to a negative but is a positive and detailed control over the [Civil Aeronautics] Board's decisions, unparalleled in the history of American administrative bodies.

"Congress may, of course, delegate very large grants of its power over foreign commerce to the President. . . . The President also possesses in his own right certain powers conferred by the Constitution on him as Commander-in-Chief and as the Nation's organ in foreign affairs." Chicago and Southern Air Lines v. Waterman S. S. Corp., 333 U.S. 103, 109 (1948)

4

The Conduct of Foreign Relations

Recognition of Foreign Governments

UNDER our system of governance, the recognition or non-recognition of foreign governments is a purely executive act, and among executive acts it is perhaps the most remote from the possibility of judicial review. The question of recognition may be surcharged with explosive overtones for both international and domestic politics, as in the case of the non-recognition of the U.S.S.R. from 1917 to 1933, in the recognition of the new state of Israel and the presidential election of 1948, or in the relationship to the Korean War and the 1952 presidential election of our continued recognition of the exiled government of Nationalist China and our refusal to recognize the Communist Peiping government. Nevertheless, attempts have been made in the past to persuade the courts to intervene in similar decisions. Thus, a federal district court held that the action of foreign states with respect to the recognition of the Confederate States of America was irrelevant in a court of the United States, which was bound to follow the decision of the "political department" of our government;[1] a taxpayer's suit to enjoin the construction of the Panama Canal failed, in part because of President Theodore Roosevelt's action in recognizing the new government of the republic of Panama;[2] and the successive grants of de facto (October 19, 1915) and de jure (August 31, 1917) recognition to the revolutionary Carranza government of the republic of Mexico were conclusive on the courts, even though this suit was begun in the trial court before either event.[3]

More recent decisions in the circuit courts of appeals are to the same effect: since the courts are bound by the action of the Chief Executive, and where necessary address their own inquiries to it, further clarification by the President, even when made after decision had been rendered in a trial court, had to be considered and was conclusive on an appellate court.[4] Although Estonia had been occupied and incorporated in the U.S.S.R. as a Soviet republic in 1940, a suit brought by AMTORG, to recover compensation for an Estonian ship requisitioned by the War Shipping Administration, was dismissed, since the President had not recognized U.S.S.R. sovereignty over Estonia and acts of the Soviet government, including nationalization and transfer in ownership of the vessel, could not be recognized by a United States court.[5]

Executive Agreements

A treaty is a presidential ordinance.[6] No attempt has been made to deal exhaustively here with the question of judicial review of treaties, but the following discussion is intended to suggest the scope of the problem and the relative freedom from judicial restraint that the President enjoys when he acts through treaties and executive agreements. Since the senatorial function of advising the President in the pre-negotiation or negotiation stages of treaties has been largely nonexistent since Washington's first term, the formulative aspects of this exercise of legislative power[7] have always reposed solely in the President. Senatorial concurrence is a procedural prerequisite to promulgation, however, and the widespread use of the executive agreement in recent years is due in part to the fact that this procedure frequently obviates the necessity for seeking congressional approval (other than for subsequent appropriations). Both treaties and executive agreements may or may not also require implementing legislation,[8] but the President's power to bind or commit the United States to any given course of action is as great under the one as under the other, at least insofar as the courts forbear to draw legal distinctions between them.[9]

Thus the Supreme Court, reversing a decision of the Supreme Court of the District of Columbia, refused to mandamus the Secretary of State to distribute funds, paid by the Mexican government to the United States for settlement of their claims, among certain mining companies whose properties had previously been expropriated by Mexico. President Arthur had re-examined the determinations of a joint claims commission and, "believing that said award was obtained by fraud and perjury," negotiated a new treaty with Mexico providing for a rehearing on these claims. Neither the fact that President Hayes had failed to carry out a statutory authorization to make the investigation that President Arthur did make, nor that the treaty was pending before the Senate in protocol form, militated against the independent constitutional power of the President to undertake or not to undertake such an investigation, to renegotiate with Mexico concerning the claims of citizens of the United States, or to pay or withhold benefits to the extent that Mexico had made funds available to our government for such a purpose. "That discretion of the Executive Department of the government cannot be controlled by the Judiciary."[10]

Although the matter has not been raised in similar form before the Supreme Court during the past three decades, we have known since 1920 that limitations of federalism that would apply in the case of a statute do not apply to a treaty, which can then authorize the adoption of a statute which, standing alone, would be unconstitutional. In other words, the scope of the substantive powers of the national government are broader (in an undefined manner) under the treaty power than its statutory powers: Article II, 2 (2) is, therefore, not merely a prescription of a particular legislative procedure, but an independent grant of substantive power.[11] Although the point has not yet been explicitly decided, the same is doubtless also true of executive agreements. Certainly, an executive agreement takes precedence over conflicting state law to the same extent that a treaty would. This was made clear in litigation arising from the executive agreement whereby the United States recognized the U.S.S.R. and the Soviet government agreed that all her assets in the United States were to be made available to pay the claims of citizens of the United States for property confiscated at the time of the revolution when the Communist government came to power. The latter arrangement was formalized in an interchange of notes on November 16, 1933, and is known as "The Litvinov Assignment." The U.S.S.R. had, of course, been unable to sue in the courts of the United States, or of the individual states, prior to this time because the previous refusal of recognition denied the Soviet government the status of a legal person.

The first of two cases to reach the Supreme Court was decided less than six months after the *Curtiss-Wright* case, and Mr. Justice Sutherland took advantage of the opportunity to write, for the Court, a long essay on the pre-eminent role of the President in the conduct of our foreign relations, in which he noted:

That the negotiations, acceptance of the assignment and agreement and understandings in respect thereof were within the competence of the President may not be doubted . . . in respect of what was done here, the Executive had authority to speak as the sole organ of [the] government . . . an international compact, as this was, is not always a treaty which requires the participation of the Senate. . . .

Plainly, the external powers of the United States are to be exercised without regard to state laws or policies . . . the same rule [as for treaties] would result in the case of all international compacts and agreements from the very fact that complete power over international affairs is in the national government and is not and cannot be subject to any curtailment or interference on the part of the several states . . . In respect of all international . . . compacts . . . State lines disappear. As to such purposes the state of New York does not exist.[12]

Five years later, the Court ruled directly on certain points expressly reserved but nevertheless discussed by Justice Sutherland in the majority opinion in the *Belmont* case. Stone, who had dissented there and was by this time the chief justice, protested vigorously that the Court was now accepting as authority for and controlling of its decision here the very statements that he had explicitly pointed out to be *obiter dicta* in the *Belmont* case, but the majority of the Court held:

The powers of the President in the conduct of foreign relations include power, without consent of the Senate, to determine the public policy of the United States with respect to the Russian nationalization decrees. . . . That authority is not limited to a determination of the government to be recognized. It includes the power to determine the policy which is to govern the question of recognition. Objections to the underlying policy as well as objections to recognition are to be addressed to the political department and not to the courts. . . . Recognition is not always absolute; it is sometimes conditional. . . . Power to remove such obstacles to full recognition as settlement of claims of our nationals . . . certainly is a modest implied power of the President who is the "sole organ of the federal government in the field of international relations.". . . Effectiveness in handling the delicate problems of foreign relations requires no less. Unless such a power exists, the power of recognition might be thwarted or seriously diluted. No such obstacle can be placed in the way of rehabilitation of relations between this country and another nation, unless the historic conception of the powers and responsibilities of the President in the conduct of foreign affairs . . . is to be drastically revised. It was the judgment of the political department that full recognition of the Soviet Government required the settlement of all outstanding problems including the claims of our nationals. Recognition and the Litvinov Assignment were interdependent. We would usurp the executive function if we held that that decision was not final and conclusive in the courts. . . .

A treaty is a "Law of the Land" under the supremacy clause (Art. VI, Cl. 2) of the Constitution. Such international compacts and agreements as the Litvinov Assignment have a similar dignity.[13]

Almost a decade elapsed before another direct challenge was raised to the constitutionality of an executive agreement, although Presidents Roosevelt and Truman came to rely increasingly upon such international agreements as instruments for making and effecting national policy. When it came, the challenge took the form of a claim that an agreement between the United States and Canada[14] was unconstitutional, because the President had failed to utilize a relevant statutory procedure, preferring to rely upon his own independent constitutional authority. This was precisely the same issue that was raised in the *Steel Seizure* case,[15] which the Supreme Court decided while this case was being appealed.

The suit arose as a civil claim for damages by the United States against a Florida importer of Canadian potatoes. The government was obligated by the Agriculture Act of 1948 to purchase all of that year's potato crop that could not be sold on the market at parity. It was a bumper crop, in both the United States and Canada. In order to protect the American market, the statute provided that after an investigation by the Tariff Commission, if the President approved its findings, he could issue a proclamation limiting imports of any commodity from a foreign country to not more than 50 per cent of the quantity admitted during a representative period, and imposing countervailing duties up to 50 per cent *ad valorem*. Instead of doing this, however, the State Department had negotiated an agreement with the Canadian government by which Canada refused to issue licenses for the export of potatoes to the United States except for use as seed; this was to be an express provision of all purchase contracts. The United States agreed, in turn, to admit Canada's seed potatoes. The proclamation procedure would have taken considerably more time to execute than did the negotiation of the agreement. The theory of the government's suit was that the defendant had sold his potatoes to the A & P, which had directed them to table use; this had necessitated government purchase of an equivalent quantity of potatoes, and the government's claim was for the value of these purchases.

In a preliminary decision on the defendant's motion to dismiss without going to trial, the trial court, relying on the *Curtiss-Wright, Belmont,* and *Pink* cases, upheld the validity of the executive agreement:

Though not a treaty, the United States–Canada agreement nevertheless had the force of law. It was an Executive Agreement. Long has it been recognized that the President through his Secretary of State or other authorized representative may, without the authorization or approval of the Congress, enter into commercial compacts. Even assuming that it could do so, the Congress did not, as the defendant argues, by the Agriculture Act of 1948 or by the Tariff Act of 1930 . . . curtail this reach of Executive authority . . . their terms disclose that each of these Acts proposed only a control of the Executive's stewardship of the Congressional power to regulate foreign commerce, which had been delegated through those Acts to the President. In them is found no design to rein the President's international bargaining powers. Moreover, when the Congress in adopting a program invests the President with means to protect it, he is not thereby ousted of any ex officio prerogative also adaptable to preserve the program. His power remains independently, though complementary and coordinate with the legislative scheme.[16]

On the merits, however, Judge Bryan dismissed the complaint, directing a verdict for the defendant on the ground that the government had failed to introduce evidence sufficient to prove the alleged breach of contract.[17] While the case was pending before the Court of Appeals for the Fourth Circuit, the Supreme Court decided the *Youngstown* case, and Chief Circuit Judge John J. Parker relied on that decision, together with Holmes' dissenting opinion in the *Myers* case,[18] in a vigorous opinion affirming the trial court's decision but holding the direct opposite on the constitutional issues. Parker thought that the breach of contract was clear, but that the executive agreement was unconstitutional "because it was not authorized by Congress and contravened provisions of a statute dealing with the very matter to which it related." Moreover:

The power to regulate foreign commerce is vested in Congress, not in the executive or the courts. . . .

The Conduct of Foreign Relations

Even though the regulation prescribed by the executive agreement be more desirable than that prescribed by Congressional action, it is the latter which must be accepted as the expression of national policy.[19]

The timing of this decision was ideal for adherents of Senator Bricker's proposal to amend the Constitution to limit the President's power to negotiate and to utilize executive agreements, and they seized upon it eagerly and gave it wide publicity. The Supreme Court held the case on its docket throughout the 1953–54 term, and finally disposed of it the following winter in a unanimous decision on non-constitutional grounds. The Supreme Court affirmed the trial court's ruling that the evidence was insufficient to support the government's claim, but was careful to note explicitly that "there is no occasion for us to consider the other questions discussed by the Court of Appeals. The decision in this case does not rest upon them."[20] It is probably justifiable to assume that the law remains as stated in the Court's own earlier decisions in *Curtiss-Wright*, *Belmont*, and *Pink*.

The Court of Claims, in fact, has gone so far as to assert — in what might be considered a dictum, however—that an executive agreement, like a treaty, will supersede an earlier act of Congress with which it is in conflict. The rule with regard to treaties is well established,[21] but the Supreme Court has not yet extended it to include executive agreements, although the logic of its other decisions in this area certainly points in this direction. This is precisely what the Court of Claims did. Having recently decided that a United States–Norway claims convention, which had been ratified by the Senate, operated to withdraw the consent of the United States, previously granted by a federal statute,[22] to be sued in the Court of Claims, the court applied the same rule to the Byrnes-Blum agreement of May 28, 1946, which provided for the French government to settle claims of French residents for property requisitioned by the armed forces of the United States in French protectorates in North Africa during World War II.[23] This attempt of a claimant to exercise an earlier statutory right to bring suit in the Court of Claims was denied. The decision was not appealed to the Supreme Court.

The Regulation of Commerce with Foreign Nations

The Constitution of the United States makes no reference to presidential authority in the regulation of commercial intercourse, while it does expressly state: "The Congress shall have power . . . to regulate commerce with foreign nations and among the several States, and with the Indian tribes."[24] Commerce with the Indians is no longer important, and, periods of emergency aside, the Congress has deliberately by-passed the President in developing administrative machinery for the regulation of interstate commerce; but the President has always exercised considerable power in the regulation of foreign commerce. The last twenty years have witnessed not only an accelerated expansion of his responsibilities in this area, but also the expression of a degree of judicial tolerance of presidential discretion that must be shocking to any who believe that the principles of federalism, separation of powers, and due process in administrative procedure are basic virtues of our constitutional system.

The roots of this development lie in an early period of our national history; as early as the War of 1812, the courts were called upon to consider the constitutionality of presidential action implementing the embargo legislation which characterized the dominant but unsuccessful national policy on the question of "foreign entanglement" during the administrations of John Adams and Thomas Jefferson, and during Madison's first term.[25] President Madison had suspended the operation of the Embargo acts against Great Britain by his Proclamation of April 19, 1809; and then, after the British government's disavowal of British Ambassador Erskine's arrangements, had revived their operation by his later Proclamation of August 9, 1809. There appeared to be no direct statutory authority for the latter proclamation. The act of March 1, 1809, had given the President power to permit, by proclamation, a renewal of intercourse — as he had done through the April 19 proclamation — but the later proclamation undertook to revive the lapsed penal provisions of the Embargo acts of December 1807, March 1808, and April 1808. None of the earlier statutes had delegated any power to the President to suspend their operation, let alone to reinstate them after they should have lapsed by their own terms; but the proclamation of August 9 recited that trade with British ports "is to be considered as under the operation of the several acts by which such trade was suspended." Moreover, the April proclamation went into effect after a day named; but the August proclamation went into effect immediately and was, from the point of view of vessels sailing from Great Britain and her colonies to the United States on and for some time after August 9, 1809, retroactive in its effect, and thereafter *ex post facto* as applied to them.

So held the courts in the only reported cases. In one, the court upheld the President's power to suspend the operation of the statute, as he did in his proclamation of April 19, even though the court recognized that his action had been based upon a mistake in fact; but at the same time denied that he had power to revive the lapsed statutes, holding that since the President had no prerogative powers and neither the act of March 1, 1809, nor the act of June 28, 1809, gave him any express authority to revive the Embargo Act, his proclamation of August 9, 1809, was founded on an "inaccurate construction of a law," and was therefore unconstitutional.[26]

The next session of the Congress, however, had proceeded to give the President express authority to do that which the courts subsequently held he had no constitutional power to do either independently or under the 1809 legislation. The act of May 1, 1810, was a two-edged sword which delegated authority to the President to revive the embargo against either England or France, depending upon which of the two he found to have been the first to cease the existing depredations against our commerce. Finding that the Berlin and Milan decrees had been revoked by Bonaparte — whereas in fact, of course, they had *not* been — Madison issued his proclamation of November 2, 1810,[27] suspending the provisions of the act of May 1, 1810, for France and reinstating as of February 2, 1811, the provisions of the act of March 1, 1809, against Great Britain. The Supreme Court had no difficulty in upholding this delegation of power to the President, and the validity of his proclamations promulgated on the basis of this statutory authority:

On the second point [was the Act of 1st of March, 1809, revived by the President's proclamation at all?], we can see no sufficient reason, why the legislature should not exercise its discretion in reviving the act of March 1st, 1809, either expressly or conditionally, as their judgment should direct. The 19th section of that act declaring that it should continue in force to a certain time, and no longer, could not restrict their power of exerting its operation without limitation upon the occurrence of any subsequent combination of events.[28]

The question of the President's power to order summary enforcement of the neutrality and embargo laws was raised at about the same time. One of the statutes referred to above, that of April 25, 1808, had authorized the collectors of the customs to detain vessels which were, in their opinion, intending to evade the embargo "until the decision of the President of the United States be had thereupon." By direction of President Jefferson, Secretary of the Treasury Gallatin issued a circular letter dated May 6, 1808, instructing the collectors to detain all vessels purporting to engage in the coastwise commerce under certain conditions, including those pertinent to the case below. One Gilchrist and others sought a writ of mandamus to force the release of their vessels by the collector of the port of Charleston, South Carolina, who justified his detention of the ships on the ground that he was bound to carry out the instructions of the President although he admitted *he* believed that Gilchrist's ship would have gone to Baltimore, for which clearance papers had been requested. The federal court decided that the President had no power of administrative direction over the collectors under the statute; his function was rather the exercise of appellate jurisdiction over the decisions of the collectors. This attribution of a judicial role to the President implied that, as a matter of practice, he could have acted only after an adverse decision on the part of a collector. Judge Johnson held that the instructions of President Jefferson were meant to be in the nature of advice only; but that if they *were* intended to restrict the discretion of the collector by substituting for his judgment that of the President, they were unconstitutional.[29]

In the somewhat better known case of *Gelston v. Hoyt*, Gelston, the collector, and Schenck, the surveyor of the customs of the district of New York, had seized on July 10, 1810, the ship *American Eagle*, which was in their judgment being fitted out to take part in the current insurrection in Santo Domingo. Such action would have been in violation of the neutrality law in effect at that time. President Madison had ordered the detention of the vessel by his specific written orders of July 6, 1810. He was empowered by an early statute[30] to act through the armed forces in circumstances when the law could not be enforced through the ordinary processes of civil government. The Supreme Court, however, ruled that the President's orders were invalid and furnished no defense for the seizure by the customs officers (who were being sued for damages at common law for trespass), because the President exceeded the scope of his delegated statutory authority in exercising his power through civil rather than military officers.[31]

It is interesting to note what the authoritative historian of the Supreme Court has remarked with respect to this case:

The Conduct of Foreign Relations

In . . . *Gelston* v. *Hoyt*, 3 Wheat. 246, there was strikingly reaffirmed the cardinal principle of the Anglo-Saxon system of law that no man — not even the President of the United States — is above the law. The question involved was whether certain Government officials, who had been sued for damages for making seizure of a vessel under alleged authority of the neutrality laws, could justify their act by alleging that it was done by express order of President Madison . . .The Court, through Judge Story, held that as no statute authorized the President to direct seizure by the civil officers, his order constituted no protection to them, if rights of an individual had been trespassed upon. Thus, for a third time and with regard to the instructions of three different Presidents . . . the Court in its short career had shown . . . its determination to prove to all that "the Constitution is a law for rulers and for people, equally in war and in peace, and covers with its shield of protection all classes of men at all times and under all circumstances."[32]

These are brave words but it might be pointed out that nobody did anything to the *President* in any of these instances. In one case, a public officer was forced to accept judicial instructions in place of those previously given to him by the President; in the other two, public officers were held personally liable for carrying out their official duties under the personal direction of the Chief Executive. Captain Little was considered to have acted like a pirate and Gelston and Schenck as though they were common brigands. As Attorney General Rush pointed out some hundred and thirty-four years ago in his argument before the Court:

[T]he defendants below, acting as innocent men, and as vigilant and meritorious public officers, are in danger of being crushed under a load of damages which could scarcely have been made more heavy if leveled at conduct marked by the most undisputed and malignant guilt.[33]

Almost a century later, when the Supreme Court again considered the question of enforcing a neutrality proclamation, Congress had provided for judicial trial of violations of the presidential ordinance.[34] President Taft's proclamation of April 12, 1912, applied the provisions of the resolution without exception or limitation to Mexico; and in a criminal prosecution for smuggling small arms and ammunition across the Mexican border near El Paso, the constitutionality of the delegation of power in this contingency legislation, and of the President's action under it, was assumed by the defendants and Court alike without discussion.[35] However, these same questions were the critical points at issue two decades later when a corporate defendant was indicted on

111

a similar charge under equivalent legislation. In response to a presidential request, Congress had adopted the joint resolution of May 28, 1934; and on that same day the President promulgated his proclamation[36] placing an embargo on the shipment of arms and munitions of war to Bolivia and Paraguay, which were at the time engaged in the Gran Chaco War. A year and a half later when the war had ended, President Roosevelt revoked this proclamation but included a saving clause expressly authorizing prosecution for acts committed in violation of the embargo during its effective period. Curtiss-Wright Export Corporation was subsequently indicted for having shipped airplane engines which were intended to be used in military aircraft in the Chaco War.

The trial was conducted before District Judge Byers, whose judicial impartiality appeared to be somewhat affected by his obvious hostility toward the government's position in this case.[37] No question was raised about the propriety of the President's issuing the embargo, but it was argued that the delegation of power to the President was invalid because of the vagueness of the congressional standards. It was also claimed that the President had failed to find certain jurisdictional facts, this being a condition precedent to the exercise of his powers under the resolution, and that he had no power to extend the period of criminal liability of the defendant beyond the effective life of the embargo itself. Judge Byers ruled that the joint resolution was unconstitutional because in delegating discretion to the President to impose an embargo on the basis of his judgment of the probable results, rather than making his action conditional upon finding existing "facts," the Congress had attempted to delegate its legislative power; but at the same time he declared that the President's formal statement of compliance with the statutory conditions was conclusive as against a demurrer. All this appears somewhat confusing in retrospect, since the trial court found, in effect, that the standards set by Congress were so inadequate that rational compliance with them was impossible, and then proceeded to demonstrate how the President had actually fulfilled them. On appeal, however, Justice Sutherland made short shrift of the questions of law raised by the facts of the case, and proceeded to embark upon his most celebrated essay on the prerogative powers of the Chief Executive in the realm of external affairs.[38]

In its political context, this opinion was remarkable,[39] for the Court was at this time still riding high in the flush of its "victory" over the

New Deal, and it was just two months later that the President came forth with his controversial proposal for "packing the court." The essence of the thesis of the opinion was that, historically, control over foreign relations was an aspect of the royal prerogative, and that the sovereign to whom such powers were transferred as the result of the revolution was the national government. Since the states had never possessed such power themselves, they could neither grant authority over foreign affairs to the newly created national government in 1789 nor withhold it. Constitutional language on the subject was declaratory only, because "powers of external sovereignty" were inherent in the status of a recognized member of the Western state system under international law. It followed logically that the constitutional limitations applicable to the exercise of powers of "internal sovereignty" were irrelevant to action in the field of foreign affairs. The unstated but clear implication was that the President's claim to such "powers of external sovereignty" was as good as that of Congress; in fact, it was probably better, since the judicial language used reinforced this proposition. The President was "The Sole Organ of the *Nation*" — not of the Constitution, or of the Congress, or even of the national government, but of the *nation*[40] — which would seem to be as close a euphemism for *"The Sovereign"*[41] as the generally contrary premises of the American constitutional system could be constrained to support:

> In this vast external realm, with its important, complicated, delicate and manifold problems, the President alone has the power to speak or listen as a representative of the nation. He *makes* treaties with the advice and consent of the Senate; but he alone negotiates. Into the field of negotiation the Senate cannot intrude; and Congress itself is powerless to invade it. . . .
>
> It is important to bear in mind that we are here dealing not alone with an authority vested in the President by an exertion of legislative power, but with such an authority plus the very delicate, plenary and exclusive power of the President as the sole organ of the federal government in the field of international relations — a power which does not require as a basis for its exercise an act of Congress. . . .[42]

The implications of this astounding hypothesis for the exercise of powers of "internal" as well as those of "external" sovereignty are truly revolutionary, as both the executive practice and the judicial decisions of the past generation have made perfectly clear.

The change that has taken place in judicial attitudes is perhaps best illustrated by comparing the decisions in two cases involving presidential licensing, the first coming up immediately after World War I and denying an attempted exercise of constitutional power; and the second, decided shortly after World War II, holding that the President's licensing power in foreign air commerce was beyond the pale of judicial review.

In the first case, Western Union had made a contract with a British cable company to set up a cable between Brazil and Miami, Florida, each laying cable to Barbados where a jointly operated way station was to be constructed. The President ordered the Navy to prevent the landing of the cable end on shore — apparently because of the monopoly rights that Brazil had granted to the British company — so the cable was anchored three miles offshore while the rest of the construction was completed. Western Union then proposed to splice in to one of their three lines laid to Cuba, but the President revoked the permit for the most recently laid cable[43] and offered a new permit for all three with the condition that they should not be used as a link in a line connecting the United States with a line enjoying an exclusive foreign monopoly. Western Union sued in the Supreme Court of the District of Columbia to enjoin the Secretaries of State, War, and Navy from interfering with its acts,[44] and the United States brought countersuit in equity to prevent Western Union from making the allegedly unauthorized cable connection. The trial court held that the President had no constitutional power to deny the facility (franchise) as a sanction, so the issue became one of congressional intent;[45] and although Congress by long acquiescence had given implicit authority to the executive to prevent the landing of a cable by a *foreign* corporation, the court decided that this authority did not extend to a domestic corporation holding a federal franchise under the Post Roads Act of July 24, 1866, and operating some cable lines expressly authorized by acts of Congress and thus subject to rate regulation and other controls by the Interstate Commerce Commission. The orders of the President were, therefore, *ultra vires* and without either constitutional or statutory authority.[46]

In the second case, the Supreme Court gave an opposite answer to a closely related legal question: the power of the judiciary to review presidential refusal of a license to a domestic corporation seeking to engage in foreign commerce, when the governing statute exempted from review only presidential orders granting or refusing licenses to foreign corporations seeking to engage in commerce with the United States. The Civil Aeronautics Act of 1938 provided that when a foreign air carrier asks for any permit of convenience and necessity, or a citizen carrier applies for a certificate to engage in any overseas or foreign air transportation, a copy of the application must be submitted to the President before a hearing is held; and any decision, either to grant or to deny, must be submitted to the President before publication and is unconditionally subject to the President's approval. Judicial review extended to "any order, affirmative or negative, issued by the [Civil Aeronautics] Authority under this Act, except any order in respect of any *foreign* air carrier subject to the approval of the President as provided in Section 801 of this Act."[47]

Soon after the statute became effective, the Circuit Court of Appeals for the Second Circuit was asked to decide whether the words "foreign air carrier" also meant citizen carriers seeking a franchise for an overseas or international route. The Civil Aeronautics Board had issued a temporary certificate, dated July 12, 1940, to American Export Airlines, Inc., to extend its service in the transportation of persons, property, and mail between the United States and France to Lisbon, Portugal. This temporary certificate was approved by the President. Pan-American Airways sought to challenge the board's decision and asked, in effect, for judicial review under Section 1006 of the statute, but the court held that such an order was not reviewable *because the President's authority to disregard the court's decision would render review futile.*[48]

This question did not reach the Supreme Court until after the war and in a different case, and when it did the Court split five to four, with Justice Jackson writing the majority opinion. The Court noted that the statute "grants no express exemption to an order such as the one before us, which concerns a citizen carrier but which must have presidential approval because it involves overseas and foreign air transportation. The question is whether an exemption is to be implied." The opinion then proceeded to underscore the inherent differences between air-borne and surface-borne transportation, domestic and foreign, and the corresponding differences in congressional policy governing their regulation. "In this case, submission of the Board's decision was made to the President, who disapproved certain portions of it and advised the Board of the changes which he required. The Board complied and submitted a revised order and opinion which the President approved."[49]

The decision was the same as that reached by the circuit court of appeals in the *Pan American Airways* case:

when a foreign carrier seeks to engage in public carriage over the territory or waters of this country, or any carrier seeks the sponsorship of this Government to engage in overseas or foreign air transportation, Congress has completely inverted the usual administrative process. Instead of acting independently of executive control, the agency is then subordinated to it. Instead of its order serving as a final [subject to judicial review, of course] disposition of the application, its force is exhausted when it serves as a recommendation to the President. Instead of being handed down to the parties at the conclusion of the administrative process, it must be submitted to the President, before publication can even take place. Nor is the President's control of the ultimate decision a mere right of veto. It is not alone issuance of such authorizations that are subject to his approval, but denial, transfer, amendment, cancellation or suspension, as well. And likewise subject to his approval are the terms, conditions and limitations of the order. . . . Thus, Presidential control is not limited to a negative but is a positive and detailed control over the Board's decisions, unparalleled in the history of American administrative bodies.

Congress may of course delegate very large grants of its [legislative?] power over foreign commerce to the President. [Citing the *Norwegian Nitrogen* and *Bush* cases, *infra*.] The President also possesses in his own right certain powers conferred by the Constitution on him as Commander-in-Chief and as the Nation's organ in foreign affairs. *For present purposes, the order draws vitality from either or both sources.*[50]

There is one matter of administrative law that this opinion leaves unresolved. The breadth of executive discretion countenanced by the Court would seem to make final not only the substantive judgment of the President, whatever it might be and irrespective of the sources or nature of the evidence on which it was based, but also departure from the procedural standards set down in the Civil Aeronautics Act and other applicable statutes, particularly the Administrative Procedure Act of 1946.

Justice Douglas pointed out in a dissenting opinion that:

Presidential approval cannot make valid invalid orders of the Board. His approval supplements rather than supersedes Board action. . . . The requirement that a valid Board order underlie each certificate thus protects the President as well as the litigants and the public interest against unlawful Board action. . . .

Today a litigant tenders questions concerning the arbitrary character of the Board's ruling. Tomorrow those questions may relate to the right to notice, adequacy of hearings, or the lack of procedural due process of law. But no matter how extreme the action of the Board, the courts are powerless to correct it under today's decision. Thus the purpose of Congress is frustrated.[51]

Some elements of what would normally be considered questions of procedure, such as the admissibility of secret evidence not of record upon which the presidential judgment may be primarily based, are very clearly not reviewable under the majority opinion; but the President should be as much concerned as the litigants before the board that the board's preliminary decision be reliable — that is, a fair and impartial judgment on the basis of the facts before it and the governing administrative policy. The object of procedural requisites is to ensure such a judgment. Why, then, should not the precedent action of the board, before its advice is given to the President, be as subject to judicial review in this sort of proceeding as its "final" judgments on questions not in the domain of foreign commerce?[52] The Court's answer here is essentially twofold: (1) the presidential power of review might affront the dignity of the judiciary by subsequently nullifying any determination they might make concerning an order of the board, thus making the action of the Court *also* not a judgment in a "case or controversy," but an advisory opinion to the Chief Executive; (2) although the statute is poorly drafted in this respect, the Congress intended all orders of the board affecting foreign commerce (i.e., within the realm of "external sovereignty") to be subject to the exclusive and final review of the Chief of State, while intending those affecting interstate and intrastate commerce (i.e., within the realm of "internal sovereignty") to be subject to the exclusive and final review of the judiciary, ultimately the Supreme Court.

Neither the Supreme Court nor the Congress has as yet analyzed the implications of this dichotomous thinking. After a somewhat turbulent period of gestation, to be described at some length in the following chapter, a different solution has been arrived at in an older and more mature system of administrative adjudication with similar characteristics: a special system of administrative courts (the Customs Court and the Court of Customs and Patent Appeals) has been created to provide systematic review of the decisions of the Tariff Commission and the President in flexible tariff rate changes, and at the same time forestall almost completely the review of the regular federal courts.

The close functional relationship between the President's action in the licensing of international air transport and his rate-making functions under the tariff laws, where in each case administrative investigation and report is a condition precedent to presidential action, was recognized by the Supreme Court itself when it cited the *Bush*[53] and *Norwegian Nitrogen*[54] cases in support of its decision in the instant *Chicago and Southern Airlines* case.

Some indication of the scope of the unfettered discretion that the President now exercises in this kind of proceeding is given by a recent decision of the Court of Appeals for the Second Circuit. This case dealt with an order of the C.A.B. for the transfer of the certificate and properties and facilities of Overseas Airlines to T.W.A. and Pan-American, including an extension of routes on a competitive basis between T.W.A. and Pan-American to London, Paris, Rome, and Frankfort. The board originally sent to President Truman an order on June 1, 1950, which he approved on June 29, 1950. On June 30, 1950, however, he verbally rescinded his approval and directed the board to return the order to him. Then on July 10, 1950,[55] the President wrote to the C.A.B., indicating *the substance of an order he would approve* and directing its submission. Such an order was approved by the C.A.B. *on that same day*, and was in turn approved by the President on the following day, July 11, 1950. Chairman Ryan of the Civil Aeronautics Board resigned as a consequence of this imbroglio, and some newspapers suggested that Pan-American Airways' campaign contributions rather than foreign policy had caused the President to change his mind. Although such a thing cannot be lightly assumed, the courts are powerless to intervene in either event under the prevailing doctrine.

The negative order argument of the dissenting justices in the *Chicago and Southern Airlines* case was specifically urged at this time, but the court, expressly following the majority opinion in that case, held that (1) a C.A.B. order on an application for approval of the transfer of a temporary certificate of public convenience and necessity for overseas or foreign air transportation from one company to another, regardless of whether the application was granted or denied, required presidential approval and was therefore not subject to judicial review; and (2) the action of the President in approving a C.A.B. order denying an application for such a transfer did not prevent him from later retracting and directing the C.A.B. to submit a different order.[56]

The Conduct of Foreign Relations

Acquisition of Territory

Perhaps the most significant fact concerning the power of the President to extend or diminish the territorial jurisdiction of the United States, acting either alone under his constitutional authority, or in collaboration with Congress, by military conquest, treaty, proclamation, executive order, or otherwise, is that it has never been directly ruled upon by the Supreme Court. Nevertheless, such action has taken place from time to time since Washington's first term, if we include — as we should — treaties with the Indian nations and tribes; it is notorious that President Jefferson considered his contemplated action in the purchase of Louisiana in 1803 to be unconstitutional but that, strict constructionist or no, he went ahead and did it anyhow.[57] Jefferson's initial attempt to acquire West Florida by the same means were frustrated, but his objective was realized when President Madison, by his proclamation of October 27, 1810, claimed title for the United States to West Florida — which had recently "revolted" from Spanish rule through the leadership of a Fifth Column of American adventurers. Prior to the post-World War II period, however, only in scattered remarks in a few cases is the question of the constitutionality of such presidential action even discussed.

Chief Justice Taney's views on the question of national sovereignty in and legislative power over our national territories are well known, and indeed, his opinion in the related case of Dred Scott was destined to become a major factor in hastening the revolution that ended in annihilating the position he sought to defend. Quite consistently (but equally erroneously, in the light of the way the Constitution was interpreted both before and after his tenure on the Court,) Taney denied to the President any legal power to acquire territory in the name of the United States by the fact of military conquest.[58] This dictum, for such it was, was later cited as the authority for a lower federal court's own *obiter dictum* to the effect that the President "had no authority to extend the Union so as to embrace within it territory acquired either by treaty or conquest without authority from the legislative branch of the Government."[59] The practice, however, has been clearly to the contrary, sometimes with specific authority delegated to the Chief Executive by statute or treaty, sometimes only with subsequent congressional approval. What is generally regarded as the leading case on this point dealt with the relatively trivial matter of the power of the President, acting under statutory powers, to assume for the United States temporary jurisdiction over uninhabited guano islands and rocks so that American entrepreneurs might have prior rights to their exploitation for commercial fertilizer over the adventurers of other countries; the Court, of course, upheld the action of the President in declaring the sovereignty of the United States over such a place, Navassa Island in the Caribbean Sea.[60]

Quite recently, the Supreme Court has been called upon to decide two groups of cases, raising on the one hand the question of presidential authority to extend United States jurisdiction to include subsoil and sea bed rights in the continental shelf beneath the high seas contiguous to the United States, and on the other, the incidental role of the President in the extension or denial of rights under national labor legislation to construction workers employed on American bases outside of the United States during World War II.

The critical legislative act in the resolution of the first matter was Presidential Proclamation No. 2667, September 28, 1945, which (omitting the "whereases") follows:

Policy of the United States with respect to the Natural Resources of the Subsoil and Sea Bed of the Continental Shelf.

*　*　*　*　*　*　*　*　*　*　*　*　*

NOW, THEREFORE, I, HARRY S. TRUMAN, President of the United States of America, do hereby proclaim the following policy of the United States of America with respect to the natural resources of the subsoil and sea bed of the continental shelf.

Having concern for the urgency of conserving and prudently utilizing its natural resources, the Government of the United States regards the natural resources of the subsoil and sea bed of the continental shelf beneath the high seas but contiguous to the coasts of the United States as appertaining to the United States, subject to its jurisdiction and control. In cases where the continental shelf extends to the shores of another State, or is shared with an adjacent State, the boundary shall be determined by the United States and the State concerned in accordance with equitable principles. The character as high seas of the waters above the continental shelf and the right to their free and unimpaired navigation are in no way thus affected.[61]

This proclamation was based directly on the President's constitutional powers rather than on any legislative delegation, since the Congress had refused to adopt legislation on this subject. The "States" referred to are of course international states, and not states of the United

States. The economic stakes involved here were high, as several states of the United States already had granted leases and licenses to private oil companies to drill and exploit the oil-bearing shale underlying what they had considered to be their coastal tidelands. They would have had unquestioned authority to do this for the beds of navigable rivers intrastate or interstate, but it is precisely the fact that these lands were at or beyond the previously claimed external borders of the United States that made this case not a matter of federal jurisdiction over public lands, but rather one of foreign relations.

The President had directed the Department of Justice to bring before the Supreme Court original suits in equity against the states of California, Louisiana, and Texas; and although the Court upheld the claim of national jurisdiction, it ignored President Truman's proclamation and rested its decision on other grounds.[62] One of the first acts of the incoming Eisenhower administration was to sponsor legislation to delegate control over oil drilling in the marginal seas to the interested states,[63] thus superseding the Truman proclamation and reversing his (and, in effect) the Supreme Court's decisions.

Equally perplexing for the Court was the matter of the extraterritorial effect of national legislation on Americans employed on bases physically occupied and controlled by the United States, but under the sovereignty of other nations. In a five to four decision, the Court construed the word "possession" in the Fair Labor Standards Act of 1938 to include American-leased bases in Bermuda. At issue was the question whether employment contracts of construction workers on the leased bases were under the wage and hour provisions of the act. The United States had acquired these bases in one of the best known of modern executive agreements, the trade of fifty "over-age" destroyers for military bases defending the Atlantic approaches to the Panama Canal. While an appeal was pending before the Supreme Court from the decision of the circuit court of appeals, the Secretary of State informed the Attorney General by letter that Great Britain unquestionably retained sovereignty over the bases in question. The Court, citing the *Jones* case, remarked that the determination of sovereignty over an area was of course for the legislative and executive departments, but that this did not prevent the courts from examining the *status* resulting from that determination.[64] There was little executive guidance for the Court's inference of an indubitably nonexistent legislative intent (in 1938) in this case; in the next one, however, the President had issued an executive order limiting the extraterritorial application of the statute, although not expressly covering the particular area involved in the litigation. Executive Order No. 8623 of December 31, 1940, issued pursuant to Section 326 of the federal eight-hour law applicable to government contractors, suspended the statute for laborers and mechanics employed directly by the government at Atlantic bases leased from Great Britain.

Reasoning that the executive order indicated a conclusion on the part of the President that the statute applied, or might apply, to these bases in the absence of action on his part, the Court nevertheless determined that this and similar executive orders suspending the operation of the statutes elsewhere in the national territories deserved "no weight as an administrative determination of the Act's applicability to localities unquestionably and completely beyond the direct legislative competence of the United States"; and on that basis, proceeded to interpret the statute not to apply to contracts of employment for construction work in Iraq and Iran during World War II.[65]

The weight to be given such executive orders was the major question for decision, however, in a case that arose before the Court of Claims. The right to be reimbursed in cash for accumulated annual leave upon separation from government employment was expressly withheld from "Alien and native labor employed outside the continental limits of the United States" by Executive Order No. 9414 of January 13, 1944. The statute upon which the executive order was based granted in general terms the right to such severance pay, but it also authorized the President to issue implementing regulations not inconsistent with the act. A Filipino native who had been employed by the United States Army in the Philippines early in the post-World War II period challenged the legality of the executive order, but the court dismissed his claim, finding that there was no conflict between the President's regulations and the statute.[66]

Executive Control over Immigration

Another aspect of the President's control over foreign relations is his power to admit, detain, expel, and exclude undesirable aliens from the United States. This power is exercised primarily by administrative regulation under a complex and extensive statutory code, which leaves relatively little personal discretion to the President. The major exception is action taken by the President as Commander-in-Chief on either constitutional or statutory authority under the war power. In a number of instances direct presidential action based on his powers in the field of foreign affairs has been challenged before the courts.

Although no such question was before the Supreme Court in the first case it heard challenging the validity of the Chinese Exclusion Act of 1892, the Court indicated in *obiter dictum* that the power to expel all resident nationals of a given state or race — the basis of classification seems to be immaterial — could be authorized by either treaty or statute, and no justiciable issue would be raised by the failure to provide for judicial review of the President's action:

In England, the only question that has ever been made in regard to the power to expel aliens has been whether it could be exercised by the King without the consent of Parliament, which passed several acts on the subject between 1793 and 1848. . . .

The power to exclude or to expel aliens, being a power affecting international relations, is vested in the political departments of the government and is to be regulated by treaty or by act of Congress, and to be executed by the executive authority according to the regulations so established, except so far as the judicial department has been authorized by treaty or by statute, or is required by the paramount law of the Constitution, to intervene. . . . For instance, the surrender pursuant to treaty stipulations, of persons residing or found in this country, and charged with crime in another, may be made by the executive authority of the president alone, when no provision has been made by treaty or by statute for an examination of the case by a judge or magistrate.[67]

The Court retreated from this position, which seemed to view the power of extradition as an inherent executive power (at least, in the absence of a relevant treaty or statute), when the question arose in a later case. The actual question involved treaty interpretation: did the President have discretionary power to order the extradition of United States citizens, wanted by France as fugitives from justice, under the treaty of 1909? That convention stated that neither France nor the United States was "bound" to turn over its own nationals; and the Court decided that this meant that the President could not do so, granting writs of habeas corpus for the release of petitioners who had been detained under preliminary extradition warrants issued by a United States commissioner in New York City. Noting that the inclusion of an exemption for her own citizens was contrary to the policy advocated by the United States but in accordance with French policy, and that some other treaties explicitly granted to the President discretion in this regard, the Court concluded that the exemption clause was deliberately inserted and had to be strictly construed. Mr. Chief Justice Hughes ruled that the extradition power was not inherent in the Chief Executive, and existed only to the extent that it was delegated by, and then in accordance with the terms of, particular treaties or statutes.[68] The case assumes some significance in that this is the only opinion announced by the Supreme Court in almost a century and a half which declares action taken by the President, or under his direct authority, in the realm of foreign affairs to be illegal.

President Wilson was given rule-making powers during time of war over the entry or departure of aliens, with supplementary licensing power (through passport visa clearance); and violations of his regulations were punishable as criminal under statutory penalties.[69] His proclamation of August 8, 1918, with a supplementary executive order, required the possession of a passport as a condition of entry for enemy aliens seeking admittance from Canada. An amendatory act of November 10, 1919, extended the life of the wartime statute to March 4, 1921; and by a later amendment of March 2, 1921, Congress extended presidential licensing power to include the entry of all aliens. Accordingly President Harding amended Wilson's executive order by his own executive order of February 1, 1922, extending the passport requirement to all aliens entering the country, including, of course, those from Canada.

A petitioner for a writ of habeas corpus alleged that Harding's executive order was invalid because the act of March 2, 1921, had "adopted" the provisions of Wilson's order of 1918, therefore "exhausting" the presidential discretion under the basic statute which Harding had sought to exercise by expanding the terms of Wilson's earlier executive order to include all aliens.[70] The effect of such an argument, if generally accepted by the courts as applicable to administrative as well as executive rule-making processes, would be to place the administrative process in a straight jacket, inhibiting necessary changes and modifications, frustrating the successful execution of almost any congressionally delegated powers, and defeating the very purpose of recourse to administrative, as distinguished from legislative, regulation. So, in effect, held a federal district court:

124

The Conduct of Foreign Relations

With respect to the executive order of President Harding, the history of the legislation and the considerations already referred to are persuasive to the effect that Congress did not say or intend to say that it adopted the executive order of President Wilson as a part of the act, and did not intend to nullify the law by tying the hands of succeeding Presidents with respect to the subject-matter involved.[71]

The question of deportation, as distinguished from denial of entry, was considered by a district court which held that the act of March 2, 1921, did *not* continue in effect the President's power under the 1918 act to deport aliens, but only the power to require visas on passports as a condition to entry. Therefore, to the extent that it dealt with deportation of aliens, Wilson's proclamation of August 8, 1918, was held invalid after March 3, 1921, the official date of the termination of World War I.[72]

A similar limitation of the President's wartime powers had already been discovered in the effect of the Immigration Act of 1924 upon the President's power to regulate the entry of *immigrant* aliens. The First Circuit Court of Appeals held that the power of the President under the 1918 act to impose, by proclamation, additional restrictions on the entry and departure of persons from the United States, continued in effect by the act of March 2, 1921, "unless otherwise provided by law," *was* otherwise provided for and was terminated for immigrant aliens by the Immigration Act of May 26, 1924.[73] Congress intended consular visas to be *convenient* but not *essential* evidence for determining the real status of non-quota immigrants returning after temporary absences; therefore, that part of President Coolidge's Executive Order No. 4125 of January 12, 1925, which required visas of *all* aliens except those reentering the United States within six months after their departure therefrom, assuming a previous lawful admittance, was held *ultra vires*. The court decided that the Immigration Act did not make possession of a visa on a passport exclusive evidence of the legal right to re-entry, but apparently contemplated an alternative remedy through proof of the facts of eligibility by an administrative hearing conducted by an officer of the Bureau of Immigration, a hearing provided for in other parts of the effective executive regulations. In a dictum, the court went on to remark that even if Congress *had* authorized the President to regulate the admission of aliens under the act of 1924 — which the court denied — the regulation in question, as construed and applied to the petitioner, would be "unreasonable and therefore invalid" as a de-

125

nial of due process of law. Expressly, then, this decision held that the rule-making powers of the President under the act of May 22, 1918, were limited in scope by the passing of the Immigration Act of May 26, 1924; thereafter only non-immigrant aliens were included.[74]

President Coolidge proceeded to amend his Executive Order No. 4125 by Executive Order No. 4476 of July 12, 1926, which required visas on passports as a condition of entry for non-immigrant aliens in substantially the same terms as the 1925 order. Far from finding any conflict with the Immigration Act of 1924, a federal district court found in the next case to arise that the President had the power to promulgate reasonable regulations or administrative orders for the admission of non-immigrant aliens under authority of Section 3 of the Immigration Act itself, and that a consul's decision on granting a visa, even if "unjustifiable," was not reviewable by the court. The court also remarked that "the ending of the war did not abrogate the presidential order as relating to passports and visas of nonimmigrants" because of the enactment of the Act of March 2, 1921.[75]

In the final case to determine the scope of the President's rule-making powers under the post-World War I immigration statutes, the President was held to have properly permitted, by his Executive Order No. 4476, certain classes of non-immigrant aliens to enter without visas: (1) those in transit through the United States to a foreign destination, and (2) those who were through passengers on vessels touching at ports of the United States. Such persons were, however, subject to regulations issued by the Secretaries of State and Labor, respectively, while temporarily within the United States.[76]

During the post-World War II period, the Court of Appeals for the District of Columbia decided that the Passport Act of 1918, and Presidential Proclamation No. 2523 of November 14, 1941, would be unconstitutional under the due process clause of the Fifth Amendment if construed (as they had been by the Immigration and Naturalization Service) to deny the right to a hearing of a legally admitted alien who sought to leave the country. This was another "security" case; a student who had entered the United States on a passport issued by the Chinese Nationalist government had been summarily detained four years later, after he had received a master's degree in oceanography, on the grounds that his skills might be used to the disadvantage of the United States by the Chinese Communists, against whom the United

States was then engaged in hostilities in Korea. The court ruled that he was entitled to a fair hearing on the question whether he should be forbidden to leave the United States for the country of which he was a national.[77]

Considerations similar to those of the Alien Enemy Act and Presidential Proclamations No. 2655 and 2662[78] but different sources of legal authority underlay the conjoint powers of the Secretary of State and the Attorney General to refuse to admit into the United States aliens who, while not necessarily *enemy* aliens, nevertheless were deemed on the basis of confidential or other information to be poor security risks. Regulations had been drafted setting up certain excludable classes, including among others those who "had advocated and acquiesced in activities contrary to decency in behalf of the Axis countries during the last world war" and those whose admission "would be prejudicial to the public interest for security reasons."[79]

As to procedure, the regulations specified that any alien who sought entry to the United States could be temporarily excluded by any official of the Department of Justice and could not be admitted but must be excluded permanently and deported unless, after the temporary action had been reported to the Secretary of State, the Attorney General was satisfied that the admission of the alien would *not* be prejudicial to the interests of the United States; and the Attorney General could reach the conclusion that he was satisfied that the alien *should* be admitted only after he had consulted with the Secretary of State. There was no requirement, however, that the Attorney General need consult the Secretary of State in the event that he was *not* satisfied that the alien might be admitted without prejudice to the public interest. The burden of proof alien petitioners had to assume and the procedural prerequisites of any attempt on their part to furnish proof made the government's position virtually unassailable; and this apart from the fact that they could hardly contravene derogatory information furnished by informers unknown and unknowable to them, especially when the information also remained confidential and could not be disclosed to them. Since the chance of subordinate administrators abusing discretion is necessarily great under such a system, it is not surprising to find many vagaries characteristic of this administrative process in the few instances in which it has thus far been challenged before the courts.

By far the most interesting case was the one that reached the Supreme Court, the so-called War Bride case.[80] Ellen Knauff was a citizen of Czechoslovakia who had fled to England when the Nazis overran her country. She served with distinction in the British Air Forces during World War II. After the war she went to the American zone of occupied Germany, where she was employed by the Department of the Army. She met and married, with the permission of the appropriate American military commander, an enlisted man in the United States Army serving in the occupation forces, and came to the United States seeking admission under the War Brides Act [81] a short time before her husband's term of enlistment was to expire and he was to return to join her in the United States. The apparent charge against her was that "She was formerly a paid agent of the Czechoslovakian Government, and reported on American personnel assigned to the Civil Censorship Division in Germany"; her claim was that she was "a victim of a foul denunciation of a woman jealous of my husband."[82] She was at first temporarily, and then permanently excluded by the Attorney General although no specific charge was ever formally made against her and she was denied any right to a hearing, either open or *in camera*, so that she might present testimony in her own behalf and answer any charges against her.

One of the anomalies in the Supreme Court's disposition of her appeal lay in the fact that the only member of the Court who knew why she had been excluded, the recently appointed justice and former Attorney General Tom C. Clark, was barred by custom from participating in the consideration of her case by the Court;[83] and since Douglas was still convalescing from a fall off a horse, the Court divided into a shaky four to three to affirm her exclusion. The plurality who spoke for the Court through Justice Minton found nothing in the War Brides Act or its legislative history to indicate that it was the purpose of Congress, by partially suspending compliance with certain requirements and the quota provisions of the immigration laws, to relax the security provisions of the immigration code. The petitioner had argued the retroactive effect of Presidential Proclamation No. 2850 of August 17, 1949, promulgated after the decision in the *Knauff* case by the Court of Appeals but before oral argument was heard by the Supreme Court. This proclamation was apparently a move on the part of the government to avoid judicial review of the inconsistency in the prior administrative practice under the regulations (whereby the Attorney

General exercised the power to exclude that was explicitly vested in the Secretary of State by Presidential Proclamation No. 2523 of November 14, 1941). The Court found this of little moment, however, since the question before it was one of *privilege*, not one of vested right. Far from finding that any merit lay in the allegation that Congress had attempted to delegate legislative power in the act of June 21, 1941, the Court held that the President possessed *independent constitutional power* to justify the exclusion program, apart from any powers vested in him by statute:

The exclusion of aliens is a fundamental act of sovereignty. The right to do so stems not alone from legislative power but is inherent in the executive power to control the foreign affairs of the nation. *United States* v. *Curtiss–Wright Export Corp.*, 299 U.S. 304; *Fong Yue Ting* v. *United States*, 149 U.S. 698, 713. When Congress prescribes a procedure concerning the admissibility of aliens, it is not dealing alone with a legislative power. It is implementing an inherent executive power.

Thus the decision to admit or to exclude an alien may be lawfully placed with the President, who may in turn delegate the carrying out of this function to a responsible executive officer of the sovereign, such as the Attorney General. The action of the executive officer under such authority is final and conclusive. Whatever the rule may be concerning deportation of persons who have gained entry into the United States, it is not within the province of any court, unless expressly authorized by law, to review the determination of the political branch of the Government to exclude a given alien. . . . Normally Congress supplies the conditions of the privilege of entry into the United States. But because the power of exclusion of aliens is also inherent in the executive department of the sovereign, Congress may in broad terms authorize the executive to exercise the power, *e.g.*, as was done here, for the best interests of the country during a time of national emergency. . . .

Whatever the procedure authorized by Congress is, it is due process as far as an alien denied entry is concerned.[84]

Justice Jackson, who observed at the time of oral argument in the case that he had had some direct personal experience in the work-ways of the office of the Attorney General and the role that that official would necessarily play in the day-to-day administrative process governing the disposition of hundreds of cases like that now before the Court, registered his dissent on the merits:

Security is like liberty in that many are the crimes committed in its name. The menace to the security of this country, be it great as it may, from this girl's admission is as nothing compared to the menace to free institution[s] inherent in procedures of this pattern. In the name of security the police state justifies its arbitrary oppressions on evidence that is secret, because security might be prejudiced if it were brought to light in hearings. The plea that evidence of guilt must be secret is abhorrent to free men, because it provides a cloak for the malevolent, the misinformed, the meddlesome, and the corrupt to play the role of informer undetected and uncorrected.[85]

After three years the government finally admitted its error in the *cause célèbre* of Ellen Knauff.[86] Following the Supreme Court's affirmation of her exclusion, she was remanded to custody at Ellis Island, after having been released on bond pending her appeal, and an unsuccessful attempt was made to get Congress to adopt a private bill specially admitting her. By then, a number of groups and organizations had become interested in her cause, and a publicity campaign spearheaded by the *St. Louis Post* ultimately bore fruit. She finally was given a hearing before the Board of Immigration Appeals, which recommended her admittance; and it was announced on November 2, 1951, that Attorney General McGrath had given his approval.[87] This, seemingly, was a happy ending for Mrs. Knauff;[88] but what of other alien immigrants who have been denied entry, and for whom such a long, costly struggle (which happened to attract the attention of the press) is not feasible? The short and sharp answer is that they are not included among the persons of whom the Fifth Amendment speaks when it states that *no person* shall be deprived of his liberty without due process of law.[89]

Notes

[1] United States v. One Hundred Barrels of Cement, 27 Fed. Cas. 292 (D.Mo.E.D., 1862), No. 15,945.

[2] Wilson v. Shaw, 204 U.S. 24, 32 (1907). Somewhat notoriously, in this instance the President waited anxiously at the moment of parturition for the revolution inaugurating the new government to come off as scheduled, so that his prepared recognition could be accorded.

[3] Oetjen v. Central Leather Co., 246 U.S. 297, 302 (1918).

[4] United States *ex rel* D'Esquiva v. Uhl, 137 F. 2d 903, 906–907 (2 C.C.A., 1943). Cf. United States v. Bussoz, 218 F. 2d 683, 686 (9 C.A., 1955), certiorari denied, 350 U.S. 824 (1955).

[5] *The Maret*, 145 F. 2d 431, 440, 442 (3 C.C.A., 1944): "Obviously the recognition or non-recognition of the Soviet Republic of Estonia is a political question for the determination of the Executive. . . . Nonrecognition of a foreign sovereign and nonrecognition of its decrees are to be deemed as essential a part of the power confided by the Constitution to the Executive for the conduct of foreign affairs as recognition."

There is a conflicting opinion — though not decision — of a federal district court. This case involved rival suitors who were claimants under the protection of the Chinese Nationalist and the People's Republic governments, respectively, for funds on deposit

The Conduct of Foreign Relations

with an American bank. The trial judge ruled that he was not obligated to decide in favor of the Nationalist claimants because of the United States' policy of non-recognition of the Peiping regime. Although the *fact* of recognition as determined by the President was conclusive upon the judiciary, it was the court's responsibility to determine the *effect* to be given to recognition and non-recognition in the decision of particular cases. The Communist-controlled corporate management, therefore, was not to be conclusively denied standing to appear before a court of the United States merely because the President refused to recognize the Peiping government. Since, however, this dispute involved a conflict in which the President had affirmatively accorded recognition to one government and explicitly denied it to the other, the court decided: "In this situation, the Court should accept, as the representative of the Chinese state, that government which our executive deems best able to further the mutual interests of China and the United States." Bank of China v. Wells Fargo Bank and Trust Co., 92 F. Supp. 920 (1950) and 104 F. Supp. 59, 66 (N.D.Calif.S.D., 1952), modified and affirmed, on other grounds, 209 F. 2d 467 (1953).

[6] James Hart, *The Ordinance Making Powers of the President* (Baltimore: Johns Hopkins Press, 1925), pp. 20, 211.

[7] *Ibid.*, p. 34.

[8] Garcia v. Pan American Airways, 50 N.Y.S. 2d 250, 251 (1944); *Opinions of the Attorney General*, 39:484 (1940).

[9] Many of the textbooks, reasoning a priori, attempt to do this, however. A typical statement is that "a treaty binds the nation, whereas an executive agreement binds only the President who makes it." Such a dictum is patently false with respect to *executed* executive agreements, and cannot be substantiated in either practice or the *decisions* (as distinguished from the dicta of some old cases) of the courts. For a more enlightened view, and a substantially correct summary of current law and practice, see F. A. Ogg and P. O. Ray, *Introduction to American Government* (New York: Appleton-Century-Crofts, 1951), pp. 710–713.

[10] Frelinghuysen, Secretary of State v. Key, 110 U.S. 63, 74–76 (1884). Cf. LaAbra Silver Mining Co. v. United States, 175 U.S. 423 (1899). The same principles apply in the case of executive agreements: B. Altman & Co. v. United States, 224 U.S. 583, 601 (1912); and State of Russia v. National City Bank of New York, 69 F. 2d 44, 48 (2 C.C.A., 1934).

[11] Missouri v. Holland, 252 U.S. 416, 432–435 (1920). On inherent powers of "external sovereignty," see generally Foster H. Sherwood, "Foreign Relations and the Constitution," *Western Political Quarterly*, 1:386–399 (December 1948). For a discussion of recent attempts to limit the scope of the treaty power and the use of presidential executive agreements, see Glendon A. Schubert, Jr., "Politics and the Constitution: The Bricker Amendment during 1953," *Journal of Politics*, 16:257–298 (May 1954).

[12] United States v. Belmont, 301 U.S. 324, 330–331 (1937).

[13] United States v. Pink, Superintendent of Insurance of the State of New York, 315 U.S. 203, 229, 230 (1942). Cf. B. Altman & Co. v. United States, 224 U.S. 583, 601 (1912).

[14] For the exchange of notes which constituted the agreement, see the Appendix to the decision of the Supreme Court in this case: United States v. Guy W. Capps, Inc., 348 U.S. 296, 305–309 (1955).

[15] Youngstown Sheet and Tube v. Sawyer, 343 U.S. 579 (1952).

[16] United States v. Guy W. Capps, Inc., 100 F. Supp. 30, 32 (E.D.Va., 1951).

[17] This oral opinion was not reported.

[18] Myers v. United States, 272 U.S. 52, 177 (1926).

[19] United States v. Guy W. Capps, Inc., 204 F. 2d 655, 658, 660 (4 C.A., 1953). Although Judge Parker did not refer to this fact, nevertheless Section 22(f) of the statute reads: "No proclamation under this section shall be enforced in contravention of any treaty *or other international agreement* to which the United States is *or hereafter be-*

131

comes a party." Italics supplied. See 62 *Stat.* 1250. Under the circumstances, the court's omission or oversight of this part of the statute on which it relied is, to say the least, curious.

[20] United States v. Guy W. Capps, Inc., 348 U.S. 296, 305 (1955).

[21] A treaty may supersede a prior act of Congress and an act of Congress may supersede a treaty: The Cherokee Tobacco, 11 Wall. 616 (1870), and cf. Horner v. United States, 143 U.S. 570 (1892).

[22] Hannevig v. United States, 114 Ct. Cl. 410 (1949). It should be noted that the convention in question provided specifically for an alternative (diplomatic) method for settling the claim of this particular plaintiff, however, with possible subsequent jurisdiction in the Court of Claims and appeal to the Supreme Court.

[23] Eltimar Société Anonymé of Casablanca v. United States, 123 Ct. Cl. 552 (1952). The ruling on the constitutional question is probably a dictum because this plaintiff had made an "election of remedy," and already had accepted a partial award from the French claims commission. It appeared that the claimant wanted dollars instead of francs.

[24] Article I, 8, (3).

[25] Only during the past few years have scholars turned to the investigation of the administrative history of this period: see Lynton K. Caldwell, *The Administrative Theories of Hamilton and Jefferson* (Chicago: University of Chicago Press, 1944); Leonard D. White, *The Federalists* (New York: Macmillan, 1948) and *The Jeffersonians* (New York: Macmillan, 1951); and James Hart, *The American Presidency in Action: 1789; A Study in Constitutional History* (New York: Macmillan, 1948). For an exploration of administrative problems in the enforcement of the embargo legislation by Jefferson, but which stops short of the action considered below, see White, *The Jeffersonians*, Chapters 29 and 30.

[26] *The Orono*, 18 Fed. Cas. 830 (C.Ct.Mass., 1812), No. 10, 585. Chief Justice Marshall, sitting in Circuit Court for North Carolina, came to the same conclusion, saying that Madison's proclamation of August 9 "was not legal": *President's Proclamation Declared Illegal*, 19 Fed. Cas. 1289 (1812), No. 11,391. A third case made the reported opinion of the judiciary unanimous on this point, and the court found that Liverpool, the intended destination of the libeled vessel, was a permitted port at the time of her capture (although the vessel was still condemned on the ground that she had sailed without posting bond as required by Section 3 of the act of June 28, 1809); the court also upheld by implication the President's power to license ships sailing to interdicted ports in the public service, as authorized by the same Section 3, when it stated that it would have condemned the vessel on the alternative ground, had the President's proclamation been valid, that she held no such presidential license. *The Wasp*, 29 Fed. Cas. 368 (C.Ct.Mass., 1812), No. 17,249.

[27] See James Richardson, *Messages and Papers of the Presidents* (Washington, D.C.: Bureau of National Literature and Art, 1907), I, 461. This proclamation, accepting the perfidious arrangements of the Duc de Cadore, French Minister of Foreign Affairs, started the sequence of events that led directly to the War of 1812. It might be noted that the chief political weapons in this period of undeclared naval warfare were the executive ordinances of the heads of the three principal nations concerned: the British Orders-in-Council, Napoleon's Berlin and Milan decrees, and the proclamations of President Madison. See especially on this point, Henry Adams, *History of the United States of America* (New York: Scribner's, 1909), Vol. V; his Chapter XIV, discussing the events of the summer of 1810, leading up to Madison's proclamations of October 27 and November 2 (annexing West Florida), is significantly entitled "Government by Proclamation."

[28] *The Brig Aurora*, 7 Cranch 382, 388 (1813).

[29] Gilchrist v. Collector of Charleston, *Ex parte* Gilchrist, 10 Fed. Cas. 355, 357 (C.Ct.S.C., 1808), No. 5420. Compare: Campbell v. Chase National Bank of the City of

The Conduct of Foreign Relations

New York, 5 F. Supp. 156 (S.D.N.Y., 1933). This interpretation of the statute foreshadows the administrative process of a much more sophisticated day, and is not dissimilar to the embargo clauses in the tariff acts of 1922 and 1930 (discussed in Chapter 5): the collectors of the customs find, as a matter of fact, that a vessel ostensibly bound for a port of the United States is really bound for a port for a foreign port in violation of the embargo; they enter what is equivalent to an intermediate order detaining the vessel; then the President makes the final determination of the cause.

[30] Act of June 5, 1794, 1 *Stat.* 384, Chapter 50, Section 7.

[31] Gelston v. Hoyt, 3 Wheat. 246 (1818).

[32] Charles Warren, *The Supreme Court in United States History* (Boston: Little Brown, 1926), I, 474–475. The other two Presidents and cases referred to were Adams and *Little v. Barreme*, and Jefferson and *Gilchrist v. Collector of Charleston.*

[33] Gelston v. Hoyt, 3 Wheat. 246, 282 (1818).

[34] "[W]henever the President shall find that in any American country conditions of domestic violence exist which are promoted by the use of arms or munitions of war procured from the United States, and shall make proclamation thereof, it shall be unlawful to export except under such limitations and exceptions as the President shall prescribe any arms or munitions of war from any place in the United States to such country until otherwise ordered by the President or by Congress." Joint Resolution of March 14, 1912, 37 *Stat.* 630, Section 1.

[35] United States v. Chavez, 228 U.S. 525 (1913).

[36] 48 *Stat.* 811, 1744.

[37] United States v. Curtiss-Wright Export Corp., 14 F. Supp. 230 (S.D.N.Y., 1936).

[38] United States v. Curtiss-Wright Export Corp., 299 U.S. 304 (1936).

[39] Particularly in that the Court was almost unanimous, with only Justice McReynolds disagreeing; Justice Sutherland's own strong views had been publicly stated in a book he wrote on the subject some 17 years earlier: see Foster H. Sherwood, "Foreign Relations and the Constitution," *Western Political Quarterly*, 1:393 (December 1948).

[40] This is a clear example of the acceptance by the Supreme Court of Theodore Roosevelt's "Stewardship Theory" of the Presidency. See Chapter 3, *supra.*

[41] Compare with the royal prerogative: "The residual powers of the Crown as the representative of the nation in foreign relations are called 'Acts of State' and are separable from those whose effect is within the realm. In general, there has been no *legal* diminution of the king's external powers comparable to the transfer of internal powers to Parliament that has taken place, thus necessitating the use of statutory ordinances (acts of Parliament) to deal with normal domestic affairs; nor has the pre-eminence of the Crown in Britain's dealings with other states ever been limited by a hostile minority in the House of Lords." Glendon A. Schubert, Jr., "Judicial Review of Royal Proclamations and Orders-in-Council," *University of Toronto Law Journal*, 9:77–78 (1951).

[42] United States v. Curtiss-Wright Export Corp., 299 U.S. 304, 319–320 (1936).

[43] The other two had been laid earlier without executive licenses.

[44] This motion was under advisement when a decision was rendered.

[45] United States v. Western Union Telegraph Co., 272 F. 311, 313 (S.D.N.Y., 1921).

[46] The United States Supreme Court reversed the lower court and directed it "to enter a decree dismissing the bill without prejudice" on consent of the parties, at 260 U.S. 754 (1922), but without opinion and "without consideration by the [Supreme] Court."

[47] Section 1006(a), 52 *Stat.* 1024. Italics supplied.

[48] Pan American Airways v. C.A.B., 121 F. 2d 810 (2 C.C.A., 1941).

[49] Chicago and Southern Air Lines v. Waterman S.S. Corp., 333 U.S. 103, 106, 110 (1948). The dissenting opinion attempted to interject overtones of the "negative order" doctrine at this point: "The Board had consolidated for hearing twenty-nine applications for certificates to engage in air transportation which were filed by fifteen applicants. The President's partial disapproval of the proposed disposition of these applica-

tions did not relate to the application involved in this case. As to them, the action of the Board stands unaltered." *Ibid.*, 116 ftn. 5. The fallacy of this approach is obvious: the President's approval of some parts of the board's order without change and of other parts only after changes had been made could hardly be said to imply a lesser exercise of presidential judgment and discretion in the one case than in the other.

[50] *Ibid.*, 109–110. Italics supplied. And see National Airlines v. C.A.A., 24 L. W. 3192 (C.A.D.C., September 15, 1955), certiorari denied 350 U.S. 948 (January 16, 1956).

[51] *Ibid.*, 116, 117–118.

[52] In the next relevant case to come before it, the Supreme Court dismissed, at 338 U.S. 947 (February 6, 1950), and on motion of the carrier, an appeal from the 2–1 decision of a three-judge district court dismissing a suit to enjoin the C.A.B. from recommending presidential approval of a permit for a foreign air carrier to make scheduled flights to and from points in the United States. The trial court had remarked in *obiter dictum* that the President had no authority to approve or disapprove the issuance of such a permit until after the board had given its advice to him, and made the findings required by Section 402(b) of the Civil Aeronautics Act of 1938 (that the carrier was ready, willing, and able to perform air transportation, and that such transportation would be in the public interest). Colonial Airlines v. Adams, 87 F. Supp. 242, 243 (D.Ct.D.C., November 16, 1949).

The Supreme Court's action constituted, of course, neither approval nor disapproval of the dictum of the lower court.

[53] United States v. Bush & Co., 310 U.S. 371 (1940).

[54] Norwegian Nitrogen Products Co. v. United States, 288 U.S. 294 (1933).

[55] See 184 F. 2d 66, 69, ftn. 2, for a copy of this letter.

[56] Trans World Airlines v. C.A.B., 184 F. 2d 66 (1950). The Supreme Court denied certiorari to review this decision in Sparks v. C.A.B., Pan American Airways, *et al.*, 340 U.S. 941 (March 5, 1951).

[57] Leonard D. White, *The Jeffersonians* (New York: Macmillan, 1951), pp. 32–33.

[58] Fleming v. Page, 9 How. 603, 614 (1850).

[59] Galban & Co. v. United States, 40 Ct. Cl. 495, 507 (1905). There was no indication that the President had any intent at this time to retain Cuba as a permanent part of the United States or under her jurisdiction other than for purposes of temporary military occupation.

[60] Jones v. United States, 137 U.S. 202, 217 (1890).

[61] 10 *Fed. Reg.* 12303. 59 *Stat.* 884.

[62] United States v. California, 332 U.S. 19, 33, 34, 45 (1947); United States v. Louisiana, 339 U.S. 699 (1950); and United States v. Texas, 339 U.S. 707 (1950). For a discussion of the states' rights point of view and a critique of the Supreme Court's position in these decisions, see Ernest R. Bartley, *The Tidelands Oil Controversy* (Austin: University of Texas, 1953).

[63] Public Law 31, 83d Congress, 1st Session, "The Submerged Lands Act," 67 *Stat.* 29 (Approved May 22, 1953).

[64] Vermilya-Brown Co. v. Connell, 335 U.S. 377, 380–381 (1948).

[65] Foley Bros., Inc. v. Filardo, 336 U.S. 281, 288–289 (1949).

[66] Luna v. United States, 124 Ct. Cl. 52 (1952).

[67] Fong Yue Ting v. United States, 149 U.S. 698, 709, 713, 714 (1893). The constitutionality of President Theodore Roosevelt's proclamation of March 14, 1907, which expressly prohibited from entry into the United States Japanese who had been lawfully admitted to residence in the Hawaiian Islands, was upheld many years later on the basis that it was explicitly authorized by the act of February 20, 1907, 34 *Stat.* 898. Kaichiro Sugimoto v. Nagle, 38 F. 2d 207, 208 (9 C.C.A., 1930).

[68] Valentine v. United States *ex rel* Neidecker, 299 U.S. 5 (1936). But cf. *In re* Kaine, 14 Howard 103 (1852).

[69] Act of May 22, 1918, 40 *Stat.* 559.

[70] Since the act of March 2, 1921, was an appropriation act, the courts would

The Conduct of Foreign Relations

doubtless have held, if it had been *Wilson's* order that was challenged, that it did constitute a ratification of his order; but the further inference by no means necessarily followed.

[71] Bennedsen v. Nelson, 2 F. 2d 296, 298 (D.Minn.4D., 1924).

[72] United States *ex rel* Swystun v. McCandless, 24 F. 2d 211 (E.D.Pa., 1928); affirmed on other grounds, 33 F. 2d 882 (3 C.C.A., 1929).

[73] Johnson v. Keating *ex rel* Tarantino, 17 F. 2d 50, 53 (1 C.C.A., 1926).

[74] The same executive order was upheld in a subsequent case as applied to non-immigrant aliens, this time against the "exhaustion of power" argument. The circuit court of appeals even went so far as to declare that the President's powers under the 1921 amendment were broader than under the wartime statute, and that he unquestionably had authority to either modify or revoke his orders. Furthermore, the action of consular officers in granting or denying visas was discretionary, and not subject to control or review by the judiciary. United States *ex rel* Johanson v. Phelps, 14 F. 2d 679, 682 (D.Vt., 1926); affirmed: United States *ex rel* London v. Phelps, 22 F. 2d 288, 290 (2 C.C.A., 1927).

[75] United States *ex rel* Grabner v. Karmuth, 29 F. 2d 314 (W.D.N.Y., 1928), affirmed by the Second Circuit Court of Appeals in 30 F. 2d 242 (1929), and certiorari denied by the Supreme Court in 279 U.S. 850 (1929).

[76] *The Alphonso XIII*, 53 F. 2d 124 (S.D.N.Y., 1931). The court did go on to add in *obiter dictum* that the President could *not* authorize by executive order the entry into the United States of *immigrant* aliens without visas, since the Immigration Act of 1924 expressly made the possession of such documents one condition of eligibility for entry.

[77] Han–Lee Mao v. Brownell, 207 F. 2d 142 (C.A.D.C., 1953). The government did not choose to seek review of this case by the Supreme Court.

[78] See Chapter 7 for a discussion of the alien enemy problem.

[79] See particularly CFR, Title 8, Sec. 175.53 and 175.57, based on presidential proclamation No. 2523 of November 14, 1941, 22 U.S.C.A. Sec. 223, and the acts of May 22, 1918, and October 16, 1918, and June 21, 1941, as amended, 22 U.S.C.A. Sec. 223.

[80] United States *ex rel* Knauff v. Watkins, 173 F. 2d 599 (2 C.C.A., 1949); affirmed: United States *ex rel* Knauff v. Shaughnessy, 338 U.S. 537 (1950).

[81] Of December 28, 1945, 8 U.S.C.A. Sec. 232–236.

[82] "Brief for the Respondent [the Department of Justice]," *In the Supreme Court of the United States*, October Term, 1949, No. 54: *United States of America ex rel. Ellen Knauff, Petitioner, v. Edward J. Shaughnessy, Acting District Director of Immigration and Naturalization Service*, pp. 5–6. It is noteworthy that, in response to the direct questioning of Chief Justice Vinson, Solicitor Monahan admitted that *he* knew the basis of her exclusion but could not, for security reasons, inform the Court; yet Attorney General Clark had apparently divulged this highly "confidential" information in his personal letter of October 4, 1948, to Joseph D. Nunan of New York! See *ibid.*, pp. 6–7, 33.

[83] As Frankfurter dryly observed in his dissenting opinion: "The Attorney General is to act on information that satisfies him; not only is there no opportunity for a hearing, but the Attorney General can lock in his own bosom the evidence that does satisfy him. 8 CFR s. 175.53, 175.57 (1949)." United States *ex rel* Knauff v. Shaughnessy, 338 U.S. 537, 548 ftn. (1950).

[84] *Ibid.*, 542–544.

[85] *Ibid.*, 551.

[86] See her book, *The Ellen Knauff Story* (New York: Norton, 1952).

[87] *In re* Knauff, 1 Ad. Law 2d 639 (1951).

[88] Her difficulties with the Immigration and Naturalization Service were not over, as it turned out. When she applied for naturalization, the same old charges were raised against her once again; and weary of the notoriety and prospect of interminable litigation, Mrs. Knauff gave up her struggle against the bureaucracy. See the *New York Times*, July 3, 1953, p. 6, col. 2. Part of my information is based on a letter from Mrs. Knauff's attorney, Alfred Feingold of New York City, dated March 5, 1954.

[80] In this regard, see particularly the dissenting opinion of Mr. Justice Jackson in Shaughnessy v. United States *ex rel* Mezei, 345 U.S. 206, 219 (1953), a 5–4 decision of the Court which followed the *Knauff* case and sanctioned life internment, by summary administrative process without a hearing, of a 25-year resident of the United States "who seems to have led a life of unrelieved insignificance."

Presidential Control over the Tariff

Reciprocal Trade Agreements

THE field of presidential legislation most cultivated by the courts has been tariff rate-making by presidential proclamation. Since a statute which levies taxes is usually considered a *sine qua non* of legislative power, and further, since administrative rate-making in public utility regulation has been a central problem in the development of American administrative law, it is astounding that — with the exception of judicial confusion and division in two of the *Insular Cases* relating to the executive tariff in the territories wrested from Spain following the Spanish-American War[1] and a single decision of the Court of Customs and Patent Appeals[2] — the judiciary has consistently upheld the action of the President in tariff rate-making. Three Supreme Court decisions[3] are of basic importance in the development of contemporary doctrines upholding delegation of legislative power to the President and presidential action under contingency legislation.

As early as 1832 the Congress, by Section 9 of the act of July 14 of that year, made it the duty of the Secretary of the Treasury, under the direction of the President, to establish from time to time such rules and regulations, not inconsistent with the laws of the United States, as the President should think proper, to secure a just, faithful, and impartial appraisal of all goods entering the country; and it was made the duty of the Secretary to report all such rules and regulations, with the reasons therefor, to the next session of Congress. Such rules and regulations governing the assessment and collection of tariff rates fixed by statute were an integral factor in the determination of the precise duties to be paid on any particular imported goods, but the Supreme Court had no difficulty in upholding the validity of the President's exercise of such rule-making power.[4]

Much more extensive, however, were the powers vested in the President by Section 3 of the Tariff Act of October 1, 1890, which gave him responsibilities similar to those delegated to him forty-four years later in the first Reciprocal Trade Agreements Act. He was authorized to negotiate with other governments to seek rate reductions on their imports from the United States, and in return to place imports from such countries on the free list by his proclamation. Various proclamations were subsequently issued relating to imports from both Latin American and European states.[5] The leading case of *Field v. Clark*,[6] however, was not brought before the Supreme Court on grounds which directly challenged the President's power to issue such a proclamation; moreover, no proclamation issued under the authority of the 1890 statute was even mentioned in the Court's opinion, which is a bit odd in view of the fact that a rather comprehensive analysis of proclamations issued under earlier contingency legislation was made in the majority opinion, and the statute itself was directly at issue.

The constitutional question discussed by the Court was that of the power of Congress to delegate authority to the President to exempt some imports from the imposition of the duties set by the statute, after his finding that such an exemption was necessary for reciprocity between the other state and the United States. The President, in other words, was empowered to determine when concessions promised by another state would be equivalent in value to those made by his own order. The majority found the delegation of authority to be valid, but as in so many other of the most important decisions of the Supreme Court, it was unnecessary for the Court to decide this important question of constitutional law in order to dispose of the case before it.

In this case Marshall Field and Company contested the validity of duties levied upon imported goods that were *not* included within the scope of any reciprocity agreement. The duties were admittedly valid if the act was constitutional, and this was the only point at issue. The Court expressly held that it was not called upon to decide whether or not the "bounties" offered by the act were valid, since the major provisions of the statute were separable; and having found that the statute was separable, the Court's duties were at an end. Under the customary practice of the Supreme Court, Marshall Field and Company had no status to challenge the power of Congress to delegate to the President duties and responsibilities, none of which had been exercised in a manner adverse to them. Furthermore, two of the members of the Court regarded the discussion in the majority opinion of delegation of power to the President to be dictum, as their concurring opinion clearly indicates.[7] Nevertheless, *Field v. Clark* has been so frequently cited by the Supreme Court and other courts and by commentators during the past sixty years that, by sheer repetition of reference, it has come to be recognized as an authoritative statement of the permissible scope of congressional delegation of rule-making power to the President.

Two decades later, however, the Supreme Court did speak directly on the legality of a reciprocal trade agreement made by the President under a delegation of statutory authority from the Tariff Act of 1897. In this case, it was not the congressional power of delegation that was at issue, but rather the status in law of an admittedly valid executive agreement. As not infrequently happens, the Attorney General was placed in the incongruous position of arguing the inapplicability of the agreement to the classification of the plaintiff importer's goods, in order to frustrate judicial review of the administrative action taken; but the Court came to a contrary conclusion, holding:

While it may be true that this commercial agreement, made under authority of the Tariff Act of 1897, s. 3, was not a treaty possessing the dignity of one requiring ratification by the Senate of the United States, it was an international compact, negotiated between the representatives of two sovereign nations and made in the name and on behalf of the contracting countries, and dealing with important commercial relations between the two countries, and was proclaimed by the President. If not technically a treaty requiring ratification, nevertheless, it was a compact authorized by the Congress of the United States, negotiated and proclaimed under the authority of its President. We think such a compact is a treaty under the Circuit Court of Appeals Act [of 1891, s. 5], and, where its construction is directly involved, as it is here, there is a right of review by direct appeal to this court.[8]

The original Reciprocal Trade Agreements Act of June 12, 1934, which had the general effect of formalizing on a multilateral basis the policy of reciprocity accepted by the Tariff acts of 1890 and 1897, was an amendment to the Tariff Act of 1930, and provided:

[T]he President, whenever he finds as a fact that any existing duties . . . are unduly burdening and restricting the foreign trade of the United States . . . is authorized . . . to enter into foreign trade agreements with foreign governments . . . and . . . to proclaim . . . modifications of existing duties and other import restrictions. [The "generalization clause" (i.e., the most-favored-nation clause) gives him power to suspend] acts or policies which in his opinion tend to defeat the purposes set forth in this section.[9]

Apparently only one case has challenged the constitutionality of this procedure, or the validity of an executive agreement entered on the basis of this statutory authority. Here, the most-favored-nation clause was attacked on the theory that "the said provision delegates to the President the power to suspend or repeal an act of Congress fixing a rate of duty" and that therefore "the order of the President suspending the application of proclaimed Swedish trade agreements rates as to importation from Germany constituted an unconstitutional exercise of legislative power."[10] As it happened, the case was dismissed on a technicality, but *Field v. Clark* and *Curtiss-Wright* would certainly have been conclusive upon a lower court passing upon this question on the merits.

The Executive Tariff in National Territories

Typical of the difficulties encountered by the judiciary in attempting to distinguish between the military and foreign relations aspects of the constitutional powers of the President has been the highly controversial matter of the executive tariff in the national territories. Historically, the problem was one of military government in the aftermath of our wars with Mexico and Spain; but since the effects of such tariff regulations were felt primarily in foreign commerce, it seems more useful to discuss the matter in this context.

Out of the Mexican War came the well-known case of *Fleming v. Page*,[11] which raised the question of whether or not the customs tariff on imports applied to goods coming from foreign territory under the temporary military subjugation of the United States. The war had begun in May of 1846, and Tampico, a seaport in the state of Tamaulipas, was garrisoned by United States troops and under our military control continuously from November 1846 until the signing of the peace treaty in May 1848. The military commander appointed courts that administered justice, and established a customs house with a collector of the customs, whom he also appointed. The schooner *Cather-*

ine, which carried the goods here in dispute, made several voyages from Tampico to the United States during the time of the military occupation. "The Mexican authorities had been driven out, or had submitted to our army and navy; and the country was in the exclusive and firm possession of the United States, and governed by its military authorities, acting under the orders of the President."[12] The Supreme Court's decision was that Tampico was a foreign port within the meaning of the Revenue Act of 1846, and that the duties it established were applicable to these cargoes. Territory under the temporary military occupation of the United States, therefore, remained foreign territory to the extent that goods imported therefrom were subject to the regular tariff.

Among the arguments raised by counsel, however, was that "A tariff was prescribed under the authority of the President, by which certain duties were levied upon goods when imported into Mexican ports when they were in our possession. Where did he get that power? Not from any act of Congress laying those duties, but in virtue of his character as commander-in-chief of the army, and in the exercise of military authority over the conquered country."[13] Although the question of the legality of the executive tariff levied upon imports at Tampico was clearly not before the Court in this case, Chief Justice Taney undertook to rule upon this point as well:

There was no act of Congress establishing a custom-house at Tampico, nor authorizing the appointment of a collector, and, consequently, there was no officer of the United States authorized by law to grant the clearance and authenticate the coasting manifest of the cargo, in the manner directed by law, where the voyage is from one port of the United States to another. The person who acted in the character of collector in this instance, acted as such under the authority of the military commander, and in obedience to his orders; and the duties he exacted, and the regulations he adopted, were not those prescribed by law, but by the President in his character of commander-in-chief. . . . The duties required to be paid . . . were nothing more than contributions levied upon the enemy, which the usages of war justify when an army is operating in the enemy's country.[14]

A similar question was raised with respect to American military occupation of Cuba, in an action for the refund of customs duties collected in Cuban ports in accordance with the President's executive order of March 31, 1900, during the period following the signing of the Treaty of Paris on April 11, 1899, and the termination of military occupation by forces of the United States on May 20, 1902. The goods involved were shipped from the United States. The Court of Claims, passing directly upon the question, followed Taney's dictum by upholding the power of the President to authorize the collection of a customs tariff for the support of our occupying forces. It is important to note, however, that in both of these cases, the occupation was temporary and designed to carry out military objectives, there having been no indication on the part of either of the political branches of our government that the United States intended to extend its sovereignty over Tampico or Cuba. Therefore, the fact that the duties were collected after the signing of the treaty of peace with Spain was not a distinguishing factor.[15]

By this time, the Supreme Court had already decided the *Insular Cases*, in which fundamental changes in the constitutional power of the national government permanently to acquire and to rule noncontiguous territory were recognized. The territories previously acquired either had been purchased or, when acquired by conquest, had been contiguous, continental territory, where the question of statehood was debated in terms of when and how, not whether and if. Perhaps the best way to sum up the legal changes resulting from the Spanish-American War is to say that a variable majority of both the Constitution and the Supreme Court followed the Flag.[16] Faced with determining the effect of the change in sovereignty over the former Spanish possessions during the period of American military occupation, the Supreme Court decided that, in the absence of special legislation, the right of the collector of the port of New York to exact duties upon imports from Puerto Rico ended with the ratification of the Treaty of Paris on April 11, 1899, because Puerto Rico ceased to be foreign territory as of that date.[17]

Another case, decided later on that same day, raised the reverse of the question: could duties be lawfully exacted in Puerto Rico on exports from the United States after that island ceased to be foreign territory? The existing Spanish tariff had been continued in effect by order of the United States military commander on July 26, 1898, and the President by his executive orders of August 19, 1898, and February 1, 1899, had ordered certain modifications but the continued collection of customs duties. The plaintiff contested the imposition of all duties under the direction of the President without statutory authorization, but the Court had precedent for upholding the validity of collections by order of the military commander and later by order of the President during the period that Puerto Rico remained foreign territory. The Court ruled that after the treaty of peace was signed, however, and Puerto Rico became part of the United States, the President could not authorize, on the basis of his constitutional powers as the Commander in Chief, a tariff on imports from the United States; this could be done only by authority of the Congress.[18] Elsewhere in the opinion, the Court used language that appeared to uphold the presidential tariff as applied to imports from *foreign* countries.[19]

It might be pointed out that our public law was shaped at this crucial period in our legal history in large measure by the predilections of a single member of the Court, Mr. Justice Brown (just as some thirty-six years later, Mr. Justice Roberts was instrumental in shaping the policies of the Nine Old Men in the transition year of 1937). There were two irreconcilable factions on the Court, with the concurring majority of the first two cases of *Delima v. Bidwell* and *Dooley I* (Fuller, Peckham, Harlan, and Brewer) convinced that a tariff could not be levied on commerce between the United States and its new island possessions; the other faction (White, Gray, Shiras, and McKenna) believed that the tariff laws applied automatically to imports from non-contiguous territories that were not "incorporated" into the United States, and hence upheld the exaction of the duties in the *Downes v. Bidwell* and *Dooley II* cases.[20] Brown wrote the opinions of the Court in each of these cases on a theory that was strictly personal and individual: that the question was one of sovereignty, and that although Congress had the power to impose a tariff, since the uniformity clause applied only to the states, Congress must explicitly indicate its intent, inasmuch as the language of the existing laws had not been drawn to anticipate and did not cover newly acquired territorial possessions. Since Brown's position was fluid while the blocs remained inflexible, and he really was in the middle between them, he was in a position to vote alternatively with both factions, and to demand, or at least to receive, the right to state the law of the case for the Court in his own way.[21] Thus the public law of the *Insular Cases* is the semantic web of a single justice who was in a position to "swing the Court" at a time of constitutional crisis.

No major change in the constitutional principles already announced was effected by the subsequent decisions of the courts, so *Dooley I* emerged as the leading case from our point of interest, holding that the President could constitutionally authorize a tariff levy on all imports of a newly conquered territory under military occupation by the United States until peace was restored and sovereignty shifted to the United States. Thereafter, he could continue to levy such a tariff, until Congress chose to act, with respect to imports from foreign countries, but could apply the tariff to imports from the United States only with statutory authorization. Thus, the tariff which had been established by the local United States military authorities, continuing in effect the Spanish duties, was valid and applicable to goods imported in Manila from Hongkong in August 1898, although the superseding presidential tariff for the Philippines created by the executive order of July 12, 1898, did not apply because neither the military authorities in the Philippines nor the plaintiff had actual notice of its existence at the time the importation took place.[22] However, the presidential tariff was a valid military order and determined the legal rate of customs duties for the Philippines from the time it went into effect on November 10, 1898, until the termination of the war on April 11, 1899.[23]

As to imports from the United States, the Supreme Court held that the executive order and the act of the Philippines Commission[24] were not intended to be interpreted to authorize the collection of the executive tariff, as the President, Secretary of War, Civil Governor, and Philippines Commission had all without exception and continuously so interpreted them; nor did the ratifying acts of March 8, 1902,[25] and July 1, 1902,[26] mean what they plainly said or what the members of Congress who voted for them thought they meant — rather, they were intended to have prospective effect only.[27] Finally, however, the Court was confronted with a third attempt at statutory ratification, this time in such unequivocal language that there was no alternative but to declare it unconstitutional or else to give effect to it:

Be it enacted . . . That the tariff duties both import and export imposed by the authorities of the United States or of the provisional military government thereof in the Philippine Islands prior to March eighth, nineteen hundred and two, at all ports and places in said islands upon all goods, wares, and merchandise imported into said islands from the United States, or from foreign countries, or exported from said islands, are hereby legalized and ratified, and the collection of all such duties prior to March eighth, nineteen hundred and two is hereby legalized and ratified and confirmed as fully to all intents and purposes

144

as if the same had by prior Act of Congress been specifically authorized and directed.[28]

But even in deciding that this statute did have the effect of retroactively approving the executive tariff up to the time when it was given
what the Court had recognized as prospective statutory authorization,
the Court applied the common-law rule of agency, which was hardly
necessary in view of their own ample precedents on this point.[29] Said
the Court:

> That where an agent, without precedent authority, has exercised in
> the name of a principal a power which the principal had the capacity
> to bestow, the principal may ratify and affirm the unauthorized act,
> and thus retroactively give it validity when rights of third persons
> have not intervened, is so elementary as to need but statement. . . .
> Congress in dealing with the Philippine Islands, *may . . . delegate
> legislative authority to such agencies as it may select* . . . the act [of
> ratification] is but an exercise of the conceded power *dependent upon
> the law of agency* to ratify an act done on behalf of the United States
> which the United States [Congress?] could have originally authorized.[30]

Presidential Rate-Making under the Flexible Tariff

Without question, the courts' most comprehensive exploration of
presidential action under statutory delegation of authority has concerned the flexible tariff laws. In the case of both the 1922 and 1930
acts, a series of cases was brought before the customs courts to feel out
the constitutionality of the legislation and to determine how close the
President could be held to the express language of the statute. After a
few years of uncertainty, the rules of interpretation were stabilized and
challenges to the exercise of presidential authority disappeared.

The so-called flexible tariff provision of the Tariff Act of 1922 was
Section 135. Subsection (a) granted authority to the President to raise
or to lower the rates of the statutory duties to a maximum of 50 per
cent if he determined, after an investigation by the Tariff Commission,
that the rates set by the statute did not equalize the costs of production between the United States and the principal competing country;
the new rates were to take effect thirty days after his public proclamation had been issued. Subsection (c) set standards for the guidance of
the President; insofar as he should find it practicable, he should consider (1) differences in conditions of production; (2) general differences
in wholesale prices; (3) subsidies granted by the foreign government;
(4) "any other advantages of disadvantages in competition." The

United States Tariff Commission was directed to make investigations, with notice and hearing, and to adopt its own rules of procedure; such investigation was expressly made a condition precedent to the issuance of a proclamation by the President. By Executive Order No. 3746 of October 7, 1922, the President directed that all petitions or applications for action or relief under the flexible section of the Tariff Act of 1922 should be filed with the Tariff Commission.

The first attempt by an importer to dispute the authority of the commission and the President turned out to be the most stubborn one, and was not finally resolved until it had been ruled upon twice by the Supreme Court and many more times by courts lower in the administrative-judicial hierarchy. Following a complaint that an increase in the rate of duty on sodium nitrate was necessary in order to equalize the difference in the costs of production in the United States and the principal competing country, Norway, the commission undertook an inquiry into the "fairness" of the statutory rate, and on September 15, 1923, made a preliminary report stating the results of its investigation. Hearings were resumed on September 26, when the principal importer was given an opportunity to offer evidence, to make oral argument, and to file briefs. On December 12, 1923, before the commission had reported to the President, the importer applied to the Supreme Court of the District of Columbia for a writ of mandamus directing the commission to disclose certain information which the commission refused to divulge on the ground that it related to trade secrets of domestic producers. That court dismissed the petition, ruling that the action of the commission had been in conformity with law. An appeal to the Court of Appeals for the District followed, but while it was pending the commission made a report to the President; and upon the basis of this report the President issued his proclamation of May 6, 1924, raising the rate of duty from three to four and a half cents per pound, the maximum change possible under his statutory powers. The Court of Appeals ventured the opinion that the information should have been given, but decided that the question had become moot by reason of the action of the President.[31] The Supreme Court agreed:

The argument is made that the President was without jurisdiction to proclaim the new tariff rate because of alleged irregularities in the conduct of the hearing before the Commission which was a prerequisite to such action by the President. But the petitioner does not attack the validity of the tariff proclaimed by the President; nor is this an appro-

146

priate proceeding in which to do so. Even if the change in the tariff rates were deemed to be ineffectual, it would not follow that it is mandatory upon the President or the Commission to institute a new hearing.[32]

Collateral attack upon the presidential judgment having failed, the Norwegian Nitrogen Products Company then protested the application of the revised rate in a direct appeal that was carried from the administrative stages of review within the Treasury Department through the customs court until, some six years later, it ultimately reached the Court of Customs and Patent Appeals (C.C.P.A.).

In the meantime, however, several cases raising related but different issues were disposed of by the customs courts. On May 19, 1924 — less than two weeks after issuing the proclamation involved in the Norwegian Nitrogen litigation — President Coolidge promulgated his proclamation raising the rate of duty on barium dioxide. In the proceedings that followed, it was conceded that all relevant acts of the President and the commission had been in conformity with the letter of the law, but it was argued that Section 315 was invalid as an unlawful delegation of legislative power. The Court of Customs Appeals upheld the delegation, asserting that the President would be held accountable by the courts for any excess of his statutory powers:

The office of the President is one of high standing and vast responsibility; public policy requires, and the courts have uniformly held, that, in the discharge of his high office, in all those matters which have been entrusted to his discretion, he is not to be interfered with or under the control of the courts. Such powers are political in their nature and for the proper exercise of these the President is responsible only to the country. . . . In the execution of such powers, the President may act unwisely and to the great injury of individual and national interests, but for such acts there can be no remedy, under our Constitution, but the political ones committed to the suffrage of the people. But when duties are imposed upon the President over and beyond his purely political ones, duties which he does not perform because of his constitutional power as Chief Executive but because the Congress has constituted him an agent for the better execution of some legislative policy, and in the execution of which powers personal or property rights are involved, then such acts are ministerial only, and are subject to review by the courts. [Citing *Marbury v. Madison.*] . . . [T]he acts of the President [under statutory delegation of authority] are entitled to no greater significance and should be measured by no other rule than that to be given and used in considering the acts of any other fact-finding official or board which the Congress may have named. . . .

[I]f . . . the President had proceeded without taking the steps directed by section 315, the importer could have set these facts out in his protest and had an adjudication thereon. . . . To deny this would be to give to the act of the President *a peculiar sanctity and inviolability not attaching to the acts of other officials of the Government performing similar fact-finding duties*; and this we are neither called upon to do nor justified by the law in doing. We are unable to see why any different rule of law should be applied to the President's finding of facts under section 315 than the one applied to the finding of valuation by an appraiser of merchandise at our ports. In such cases, while the courts have held the finding of valuation made by the appraiser to be conclusive, if he proceeds upon a wrong principle, contrary to law, his acts are subject to judicial control and correction.[33]

Finally, and two years after Section 315 of the 1922 Tariff Act had been superseded by Section 336 of the 1930 act, a number of decisions of the customs courts were appealed to the C.C.P.A., including several (which were reversed) that were adverse to the constitutionality of Section 315 and presidential action thereunder; and the broad scope of executive discretion under the statute was strikingly affirmed in a series of five decisions handed down by the C.C.P.A. on May 2, 1932.[34] Together, these cases constitute the definitive judicial interpretation of presidential action under the Tariff Act of 1922.

The first of these cases, *Foster I*, concerned President Coolidge's proclamation of January 17, 1929, raising the rates on polished plate glass, unsilvered. Relying upon the dicta of the lower court's opinion in the *Hampton* case, the importer urged that "The action of the President in determining and proclaiming the increased rates of duty specified in said proclamation was erroneous, *ultra vires*, illegal and void." The government, on the other hand, denied the possibility of any sort of judicial review:

the proclamation of the President, made in pursuance of the authority of said section 315 (a), is in itself proof of compliance by the President with the provisions of law and of the facts it recites; that said proclamation may not be either directly or collaterally attacked, that it is beyond the jurisdiction of either the United States Customs Court or this court to enquire the steps taken prior to the issuance of said proclamation.[35]

The court held that it was bound, by the decision in the *Hampton* case, to accept the basic premises that the President's power was limited by the statute delegating his authority, that fact-finding by the commission was a condition precedent to his own action, and that express noncompliance with the statutory conditions (such as changing a rate by more than 50 per cent, transferring an item from the free list to the dutiable list, changing the form of a duty, or basing his action upon an improper or completely irrelevant investigation by the commission) would result in a decision by the court that the President's action was *ultra vires*.[36] The report of the commission, however, was in no way conclusive upon the President;[37] and the only form of relief available under the statute was by direct attack protesting duties levied and collected under the proclamation. His formal statement of compliance was not conclusive evidence that he had complied with the statutory conditions, although there was a rebuttable presumption to this effect whether he said so or not;[38] and a mistake in fact in the investigation of the commission would not invalidate action of the President based thereon.[39]

The second case, an intermediate decision in the *Norwegian Nitrogen Products* series, was the one which reached the Supreme Court, and will be discussed below. The third was an appeal from a decision of the Third Division of the Customs Court, which not only had held President Coolidge's proclamation of June 8, 1927 (in which the President had very literally "filled in the details" of a statute by particularizing the statutory definition of a class of goods), to be "Executive despotism," but also had gone out of its way to strike down Section 315.[40] But the C.C.P.A. reversed, pointing out that:

the statute did not provide that the Tariff Commission should fix the duties, nor that it should make findings upon which proclamations of the President should be based. The findings contemplated by the statute were to be made by the President. . . .

[A]nd it is immaterial what opinions were entertained by the investigators, or by the members of the Tariff Commission, as a result of such an investigation.[41]

In the fourth case, the Second Division of the Customs Court had followed the lead of the Third Division and had invalidated the presidential proclamation of February 12, 1926, raising the duty on men's straw hats, together with Section 315 of the statute.[42] On the authority of this holding, this court subsequently had decided that the statute gave the President no authority to include transportation costs as a factor in ascertaining the differences between domestic and foreign costs of production, and that in any event both the statute and the proclamation were invalid as applied to the plaintiff.[43] The C.C.P.A. reversed both of these decisions, ruling that when the record disclosed nothing to the contrary, the legality of the commission's investigation was to be assumed,[44] and that congressional silence was equivalent to consent to the President's power to include transportation charges as a factor in computing comparative costs of production.[45]

In the *Norwegian Nitrogen* case, the power of the commission to withhold information, to deny cross-examination of witnesses and its own investigators, and to withhold part of the record from public scrutiny was still the question at issue, as it had been in the earlier proceeding. The C.C.P.A. pointed out that the scope of review under Section 315 was not as broad as that provided for under Section 316, relating to unfair competition, where an appeal to the court on questions of law was expressly permitted. The right of any review by the customs courts under Section 315 existed only by inference, since statutory appeal was neither expressly provided for nor expressly denied. "The hearing before the Tariff Commission was not a judicial inquiry," so it was held to be valid. Then, reaching for a question that the facts of this case did not present, the C.C.P.A. asked itself: would a presidential proclamation clearly disregarding in its entirety the weight of a unanimous report of the Tariff Commission be valid? And answered:

There is nothing in the section which prevents him from making such inquiries as he deems proper or from ignoring everything that is done by the commission. . . .

It is our view that whether the President did or did not rely, wholly or in part, upon an investigation made by himself is immaterial.[46]

Upon appeal, the Supreme Court, faced with the same legal questions that it had considered to be moot seven years earlier, again refused to examine in any respect the merits of the increase in duty as such, but the Court did rule directly on the validity of the administrative procedures followed by the commission and the President. Justice Cardozo's opinion is certainly not typical of those of the Supreme Court that deal with the scope of judicial review of the administrative procedure of regulatory commissions, or of the standards invoked from the Fifth Amendment for due process in administrative hearings by regulatory commissions. The much greater scope of executive and administrative discretion in the regulation of foreign commerce than in the regulation of domestic commerce was again affirmed by the Supreme Court's decision that in hearings before the Tariff Commission

Presidential Control over the Tariff

1. The right of a party adversely affected by an increase in a tariff duty does not include the right of:
   a. Access to all data collected by the Commission.
   b. Cross-examination of investigators and competitors upon such data.
2. Notice of hearing to those affected by a change in import duties is *not* required.
3. Congressional acquiescence in administrative practice may be inferred from Congressional silence extending over a period of years.
4. No one has a legal right to the maintenance of an existing tariff rate or duty.
5. The refusal of the Commission to disclose data regarding the cost of production in the United States, because this could not be done without identifying the competitor, was held to be:
   a. Not unfair, when the plaintiff has refused to reveal his own costs of production.
   b. Not a violation of the rules of the Commission to the effect that persons who have entered an appearance may examine records of the Commission *"except* such portions as relate to trade secrets and processes."
6. What issues from the Commission as a report and recommendation to the President may be accepted, modified, or rejected by him.[47]

There were only two later decisions. In one, the necessity for a "legal" investigation by the Tariff Commission as a condition precedent to a lawful proclamation by the President was reaffirmed as a matter of principle;[48] and upon rehearing of the *Foster* case, the C.C.P.A. went beyond its previous opinion, which it affirmed, to declare:

When the proclamation became effective, the rates named therein were, in legal effect, the rates prescribed by Congress, acting through a validly delegated authority, and had the same effect as if Congress had, by direct enactment, amended the Tariff Act of 1922 insofar as the same related to rates of duty upon cast polished glass, unsilvered.[49]

This left the scope of judicial review under the 1922 statute as follows: error in law and fact of the commission were not reviewable; the judgment of the President could not be re-examined in the courts; only the question of adherence to the prescribed statutory procedures could be raised.[50] But analysis of these decisions reveals that in no case was either a proclamation of the President or the delegation of power to him ultimately held invalid. The courts discuss various ways in which the President might exceed his authority, but they do not find that he has done so. They prescribe in some detail the requirements of the hearing process of the Tariff Commission, but this is in no way a direct limitation upon the power of the President, since he can completely disregard the recommendations resulting from such a hearing. The only specific rule applicable to the President is that the commission must act before the President can act; his discretion within the scope of his delegated authority is limited only to the extent that he cannot exercise it until certain facts have been made available for his consideration, although he may evaluate such information as he sees fit, and other and secret data may be persuasive in his judgment.

Presidential Regulation of Unfair (Foreign) Trade Practices

The President's power to proclaim an embargo-in-reverse, by excluding goods from entry into the United States under certain circumstances, has been an accepted part of our tariff machinery for the past three decades. The current statutory provision reads:

Section 1337 *Unfair practices in import trade.*

(e) *Exclusion of articles from entry.* Whenever the existence of any such unfair method or act shall be established to the satisfaction of the President he shall direct that the articles concerned in such unfair methods or acts, imported by any person violating the provisions of this Act, shall be excluded from entry into the United States, and upon information of such action by the President, the Secretary of the Treasury shall, through the proper officers, refuse such entry. The decision of the President shall be conclusive.

(f) *Entry under bond.* Whenever the President has reason to believe that any article is offered or sought to be offered for entry into the United States in violation of this section but has not information sufficient to satisfy him thereof, the Secretary of the Treasury shall, upon his request in writing, forbid entry thereof until such investigation as the President may deem necessary shall be completed; except that such articles shall be entitled to entry under bond prescribed by the Secretary of the Treasury.

(g) *Continuance of exclusion.* Any refusal of entry under this section shall continue in effect until the President shall find and instruct the Secretary of the Treasury that the conditions which led to such refusal of entry no longer exist.[51]

The United States Supreme Court has remarked on the functional relationship between the President's action in approving "Codes of Fair Competition" under the National Industrial Recovery Act and his authority to exclude goods from entry in order to counteract the effect of unfair acts and methods of competition in the importation of goods from abroad.[52] No such power to determine what constitutes either fair or unfair competition, except for that under the unconstitutional National Recovery Administration, has ever been given to the President or to officers under his power of direction with respect to domestic industry and production. Congress has seen fit to relegate such powers to the independent regulatory commissions:[53] the Interstate Commerce Commission, the Federal Trade Commission, the Federal Communications Commission, the Securities and Exchange Commission, the National Labor Relations Board, and the Civil Aeronautics Board. While the Secretary of Agriculture has comparable powers under the Packers and Stockyards Act of 1921, the Supreme Court has expressly held that the Secretary must *personally* exercise his quasi-judicial duties under this statute.[54]

Larkin, who has made the definitive study in this area, points out that most of the cases coming up under Section 337 during the early years of experience under the statute involved "unfair trade practices" which were almost without exception patent infringement cases.[55] The Tariff Commission, moreover, has no authority to decide upon the validity of patents as such, that being an "inherently" judicial function — although, of course, quite proper for the determination of the agency which reviews the Tariff Commission's findings of law, the Court of Customs and Patent Appeals.

Only one challenge was raised to the constitutionality of Section 316 under the 1922 statute, and here the question of the constitutionality of the President's actions was discussed only in a dissenting opinion. The Tariff Commission had made an investigation and reported its findings and made recommendations to the President to the effect that Frischer and Company had engaged in unfair competition in the form of the infringement of a patent held by the Bakelite Corporation, and that the imported goods complained of should be excluded from the United States.[56] The Court of Customs Appeals affirmed the findings of the Tariff Commission,[57] and the importer appealed to the Court of Customs and Patent Appeals, which upheld the validity of the congressional delegation of authority in Section 316, finding that the President acted thereunder only as a fact-finding agency to carry out the policy fixed by Congress; that appeals to the courts were on questions of law only; that the commission had the power to withhold information (in this case, the trade secrets of the complainant) in an adversary action, thus restricting the possibility of cross-examination of all relevant evidence on which the commission acted; that the findings of the commission, if supported by substantial evidence, were conclusive; and that in this case, the commission's findings as to the importer's unfair trade practices, which led to the recommendation of the embargo, were sustained by the evidence.[58]

Judge Garrett dissented, noting that the court had followed the *Hampton* decision[59] and apparently assumed an equivalence in the President's powers under Section 315 (the flexible tariff) and Section 316 (the power to exclude). He found the two sections quite different, and worried about the conclusiveness of presidential determinations as fixed by the statute, and his power to make decisions which in effect could disregard the judicial findings of law as well as the commission's findings of fact. Garrett correctly pointed out that Congress intended the Tariff Commission to function as an advisory body, while vesting the discretion to act solely in the President; the commission was an agency to guide the exercise of his discretion, not to exercise it for him; but the concept of "unfair methods," argued Garrett, was utterly insufficient as a legislative standard:

What the Commission does is certainly a part of what the President is charged with the responsibility of finally doing. He may do it with or without the Commission's aid. If he does it without, there is no court review provided. . . . If the aid of the Commission is invoked, as has been done in the instant case, thereby making possible a limited court review, the President may disregard both the findings of the Commission and courts, make his own findings as to law and fact, and direct the levy of additional duties, or he may declare an embargo, if he finds the case "extreme." [There seems to be committed to the President of the United States the authority and duty of making findings not only of fact but of law.]

[I]f the Supreme Court shall take the jurisdiction provided for it by the statute, in this or some similar case, and pronounce a judgment upon the merits as this court is doing, it will have no greater binding effect as a judgment at law than our own. By its own force, such judgment can exercise no control over the actions of the executive under this section.[60]

Which is all perfectly true, but one is tempted to ask: so what? The decisions to initiate (or not) governmental suits before the courts, and to appeal (or not) adverse decisions of lower courts — to suggest only two of many examples — certainly give the President control over the "binding effect" of judicial judgments. Here the President had discretion to act and he acted. The fact that a judicial decision may or may not have been one of the factors that he took into consideration in exercising his discretion gives him an appellate authority over the courts to no greater extent than when he pardons a convicted criminal shortly after a federal court, perhaps the Supreme Court, has handed down its decision, and there certainly is no question but that this is within his constitutional discretion.

Only two cases have challenged the validity of Section 337 of the 1930 statute as an unconstitutional delegation of legislative power to the President, and the Court of Customs and Patent Appeals decided both of them *seriatim* on May 23, 1934, on the authority of the ruling in the *Frischer* case. The important difference was that the majority were induced to consider the role of the President in these cases, where they had remained silent on this point in the earlier decision. Thus, in the first case:

Appellants also contend that the section is unconstitutional for the reason that it is indefinite and leaves the determination of what are unfair methods and unfair acts to the Tariff Commission, and for the further reason that it attempts to delegate to the President judicial powers. In the Frischer Case, supra, we held that the predecessor Section 316 of the Tariff Act of 1922 (19 USCA sections 174–180) was constitutional. . . . Appellants have attempted to point out differences between the predecessor provision of the Tariff Act of 1922 and that of the Tariff Act of 1930 now under consideration . . . we see no merit whatever in the contention. No differences between said provision of the Tariff Act of 1922 and that of the Tariff Act of 1930 here in controversy have been pointed out that would cause us to regard this court's holding in the Frischer Case, supra, as not controlling of the issue of constitutionality in the case at bar.[61]

In the second case, the majority held:

The Commission and the President, both may, in the first instance, assume the validity of patents duly issued and certified by the United States Patent Office. Upon their invalidity being declared by legal authority, it is the duty of the President, under said Section 337 (g) . . . to correct any order issued and based thereon.[62]

Such a duty, it might be added, would be a moral duty, not a legal duty. The statute includes no such requirement, and certainly no court could mandamus the President so to act; it is also almost inconceivable, for reasons that will be developed more fully later, that any court would hold his order invalid because of his failure to modify it to take into account a change in the data on which it was based. As Judge Garrett, this time concurring, reminded his colleagues:

I do feel impelled to state that, in my judgment, the issues before us do not require any declaration by us as to the duty of the President in the event some court of competent jurisdiction declares invalid a patent upon which an embargo has been predicated. Our jurisdiction under Section 337 (19 USCA s. 1337) extends alone to a review of the report of the Tariff Commission, and that upon questions of law only, and we have nothing to do in the instant proceeding with defining the President's duties. Under the section the President may act upon the report of the Tariff Commission, or he may act independently of it. I am unable to see wherein it is incumbent upon this court, under the limited duty which the statute devolves upon it, to essay a declaration as to what the duty of the Executive may be under some possible future condition.[63]

A Somewhat Less Flexible Tariff?

The Supreme Court, by inflating statutory language that Congress had intended to be restrictive, construed the 1930 statute to bring about a return to the *status quo ante*. But as enacted, important changes had been made in Section 336 of the Tariff Act of 1930.[64] The broad discretion vested in the President by Section 315 was transferred, in substantial measure, to the Tariff Commission by Section 336, leaving the President with the much narrower power of veto over the sublegislation recommended to him by the administrative agency. This change in the statutory language was soon reflected in the decisions of the C.C.P.A., which came to view the President more and more, during the first decade of experience under the new law, as a kind of administrative agency himself; and which further limited the range of his discretion under the act to approving *only those changes justified by the weight of evidence* in the commission's report, through application of the doctrine of jurisdictional fact (because their own review under Section 333, although greater than under the 1922 statute which made no express provision for judicial review, was explicitly limited to questions of law). This tendency within the C.C.P.A. continued until 1939, when a divided court for the second time held a presidential proclamation invalid. On this score, however, they were soon decisively reversed by the Supreme Court in the *Bush* case, *infra*, which apparently resolved all latent doubts as to the scope of the

President's powers, for there has been only one relevant case since the latter decision, and that follows it.

At first the C.C.P.A. saw no difference in the President's powers under the two statutes. Thus, when the Second Division of the Customs Court held invalid President Hoover's proclamation of February 5, 1931, because he had added to the list of the statutory paragraph certain *eo nomine* classifications[65] and because Section 336 was considered to have delegated authority to him to "write new provisions into the tariff laws," and was therefore unconstitutional,[66] the C.C.P.A. reversed, finding no substantial difference between the procedures outlined in Section 315 and those in Section 336, and upholding the constitutionality of the latter on the basis of its own numerous prior decisions upholding the former. This court also announced that it would apply the same general principles in interpreting the 1930 act as it had followed in the case of the 1922 act; and that in any event, the Supreme Court's decision in the *Hampton* case (under the 1922 act) was controlling in the case at bar.[67]

The trend in the other direction began with the remarks of Judge Lenroot in a case decided two years later:

Under the provisions of section 336 of the Tariff Act of 1930 . . . the President, in forming his judgment, is confined to a consideration of the facts secured by the Tariff Commission in its investigation, and is further limited to approval of the rates specified by the Commission if he finds, from such investigation, that the rates so specified are necessary to equalize costs of production.

We can find nothing in the statute which limits the President to a consideration of *the report* of the Tariff Commission, but we think the fair construction of section 336 is that the President, upon a report coming to him from the Tariff Commission, may require such Commission to place before him *all the facts secured by it* in its investigation, and *from such facts* the President may determine whether *the rates specified* in the report of the Commission should be approved.[68]

The following year, the court, speaking through Judge Hatfield, pushed this doctrine to its next logical step: the President was limited to the evidence adduced before the Tariff Commission, and his duty was to approve the recommendations of the commission if in his judgment the evidence supported their findings. But "reasonable public notice" was an essential element of a "legal investigation" by the Tariff Commission, which was a prerequisite to presidential action. Notice in this case was not reasonable, since the Tariff Commission had announced that its investigation would relate to optical instruments "used by" the Army and Navy, and this same language was followed by the proclamation; actually, said the court, it was clear from the record that the investigation had been extended to include optical instruments "suitable for use" by the armed services, to the detriment of the plaintiff, who had not been represented at the hearing. Consequently, the court held "that the proclamation of the President was without authority of law, illegal, and void." [69]

A year later, however, the court swung back temporarily toward the earlier pattern of decisions in two opinions that it delivered on November 9, 1936. The first raised no constitutional issues, but the court, disregarding the testimony of expert (but interested) witnesses, resolved the legal question whether "infants underwear" properly referred to children under two or under six years of age by consulting the dictionary definition of infant and *on that basis* accepting the presidential interpretation of six years.[70] The other case raised, with respect to Section 336, the same question that had been so bitterly contested by the Norwegian Nitrogen Products Company under the 1922 act: the power of the commission to withhold information on which its decision was in part based. The appeal here was by a domestic manufacturer, protesting the somewhat unusual circumstance of a *decrease* in the tariff rates on imported hay and manure forks. The original investigation of the commission into the statutory rates had followed on the heels of the adoption of the statute itself, having been directed by Senate Resolution No. 295 of June 18, 1930. President Hoover had refused to approve the commission's report of December 14, 1932, and had directed the commission to undertake the investigation which resulted in the commission's supplemental report of February 24, 1933. Although the latter report went to President Hoover, he took no action upon it, and it was subsequently approved by President Roosevelt, who used it as the basis for his Proclamation No. 2044 of April 3, 1933, announcing the maximum permissible decrease in the statutory rates of duty on various agricultural hand tools. The appellant sought to have the members of the Tariff Commission called as witnesses to show "whether any additional information had been presented to the President, except that which was contained in the formal report," hoping, of course, to attack the validity of the proclamation by proving that he had acted on the basis of confidential information not of record. The court denied this request and upheld the proclamation, largely on the basis of the Supreme Court's decision in *Norwegian Nitrogen Products II* under the earlier statute, declaring:

The communications which the individual members of the United States Tariff Commission may make, or fail to make, to the President, aside from the report and findings of the commission as specified by law, are not matters of public record, and in our opinion, are not subject to investigation by this court.[71]

The judicial pendulum reversed itself sharply again in the very next case, in substantial measure, however, because of the fortuitous circumstance that John Parker, chief judge of the Second Circuit Court of Appeals and an old foe of bureaucracy, sat by special assignment with the C.C.P.A. on this case during the absence of one of the regular members of that court. He also delivered the opinion for the court,[72] and although he upheld the validity of the presidential proclamation, he did so only after subjecting the recommendations of the commission, on which it was based, to the "substantial evidence" test, remarking: "It is settled that, where an order of a commission can be made only after hearing, it is void if unsupported by the evidence. *Chicago Junction* case, 264 U.S. 258."[73] But this ignores the clear differentiation made by the Supreme Court only three years previously in *Norwegian Nitrogen Products II* between the hearing process of a fact-finding body like the Tariff Commission and the control process of an "independent" regulatory commission such as the Interstate Commerce Commission, and this apart from the differences between the regulation of foreign and interstate commerce.

The dissenting judges were even more explicit. Judge Bland declared: "I find no substantial evidence in the record from which the commission or the President might properly conclude that there was such an article [as dried egg powder] produced."[74] Judge Garrett accused his colleagues of deliberately avoiding a conflict with the President,[75] even though such a conflict was basic to a resolution of the issues raised by the case:

In the final analysis the precise question here involved is that of the validity of the President's proclamation, not the validity of the commission's procedure or report. . . .

[I]t seems to me upon the facts developed by the commission's investigation the non-existence of a domestic albumen drying industry was established and hence that there was no valid basis for that part of the Executive proclamation relating to that product.[76]

However, it was the opinion of Judge Hatfield, who specially concurred in the result only, that charted the course to be followed by the Supreme Court when a suitable case finally reached it a year later. In essence, his position was that, whatever changes the 1930 act may have intended in the relations between the commission and the President, it did not expand the scope of judicial review beyond the standards set by the Supreme Court for the 1922 statute:

I am of the opinion that the findings and the proclamations of the President are legislative in character, and the prescribed forms of legislation having been regularly observed as they were in the instant case, are not subject to impeachment in any judicial proceeding, and that the proclaimed rate of duty here involved is "as conclusive as though fixed by the statute itself."[77]

As might have been anticipated, the court[78] was forced less than nine months later to declare that the *Moss* decision was not controlling, in the face of a request to have the testimony of the President taken with respect to the facts upon which he based his judgment. The proclamation in question had been signed by Hoover on December 2, 1931, so the issue was decidedly different than would have been a request for the interrogation of an incumbent President. As a private citizen in 1939, Hoover might not have enjoyed the immunity attaching to the office which would ordinarily render futile such a demand.[79] Neither can the President be compelled to consider the data in terms of which he is "required" to make his decision.[80] The combined effect of these two facts is to render pointless the attempts of Congress to transfer to the commission, by Section 336, the large area of discretion which Section 315 had recognized as properly vested in the President. The courts cannot get inside either the President's mind[81] or the White House Office to ascertain what factors have determined his decision one way instead of another, irrespective of the substance, weight, or conclusiveness of the evidence accompanying the commission's report.

The high-water mark in the scope of judicial review that the Court of Customs and Patent Appeals was willing to claim for itself was reached in the *Bush* case, which was also a three to two decision.[82] The question presented was whether the Tariff Commission had any statutory authority to take the period from December 1, 1930, to September 30, 1932, as a representative period with respect to the invoice price of values in Japanese currency, and, because "the exchange rate of the Japanese yen for the dollar" was much below par in 1932, use the average rate of exchange during the year 1932 for the purpose of ascertaining the weighted average of invoice prices in United States currency for the period from December 1, 1930, to September 30, 1932. The court held that the commission's "mistake in law" invalidated the President's proclamation of May 1, 1934, increasing the customs duty on canned clams:

It clearly appears from the commission's report that its investigation . . . and its findings . . . were based upon an erroneous conception of the statutory provision. . . .

[A] legal investigation by the Tariff Commission . . . has not been made. . . .

We must hold, therefore, that as the investigation made by the Tariff Commission was illegal . . . the proclamation of the President, based upon such investigation, was without authority of law, illegal, and void.[83]

Making an abrupt about-face from his position in the *Moss* case, Judge Lenroot now dissented:

The predecessor of section 336 was section 315 of the Tariff Act of 1922. One of the principal differences between the two sections is that in section 315 the President, in arriving at his determination, was not confined to a consideration of the facts secured by the commission, while under section 336 he is so limited. . . .

[U]nder the Tariff Act of 1930 the President is bound by the testimony adduced before the commission, while under the act of 1922 he was not. . . . Here, as there, the President is not bound by *the findings* of the commission, and here, as there, it is fallacious to argue that error committed by the Tariff Commission in *its findings* "may invalidate the President's finding and proclamation."[84]

The Supreme Court granted certiorari and reversed in a decision that is now recognized as the leading case on the President's powers under the flexible tariff. If this case could have been decided ten years earlier, most of the foregoing litigation would have been obviated. The essence of the decision was that, since the statute was silent as to how foreign exchange value was to be determined, the Court would not disturb the President's judgment *no matter what method* he should adopt. His judgment as to facts, after he followed the procedures outlined in the act, was held to be not subject to re-examination by the judiciary; in other words, his acceptance of the commission's fact-finding made it *substantively conclusive.* His judgment that it was *necessary* to change existing tariff rates and to adopt those recommended by the commission in order to accomplish the purposes of the act was likewise immune from judicial review:

[T]he . . . Act . . . does not permit judicial examination of the judgment of the President that the rates of duty recommended by the Commission are necessary to equalize the differences in the domestic and foreign costs of production. . . .

In substance and to a great extent in form . . . the action of the Commission and the President is but one stage of the legislative process. . . . And the judgment of the President that on the facts, adduced in pursuance of the procedure prescribed by Congress, a change of rate is necessary is no more subject to judicial review under this statutory scheme than if Congress itself had exercised that judgment. . . .

For the judiciary to probe the reasoning which underlies this Proclamation would amount to a clear invasion of the legislative and executive domains. . . . Here the President acted in full conformity with the statute. No question of law is raised when the exercise of his discretion is challenged.[85]

The Court did, however, state that the Customs Court would be justified in holding a presidential proclamation invalid on any of the following grounds: (1) The Tariff Commission did not make an investigation as prescribed by statute. (2) The President acted contrary to the provisions of the statute. (3) The commission's actions were not fair and impartial.

There has been only one subsequent and relevant decision.[86] Here an old horse was trotted out to be whipped again, but without success. The *Duche* case raised the identical substantive issue — the rate of duty on dried egg albumen — and challenged the same presidential proclamation of June 24, 1931, T.D. 44887, that was involved in the *Moss* case. But Judge Hatfield's concurring opinion in *Moss* was expressly followed by the majority in the *Duche* case, which ruled that the Supreme Court's decision in *Norwegian Nitrogen Products II,* holding presidential action valid if procedurally consistent with the Tariff Act (of 1922), was also applicable and to be followed in this decision under the 1930 act. Particularly was that case to be followed on the point that hearings before the Tariff Commission are *not* judicial in nature, and that confidential information may be relied on by either the commission or the President, or both. In accordance with the Su-

162

preme Court decision in the *Bush* case, the C.C.P.A. held that it had no power to review the fact-finding of the commission.

As the result of the Supreme Court's liberality in the *Bush* case and the consequent acquiescence of the C.C.P.A. in the *Duche* case, it is now considered that there are no significant differences between Section 315 and Section 336 insofar as the judiciary and the scope of judicial review are concerned; so the President emerges in law as he had been all along in practice: immune from any effective control by these specialized administrative courts, unless he should make some flagrant departure from the limited procedural standards outlined by the statutes — which he could not afford to do, in any event, *for political reasons*.

In spite of the fact that presidential rule-making has been more thoroughly and systematically subjected to judicial scrutiny here than in any other substantive area, in only a single instance has a presidential proclamation under either of the flexible tariff acts been held unconstitutional after the final judicial disposition of the case challenging its validity, and that exception was clearly overruled in the first subsequent C.C.P.A. case to reach the Supreme Court.

The decisions of these administrative courts, and even more so the four decisions of the Supreme Court, have laid the basis for the exercise of a pattern of executive power which has importance far transcending the substantive issues involved in the flexible tariff cases. The rudiments of the design are disarmingly simple: vest power in the President by statutory delegation, guide his discretion with a mandatory fact-finding process, and then recognize that he may also depend upon confidential sources of information in coming to a decision. This adds up to executive finality, because the resulting presidential regulations are practically unimpeachable: neither administrative advice nor the political judgments of the President are subject to judicial review.

Notes

[1] Dooley v. United States, 182 U.S. 222 (1901); Lincoln v. United States, 197 U.S. 419 (1905), 202 U.S. 484 (1906).

[2] Carl Zeiss, Inc. v. United States, 23 C.C.P.A. (Customs) 7 (1935).

[3] Field v. Clark, 143 U.S. 649 (1891); Hampton & Co. v. United States, 276 U.S. 394 (1927); United States v. Bush & Co., 310 U.S. 371 (1940).

[4] Albridge v. Williams, 3 How. 9 (1845).

[5] See, for example, Harrison's proclamation of July 31, 1891, exempting certain items from the tariff of the act of October 1, 1890, with the object of securing reciprocal trade between the United States and Spain. Richardson, *op. cit.*, IX, 148.

THE CHIEF OF STATE

[6] 143 U.S. 649 (1891).

[7] The reporter labels this opinion by Justice Lamar and Chief Justice Fuller a "dissent," but it is evident that they in fact voted with the majority on the question of the disposition of the case, but disagreed as to the constitutionality of Section 3 of the act of 1890, which they correctly argued was an issue not properly before the Court.

[8] B. Altman & Co. v. United States, 224 U.S. 583, 601 (1912).

[9] Section 350(a), 48 *Stat.* 943–944.

[10] Wislar v. United States, 97 F. 2d 152, 154 (C.C.P.A., 1938). Other cases have been concerned with the effect of exceptions to most-favored-nation clauses, which could be made by either Congress or the President. Thus, the exclusive preference given to Cuban imports under the Cuban Trade Agreement of 1934, modifying the Cuban Treaty of 1902, did not extend to countries with which the United States has either conditional or unconditional trade agreements because of the intent of Congress to create an exception in the case of Cuba, Louis Wolf & Co. v. United States, 107 F. 2d 819 (C.C.P.A., 1939); and the trade agreement with the United Kingdom, T.D. 49753, did not apply to importations from Germany because of the express prior exception created by presidential proclamation, T.D. 49752, excluding German merchandise from the benefits accorded in trade agreements, United States v. Mill and Mine Supply Co., 30 C.C.P.A. (Customs) 128, 133 (1942).

[11] 9 Howard 603 (1850).

[12] *Ibid.*, 614.

[13] *Ibid.*, 612.

[14] *Ibid.*, 616.

[15] Galban & Co. v. United States, 40 Ct. Cl. 495 (1905); affirmed in 207 U.S. 579 (1907).

[16] See Pedro E. Abelarde, *American Tariff Policy towards the Philippines* (New York: King's Crown Press, 1947), p. 39. For more recent judicial comment on the question Does the Constitution Follow the Flag? See separate and delayed concurring opinion of Justice Douglas, Hirota v. MacArthur, 338 U.S. 197, 204 (June 27, 1949); and the dissenting opinion of Justices Black, Douglas, and Burton in Johnson v. Eisentrager, 339 U.S. 763, 796–797 (June 5, 1950).

[17] DeLima v. Bidwell, 182 U.S. 1 (1901). Although there was a loophole until May 1, 1900, Congress had already remedied this situation and applied the Dingley Tariff to Puerto Rican exports to the United States by the adoption of the Foraker Act which became effective on that date, and which was upheld as constitutional in a later decision on the same day, Downes v. Bidwell, 182 U.S. 244 (1901).

[18] Dooley v. United States (Dooley I), 182 U.S. 222, 235–236 (1901). There is little question but that the President intended the tariff to be used to pay part of the costs of military occupation throughout the period of occupation and military rule, which extended on into the period after Puerto Rico had become a possession of the United States. Nevertheless, the Court avoided an express ruling that the executive orders were unconstitutional by indulging the presumption that the President did not intend to exceed his constitutional powers. The power of Congress to levy a tariff on imports to Puerto Rico from the United States, by the adoption of the Foraker Act, was subsequently upheld in the second *Dooley* case, Dooley v. United States, 183 U.S. 151 (1901).

[19] 182 U.S. 222, 234. But what have the tariff *laws*, in substance or spirit, to do with military contributions upon the enemy? And who was the "enemy" after the peace treaty had been signed? Certainly, the United States was not legally at war with any of its new possessions. If the President could, as Commander in Chief, levy a tariff on Puerto Rican imports from foreign countries after Puerto Rico had become national territory of the United States, and the Congress could levy a tariff on Puerto Rican imports from the United States, a rational basis for the Court's distinction is most difficult to comprehend.

164

Presidential Control over the Tariff

[20] Therefore, the question of whether, under the theory of separation of powers, the possessor of authority to levy such tariff duties was the Congress alone, or the President also, was at best an incidental and collateral issue which was subordinated in the thinking of the justices to the more fundamental question of whether there was any constitutional power for the national government to place such a tax upon what was clearly no longer *foreign* commerce.

[21] The fragmentation of the Court was so complete by the time *Downes v. Bidwell* (upholding the statutory tariff on imports to the United States from Puerto Rico) was reached that there wasn't even a majority opinion: Brown "announced the conclusion and judgment of the court"; White, Shiras, and McKenna concurred together in a different opinion; Gray concurred separately; Fuller, Brewer, and Peckham joined in a dissenting opinion; and Harlan dissented separately.

[22] Ho Tung & Co. v. United States, 42 Ct. Cl. 213, 227–228 (1907). The Secretary of War had, in any event, directed by his own order of October 13, 1898, that the presidential tariff should not go into effect until November 10, 1898.

[23] Lincoln v. United States; Warner, Barnes & Co., Ltd., v. United States, 197 U.S. 419, 429 (1905). For the text of the executive order of July 12, 1898, see Senate Documents, 56th Cong., 1st Sess. (1899–1900), Vol. XXV, p. 269; for a general documentation of this subject, see Charles E. Magoon, *Reports on the Law of Civil Government in Territory Subject to Military Occupation by the Military Forces of the United States* (Washington, D.C.: GPO, 1902), pp. 210–251; for congressional debate on the statutes which were enacted in an unsuccessful attempt retroactively to approve the collection of duties on imports from the United States under the executive order, see 35 *Congressional Record*, Part VII, p. 6867; 35 *Congressional Record*, Part VI, p. 5730; 40 *Congressional Record*, Part X, pp. 9407, 9514–9515; and for the "inside story" by the sponsor of the ratifying statute, who was also the first civil governor of the Philippines responsible for the collection of the tariff under the act of the Philippines Commission, see William Howard Taft, *Our Chief Magistrate and his Powers* (New York: Columbia University Press, 1916), pp. 99–102.

[24] For five years until the organic act for the Philippines was adopted, the Philippines (Taft) Commission enacted legislation for the territory "By authority of the President of the United States." The executive order was superseded by the act of the Philippines Commission effective September 6, 1901.

[25] 32 *Stat.* 54

[26] 32 *Stat.* 691, especially Section 2.

[27] Lincoln v. United States, 197 U.S. 419, 429 (1905), unanimous opinion; approved on rehearing with two members dissenting, 202 U.S. 484, 498, 500 (1906). By implication only, the latter opinion appears to indicate that the Court may have considered the executive tariff to have been ratified by the act of July 1, 1902, as applied to goods imported from *foreign* countries, but the Court was never called upon to decide this point. What the Court said was that while the statute was so ambiguous that it could not be construed retroactively to ratify the duties in controversy, there were nevertheless duties which had been levied and collected other than those in controversy to which the act clearly applied; and that the question of validity *as to them* was put to rest by this ratification (which seems to be a somewhat ambiguous statement in its own rights.) See particularly Taft, *op. cit.*, pp. 101–102; the remarks of Representative Olmstead, 40 *Congressional Record*, Part X, p. 9407; and Paragraph 5 of the Spooner Bill, S. 6362, introduced June 5, 1906, 40 *Congressional Record*, Part X, p. 9514.

[28] Act of June 30, 1906 (34 *Stat.* 636), a rider to a deficiency appropriation bill. How Congress could thus ratify an executive order during a period in which, according to the decision in the first *Lincoln* case, *supra*, the order was neither in effect *nor intended to be in effect*, the Court does not explain. Even for the Supreme Court, rationalization of the ratification of a legally nonexistent executive order posed certain inherent difficulties.

It might seem that the language quoted above was as comprehensive in its terms as a Congress which had been twice frustrated could make it, but such did not prove to be the case. Seven years later, the Court held that the executive orders of July 12, 1898, and December 21, 1898 (which directed the collection of duties during military occupation at ports and places in the possession of the forces of the United States) did not authorize the collection of duties on goods imported into ports of the Philippine Islands under the control of the *de facto* insurgent government (which enacted its own import duties); and this collection was not ratified by the act of June 30, 1906. MacLeod v. United States, 229 U.S. 416 (1913).

[29] For instance, The Prize Cases, 2 Black 635 (1863).

[30] United States v. Heinszen, 206 U.S. 370, 382, 385, 386 (1907). Italics supplied. This is precisely the sort of judicial process which Justice Robert Jackson criticized in his *The Struggle for Judicial Supremacy* (New York: Knopf, 1941), especially Chapter IX: the decision of fundamental questions of public law and public policy as though the issue were a question of the property rights of individual citizens. As a dissenting justice in one of the *Insular Cases* put it, the majority opinion (by Brown) discussed sovereignty as though it were akin to gaining a clear title to a piece of real estate! But compare the dissenting opinion of Justice Frankfurter in United States v. California, 332 U.S. 19, 45 (1947).

White, who delivered the opinion for the Court and the language quoted above, was elevated to the position of chief justice by Taft in 1910. For Taft's own interesting comment on the relationship between this decision and White's promotion, see Taft, *op. cit.*, p. 102.

[31] Norwegian Nitrogen Products Co. v. United States Tariff Commission, 6 F. 2d 491 (C.A.D.C., 1925).

[32] Norwegian Nitrogen Products Co. v. United States Tariff Commission (Norwegian Nitrogen I), 274 U.S. 106, 112 (1927).

[33] J. W. Hampton, Jr. & Co. v. United States, 14 C.C.A. 350, 367–369 (1927). Italics supplied. Of course, the point in Congress having selected the President for participation in this administrative process is precisely that he is *not* an appraiser of merchandise; he is the "sole organ of the nation" in its relations with other states, and is in a position to have access to information available to no one else, in addition to that furnished him by the Tariff Commission, in coming to a decision with respect to changes in tariff rates, the effects of which can obviously never be felt exclusively in this country. Furthermore, the President *does* enjoy a peculiar sanctity and inviolability; see Chapter 11, *infra*. Notoriously, members of the Congress, officials of the government who perform similar fact-finding duties, enjoy a peculiar sanctity and inviolability when engaged in committee investigations, and are largely immune from judicial review.

The Supreme Court affirmed this decision of the Court of Customs Appeals, but ignored the long dictum quoted above, and confined its discussion to the only question actually before either court: the validity of the delegation of power to the President, which was upheld. Hampton & Co. v. United States, 276 U.S. 394 (1928).

[34] Foster v. United States (Foster I), 20 C.C.P.A. (Customs) 15 (1932), affirmed on rehearing, 26 C.C.P.A. (Customs) 59 (1938), and not appealed to the Supreme Court. Norwegian Nitrogen Products Co. v. United States, 20 C.C.P.A. (Customs) 27 (1932); affirmed in 228 U.S. 294 (1933) and discussed below. United States v. Fox River Butter Co., 20 C.C.P.A. (Customs) 38 (1932); c.d. 287 U.S. 628 (1932). United States v. Blandamer, 20 C.C.P.A. (Customs) 45 (1932); c.d. 287 U.S. 628 (1932). United States v. S. Leon & Co., 20 C.C.P.A. (Customs) 49 (1932); c.d. 287 U.S. 628 (1932).

[35] 20 C.C.P.A. (Customs) 15, 18, 20–21 (1932).

[36] "The question of whether the President has proceeded in conformity with the law in proclaiming certain changes in customs duties is . . . a justiciable one which may be adjudicated in the proper forum." *Ibid.*, 23.

[37] "[I]ts conclusions and report thereon, if any, are not, under this statute, binding upon the President. He may follow or disregard them. He may use information derived

from other departments of the Government or other sources in his investigation and finding." *Ibid.*, 22.

[38] *Ibid.*, 25.

[39] "He may arrive at his conclusions from information . . . which . . . may be privately conveyed and confidentially received . . . it is fallacious to argue that possible error committeed by the Tariff Commission, or failure of proof before that body, may invalidate the President's finding and proclamation . . . hearing before the United States Tariff Commission is provided by law 'to assist the President,' not to control him." *Idem.*

[40] Fox River Butter Co. v. United States, T.D. 44667 (1931).

[41] 20 C.C.P.A. (Customs) 38, 44 (1932).

[42] Harry Blandamer v. United States, T.D. 45083 (1931).

[43] S. Leon & Co. v. United States, T.Ab. 17508 (1931). This was the identical argument raised before and rejected by the Supreme Court with respect to Section 336 of the 1930 statute in United States v. Bush & Co., 310 U.S. 371 (1940), *infra*.

[44] United States v. Blandamer, 20 C.C.P.A. (Customs) 45, 49 (1932).

[45] United States v. S. Leon & Co., 20 C.C.P.A. (Customs) 49, 53 (1932).

[46] Norwegian Nitrogen Products Co. v. United States, 20 C.C.P.A. (Customs) 27, 34 (1932).

[47] Norwegian Nitrogen Products Co. v. United States (Norwegian Nitrogen II), 288 U.S. 294 (1933).

[48] Akawo & Co. v. United States, 77 F. 2d 660 (C.C.P.A., 1935).

[49] Foster v. United States, 26 C.C.P.A. (Customs) 59, 62 (1938).

[50] It is interesting to note that both the acceptance of executive regulations as statutory amendments and the institutionalization of formal administrative advice to the Chief Executive, who must consider without necessarily following, are much more common in British than in American practice. See, on the first point, Henry VIII's Statute of Proclamations ("The King, for the time being, with the advice of his Council, or the more part of them, may set forth proclamations under such penalties and pains as to him and them shall seem necessary, which shall be observed as though they were made by Act of Parliament"; (1539) 31 Henry VIII, c. 8, s. 1) and the discussion in Schubert, "Judicial Review of Royal Proclamations and Orders-in-Council," *University of Toronto Law Journal*, 9: 92–93; and Bernard Schwartz, *Law and the Executive in Britain: A Comparative Study* (New York: New York University Press, 1949), pp. 50–64. On the second point, see Rex v. Home Secretary; *Ex parte* Lees (1941) 1 K.B. 72; and the comment in Schubert, *loc. cit.*, pp. 100–102.

[51] Tariff Act of June 17, 1930, Sec. 337 (46 *Stat.* 704; F.C.A. Title 19 s. 1337). The only material differences between the President's embargo power under this section and that under Section 316 of the Tariff Act of 1922 are these: (1) Section 316 of the 1922 act authorized Supreme Court review of the customs court decisions, by certiorari, whereas Section 337 made the decision of the Court of Customs and Patent Appeals final; and (2) the alternative remedy of additional penalty duties which the President was empowered to prescribe under Section 316 are dropped from Section 337, leaving exclusion as the only authorized sanction.

[52] Schechter v. United States, 295, U.S. 495, 533 ftn. 12 (1935).

[53] One obvious explanation is that the Congress has refrained from delegating such powers to the President in order to ensure review by the regular federal courts of the administrative action taken.

[54] Morgan v. United States, 298 U.S. 468 (1936).

[55] John Day Larkin, *The President's Control of the Tariff* (Cambridge: Harvard University Press, 1936). In domestic trade, the problem of patent infringement is one for the regular federal courts, although the pooling, suppression, and cross-licensing of patents has increasingly tended to assume importance in the work of the Federal Trade Commission, supposedly in forestalling the growth of monopoly and recourse to monopolistic practices.

167

[56] The Tariff Commission had previously on April 16, 1926, made its report to President Coolidge recommending temporary exclusion of the articles complained of pending the completion of the commission's investigation. On the basis of this report, the President had promulgated an exclusion order on April 22, 1926. The following December 2, 1926, the commission recommended modification of the exclusion order because Bakelite's patent expired on December 6, 1926. A modifying order was accordingly issued by the Secretary of the Treasury, by direction of the President.

[57] An attempt to prohibit the Court of Customs Appeals from entertaining the appeal from the Tariff Commission failed in *Ex parte* Bakelite Corporation, 279 U.S. 438 (1929).

[58] Frischer & Co. v. Bakelite Corp., 39 F. 2d 247 (1930); c.d. sub. nom. Frischer & Co. v. Tariff Commission, 282 U.S. 852 (1930). The last chapter on this particular exclusion order was written by the Circuit Court of Appeals for the Second Circuit in Frischer & Co. v. Elting, 60 F. 2d 711 (1932), which held that the President's order to a customs collector to export the excluded merchandise was final.

[59] J. W. Hampton, Jr. & Co. v. United States, 14 C.C.A. 350, and 276 U.S. 394 (1928).

[60] 39 F. 2d 247, 263 (C.C.P.A., 1930). A similar conclusion was reached by the Supreme Court in Chicago & Southern Air Lines v. Waterman S.S. Co., 333 U.S. 103 (1948), discussed in Chapter 4, above.

[61] *In re* Northern Pigment Co., 71 F. 2d 447, 456–457 (1934).

[62] *In re* Orion Co., 71 F. 2d 458, 468 (1934).

[63] *Idem.*

[64] 46 *Stat.* (Part I) 701.

[65] He had actually made subclassifications within some of the statutory classifications. This was absolutely necessary in order to carry out the purposes of the act. As the *Fox River* decision had pointed out, there might be over a hundred distinct varieties of cheese included within the statutory classification, some of which were competitive with domestic manufactures and some of which were noncompetitive. It was essential to distinguish between these in order to equalize differences in the costs of production, as the act required.

[66] Sears, Roebuck & Co. v. United States, T.D. 45534, 61 T.D. 679, 686 (1932).

[67] United States v. Sears, Roebuck & Co., 20 C.C.P.A. (Customs) 295, 304 (1932).

[68] Feltex Corp. v. Dutchess Hat Works, 21 C.C.P.A. (Customs) 463, 476 (1934). Italics supplied.

[69] Carl Zeiss, Inc. v. United States, 23 C.C.P.A. (Customs) 7, 14, 16 (1935). No petition for a writ of certiorari was filed by the solicitor general in this case, but the decision was implicitly overruled (although not directly mentioned) by the Supreme Court when it decided the *Bush* case, *infra*, a few years later.

[70] United States v. Best & Co., 86 F. 2d 23 (C.C.P.A., 1936).

[71] Union Fork & Hoe Co. v. United States, 86 F. 2d 423, 428–429 (C.C.P.A., 1936). The court also specifically disclaimed any right to review the weight or sufficiency of evidence on which the commission based its report where an investigation had been made, and held that they could not hold the proclamation invalid for lack of a proper investigation where the commission had complied with the procedural prerequisites by holding a public hearing, with due notice for domestic producers, and this appeared in the record.

[72] This case split the court wide open, with five judges writing four different opinions, so there was no majority opinion. Since Judge Lenroot accepted Judge Parker's statement, it became the official opinion of the court.

[73] David Moss & Co. v. United States, 26 C.C.P.A. (Customs) 381, 384 (1939). To Judge Parker, a commission was a commission, and a bureaucrat was a bureaucrat.

[74] *Ibid.*, 398. Actually, his other remarks indicated that what he really insisted upon was the preponderance or weight of evidence in support.

In another case decided later the same year, the primary issue was whether the classification made by the same proclamation at issue in the *Moss* case, that of June 24, 1931, was correct. The court examined the facts underlying the commission's recommendation of this classification, and found that the *weight of evidence* did support their findings. Oppelman v. United States, 27 C.C.P.A. (Customs) 227 (1940).

[75] The same charge that was later levied against their respective colleagues by Judge Denham of the Circuit Court of Appeals for the Ninth Circuit in the *Korematsu* case and by Justice Roberts in his separate concurrence to the Supreme Court's decision in the *Endo* case. See Chapter 7.

[76] David Moss & Co. v. United States, 26 C.C.P.A. (Customs) 381, 393, 396 (1939).

[77] *Ibid.*, 392. It is interesting to note that the decision of the majority in this, the *Moss* case, was expressly overruled a decade later in T. M. Duche & Sons, Inc. v. United States, 36 C.C.P.A. (Customs) 19 (1948), in view of the intervening decision of the Supreme Court in the *Bush* case, *infra*, which was expressly followed. Judge Hatfield himself was, of course, with the majority in the *Duche* decision; Presiding Judge Garrett, whose dissent was quoted above, dissented in the later case as well.

[78] This time, without the assistance of visiting Judge Parker.

[79] See Chapter 11, *infra*; and for a unique attempt to sue a former President for his official acts while in office, see Livingston v. Jefferson, 15 Fed. Cas. 660 (C.Ct.Va., 1811), No. 8411.

[80] Westergaard Berg-Johnson Co. v. United States, 27 C.C.P.A. (Customs) 207, 215–216 (1939).

[81] Compare the dictum of the second Morgan case: "we agree with the Government's contention that it was not the function of the [trial] court to probe the mental processes of the Secretary [of Agriculture] in reaching his conclusions if he gave the hearing which the law required." Morgan v. United States, 304 U.S. 1, 18 (1938).

[82] Bush & Co. v. United States, 27 C.C.P.A. (Customs) 64 (1939).

[83] *Ibid.*, 72–73.

[84] *Ibid.*, 75–76. Italics supplied.

[85] United States v. Bush & Co., 310 U.S. 371, 379–380 (1940).

[86] T. M. Duche & Sons, Inc. v. United States, 36 C.C.P.A. (Customs) 19, 26 (1948), certiorari denied, 336 U.S. 931 (1949).

III

The Commander in Chief:
Imperium in Imperio

"If the Fathers of the Constitution intended that a dictatorship should exist under any emergency, they would not leave it to the chief executive to assume it when he may, in his discretion, declare necessity required it. . . . That the president can of his own accord assume dictatorial power, under any pretext, is an extravagant presumption." Jones v. Seward, 40 Barbour (N.Y.) 563, 570 (1863)

"In these days of lightning war this country does not have to submit to destruction while it awaits the slow process of Constitutional amendment." United States v. Gordon Hirabayashi, 46 F. Supp. 657, 662 (1942)

"Executive power over aliens, undelayed and unhampered by litigation, has been deemed, throughout our history, essential to war-time security. . . . The resident enemy alien is constitutionally subject to summary arrest, internment and deportation whenever a 'declared war' exists Courts will entertain his plea for freedom from Executive custody only to ascertain the existence of a state of war and whether he is an alien enemy and so subject to the Alien Enemy Act. Once these jurisdictional elements have been determined, courts will not inquire into any other issue as to his internment." Johnson v. Eisentrager, 339 U.S. 763, 774–775 (1950)

"Even though 'theater of war' be an expanding concept, we cannot with faithfulness to our constitutional system hold that the Commander in Chief of the Armed Forces has the ultimate power as such to take possession of private property in order to keep labor disputes from stopping production. This is a job for the Nation's lawmakers, not for its military authorities." Youngstown Sheet & Tube Co. v. Sawyer, 343 U.S. 579, 587 (1952)

6

Military Necessity and Executive Power

Military Command

CALLING OUT THE TROOPS

THE power of military command sometimes has been confused with the power to raise armies. It would certainly appear at first blush that the President has no constitutional power to create the armies that, once they are raised and equipped, are subject to his command.[1] Nevertheless, the President has always been delegated considerable discretion in implementing the plans of Congress, especially with respect to the circumstances in which the reserves might be called up for temporary duty in time of national emergency proclaimed by the President himself. This was true in George Washington's time, as it is today.

The act of February 28, 1795, authorized the President to call out the militia in cases of actual invasion, or of imminent danger of invasion; and in cases of insurrection in any state against the government thereof, on the application of the state legislature, or the governor when the legislature was not in session. Two well-known early decisions of the Supreme Court upheld the exclusive and conclusive power of the Commander in Chief to determine both the fact of the existence of such an emergency and the necessity for and conditions governing the use of troops. In the first instance, the Court ruled against the claimed right of a militiaman to dispute the orders and judgment of the President;[2] and in the second case, the Supreme Court ruled against judicial review by the courts themselves.[3] There were, of course, several other early occasions on which the President called out the militia, but they did not lead to cases challenging the authority of the President before the Supreme Court.[4] These two cases that did, arising from the War of 1812 and from Dorr's Rebellion in Rhode Island, laid the cornerstone for the legal edifice supporting the theory under which President Lincoln prosecuted the Civil War. Thus, although Justice Woodbury dissented in *Luther v. Borden*, he agreed with Chief Justice Taney and the rest of the Court that there was no doubt about the President's power to intervene:

But he issued no orders or proclamations. Had he done so, and marched troops, though the action of the Executive under the standing law is not waging war, yet, I concede, it is attempting to suppress domestic violence by force of arms, and in doing it *the President may possess and exert some belligerent rights in some extreme stages of armed opposition. . . .* The President has been considered the paramount and final judge as to this, whether in invasion or rebellion; and not the governors or legislatures of States. This was fully settled during the war of 1812 with England. (3 Story's Com. on Const. sec. 1206; 11 Johns. (N.Y.) 150.) He may then issue his proclamation for those in insurrection to disperse, and, if not dispersing, he may afterwards call out the militia to aid in effecting it.[5]

During the early months of the Civil War, Lincoln justified his action in calling out the militia, raising an army of volunteers, and exercising belligerent rights against the "rebels" on the basis of his statutory powers under the act of 1795 together with his implied constitutional powers flowing from his status as Commander in Chief. He issued two proclamations to raise an army before the Congress was convened. By the first, issued on April 15, 1861, he delayed calling Congress into special session for almost three months (the date set by the proclamation was July 4, 1861). In the meantime, since the laws could not be enforced by the ordinary processes of government in certain states, President Lincoln announced that by authority of "the power in me vested by the constitution and laws" he was calling out 75,000 militia to suppress "combinations" in certain named states; and he called upon loyal citizens resident therein to support the Union.[6] Two weeks later, on May 3, 1861, the President found that the existence of an emergency requiring "immediate and adequate measures" to save the Union made indispensable the need for additional troops.[7] The "combinations" of April 15 had by now become "insurrectionary combinations." It is also noteworthy that in the second proclamation Lincoln made no pretense of invoking any statute as the source of his authority, relying instead upon the formal assumption of his title of "Commander in Chief." As such, he apparently assumed himself to possess, in the interim until Congress should meet, the full scope of the national war power as the military leader of the nation, including those rights accruing to a belligerent under the law of nations. His proclamation called into the service of the United States 42,034 volunteers, ordered the enlargement of the regular Army, and directed the enlistment of additional seamen. It could hardly be claimed that the act of 1795 contemplated such action as this, so the proclamation anticipated congressional acquiescence by promising that "The call for volunteers hereby made and the direction for the increase together with the plan of organization adopted for the volunteer and for the regular forces hereby authorized, will be submitted to Congress as soon as assembled." Thus presented with a *fait accompli*, Congress did proceed to ratify both of these proclamations by the act of August 6, 1861.

The earlier proclamation calling up the militia does not appear to have been challenged in the courts; and the constitutionality of the proclamation of May 3 was upheld by the Supreme Court in *United States v. Hosmer*, where a veteran's right to a bonus, which depended upon General Order No. 15 of the War Department of May 4, 1861, was conditioned upon the legality of his enlistment in the Army. Hosmer was one of those who had volunteered in response to the President's call; needless to say, it would have entailed harsh judgment to have denied his claims as a patriotic citizen, even though the war had been over for five years when the Court acted. Expressing some doubts as to what might have been the constitutional status of the naked proclamation resting only on the authority under which the President presumed to issue it (and action subsequently was taken), the Supreme Court found that the Bill of Indemnity conclusively laid to rest all such questions:

The 3rd section of the Act of August 6th, 1861 [12 Stat at L. 326], declares that "all acts, proclamations, and orders of the President of the United States, after the 4th of March, 1861, respecting the army and navy of the United States, and calling out or relating to the militia or volunteers from the States, are hereby approved, and in all respects legalized and made valid, to the same intent, and with the same effect, as if they had been issued and done under the previous express authority of the Congress of the United States."

This made the case of the petitioner complete. It was unquestionably within the proclamation and orders *thus legalized*.[8]

MILITARY CONSCRIPTION OF MANPOWER

The mass citizen army is a characteristic of modern warfare, and the draft was used for the first time in the United States in our first modern war, the Civil War. The action of President Lincoln in raising such an army under delegated statutory authority was upheld in several cases decided by state courts. An act of July 17, 1862 (which amended the act of February 28, 1795), empowered the President to make necessary rules and regulations for drafting the militia in cases where the laws of the states had not made a sufficient provision for that purpose. The formal distinctions in classifying executive orders which we draw today were unknown at this time (the numbered series of executive orders begins with Lincoln's first term), and Lincoln acted through the agency of the War Department. General Order No. 99 set up the method of selecting, drawing, and enforcing the attendance of the militia in the respective states; and General Order No. 104 provided for the arrest of persons absenting themselves to avoid being drafted into military service. The Court of Common Pleas of Dauphin County, Pennsylvania, decided that the President's order "must be considered as having all the force of a law, the same as if specially set forth at length in the act";[9] and the Supreme Court of Wisconsin also expressly upheld the validity of these regulations. The argument that the President had been unconstitutionally delegated legislative power was expressly rejected on the now-familiar basis that in merely filling in the details of the statute he was undertaking a necessary part of his function of executing its provisions;[10] and the same court confirmed this decision four years later in a postwar suit for civil damages against the wartime chief executive of the state.

Drueker, one of the leaders in the mob riots against the draft in Wisconsin, had been held in military custody by Governor Salomon for twelve days before he was transferred to the custody of federal officials. The governor asserted that he had held Drueker "no longer than in my opinion . . . was necessary to suppress the insurrection and enforce the laws," and pointed to *Martin v. Mott* in justification of his own actions and the presidential regulations on which they were based. The Supreme Court of Wisconsin agreed, and wrote an opinion which recognized the governor as an agent of the President, even going so far as to suggest that the governor's discretionary actions which were challenged in this case must "be regarded, in a certain sense, as the acts of the president." [11]

Apart from the question of the validity of the statute and regulations, and the power to prevent active interference with the system of induction, there remained the power of the President to cause the arrest of draft dodgers for the purpose of forcibly inducting them into military service. This, too, was approved by the Supreme Court of New Hampshire. [12]

The Supreme Court of the United States was not called upon to face these constitutional questions until it decided the *Selective Draft Law* cases half a century later. [13] The authority of Congress to delegate power to the President by the National Defense Act of June 3, 1916, and the Selective Draft Law of May 18, 1917, already had been upheld by a federal district court; [14] this decision also had upheld the President's action in ordering the compulsory induction into the service of the United States of all officers and enlisted men of the National Guard. It is true that the pattern of administrative controls set up under the World War I statute was more complex than that of the Civil War, and was keyed to local civilian rather than to federal military enforcement processes, but the issue had been foreclosed to those who sought at this late date to challenge President Wilson's authority. The legal and practical precedents had been nailed down by the uncontravened constitutional example established by Lincoln in the much more raw and desperate circumstances of the Civil War. Certainly the delegation of power to the President in the 1917 statute was exceptionally broad, [15] and the arguments against it pressed upon the Court were equally so. [16] The Supreme Court did not deem it necessary or expedient to consider such questions, however, and summarily rejected the challenges to the President's power on the ground that *they had already been conclusively determined.* [17] This judgment came at the tag end of a unanimous opinion that otherwise was preoccupied with an exhaustive review of federal-state questions, all of which had been settled in the period before or during the Civil War. Nevertheless, the accepted rule associated with this case is that Congress may delegate authority to the President to raise an army by selective draft. Congress sets the major policy, defines the power delegated to the President, and gives him authority to draw up an administrative plan for implementing the legislative policy, together with the power to subdelegate his powers to federal and state officials.[18]

The President's power to subdelegate his statutory powers to raise an army under the later Selective Service and Training Act of 1940 was upheld by the Supreme Court in an opinion which assumed the constitutionality of the statute itself, even though it had been adopted at a time when the United States was still technically at peace.[19] Both the Selective Service and Training Act of 1948 and President Truman's Proclamation No. 2799, which established the legal obligation for registration under the statute, were expressly upheld as constitutional in a criminal case involving defendants who had failed to register.[20] And the Supreme Court subsequently upheld the President's discretionary power to refuse to grant a commission to a drafted physician who refused to execute an oath and an affidavit disavowing affiliation with the Communist party or other "subversive" organizations.[21]

The integrated administrative system established on the basis of presidentially authorized Selective Service Regulations was challenged by a conscientious objector who denied that the President had any power to assign him, against his will, to "work of national importance." The Court of Appeals for the First Circuit affirmed the conviction, after a jury trial, of this objector who had refused to go to a work camp. The court rejected his contentions that the act unconstitutionally delegated legislative power to the President by failing to establish any standards to guide the President in determining what was "work of national importance." It certainly did not authorize the "internment" of conscientious objectors in "concentration camps" as the appellant claimed; and neither would the court undertake to say that labor in a national forest was not "work of national importance."[22] An equally unsuccessful attempt to attack the relevant rules and regulations, as being inconsistent with the statute on which they were based, was made on behalf of six objectors who had been convicted and imprisoned for having gone A.W.O.L.; and in this case an attempt was made to appeal to the Supreme Court, but certiorari was denied.[23] It is interesting to note that the two Supreme Court decisions most heavily leaned upon as precedents by the Circuit Courts of Appeals in these two cases involving conscientious objectors were *Ex parte Quirin*,[24] upholding the power of the military to try enemy spies before a special military commission, and *Hirabayashi v. United States*,[25] which approved a military curfew as applied to enemy aliens (and to American citizens who looked like enemy aliens). The curfew had been in effect in west coast cities during the first months of the war, when the possibility of invasion by a Japanese fleet seemed not impossible.

Only state courts had ruled upon the constitutionality of congressional delegation of power to the President under the Civil War draft law, and no cases challenging such delegation under World War II legislation ever reached the Supreme Court. The result of the Court's avoidance of the fundamental constitutional questions raised by the World War I *Arver* case has been that the power of the Commander in Chief to raise armies, with either prospective or retroactive approval by Congress, is now taken for granted on the basis of what was in fact done during our last three major wars; but the Supreme Court of the United States has not yet squarely faced the basic issue. Perhaps this is of little moment, since such a decision coming now would be anticlimactic; it is unthinkable that the Supreme Court should hold against the power of Congress and the President to raise armies by conscription in peacetime, limited or unlimited national emergency short of war *de jure*, or otherwise. Since this area of constitutional power has passed beyond the pale of justiciable controversy into the nebulous confines of a political question, the unlikely event of disagreement between the President and Congress — which would most likely mean independent presidential action based on the Lincolnian interpretation of the role of the Commander in Chief — would appear to be equally immune from any judgment on the part of the courts.

Military Justice

MILITARY LAW

As the Commander in Chief, the President has from the beginnings of our government functioned as the highest court of appeal for those subject to military law. As the Supreme Court put the matter some time ago, "To those in the military or naval service of the United States the military law is due process." [26] Consonant with such a premise, the decisions of courts-martial are not in any case subject to the direct review of the regular courts, and there have been exceedingly few instances in which the judgments of courts-martial have been subjected successfully to collateral attack in the courts. The rule followed consistently by the Supreme Court is that the only question open to the ex-

amination of the civil courts, when an attempt is made (almost invaria-
bly through the writ of habeas corpus) to impeach the judgment of a
court-martial, is that of jurisdiction. In other words, if the accused was
in fact subject to military law, if the offense was within the scope of
military law, and if the court-martial was lawfully constituted — i.e.,
according to the orders of a military commander authorized to appoint
the court-martial that acted — it is the duty of the civil court to dismiss the petition.[27] In a recent decision on this point, the Supreme
Court went even further and held that, as in cases arising under state
court systems, a person convicted by a court-martial must exhaust all
administrative remedies, including any made available after the petition for a writ of habeas corpus has been filed in a federal district court,
before such a federal court would be justified in granting a hearing to
entertain collateral attack on the court-martial's judgment. The Court
added that "Congress was legislating as respects tribunals over which
the civil courts have traditionally exercised no power of supervision or
review. See *In re Grimley*, 137 U.S. 147, 150. These tribunals have operated in a self-sufficient system, save only as habeas corpus was available to test their jurisdiction in specific cases."[28]

The Supreme Court's future position on precisely what is involved
in a civil court's examining the basis of a court-martial's "jurisdiction,"
is somewhat uncertain as the result of the fragmentation of the Court
in another recent case.[29] Three enlisted men were convicted by Air
Force courts-martial on Guam of having committed the crimes of rape
and murder, and they were sentenced to death, with the approval of
the President. The district court dismissed their petitions for habeas
corpus, finding that the prisoners were subject to the jurisdiction of
the courts-martial by which they had been tried.[30] The Court of Appeals of the District of Columbia affirmed the dismissal of the petitions, but only after an extensive review of the court-martial records,
basing its decision on the merits.[31] Four members of the Supreme
Court joined in an equivocal opinion stating that the review by civil
courts of court-martial decisions extends only to the question of jurisdiction, and that "the Court of Appeals may have erred in reweighing
each item of relevant evidence in the [court-martial] trial record"; but
instead of vacating that possibly erroneous judgment and affirming the
district court, the judgment of the Supreme Court was to affirm that
of the Court of Appeals! Jackson and Minton concurred, the latter, at

least, on the grounds that jurisdiction meant jurisdiction, and not trial procedure. Douglas and Black dissented, thinking that the district court should have granted trial *de novo* on the constitutional issues relating to the petitioners' claims of coerced confession by pretrial "torture." Frankfurter thought that the case should have been reargued to consider (1) whether the concept of "jurisdiction" should be expanded to include a review of the fairness of military trial procedure "on the whole record" — thus seeming to assimilate the "substantial evidence test" applicable to the review of judgments of certain administrative tribunals;[32] and (2) the question, which the Court had been evading for years, "whether an American citizen detained by federal officers outside of any federal judicial district, may maintain habeas corpus directed against the official superior [in this case, Secretary of Defense Charles Wilson] of the officers actually having him in custody."[33]

In another recent case, however, the Supreme Court did find a jurisdictional defect which served as the basis for the release on habeas corpus of a petitioner who had been convicted by a Navy court-martial. A Navy enlisted man had re-enlisted in 1946, the day after the expiration of a former enlistment during which he had been a prisoner of war and allegedly had mistreated other Navy enlisted personnel who were also prisoners of war in the same Japanese camp. The Court held that in the absence of statutory authority, the Secretary of the Navy had no power to expand by a Navy regulation (which was, of course, approved by the President) the scope of court-martial jurisdiction to include an offense committed during the period of a prior enlistment.[34] However, the Supreme Court was expressly overruled on this point the following year when Congress enacted the *Uniform Code of Military Justice*.[35]

The Congress, in turn, was soon reversed by the Supreme Court, whose rejoinder took the form of a ruling that Article 3(a) of the *Uniform Code of Military Justice* violated the Fifth Amendment. This was only the fourth time in a decade that the Supreme Court had declared an act of Congress to be unconstitutional. The petitioner here was a civilian, a former serviceman who had been arrested in Pittsburgh, transported by the Army across the sea to Korea, and there tried by court-martial for an offense committed during his period of military service. The question was one of jurisdiction, for the military admittedly lacked jurisdiction if Article 3(a) of the *Code* (extending court-martial jurisdiction to cover civilians who had committed military offenses before their separation from the armed services) could not be supported by the power of Congress under Article I, together with the Necessary and Proper Clause, "To make Rules for the Government and Regulations of the land and naval Forces." "And this assertion of military authority over civilians," remarked Black for the majority, "cannot rest on the President's power as commander-in-chief, or on any theory of military law." [36] He added that Congress could, if it so chose, provide for the trial of such offenses in the regular federal district courts. Reed, dissenting, noted tartly that the Supreme Court had suffered no qualms in approving the extension of court-martial jurisdiction over civilians who refused induction during World War II.[37]

Apart from their precedent value in determining the scope of judicial review of court-martial proceedings, the substantive law of the preceding cases has been largely supplanted by the *Uniform Code of Military Justice*. An integrated system of administrative adjudication, in many respects similar to the separate system created for customs appeals, but without access to the Supreme Court through certiorari, has been set up by statute with ultimate administrative finality reposing in the President. Within this new hierarchy are five possible stages of review of the decisions of courts-martial. The first two stages, applicable in all except minor cases, consist of the commanding officer who appointed the court-martial and the departmental board of review for the service concerned; review here extends to the facts, the law, and administrative policy. Appeal to a three-member civilian Court of Military Appeals (with a status generally similar to that of the United States Tax Court) exists (1) in all cases affecting an officer of general or flag rank or when the sentence extends to death; (2) if so ordered by the judge advocate general; and (3) by certiorari to the boards of review (the review here is only on the record with respect to questions of law). Cases where the sentence extends to the dismissal of any officer must be approved by the secretary of the department concerned, and those affecting general officers or in which a death sentence has been decreed must be approved by the President.[38] The President also is given explicit authority to prescribe rules of court-martial procedure, to determine by regulation inter-service court-martial jurisdiction, to prescribe maximum punishments for offenses covered by the

Code, and "to delegate any authority vested in him under this chapter, and to provide for the subdelegation of any such authority." [39]

In one of the first cases to come before it, the new Court of Military Appeals ruled that the statute, the *Uniform Code of Military Justice,* and Executive Order No. 10214, the *Manual for Courts Martial 1951,* "are on the same level and that the ordinary rules of statutory construction apply." [40] Therefore, both should be construed so that effect is given to every provision of each; and both "should be construed so that no part will be inoperative, void, or ineffective." Specifically, where Article 51 (c) of the *Code* did not expressly require the law member of the trial court-martial to instruct the court as to the elements of each offense charged, "including those in which a plea of guilty has been entered," and this language was added by paragraph 73(b) of the *Manual,* there was no inconsistency and the military courts would enforce the additional requirement, since "the President has been expressly authorized to prescribe rules of procedure for courts martial (Uniform Code of Military Justice, Article 36)." [41] The exercise of the President's procedural rule-making power was upheld again in a subsequent case as merely "filling in the details" of the statute, the court adding that:

We conclude that Congress intended that the President should be fettered only to the extent that his orders must be consistent with and not contrary to the Act, and that he be permitted to exercise his discretion in prescribing the manner of prosecution so long as he provided a method by which all offenses could be prosecuted. [42]

This meant that even though Article 36 of the *Code* directed the President to establish by his regulations a procedure, including modes of proof, which should as far as practicable apply the rules of evidence generally recognized in the trial of criminal cases in the United States district courts, the President did not abuse his discretion in having provided, in paragraph 143(a) of the *Manual,* for the use of fingerprint evidence in certificates of identity not admissible in the civil courts. [43]

The rule established by the regular courts themselves governing the permissible scope of judicial review is given express statutory confirmation by Article 76, "Finality of court-martial judgments":

The appellate review of records of trial provided by this code, the proceedings, findings, and sentences of courts-martial as approved, reviewed, or affirmed as required by this code, and all dismissals and discharges carried into execution pursuant to sentences by courts martial following approval, review, or affirmation as required by this code, shall be final and conclusive, and orders publishing the proceedings of courts-martial and all action taken pursuant to such proceedings shall be binding upon all departments, courts, agencies, and officers of the United States, subject only to action upon a petition for a new trial as provided in Article 73 and to action by the Secretary of a Department as provided in Article 74, and the authority of the President.

An attempt to persuade the Court of Appeals of the District of Columbia to exercise appellate jurisdiction to review a decision of the Court of Military Appeals, because constitutional questions were raised and on the theory that the Court of Military Appeals was an "administrative agency," failed.[44] No attempt was made to induce the Supreme Court to review this case by certiorari, nor would it appear that the Supreme Court has the authority to review directly by certiorari the decisions of the Court of Military Appeals — as it does the decisions of such "legislative courts" as the Court of Claims and the Court of Customs and Patent Appeals.[45] The rule under the *Uniform Code* is the same as always: the highest reviewing authority for the system of military courts is the President.

MARTIAL LAW

The jurisdiction of United States courts-martial is limited to those serving in the armed forces, certain categories of reserve and retired personnel, prisoners of war (subject to applicable provisions of treaties, executive agreements, and international law), and persons employed by or accompanying the armed forces beyond the continental limits of the United States.[46] Nevertheless, where martial law has been declared and the privilege of the writ of habeas corpus suspended, any civilian may find himself amenable to trial not before the regular civil courts but by the order of or under regulations promulgated by a military commander, by one of a miscellany of *ad hoc* tribunals composed of officers of the armed services and usually designated as provost courts, military commissions, or military boards. The judgments of such military courts are no more subject to review in the regular civil courts than are those of courts-martial. Although it is highly exceptional for court-martial cases to raise serious constitutional issues touching the authority of the President, it is customary for cases involving the trial of civilians by military tribunals to bristle with such issues. The limited experience of Americans in such matters to date, however, affords no basis for optimism about the ability of the civil courts to intervene in or frustrate the administration of military justice. When direct conflict between the courts and the military arises — and this has rarely happened in the past — the judges must bow to superior force. It is the President and not the Supreme Court who is the Commander in Chief and in those rare instances in which he has yielded to the exigencies of the demands of the public safety, due process of law and military expediency have exhibited a notable tendency to coalesce.

The action of the President in suspending the writ of habeas corpus during the Civil War, and his approval of suspension in Hawaii during World War II, led to direct challenges in the courts to the authority of the Commander in Chief to order the trial of civilians by military courts when the regular courts might have exercised jurisdiction. It is true that the Supreme Court has held both the Civil War and the Hawaiian episodes to have been unconstitutional;[47] but in each instance a successful challenge was possible only retroactively after the cessation of hostilities, which could under any circumstances have justified the judgment of the military. These matters have been so well and so recently discussed by Professor Rossiter that little needs to be added here.[48]

The first of a succession of orders and proclamations by Lincoln suspending the writ covered originally only the critical main line of communications between Washington and Philadelphia and ran almost entirely through territory in which sympathy for the Confederacy was very high, but ultimately embraced all of the United States. It was challenged almost immediately and at the highest possible level of executive-judicial conflict in the celebrated case of *Merryman*. Here President Lincoln personally directed the commanding officer of Fort McHenry in Baltimore to refuse to deliver up the body of the petitioner to Chief Justice Taney, who retaliated by writing an opinion in which he explicitly ruled that "the president has exercised a power which he does not possess under the constitution."[49] The subsequent adverse decisions of several state and lower federal courts were bound to be anticlimactic under these circumstances, and they serve chiefly to drive home the point, already made abundantly clear in the *Merryman* case, that the civil courts have no power to interfere with or control the actions of the Commander in Chief if he wills otherwise.

The first general suspension of the writ was accomplished through a War Department General Order of August 8, 1862, signed by Secretary of War Stanton "by direction of the President," and applicable in the case of all draft evaders and persons arrested for disloyal practices; the following month the President suspended the writ throughout the loyal states by his proclamation of September 24, 1862.[50] In the first case to challenge these military orders, the federal court for the northern district of New York ruled that the President had no constitutional power to suspend the writ of habeas corpus at any time without the authority of an act of Congress, but the petitioner, who had been arrested under Stanton's order, was effectively removed from the jurisdiction of the court on War Department orders which caused his transfer to the jail in the District of Columbia; and the local United States marshal had, in any event, refused to serve the writ issued by the court because of his own contrary instructions from the War Department.[51] But in an action for damages for false imprisonment by the American minister to Bogotá, who had been arrested on his return to the United States by order of Secretary of State Seward under direction of the President, the highest court of New York denied the United States attorney's motion to transfer the case to the local federal circuit court under the Habeas Corpus Act of 1863. This court was unequivocal in its denial of any power in the President to issue his proclamation of September 24, 1862. The New York court held that the President of the United States, whether in his civil capacity or as Commander in Chief of the Army and Navy, had no power during a rebellion or insurrection to arrest or imprison civilians or to subject them to military law without an order, writ, or precept or process of some court of competent jurisdiction. Any claim to such power was considered to be so destitute of color that it could not even constitute a case arising under the Constitution of the United States so as to give original jurisdiction to the federal courts.[52]

Lincoln's proclamation of September 24, 1862, was also held to be unconstitutional by the Supreme Court of Wisconsin, in an opinion that follows very closely the reasoning of the *Merryman* case; in this case a civilian had been arrested by the military for participation in a draft riot.[53] Several years after this proclamation, which rested on the direct constitutional powers of the President, had been superseded by one based on a statutory delegation of authority, and after the war itself was over, a federal court in California gratuitously observed that the 1862 proclamation had been unconstitutional, because "there are some things too plain for argument, and one of these is, that by the constitution of the United States the president has not the power to suspend the privilege of the writ, and that congress has. The power of the president is executive power — a power to execute the laws, but not to suspend them."[54] However, it should not be forgotten in conjunction with these decisions by state courts and the lower federal judiciary that political opposition to the administration was as intense and bitter in some of the states of the Union as it was in the states of the Confederacy.

The Habeas Corpus Act of 1863 contained, in addition to its blanket ratification of antecedent unconstitutional executive action, a delegation of prospective authority for the President to suspend the privilege of the writ of habeas corpus. Acting on the basis of this power, the President issued his proclamation of September 15, 1863, expanding the scope of his proclamation of the previous year to include both a suspension of the writ and a declaration of martial law effective throughout the United States. Unlike the earlier orders and proclamation, the form of this proclamation was normal: the President claimed both the Constitution and the statute as authority; he declared a rebellion to have been in existence on March 3 and still to exist; and he stated that in his judgment the public safety "does require that the privilege of the said writ shall now be suspended," with respect to prisoners of military, naval, or civil officers who are prisoners of war, spies, aiders or abettors of the enemy; military and naval personnel; deserters; those otherwise amenable to military law; draft resisters; and those committing "any other offense against the military or naval service."[55]

In all except one of the cases in which it was challenged during the remainder of the war, the validity of this proclamation was upheld, in several instances by the same courts that had held the 1862 proclamation to be void and unconstitutional.[56] In fact, the District of Columbia court went so far as to hold that the delegation of power to the President (to suspend the privilege of the writ of habeas corpus) in the Habeas Corpus Act was invalid, since the power to suspend the writ was invested in the President by the Constitution, and this statute which purported to limit or control the discretion of the President was unconstitutional as a legislative attempt to encroach upon the area of executive discretion![57]

During the period of the war, only one case reached the Supreme Court in which a challenge to the system of military trials of civilians was directly raised. This case involved the notorious Copperhead agitator Clement L. Vallandigham. The Supreme Court, however, did not pass upon the question of the constitutionality of the Army regulations under which Vallandigham (and later Milligan) were tried, nor did it reach the merits of the issue of Vallandigham's detention and trial, because it ruled that the authority of a military commission was not judicial in the sense that judicial power is granted to the courts of the United States. The judgment of such a tribunal could not, therefore, be reviewed by a civil court by writ of certiorari. Since the Supreme Court had no original jurisdiction to issue writs of habeas corpus,[58] it had no jurisdiction to hear Vallandigham's case. The question of the validity of the presidential proclamations suspending the writ of habeas corpus was therefore not discussed by the Court in its opinion.[59]

The relatively few cases involving the trial of civilians by military commissions during the Civil War is explicable, therefore, not by the paucity of incidents, for there were quite literally thousands such;[60] but rather by the fact that judicial review was almost impossible to achieve. Since review by certiorari was not possible, the only way to get a case before the courts was to ask the judiciary to consider the question of the constitutionality of the President's suspension of the privilege of the writ of habeas corpus. The Supreme Court was unwilling to do this until the war was over and Lincoln was dead.

Although the Supreme Court decided the *Milligan* case on April 3, 1866 — *the day following* that on which the President had issued his proclamation declaring that peace had been restored throughout the United States — the Court delivered no opinion until December 17, 1866.[61] By this time, the shouting and the tumult had died and the captains and the kings had departed either for home, the Freedmen's Bureau, or the army of occupation; and the problems of prosecuting the war to a successful military conclusion and the holding of fifth columnists in protective custody, or hanging them, had been replaced by the characteristic problems of reconstruction and normalcy. By its opinion in the *Milligan* case, the Supreme Court recognized the constitutional power of Congress to suspend the privilege of the writ of habeas corpus and to delegate such power to the President; and it held that what we should now call "the clear and present danger test" should determine the circumstances in which the imposition of martial law with its consequent trial of civilians by military commissions would be justifiable under the Constitution.[62] The decision was that since Congress had not clearly authorized the imposition of martial law in the loyal states, the President's action in this regard and that of the military in carrying out his orders were unconstitutional.

Three quarters of a century later, the Supreme Court was faced again with the responsibility of deciding a case in which the authority of the President to order the trial of fifth columnists by military commission, rather than by indictment in the civil courts on the charge of espionage, was directly challenged. It is perhaps unfortunate that the Supreme Court felt compelled to speak at all in this case, because it was impossible for the Court publicly to take a position in opposition to the Commander in Chief on the set of facts outlined below without at the same time striking a very real and very serious blow against national unity and, therefore, national security. The effect of creating a verbal rationale to add the stamp of judicial approval to what the President had decided it was necessary to do was, on the one hand, to add another buttress to the legal structure of a monolithic executive that needed no such additional support, and on the other hand to utter language that would thenceforth be available for almost indiscriminate application — and the case has since been frequently cited as a precedent — to factual situations in no way even remotely similar to this unique episode.

Seven Nazi agents who had been trained as saboteurs were landed from German submarines off the coasts of Long Island and Florida on June 13 and 17, 1942. They were apprehended almost immediately by agents of the Federal Bureau of Investigation of the Department of Justice. On July 2, 1942, the President issued his Proclamation No. 2561,[63] defining liability for the crime of unlawful belligerency and limiting the scope of judicial review of the trial of persons accused of such a crime; on the same day he also issued his executive order[64] appointing a military commission and defining its procedure. The F.B.I. then turned the prisoners over to the Army, and they were subsequently brought to trial. Although the District Court for the District of Columbia denied the applications of counsel for the accused to file petitions for writs of habeas corpus in that court, the Supreme Court, in a special term convened on July 29, 1942, assumed jurisdiction specially for the purpose of determining whether it had jurisdiction. The Court heard oral argument on that day and on the 30th, and announced its decision in a *per curiam* opinion delivered on July 31. An extended unanimous opinion was subsequently filed on October 29, 1942.

Of course the Court found that these petitioners were properly subject to military law and amenable to trial according to the procedures set up by the President; and having thus gone through the ritual of maintaining the dignity of judicial office and the independence of the judiciary, the Court retired from the scene of battle. A major issue in the *Milligan* case, the question of the independent constitutional power of the President, in the absence of a statutory delegation of authority, to suspend the privilege of the writ of habeas corpus — and it certainly could not be denied that Proclamation No. 2561 purported to do that — was not even touched upon in the opinion of the Supreme Court.[65]

In the summer of 1942, when Pearl Harbor was only seven months past, the Japanese Imperial Armies and Navy were as yet unchecked in their expansion toward Australia, the possibility of invasion or at least attack on the west coast seemed very real, the loss of Alaska was not deemed improbable, and the continent of Africa appeared about to fall in the lap of the Desert Fox, *Ex parte Milligan* and the procedures utilized by Lincoln to cope with the disloyalty of Sons of Liberty and Peace Democrats seemed a long way off in a dimly remembered past. And so they were. In 1942, the fifth columnists to be dealt with were these Nazis who had sneaked into the country to commit deliberate and well-planned acts of sabotage and espionage. So the *Milligan* case was summarily put to one side with a remark that it was "inapplicable to the case presented by the present record." And, of course, it was, because Milligan, a citizen and resident of the United States, was tried by the military for *treason,* a crime that is uniquely given both substantive and procedural definition and limitation by the Constitution itself; but these petitioners were enemy aliens who were legally incapable of committing treason against the United States.

So the writ did not issue. The rule of the case, which is of the utmost importance because of its value as a precedent in the later trials of war criminals, *who were also charged with the crime of unlawful belligerency,* was that enemy aliens who violate the international or common law of war may be tried in time of war before military commissions under orders of the President. He, in turn, acts both under authority delegated by Congress and in his independent constitutional capacity as the Commander in Chief.

MILITARY GOVERNMENT

The third major facet of the status of the President as Commander in Chief relates to his power to institute a system of military government, or to maintain military control over existing or newly created agencies of civil government, in territories wrested from an enemy by conquest or cession. Fragments of the systems of occupation government set up following all the wars to which the United States has been a party during the last century, except World War I, have been brought under the purview of the courts, although special problems have been created in this regard during the post-World War II period by the trial of so-called war criminals under both unilateral and international auspices.

Only one case has held against an exercise of presidential power of this sort, and this was the first one to reach the Supreme Court. During the war with Mexico, *The Admittance* was captured, while trading with the enemy, as a prize of war by Captain Montgomery, U.S.N. Under express authorization of the President, the military governor of California had established a prize court at Monterey, because prize crews could not be spared by the Navy to bring captured vessels around Cape Horn to a port of the United States. The ship and its cargo were condemned by the Monterey prize court on June 1, 1847. Speaking for the Court, Chief Justice Taney ruled that neither the President nor the military commander could establish a court of prize, competent to take jurisdiction of a case of capture, whose judgment would be conclusive on the regular federal courts, and rejected the plea of military necessity set up as a defense for the presidential orders:

The courts, established or sanctioned in Mexico during the war by the commanders of the American forces, were nothing more than the agents of the military power, to assist it in preserving order in the conquered territory . . . while it was occupied by the American arms. . . . They were not courts of the United States, and had no right to adjudicate upon a question of prize or no prize. And the sentence of condemnation in the court at Monterey is a nullity. . . . Under the Constitution of the United States the judicial power of the general government is vested in one Supreme Court, and in such inferior courts as Congress shall from time to time ordain and establish. Every court of the United States, therefore, must derive its jurisdiction and judicial authority from the Constitution or the laws of the United States. And neither the President nor any military officer can establish a court in a conquered country, and authorize it to decide upon the rights of the United States, or of individuals in prize cases, nor to administer the law of nations.[66]

Taney's precedent has never been followed. In fact, his own Court began the development of a divergent series out of which has evolved the modern principle that, far from lacking the constitutional power to create both civil and military courts in occupied territory, the President's instrumentalities "outside of the Realm" are effectively beyond the pale of judicial review.[67] Just two years after the decision in *Jecker v. Montgomery*, the Court decided that the civil government established by the President in California (including the civil courts) continued, from the necessities of the case, until Congress provided for a territorial government by statute;[68] and in the next such case to come before it, the Court upheld the constitutionality of the presidentially created system of government for New Mexico from the time of the cession until Congress acted to organize the territory.[69]

Only a few years after the Supreme Court had thus approved the role of the President in the transition to the status of organized national territories of the lands wrested from the enemy in the Mexican War, the Civil War had broken out and similar questions stemming from it were brought before the Court. Following the capture of New Orleans by the military forces of the Union, the President promulgated, without previous statutory authorization, his proclamation of October 20, 1862, establishing the Provisional Court for Louisiana. Stating that insurrection had swept away the civil institutions of the state, including the judiciary, so that it had become necessary to hold Louisiana in military occupation, and that some judicial tribunal capable of administering justice was indispensable there, the proclamation announced the creation of a provisional court of record for the state of Louisiana and appointed Charles A. Peabody to be judge. The President defined both the jurisdiction and procedure for the new court, "conforming his proceedings so far as possible to the course of proceedings and practice which has been customary in the courts of the United States and Louisiana, his judgment to be final and conclusive." This combined state-

and-federal court was also delegated such rule-making powers as would be necessary to the exercise of jurisdiction, and the power of appointing officers of the court; the proclamation itself set official salaries for the court and its attendants and provided for payments to be made out of the War Department contingent fund.

A clearer example of executive legislation keyed, if to any recognizable constitutional source of authority, to the status of the Commander in Chief would be difficult to find; and in this, as in many other exercises of presidential power in wartime, it is neither wise nor accurate to "soften with a quasi" what was done. This presidential proclamation was *legislation*; it was not, as some writers on the subject would say, "sub-legislation," "quasi-legislation," or "co-legislation." On the basis of the same underlying theory, the President subsequently set up civil governments under military control in every one of the states that had been in rebellion. To speak of the President's plan of reconstruction, which became a working reality in the occupied Confederacy, as something different in legal effect from the congressional plan that replaced it after Lincoln's death (and Johnson's failure to carry out Lincoln's program) is to indulge in the most patent of legal fictions. The Constitution unquestionably vests the power to create inferior courts in the Congress; but the President's court in New Orleans was upheld as constitutional in no fewer than five different cases.[70]

Similar decisions were rendered upholding the constitutionality of presidential reconstruction in other states of the Confederacy. So held the Supreme Court of Tennessee;[71] and the High Court of Errors and Appeals of the State of Mississippi ruled that "The President could create courts of justice [in the conquered territory of Mississippi] or not, at his discretion."[72] In the case of Texas, President Johnson had appointed a provisional governor and created a provisional system of civil government by his proclamation of June 17, 1865. The Supreme Court subsequently held, in effect, that the acts of this presidentially ordained government were valid and enforceable in the courts, whereas the acts of the *de facto* insurgent government were not.[73]

In an almost continuous sequence of cases arising from two different wars and extending over a quarter of a century in time (1851–1875), the judiciary thus had established the clear principle, in recognition of what had come to be established executive practice, that the President may create either civil or military government, including courts of justice, in the absence of congressional legislation creating a system of organized civil government for newly acquired territories. The pattern thus established, which with very few exceptions has been followed since that time, includes an initial period of military government followed by a presidentially sponsored civil government created under the auspices and protection of United States military forces. This is followed in time by a civil government with a statutory basis and the status of an organized territory, after which the alternative options of statehood or independence (or now, trusteeship) are, at least in theory, available. The President is the ultimate lawmaker for the resident populace of the occupied territory throughout the first two stages of this evolutionary process, both by logic and necessity.

When comparable issues arose again after the Spanish-American War, the Supreme Court was not entirely without precedent when it was called upon to resolve at least some of the facets of the underlying problem of the extent to which "the Constitution followed the Flag." Accordingly, the relevant cases merely applied the already established principles to new factual situations.[74] As the Court stated in the most recent case in this series:

[P]ending the action of Congress, there is no *civil* power under our system of government, not even that of the President *as civil executive*, which can take the place of the government which has ceased to exist by the cession. . . . The authority to govern such ceded territory is found in the laws applicable to conquest and cession. That authority is the military power, under the control of the President as Commander-in-Chief. . . .

[W]hatever may be the limits of the military power, it certainly must include the authority to establish courts of justice, which are so essential a part of any government.[75]

Forty years were to elapse before such issues were to be raised before the Supreme Court again. The first war criminal to be tried under Proclamation No. 2561 of July 2, 1942 — the basic authority for the trial of the spies in the *Quirin* case — was General Tomoyuki Yamashita, the former Japanese military commander in the Philippine Islands. By direction of the President, the United States Joint Chiefs of Staff had on September 12, 1945, instructed General Douglas MacArthur, the commander in chief of United States armed forces in the Pacific theater, to proceed with the trial before appropriate military tribunals of such Japanese war criminals "as have been or may be apprehended." On September 24, 1945, General MacArthur ordered General Styer to try General Yamashita on the charge of "unlawful belligerency" — the same charge lodged against the Nazi saboteurs. This order was accompanied by detailed rules and regulations prescribed by General MacArthur for the trial of war criminals.

Of course, important factual differences distinguished the behavior proscribed as unlawful belligerency in the case of the Nazi saboteurs from what Yamashita had done, but the *Quirin* case assumed importance now because it was considered to have foreclosed the issue of the validity of Proclamation No. 2561. Scant attention was paid by Chief Justice Stone, who delivered the majority opinion, to the question of presidential authority, which was assumed to exist; and the dissenting justices were preoccupied with the patent lack of due process in the trial.[76] Masaharu Homma succeeded to both Yamashita's command in the Philippines and his fate. The directive prescribing the regulations governing his trial was issued by General MacArthur on December 5, 1945, and an application on his behalf for writs of habeas corpus and prohibition was denied by the Supreme Court, without an opinion by the majority, one week following their decision in the *Yamashita* case and on the authority of that decision.[77]

The outcome of cases involving other "war criminals" was clearly foredoomed by the decision in Homma's case, although there still remained the matter of the status of *political*, as distinguished from *military*, war criminals. Some of the Japanese political leaders, including former Premier Tojo, did not attempt to appeal their sentences to the Supreme Court of the United States, but several others, including Hirota, Dohihara, and Kido, did petition the Court for writs of habeas corpus. During the intervening two years, literally dozens of petitions, primarily on behalf of those convicted by the Nuremburg and satellite military and civil tribunals in Germany, had been dismissed by a divided Court. Justices Murphy, Rutledge, Douglas, and Black wished at least to hear argument; Vinson, Reed, Burton, and Frankfurter were convinced that the issues were foreclosed to all war criminals; and Jackson, although his position was clear in view of his personal role as chief prosecutor at the Nuremburg trials, abstained from participation because of personal interest. However, Jackson joined to create a majority in favor of argument being heard by the full Court on the petitions for the writ in behalf of the "Japanese War Lords" because, in his own words:

[T]he issues here are truly great ones. They only involve decision of war crimes issues secondarily, for primarily the decision will establish or deny that this Court has power to review exercise of military power abroad and the President's conduct of external affairs of our Government. The answer will influence our Nation's reputation for continuity of policy for a long time to come. For these reasons I decided at Saturday's conference to break the tie in the Japanese cases.[78]

The unanimous *per curiam* decision of the Court was announced just two weeks later, on December 20, 1948:

We are satisfied that the tribunal sentencing these petitioners is not a tribunal of the United States. The United States and other allied countries conquered and now occupy and control Japan. General Douglas MacArthur has been selected and is acting as the Supreme Commander for the Allied Powers. The military tribunal sentencing these petitioners has been set up by General MacArthur as the agent of the Allied Powers.

Under the foregoing circumstances the courts of the United States have no power or authority to review, to affirm, set aside or annul the judgments and sentences imposed on these petitioners and for this reason the motions for leave to file petitions for writs of *habeas corpus* are denied.[79]

Justice Douglas had joined in the majority opinions dismissing the petitions of Yamashita and Homma. In his concurring opinion in this case, filed some six months after the Court announced its decision, he expressed much more precisely the considerations that doubtless underlay the brief *per curiam* opinion of his brethren:

We need not consider to what extent, if any, the President, in providing that justice be meted out to a defeated enemy, would have to follow (as he did in *Ex parte Quirin* . . . and *In re Yamashita* . . .) the procedure that Congress had prescribed for such cases. Here the President did not utilize the conventional military tribunals provided for by the Articles of War. He did not act alone but only in conjunction with the Allied Powers. This tribunal was an international one arranged for through negotiation with the Allied Powers. . . .

Agreement with foreign nations for the punishment of war criminals, insofar as it involves aliens who are the officials of the enemy or members of its armed services, is a part of the prosecution of the war. It is a furtherance of the hostilities directed to a dilution of enemy power and involving retribution for wrongs done. It falls as clearly in the realm of political decisions as all other aspects of military alliances in furtherance of the common objective of victory. Cf. *Georgia* v. *Stanton*, 6 Wall (50, 71). . . .)

When the President moves to make arrangements with other nations for their trial, he acts in a political role on a military matter. His discretion cannot be reviewed by the judiciary. . . .

For the capture and control of those who were responsible for the Pearl Harbor incident was a political question on which the President as Commander-in-Chief, and as spokesman for the nation in foreign affairs, had the final say.[80]

There would seem to be little left for anyone else to say concerning the status of war criminals before the Supreme Court. The definition of their crimes, their trial, and their punishment, whether they are enemy generals or enemy politicians, is a matter for the President, acting for the United States alone or in association with our military allies, to decide.

There remained only the problem of the lesser fry. Even though hundreds of the more important political and military enemy leaders were brought to trial before international tribunals of one sort or another in Germany and Japan,[81] thousands of others could feasibly be dealt with only through "de-Nazification" procedures before domestic tribunals sponsored by international agreements, military provost courts, or civil courts created under the auspices of the United States military commanders; and the customary problems of occupation administration evoked the exercise of judicial powers abroad over the affairs of both the occupation forces and the civilian populace.[82] Some of the latter category came under the jurisdiction of regular courts-martial, but most, as in the past, were subject to special courts created under the authority of the President. Although most petitioners seeking review by the Supreme Court of the judgments of such tribunals were singularly unsuccessful in getting the court even to assume jurisdiction to ascertain whether it had jurisdiction, the Court finally did render a decision five years after the hostilities of World War II had ended. The Supreme Court then ruled that enemy aliens had neither a constitutional nor a statutory right to the writ of habeas corpus, although it also pointed out that the question of the legal right of American citizens tried by military commissions abroad to invoke the jurisdiction of a federal district court, which had been expressly reserved in *Ahrens v. Clark*,[83] remained reserved, as not raised in this case. Justice Jackson expanded a bit more the principle of presidential irresponsibility

—at least to the courts—for acts of state in which the military and foreign relations facets of his constitutional authority tended to coalesce, and five other members of the Court accepted this interpretation. In his words:

Certainly it is not the function of the Judiciary to entertain private litigation—even by a citizen—which challenges the legality, the wisdom or the propriety of the Commander-in-Chief in sending our armed forces abroad or to any particular region. . . . The issue tendered . . . involves a challenge to conduct of diplomatic and foreign affairs, for which the President is exclusively responsible. *United States* v. *Curtiss-Wright Corp.*, 299 U.S. 304; *Chicago & Southern Air Lines* v. *Waterman Steamship Corp.*, 333 U.S. 103.[84]

Two years later, the Court faced the question of the power of such military courts to try civilians who were citizens of the United States. The wife of an American army officer on occupation duty in Germany had shot her husband. She was tried and convicted of murder by a civil court of the United States zone of occupation, and subsequently she was committed to the Federal Reformatory for Women in West Virginia.[85] Since her jailer was clearly within the territorial jurisdiction of a federal district court, there was no question of her procedural right to petition for a writ of habeas corpus; but her substantive constitutional rights appeared to be no greater than (or different from!) those of the war criminals, because the Supreme Court stated (with only Justice Black dissenting) that:

The key to the issue is to be found in the history of United States military commissions and of United States occupation courts in the nature of such commissions. Since our nation's earliest days, such commissions have been constitutionally recognized agencies for meeting many urgent governmental responsibilities related to war. They have been called our common-law war courts. They have taken many forms and borne many names. Neither their procedure nor their jurisdiction has been prescribed by statute. It has been adapted in each instance to the need that called it forth. See *In re Yamashita*, 327 U.S. 1, 18–23.

In the absence of attempts by Congress to limit the President's power, it appears that, as Commander-in-Chief of the Army and Navy of the United States, he may, in time of war, establish and prescribe the jurisdiction and procedure of military commissions, and of tribunals in the nature of such commissions, in territory occupied by Armed Forces of the United States. His authority to do this sometimes survives cessation of hostilities. The President has the urgent and infinite responsibility not only of combating the enemy but of governing any territory occupied by the United States by force of arms.[86]

Inter arma silent leges.

Notes

[1] "The Congress shall have Power . . . To raise and support Armies . . . To provide and maintain a Navy; To make Rules for the Government and Regulation of the land and naval Forces; To provide for calling forth the Militia to execute the Laws of the Union, suppress Insurrections and repel Invasions; To provide for organizing, arming, and disciplining, the Militia, and for governing such Part of them as may be employed in the Service of the United States. "Constitution of the United States, Article I, 8 (12)–(16).

It might be noted that in English law, the power to wage war and to call up troops were both elements of the direct Prerogative of the Crown incident to the status of the King as Commander in Chief of the Army and Navy. Joseph Chitty, Jr., *Prerogatives of the Crown* (London, 1820), p. 44; compare, however, Luther v. Borden, 7 How. 1, 76 (1849).

[2] Martin v. Mott, 12 Wheat. 19, 29–31 (1827).

[3] Luther v. Borden, 7 How. 1, 43–44 (1849). For a discussion of these two cases, see Clinton Rossiter, *The Supreme Court and the Commander in Chief* (Ithaca: Cornell Press, 1951), pp. 14–17.

[4] For an excellent study of these earlier as well as later incidents, see Bennett M. Rich, *The Presidents and Civil Disorder* (Washington, D.C.: Brookings, 1941), *passim.*

[5] How. 1, 76–77 (1849). Italics supplied.

[6] James Richardson, *Messages and Papers of the Presidents* (Washington, D.C., 1907), VI, 13.

[7] *Ibid.,* p. 15.

[8] 9 Wall. 432, 434 (1870). Italics supplied.

[9] Commonwealth *ex rel* Wendt v. Andreas, 2 Pitts. Rep. (Pa.) 402, 404 (1863); and see Kneedler v. Lane, 45 Pa. 238 (1863), upholding the constitutionality of the national power of conscription per se.

[10] *In re* Griner, 16 Wis. 423 (1863).

[11] Druecker v. Salomon, 21 Wis. 621, 631 (1867).

[12] Allen v. Colby, 47 N.H. 544, 547–548 (1867).

[13] Arver v. United States, 245 U.S. 366, 389 (1918).

[14] *Ex parte* Dostal, 243 F. 664 (N.D. Ohio E.D., 1917).

[15] Including the power (1) in his discretion, to organize by voluntary enlistment four divisions of infantry; (2) to issue a proclamation announcing the necessity of their service, and thereby making subject to duty in the national army for the period of the existing emergency all male citizens between the ages of 21 and 30; (3) to issue a further proclamation causing 500,000 enlisted men to be selected for service from among those eligible; (4) in his discretion, if he deemed it necessary, to issue a further proclamation calling up an additional 500,000 men for duty; (5) in his discretion, to create local boards to consider claims for exemption based on statutory *or other grounds*; and (6) to define and arrange for noncombatant service for those who received statutory exemption on religious grounds. 40 Stat. 76.

[16] That the act and regulations thereunder were invalid in that Congress had attempted to delegate legislative power to the President and to other officials of the national or state governments; that the act was unconstitutional because it authorized the President "to raise an army," while the Constitution confers this power upon the Congress alone; and that the act was unconstitutional because it gave to the President the power to create "courts of justice."

[17] The precedents which the Court found determinative were Field v. Clark, 143 U.S. 649 (1892), which related to the peacetime delegation of power to the President to bring

about tariff reductions through the negotiation of reciprocal trade agreements, and Buttfield v. Stranahan, 192 U.S. 470 (1904), which concerned the seizure of eight packages of tea determined to be of inferior quality by subordinates of the Secretary of the Treasury, acting under regulations he had approved under powers delegated to him in the Tea Inspection Act of March 2, 1897.

[18] A subsidiary question was that of the power of the President to organize within the states a militia to replace the National Guard, which had been called into federal service for the duration of the war. This was upheld in a court-martial case, Kahn v. Anderson, 255 U.S. 1, 7 (1921), where the legality of the military court had been challenged, in part, because one of the members was an officer in such a militia unit.

[19] Billings v. Truesdell, 321 U.S. 542, 551–552 (1944). But see the *Uniform Code of Military Justice*, 50 U.S.C.A. sec. 551, 552 (approved May 5, 1950), Art. 2(1), defining persons subject to the code; and see in this regard S. Rep. 486, 81st Cong., 1st Sess. (June 10, 1949): "In order to leave no doubt as to the point where an inductee will be subject to the code, this subsection is now consistent with the Selective Service Act of 1948 to provide that jurisdiction will not be obtained over those who attempt to avoid selection or induction. Jurisdiction over these persons will continue to reside in the Federal Courts."

[20] United States v. Henderson, 180 F. 2d 711 (7 C.C.A., 1950), certiorari denied, 339 U.S. 963 (1950), and rehearing denied, 340 U.S. 846 (1950).

[21] Orloff v. Willoughby, 345 U.S. 83 (1953).

[22] Weightman v. United States, 142 F. 2d 188, 190–192 (1 C.C.A., 1944).

[23] Kramer v. United States, 147 F. 2d 756 (6 C.C.A., 1945); 324 U.S. 878 (1945).

[24] 317 U.S. 1 (1942).

[25] 320 U.S. 81 (1943).

[26] Reaves v. Ainsworth, 219 U.S. 296, 304 (1911).

[27] Among the numerous cases, the following are most significant. All these involve direct challenges to presidential rule-making, discretion (or the failure to exercise it) in the review of sentences, or subdelgation to military subordinates of some aspects of these powers: *Ex parte* Reed, 100 U.S. 13 (1879); Runkle v. United States, 122 U.S. 543 (1887); United States v. Page, 137 U.S. 673 (1891); Mullan v. United States, 140 U.S. 240 (1891); United States v. Fletcher, 148 U.S. 84 (1893); Swaim v. United States, 165 U.S. 553 (1897); Mullan v. United States, 212 U.S. 516 (1909); Givens v. Zerbst, 255 U.S. 11 (1921); Humphrey v. Smith, 336 U.S. 695 (1949); and Sima v. United States, 119 Ct. Cl. 405 (1951). For a discussion of some of these cases, see Rossiter, *op. cit.*, 102–109.

[28] Gusik v. Schilder, 340 U.S. 128, 132 (1950).

[29] Burns v. Wilson, 346 U.S. 137 (June 15, 1953).

[30] Dennis v. Lovett, 104 F. Supp. 310 (1952), and Burns v. Lovett, 104 F. Supp. 312 (1952).

[31] Burns v. Lovett, 202 F. 2d 335 (1952).

[32] Universal Camera Corp. v. N.L.R.B., 340 U.S. 474 (1951).

[33] Burns v. Wilson, 346 U.S. 137, 851 (October 12, 1953). In dismissing the petitions of convicted "war criminals" for lack of jurisdiction, the District Court of the District of Columbia had ruled that ". . . the President, as Commander in Chief of the Army, has complete and paramount authority over enemy aliens captured by arms on foreign soil. The writ of habeas corpus does not run against the Commander in Chief in such a situation. As a corollary, the writ does not run against the Secretary for the Army." Toulo Shigakura v. Royall, 89 F. Supp. 711, 713 (1948); also 89 F. Supp. 713, 715 (1949). This case was not appealed, but see Johnson v. Eisentrager, 339 U.S. 763 (1950), discussed below in this chapter.

[34] United States *ex rel* Hirshberg v. Cooke, 336 U.S. 210, 217–219 (1949).

[35] Public Law 506, approved May 5, 1950, Article 3(a) (50 U.S.C.A. sec. 553); and see S. Rep. 486, 81st Cong. 1st Sess., June 10, 1949, reprinted in *United States Code Congressional Service* (1950), p. 2222.

Military Necessity and Executive Power

[36]United States ex rel Toth v. Quarles, 350 U.S. 11, 14 (November 8, 1955).

[37] The Supreme Court's decision in the *Toth* case immediately provoked a conflict among the circuits concerning the constitutionality of another provision of the *Code*: Article 2(11), which provides for trial by court-martial of accompanying dependents of military personnel in overseas posts of duty. In each of two cases, a wife who had killed her army officer husband had been tried by court-martial overseas. Both women were back in the United States at the time *Toth* was decided, Clarice Covert awaiting a second trial by court-martial (after the reversal by higher military authority of her earlier conviction) and Dorothy Krueger Smith in confinement in the Federal Reformatory for Women under sentence of a court-martial. Each brought a habeas corpus action in the federal district court having jurisdiction over her jailer. One court, reading the *Toth* case to mean that "the Supreme Court says . . . a civilian is entitled to a civilian trial," ruled that Article 2(11) violated the Fifth and Sixth amendments and was unconstitutional. Covert v. Reid, 24 L.W. 2238 (D.Ct.D.C., November 22, 1955). The other court did not consider the *Toth* decision to apply, because Mrs. Smith was in Japan at the time of her offense and trial. The relevant precedent, therefore, was Madsen v. Kinsella, 343 U.S. 341 (1952) (discussed below at the end of this chapter). Krueger v. Kinsella, 137 F. Supp. 806 (D.Ct.S.D.W.Va., January 6, 1956). A bare majority of the Supreme Court thought the *Toth* precedent "clearly distinguishable," and ruled that Article 2(11) was constitutional and "that military jurisdiction, once validly attached, continues until final disposition of the case." Reid v. Covert, 351 U.S. 487, 491–492, and Kinsella v. Krueger, 351 U.S. 470 (June 11, 1956). Four dissenting justices complained that the majority had forced the issue by deciding the cases before the Court could give them adequate consideration.

[38] 50 U.S.C.A. sec. 651–658. See also James Snedeker, *Military Justice under the Uniform Code* (Boston: Little, Brown, 1953), pp. 31, 35–48.

[39] 50 U.S.C.A. sec. 611, 577, 637, 736.

[40] United States v. Lucas, 1 C.M.R. 19, 22 (1951). This precedent was followed and somewhat extended in United States v. Sonnenschein, 1 C.M.R. 64, 67 (1951), where the court announced that the *Code*, the *Manual*, and the Articles of War would be regarded as sharing a similar authoritative position.

[41] United States v. Lucas, 1 C.M.R. 19, 22 (1951).

[42] United States v. Merritt, 1 C.M.R. 56, 61–62 (1951).

[43] United States v. White, 14 C.M.R. 84 (1954).

[44] Shaw v. United States, 209 F. 2d 811 (C.A.D.C., 1954).

[45] "Nothing in the Uniform Code confers upon this court or any other court the power to review the decisions of the Court of Military Appeals." *Ibid.*, 812. And see Lewis Mayers, *The American Legal System* (New York: Harper, 1955), p. 524.

[46] 50 U.S.C.A. sec. 552. See footnote 37, supra.

[47] *Ex parte* Milligan, 4 Wall. 2 (1866); Duncan v. Kahanamoku, 327 U.S. 304 (1946).

[48] *Op. cit.*, pp. 18–39, 54–59.

[49] *Ex parte* Merryman, 17 Fed. Cas. 144, 148 (C.Ct.Md., 1861), No. 9487.

[50] Richardson, *op. cit.*, IV, 98; the proclamation is also reprinted by Rossiter at pp. 26–27. It is a curious document in that, contrary to usual practice, the President nowhere in it undertakes to cite the basis for the authority under which he purports to act, nor does he identify himself as President, Commander in Chief, or otherwise. This proclamation was doubtless written by Stanton, too.

[51] *Ex parte* Benedict, 3 Fed. Cas. 159 (September 30, 1862), No. 1292. In *Ex parte* Field, 9 Fed. Cas. 1 (1862), No. 4761, the Circuit Court for Vermont avoided the constitutional issue by deciding that, although Stanton's order was invalid as construed and applied in this case, the President had *not* authorized it; and the proclamation of September 24 was held to have been authorized by the act of 1795. In *In re* Spangler, 11 Mich. 298 (1863), however, the Supreme Court of Michigan directed the dismissal of a petition for a writ of habeas corpus, where a draft commissioner made return that he held Spangler under the military authority of the United States. The state court

THE COMMANDER IN CHIEF

ruled that where one was imprisoned under the authority of the federal government, the state judiciary had no jurisdiction to inquire into the legality of the imprisonment on habeas corpus.

[52] Jones v. Seward, 40 Barbour 563 (1863).

[53] *In re* Kemp, 16 Wis. 359 (1863). The court expressly ruled that the power to suspend the writ was a legislative and not an executive power, and therefore could not in any case be constitutionally exercised by the President, as Commander in Chief or otherwise; as to the petitioner, the court decided that a writ of attachment *should* issue against the military commander in whose custody he remained, but that in view of the certain superior force of the military, it would not.

[54] McCall v. McDowell, 15 Fed. Cas. 1235, 1245 (C.Ct.Cal., 1867), No. 8673. The real issue in this case related to the validity of General Order No. 27 of April 17, 1865, issued by the commanding general of the Department of the Pacific, under which a civilian had been summarily arrested and imprisoned on the charge of having publicly approved of the assassination of Lincoln. By this time, the Supreme Court had, of course, already handed down its decision in the *Milligan* case, *infra*.

[55] Richardson, *op. cit.*, IV, 170–171.

[56] *In re* Fagan, 8 Fed. Cas. 947 (D.Mass., 1863), No. 4604; *In re* Dunn, 8 Fed. Cas. 93 (S.D.N.Y., 1863), No. 4171; *In re* Oliver, 17 Wis. 681 (1864). In the latter case, for instance, the Supreme Court of Wisconsin upheld both the statute and the proclamation as being elements in a constitutional congressional plan of contingency legislation, and denied that there had been any delegation of "legislative power." But see Griffin v. Wilcox, 21 Ind. 370 (1863), holding the Indemnity Act of 1863 to have violated both the Fourth and Fifth amendments, essentially on the states' rights basis, however, that neither the President nor the Congress had any power to suspend the issuing of the writ of habeas corpus by a *state* court.

[57] *In re* Dugan, 6 D.C. 131 (1865). Dugan had been arrested by the military and was detained in a military prison; and the return to the writ included an order personally signed by Lincoln stating that Dugan was held by the President's own order and that "this writ of *Habeas Corpus* is suspended." It is apparent from reading this opinion that the court resolved its dilemma in a manner that permitted it to maintain its own dignity by the exercise of the highest form of its power: declaring a statute unconstitutional. If it had found the act unconstitutional on the grounds of unlawful delegation of legislative power, however, it would have come into direct conflict with the President and the military; by ruling on the grounds that it did accept, it was able to appear to uphold the constitutional principle of the independence of the courts, the Chief Executive, and the Congress while at the same time bowing to the inevitable, because it was clear that nothing the court could do would affect the status of the petitioner.

[58] Marbury v. Madison, 1 Cranch 137 (1803); and see the subsequently decided *Ex parte* McCardle, 7 Wall. 506 (1869).

[59] *Ex parte* Vallandigham, 1 Wall. 243 (1864). For additional discussion of this case, see Rossiter, *op. cit.*, pp. 28–30.

[60] James G. Randall, *Constitutional Problems under Lincoln* (New York: Appleton, 1926), pp. 147, and 152 ftn. 25.

[61] *Ex parte* Milligan, 4 Wall. 2 (1866).

[62] The majority thought that no such justification was shown to have existed in Indiana in the case at bar, although the chief justice and three other justices differed with the Court on this point in their concurring opinion.

[63] 7 *Fed. Reg.* 5101.

[64] Unnumbered, 7 *Fed. Reg.* 5103.

[65] *Ex parte* Quirin, 317 U.S. 1 (1942). A majority of the full Court did not agree on the question whether the President, in the absence of statutory authority to create the military commission under the Articles of War (or even in the face of conflicting requirements in the Articles of War) could nevertheless authorize his action on the basis of his constitutionally invested powers as Commander in Chief. *Ibid.*, 28–29, 46–47.

Military Necessity and Executive Power

[66] Jecker v. Montgomery, 13 How. 498, 515 (1851). Compare, *The Zamora* (1916), 2 A.C. 77.

[67] Compare Colenso v. Gladstone (1863), 12 Jur. N.S. 971; and see Glendon A. Schubert, Jr., "Judicial Review of Royal Proclamations and Orders-in-Council," *University of Toronto Law Journal*, 9:69, 84–85 ftn. 57 (1951). Cf. Rossiter, *op. cit.*, pp. 120–126.

[68] Cross v. Harrison, 16 How. 164 (1853).

[69] Leitensdorfer v. Webb, 20 How. 176, 178 (1857). Accord: Ward v. Broadwell, 1 N.M. 75, 83 (1854).

[70] United States v. Reiter, 27 Fed. Cas. 768, 779 (1865), No. 16,146; The Grapeshot v. Wallerstein, 9 Wall. 129, 132–133 (1870); Lewis v. Cocks, 90 U.S. 466 (1874); Burke v. Tregre and Miltenberger, 86 U.S. 519, 524–525 (1873); and Mechanics & Traders' Bank v. Union Bank, 25 La. Ann. 387, 388 (1873), affirmed in Mechanics & Traders' Bank v. Union Bank of New Orleans, 89 U.S. 276, 296–297 (1875).

[71] Rutledge v. Fogg, 43 Tenn. (3 Cold.) 554, 91 Am. D. 299, 303 (1866); Hefferman v. Porter, 6 Cold. 391, 98 Am. D. 459, 463 (1869).

[72] Scott v. Billgerry, 40 Miss. 119, 137 (1866).

[73] Texas v. White, 74 U.S. 700 (1869).

[74] Neely v. Henkel, 180 U.S. 109, 124 (1901); Galban & Co. v. United States, 40 Ct. Cl. 495, 505, 507 (1905), affirmed in 207 U.S. 579 (1907).

[75] Santiago v. Nogueras, 214 U.S. 260, 265–266 (1909). Italics supplied. See also Basso v. United States, 40 Ct. Cl. 202 (1905).

[76] In the Matter of the Application of Yamashita, 327 U.S. 1, 11 (February 4, 1946). For a full development of the background of the case by one of Yamashita's counsel, see A. Frank Reel, *The Case of General Yamashita* (Chicago: University of Chicago Press, 1949), *passim*.

[77] Homma v. Patterson, 327 U.S. 759 (1946).

[78] Hirota v. MacArthur, 335 U.S. 876, 879–880 (1948).

[79] Hirota v. MacArthur, 338 U.S. 197, 198 (1948). Six justices joined in the opinion; Jackson did not participate; Rutledge reserved decision and the announcement of his vote until a later time, but no such announcement was made prior to his death on September 10, 1949; and Douglas concurred separately, but his opinion was not filed until the final decision day for the term, June 27, 1949.

[80] Hirota v. MacArthur, 338 U.S. 197, 208–209, 215 (1949).

[81] In this regard see particularly the article of Charles Fairman, "Some New Problems of the Constitution Following the Flag," *Stanford Law Review*, 1: 587–645 (1949).

[82] See Charles Fairman, "Some Observations on Military Occupation," *Minnesota Law Review*, 32: 319–348 (1948).

[83] 335 U.S. 188, 192 ftn. 4 (June 21, 1948), where it was held that only the federal district court having territorial jurisdiction over a federal prisoner has the power to issue a writ of habeas corpus in his behalf.

[84] Johnson v. Eisentrager, 339 U.S. 763, 789 (June 5, 1950).

[85] By Amendment No. 2 to Law No. 1 of the United States High Commissioner, effective January 1, 1950, the name of the courts was changed from "United States Military Government Courts for Germany" to "United States Courts of the Allied High Commission for Germany." 15 Fed. Reg. 71, 2086. Yvette Madsen was tried by one of these courts. She was turned over to the United States Attorney General, upon affirmation of her sentence by the Court of Appeals of the United States Courts of the Allied High Commission for Germany.

[86] Madsen v. Kinsella, 343 U.S. 341, 346–348 (1952). And see ftn. 37, *supra*.

The Fifth Column

The Alien Enemy Act of 1798

THE act of July 6, 1798, delegated to the President the authority to prescribe rules and regulations for the control of alien enemies in time of war. President Madison was the first to use this authority. After the outbreak of the War of 1812, he issued regulations and directives through the Department of State and the Commissary-General of Prisoners ordering the exclusion of British subjects from a zone forty miles from tidewater. Lockington, an enemy alien and British subject, had been permitted to go from Philadelphia to Reading. When the United States marshal in Philadelphia subsequently found him in Philadelphia contrary to the regulations and he refused to return to Reading, the marshal arrested Lockington on October 9, 1813. Since Lockington also refused to take a "parol of honor," he was kept in jail until April 14, 1814, when he signed the parol and was released. He had in the meantime attempted unsuccessfully to secure his release by habeas corpus from the chief justice and from the Supreme Court of Pennsylvania.[1] His subsequent action for assault and battery and false imprisonment against United States Marshal Smith was dismissed by the federal Circuit Court for Pennsylvania, which laid down an authoritative interpretation of the statute which has since been followed by courts and Presidents alike without significant deviation. Speaking through Supreme Court Justice Washington, the court held that the actions of Marshal Smith's administrative superiors were to be considered as "the public acts of the President" and that "the authority of the marshal to carry into execution the regulations and orders of the president, is implied in the power conferred on the president to establish those regulations." It was further held that internment by summary executive action, as in this case, or internment resulting from the sentence of a court after a criminal trial, were alternative and independent means, and that the judiciary should, when called upon to act, base their decisions on the executive regulations. A broader scope of executive discretion under a statute than that recognized by Justice Washington would be difficult to imagine:

First, the power of the president under the first section of the law, to establish by his proclamation or other public acts, rules and regulations for apprehending, restraining, securing, and removing alien enemies, under the circumstances stated in that section, appears to me to be as unlimited as the legislature could make it.[2]

It was precisely a century before the presence of alien enemies in our midst arose again as a problem. President Wilson, in his proclamations of April 6 and December 11, 1917, gave to the United States marshals summary power to arrest alien enemies on suspicion and to cause their detention in protective custody for an indeterminate period of time. The statute of 1798 was also amended for the first time on April 16, 1918, in order to make it applicable to women as well as to men. None of the World War I cases reached the Supreme Court, but there were several in the lower federal courts challenging various facets of the Attorney General's administration of the presidential directives.

The arrest of a German citizen was held to be the act of the President, conclusive, and not subject to judicial review;[3] it was decided that the presidential determination of the necessity for the internment of alien enemies was not reviewable, that the President could not be required to disclose the basis for the issuance of the arrest warrant, that the procedures adopted and ordered by the President could not violate due process if in accordance with the terms of the statute delegating his authority,[4] and that the provision for the judicial trial of alien enemies was an alternative remedy which in no way limited the powers of the President.[5] The President's determination that a person was in fact an alien enemy was held to be not subject to judicial review, although this court actually applied the doctrine of jurisdictional fact and affirmed, on the merits, the President's finding that the petitioner was a German national.[6] The constitutionality of the statute was questioned for the first time in 120 years, on the grounds that it authorized the deprivation of enemy aliens' liberty without due process of law; but the Ninth Circuit Court of Appeals stated the common-law rule[7] and noted that there was nothing in the Constitution or laws of the United States to change it.[8] The Attorney General's contention, that the "President's" determination (i.e., the determination of the Attorney General's administrative subordinates) of the status of a petitioner was conclusive on the courts, was avoided by one court which found that the petitioner before it had failed to sustain the burden of proof necessary to overcome the presumption in law of the legality of his detention;[9] but in a contemporaneous decision, this proposition was rejected by a court which ordered the release of an American citizen who had been interned, noting that the writ of habeas corpus had not been suspended and that the statute related to the *civil* power of the Chief Executive.[10] In the latter case, the court stated that judicial review of the presidential determination of alien enemy status was proper because no hearing preceded the summary administrative action; but that if the statute *had* required an administrative hearing of some sort to be given enemy aliens placed under restraint, then the administrative determination would be conclusive and not subject to review.

Such refinements in administrative procedure as a formal system of administrative review and a formal decision by the Attorney General did not become institutionalized, however, until World War II.[11] Acting upon the petition of an admitted alien who was held in custody as an enemy alien after a hearing before an alien enemy hearing board, and after consideration of the evidence by the Attorney General, a district court narrowed the scope of judicial review somewhat but ignored the dictum of the *Gilroy* case by making its own independent determination that the relator was in fact a "denizen" of Germany.[12] The court held that the administrative hearing and review did not negate the possibility of judicial review, but merely fortified somewhat the pre-existing assumption of legality in favor of the government. On the other hand, an executive search warrant was held to be sufficient authorization for a search by a federal agent seeking evidence to incriminate a member of the United States branch of the Nazi party, on the basis that the use of such a warrant was "justifiable" to search for property unlawfully held by an alien enemy.[13] The exclusion of enemy aliens as a group from identity with those "persons" guaranteed protection against the possibility of arbitrary executive action would appear to be just as complete in the case of the Fourth Amendment as in that of the Fifth.

After the close of World War II, only a few months elapsed before the Cold War began. Two dominant problems characterized this new period: what to do about the more dangerous of the alien enemy internees of World War II, and how to redefine "alien enemies" to exclude the Germans, Italians, and Japanese who had become in effect, if not in law, our friends and allies, and to include our erstwhile partners of the late war, the Russians, and their Communist associates in other states, who had become our new enemies.

Two major acts of presidential legislation underlay the two different but closely related administrative programs created for the purpose of expelling undesirable alien enemies. Presidential Proclamation No. 2655 of July 14, 1945, and the regulations of the Attorney General thereunder,[14] provided for the deportation on the order of the Attorney General, after a hearing before an alien repatriation board, of any alien dangerous to the public peace and safety of the United States, interned or found within the United States, who owed allegiance to an enemy government and adhered to that government, *and* who refused to depart voluntarily from the United States within thirty days after notice from the Attorney General. The alternative procedure was based on the postwar hemispheric defense agreements, specifically Resolution VII of the Conference of American States, as well as the Alien Enemy Act of 1798; and Presidential Proclamation No. 2662 of September 8, 1945, directed the Secretary of State to order the deportation of aliens whose continued residence *in the western hemisphere* "is deemed by [him] prejudicial to the future security or welfare of the Americas."

An early attempt to enjoin the Secretary of State from deporting certain interned aliens was held to be premature, since no hearings had as yet been held for them and no removal orders issued, so that their imminent deportation to Germany, although likely, was not absolutely certain;[15] and in an independent attempt to enjoin the Attorney General in a parallel case involving internees for whom the administrative process had matured and removal orders had been issued, the Court of Appeals of the District of Columbia brushed aside challenges to the constitutionality of the statute, Presidential Proclamation No. 2655, and the regulations of the Attorney General thereunder, noting that:

As a practical matter, it is inconceivable that before an alien enemy could be removed from the territory of this country in time of war, the President should be compelled to spread upon the public record in a judicial proceeding the method by which the Government may detect enemy activity within our borders and the sources of the information upon which it apprehends individual enemies. No constitutional principle is violated by the lodgment in the President of the power to remove alien enemies without resort or recourse to the courts.[16]

Early in January 1947, however, Presidential Proclamation 2662 was held to be in part unconstitutional to the extent that, in failing to provide for the voluntary departure of aliens whose continued presence was inimical to hemispheric security, it was inconsistent with the Alien Enemy Act of 1798 on which it was in part based, since that statute authorized the President to provide for the removal of those alien enemies who, not being permitted to reside within the United States, *refused or neglected* to depart therefrom.[17] The petitioner here had been turned over to the United States in 1942 by the government of Costa Rica for internment in the United States until he could be deported as a dangerous enemy alien; but the Secretary of State had not proved or offered to prove that Von Heymann had refused to leave the United States, thus denying him the option of returning to German territory.[18] Almost two years later, the same court held that the State Department's practice of blacklisting dangerous enemy aliens subject to expulsion orders did not interfere with their voluntary departure as long as there was *any* country to which they might go and be admitted; the blacklists were, in any event, merely advice from the State Department to certain foreign governments.[19] The effect of the *Von Heymann* decision was to expand the scope of judicial review under both proclamations so that two questions could thence be independently determined by the courts: (1) Was the relator in fact an alien enemy? and (2) Was the relator given an opportunity to depart "voluntarily" from the United States before the execution of a deportation order against him?

Apparently, however, there were no time limitations as to when, if at all, an enemy alien might be given a hearing and a decision made to expel or deport him; he could be interned without a hearing for an indeterminate period since the wartime powers carried over without diminution into the postwar period:

The wording of Section 21 of the Act places no such restriction on the word "removal." Under this section, an enemy alien may be removed to any place within the confines of the United States, or he may be expelled or deported to another country. . . . The fact that the latter countries have surrendered unconditionally, and that the President of the United States has officially proclaimed that hostilities have ceased, has not officially terminated the war. No peace treaty between the United States and Japan has been signed and ratified by the Senate, nor has any joint resolution by Congress or executive proclamation been made terminating the war. . . . Until the war between the United States and Japan is officially proclaimed to be at an end, Japan is a hostile or enemy nation within the meaning of the Act.[20]

It was not until 1948, exactly a century and a half after Congress enacted the Alien Enemy Act, that a case under it and challenging its constitutionality finally reached the United States Supreme Court. A divided Court upheld in strong language both the statute and the executive and administrative action implementing it, with the minority of four justices equally vigorous in their dissent. By this time, the argument that presidential power under the statute had lapsed because of the restoration of peace (or at least, the termination of the war) was already foreclosed because of the Supreme Court's recent decision in *Woods v. Miller*,[21] so the only real issue before the Court was that of the constitutionality of the statute and the executive action taken under it, and *this* issue was foreclosed, in the judgment of the majority, by the interpretation heretofore given by courts and Presidents alike since the closing years of the eighteenth century:

War does not cease with a cease-fire order, and power to be exercised by the President such as that conferred by the Act of 1798 is a process which begins when war is declared but is not exhausted when the shooting stops. . . . It is not for us to question a belief by the President that enemy aliens who were justifiably deemed fit subjects for internment during active hostilities do not lose their potency for mischief during the period of confusion and conflict which is characteristic of a state of war even when the guns are silent but the peace of Peace has not come. These are matters of political judgment for which judges have neither technical competence nor official responsibility. . . .

The Act is almost as old as the Constitution, and it would savor of doctrinaire audacity now to find the statute offensive to some emanation of the Bill of Rights. The fact that hearings are utilized by the

Executive to secure an informed basis for the exercise of summary power does not argue the right of courts to retry such hearings, nor bespeak denial of due process to withhold such power from the courts. . . .

Accordingly, we hold that full responsibility for the just exercise of this great power may validly be left where the Congress has constitutionally placed it — on the President of the United States. The Founders in their wisdom made him not only the Commander-in-Chief but also the guiding organ in the conduct of our foreign affairs. He who was entrusted with such vast powers in relation to the outside world was also entrusted by Congress, almost throughout the whole life of the nation, with the disposition of alien enemies during a state of war. Such a page of history is worth more than a volume of rhetoric.[22]

"Americans Betrayed" [23]

All aliens in the United States were subjected to a licensing system by the Alien Registration Act of 1940. Such control was certainly not unreasonable in view of the imminence of the involvement of the United States in both the European and Sino-Japanese conflicts, particularly since it was known that such potentially dangerous groups as the Bund and the Black Dragon Society included many aliens in their membership. After war had actually come, however, the United States embraced a theory somewhat foreign to the general assumptions of the Anglo-Saxon legal order (but quite consonant with such immigration legislation as the Chinese Exclusion Act of 1882, the National Origins Act of 1921 and as amended, and the Displaced Persons Act of 1948) to the effect that the individual behavior of alien enemies could be predicted in terms of their racial or national origins. The Italians, since it was well known that they were a jovial, warm-blooded people addicted to raising large families, were soon in effect removed en bloc from the category of alien enemy; the Germans, a thrifty, industrious lot who suffered the periodic misfortune of being misled by false prophets, were arraigned individually and dealt with accordingly; but the Japanese, a strange, unknowable, mysterious group who competed unfairly with American labor and businessmen, were dispossessed of their homes and property and placed in concentration camps.[24] So much for equality under the law.

The basic law authorizing the detention of all persons (including citizens of the United States, "friendly aliens," and enemy aliens alike) in protective custody for the duration of the emergency was Executive Order No. 9066,[25] authorizing the Secretary of War and military commanders whom he might designate to prescribe military areas from or in which any or all persons might be excluded, expelled, restricted, or otherwise subjected to whatever regulations the Secretary of War or the appropriate military commanders might impose *in their discretion*. No direct sanctions were provided by this executive order, but the clear implication was military arrest and confinement. The fear of judicial frustration (doubtless without foundation) caused a month's delay during which plans were being developed and little or no attempt was made to implement the order and restrain individual behavior; but by the act of March 21, 1942,[26] Congress specifically ratified Executive Order 9066 and provided for enforcement by criminal prosecution of violators in the regular federal courts. Within eight months, a minority group of over a hundred thousand people had been rounded up, transported hundreds of miles away from the seacoast, and "relocated" for the next several years.[27]

German aliens, who were concentrated primarily near the eastern seaboard, were handled quite differently. Those relatively few who were deemed sufficiently dangerous to warrant their internment were arrested through civil processes under the authority of the Alien Enemy Act, as discussed above. Those who were considered to be disaffected but not to a degree to warrant their incarceration were expelled and excluded from vital defense and military areas by individual exclusion orders, which were functionally administrative injunctions issued in the name of the appropriate military commanders. The government was consistently unsuccessful in those few instances in which challenges to this program were raised in the eastern federal courts, and was conspicuously loath to push these cases on to the Supreme Court where the question of constitutionality could be definitively established.

Olga Schueler, a United States citizen by the naturalization of her husband, managed a restaurant in Philadelphia; after having exhausted her administrative remedy — a hearing, with an appeal to the commanding general — in a vain endeavor to ascertain the cause of her exclusion from the eastern military area,[28] she sought and procured from a district court a declaratory judgment that Lieutenant-General Hugh Drum's order was invalid.[29] At the same time, another district court reached a similar conclusion in the case of Maxmilian Franz Joseph Ebel, who, although a naturalized American citizen, was avidly pro-Nazi, and had been the local Fuehrer of the Boston Bund before its dissolution. Although he had been given a hearing, "No opportunity for cross examination of witnesses was afforded him, nor was he informed of the nature and cause of the accusations against him"; the court held that such restraint upon the liberty of a United States citizen was unreasonable, and was not justified by military necessity at the time of its application. So the order was invalid and Ebel's injunction was granted; again, the government did not choose to appeal.[30]

The third case related to the lesser sanction of dismissal from employment in a "sensitive" industry. The commanding general of the First Service Command had directed in a letter of August 12, 1943, the dismissal of Hans Von Knorr, whom he had found to be subversive, from his employment by the Cities Service Corporation. Although the district court held that the order was authorized by Executive Order 9066 and that the penalties of the act of March 21, 1942, would have been applicable to a violation of the order by the employer,[31] this ruling was vacated by the First Circuit Court of Appeals because the Secretary of War had not designated General Miles to act under the executive order.[32] That court, at least, was willing to subject the procedures followed by the military to judicial review. The general predisposition of federal judges on the west coast, however, was considerably less intransigent than that of their brethren of the east, and the Ninth Circuit Court of Appeals rejected an attempt to enjoin an individual exclusion order, holding that the question of validity could only be raised as a defense to enforcement proceedings.[33]

Citizens of Japanese descent didn't make out so well as the German-Americans. Mary Ventura was the first to get her case into court. She had the misfortune to have her case heard before Judge Black of the Seattle federal district court, who began his opinion by disposing of *Ex parte Milligan* as "that United States Supreme Court decision of about seventy-six years ago." Her petition for habeas corpus was dismissed on the ground that the curfew and restriction orders to which she was subject placed her in "moral restraint," not physical custody. The court incidentally displayed his erudition and familiarity with such subversive organizations as the Sons of Liberty and the Copperheads when he remarked: "In the Civil War . . . [t]hey never had to think then of fifth columnists far, far from the forces of the enemy successfully pretending loyalty to the land where they were born who, in fact, would forthwith guide or join any such invaders." Blitzkrieg was for him sufficient warranty for substituting the doctrine of military necessity for the due process of law required by the Constitution; it is frightening to contemplate what might have been done, or might be done in the name of the Atom Bomb!

The orders and commands of our President and the military forces as well as the laws of Congress, must, if we secure that victory that this country intends to win, be made and applied with realistic regard for the speed and hazards of lightning war. . . .

I do not believe that the Constitution of the United States is so un-fitted for survival that it unyieldingly prevents the President and the Military, pursuant to law enacted by the Congress, from restricting the movement of civilians such as petitioner, regardless of how actually loyal they perhaps may be, in critical areas desperately essential for national defense.

Aside from any rights involved [and there seem to be no rights in-volved] it seems to me that if petitioner is as loyal and devoted as her petition avers she would be glad to conform to the precautions which Congress, the President, and the armed forces [the three branches of our government in time of war?], deem so requisite to preserve the Constitution, laws and institutions for her and all Americans, born here and naturalized.[34]

On the basis of information supplied by a Federal Bureau of Investi-gation agent, Lincoln S. Kanai was arraigned before a district court in Wisconsin on the charge of having willfully violated various restriction and exclusion orders promulgated by Commanding General DeWitt of the Western Defense Command. Judge Duffy noted that "Petitioner frankly admits that he is a full-blooded Japanese" and held that he would not rule upon the constitutional question,[35] reserving that for the criminal court before whom the petitioner would be tried. Kanai was a Nisei, a citizen of the United States by birth under the rule of *jus soli*; he sought to question the legality of his detention by writ of habeas corpus. The record does not disclose that he was charged with the crime of being of Japanese descent, but this is the only matter considered by the court.[36]

The limited scope of review in cases arising out of defense to crimi-nal prosecution, however, was illustrated in the trial in Judge Black's court of an American college student, Gordon K. Hirabayashi, for the violation of curfew and exclusion orders. Upholding the constitution-ality of the executive order, statute, and military orders, Judge Black based his decision on grounds of racial mythology which, while if emanating from a Nazi court would not have seemed out of context, sound fantastic and unreal coming from the mouth of an American judge only a decade ago:

[The Japanese] make diabolically clever use of infiltration tactics. They are shrewd masters of tricky concealment among any who resemble them. With the aid of any artifice or treachery they seek such human camouflage and with uncanny skill discover and take advantage of any disloyalty among *their kind*. . . .

[C]ertainly in time of war a technical right of an individual[37] should not be permitted to endanger all of the constitutional rights of the whole citizenry. . . .

And this court will not question in this time of war the wisdom or necessity of the curfew or evacuation orders with respect to those of Japanese ancestry which are involved in this proceeding. The situation is too grave — the menace too great. . . . In these days of lightning war this country does not have to submit to destruction while it awaits the slow process of Constitutional amendment.[38]

There was only one dissenting judicial voice, and that was raised only in a dictum. In an opinion obviously based upon the rationale of *Ex parte Milligan*, a district court observed that "While the orders of General DeWitt, therefore, were void as respects citizens, unquestionably . . . the regulations . . . are thus valid with respect to aliens";[39] and Yasui, who had dual citizenship at the time he reached his majority, was held to have renounced his United States citizenship by his disloyal acts in the months before war was declared.

The cases of Hirabayashi and Yasui were appealed to the Supreme Court which decided them together on June 21, 1943. The scope of this decision was incredibly narrow in view of the magnitude of the issues involved, raised by the facts, and argued before the Court. It was held lawful for the military commander of the Western Defense Command to impose curfew restrictions upon American citizens of Japanese ancestry *as of May 1942* and in the light of the *then* prevailing military conditions; ignored were the major questions: (1) Was there an unconstitutional subdelegation of power to the military commander? and (2) Did the discrimination against American citizens of Japanese ancestry violate the due process clause of the Fifth Amendment?

How could the Court avoid the seemingly inescapable constitutional issues? Hirabayashi had been given concurrent sentences for violating Civilian Exclusion Order No. 57 and Public Proclamation No. 3 (the curfew order); the Court limited its consideration to the latter on the ground that his conviction would be sustained if either count were valid. In any event, the basis of the authority of the curfew order lay in the war power, which the Court viewed as a transcendental excrescence of the totality of the combined powers of the President and the Congress; such a definition made any question keyed to the doctrine of the separation of powers simply irrelevant. As for Yasui, the judgment of the district court respecting his loss of citizenship was vacated because this was an irrelevant issue; as the Court had just decided with respect to Hirabayashi, the curfew order was valid as applied to citizens.[40]

Six months later, the Ninth Circuit Court of Appeals faced the specific question left unanswered by the Supreme Court's decision in the *Hirabayashi* case when another American citizen, Fred Korematsu, was indicted for having violated Civilian Exclusion Order No. 34, promulgated by General DeWitt on May 3, 1942. The majority opinion, however, simply stated that *in principle*, the Supreme Court had already affirmed the validity of exclusion orders by its decision in the *Hirabayashi* case, which this court purported to follow. In a concurring opinion, Judge Denham took both his colleagues and the Supreme Court to task for their failure to muster the moral courage necessary to carry out their judicial duty of dealing with the issues raised by the cases before them:

[T]he opinion of this court disposes of Korematsu's major contentions without their mention, much less their consideration. Outstanding is the avoidance of the question of imprisonment and deportation. It is buried in the euphemism "evacuation," without suggestion of its forced character or its accomplishment by compulsory confinement. . . . [The Supreme Court in its opinion in the *Hirabayashi* case discusses the curfew order as though it were] analogous to the control of civilians by lines about a burning building, established by the police or firemen, or the requirement of citizens to remain indoors during the brief period of a blackout. . . .

The Supreme Court refused to consider the validity of the orders to report for imprisonment. . . .

Here is no resemblance to the orders leading to the imprisonment of men, women and children en masse in assembly center stockades for deportation. . . .

Korematsu's contention, in effect, is that his conviction was for the crime of not moving out of San Leandro *into imprisonment in an assembly center*. An inspection of the series of orders affecting him shows his position to be well taken. *These orders at once required him not to leave and not to remain in the area.* His sole alternative was imprisonment. . . .

In the course of the hearing, the Government admitted that not one of these 70,000 Japanese descended citizen deportees had filed against him in any federal court of this circuit an indictment or information charging espionage, sabotage or any treasonable act. This admission covered the five months from Pearl Harbor to General DeWitt's deportation order of May 10, 1942. . . .

Imprisonment without trial is a denial of the due process of the Fifth Amendment and such orders are the equivalent of lettres de cachet so far as the physical effect of the bodies of these citizens is concerned. It would be like the hypocrisy of the phrase "voluntary evacuation" to contend otherwise.[41]

The Supreme Court did not pass upon Korematsu's appeal for another year. On December 18, 1944, they narrowed the point for their consideration to that of the separate and individual constitutionality of Civilian Exclusion Order No. 34 as applied to Korematsu personally in *May of 1942*: this they held to be within the scope of the war power as they had previously defined it in the *Hirabayashi* case.[42] Frankfurter, concurring separately, thought that the Court had no jurisdiction because the treatment accorded the minority group in this case raised only political questions.[43]

On the same day, the Court decided the *Endo* case. Mitsuye Endo, a civil servant of the state of California and a citizen of unquestioned loyalty, had been detained in the Sacramento Assembly Center from May 15 to 19, 1942; and in the Tule Lake Relocation Center from May 19, 1942, until December 1944. The precise question presented in her appeal related to the validity of the denial of her application for leave from the Tule Lake Center. It may be of interest, however, to trace the bare legal outlines of the antecedent administrative and military process which the Court found it unnecessary to examine in the disposition of her petition for habeas corpus.

Miss Endo's expulsion was effected by Civilian Exclusion Order No. 52, dated May 7, 1942, and effective May 16, 1942; this order, together with the remainder of Civilian Exclusion Orders Nos. 1–99, was ratified by Public Proclamation No. 7 of June 8, 1942.[44] Public Proclamation No. 8 of June 27, 1942[45] confirmed Civilian Restriction Order No. 1 of May 19, 1942, which authorized detention of evacuees in assembly centers or relocation centers (unless exceptions were made by direct order of General DeWitt), and the promulgation of restrictions on the rights of evacuees to enter, remain in, or leave the War Relocation Project Areas (i.e., the six relocation centers located in the Western Defense Command). The four centers outside of the Western Defense Command were each designated as a military area by the Secretary of War in his Public Proclamation No. WD1 of August 13, 1942,[46] which also provided that all persons of Japanese ancestry in such areas were required to remain there unless written authorization to leave was obtained in each case from the Secretary of War or the director of the War Relocation Administration; violations of any of these orders or proclamations were punishable under the act of March 21, 1942.

By letter of August 11, 1942, General DeWitt authorized the W.R.A. (pursuant to Public Proclamation No. 8) to issue permits for persons to leave the areas within the Western Defense Command. By virtue of that delegation and the direct authority conferred by Executive Order No. 9102, the W.R.A. was given control over both the ingress and the egress of evacuees from the Tule Lake Relocation Center. Then on February 16, 1944, Executive Order No. 9423 amended 9102 and transferred the W.R.A. from the Office for Emergency Management (in the Executive Office of the President) to the Department of the Interior. Perhaps this constituted recognition that the continued detention of the Japanese-Americans was no longer an emergency measure, but had become a stabilized permanent program somewhat akin to the administration of Indian Affairs. The Secretary of the Interior, by Administrative Order No. 1922 of February 16, 1944, authorized the director of the W.R.A. to perform under the Secretary's supervision and direction the functions transferred to the department by Executive Order No. 9423. The first leave procedure was contained in Administrative Instruction No. 22 of July 20, 1942, revised November 6, 1942, and superseded as a supplement to the *Regulations* by Section 60 of the *Handbook* of July 20, 1943. The *Regulations*, issued September 26, 1942,[47] and revised January 1, 1944,[48] stated in detail the law governing the issuance of leave clearances and indefinite clearances; the *Handbook* was for the guidance of the public (or more specifically, the evacuees).

Only the *Revised Leave Regulations* were considered by the Supreme Court. They and they alone were in part invalidated as of December 18, 1944, as applied to citizens of unquestioned loyalty such as Miss Endo:

We are of the view that Mitsuye Endo should be given her liberty: In reaching that conclusion we do not come to the underlying constitutional issues which have been argued. For we conclude that, whatever power the War Relocation Authority may have to detain other classes of citizens, it has no authority to subject citizens who are concededly loyal to its leave procedure.[49]

Her liberty? But she still could not return to her home in Sacramento. She still was subject to military restrictions upon her right to travel through the territory of the Western Defense Command, and still was excluded from residence therein. Among the phases of the program *not* passed upon by the Supreme Court remained:

1. The detention of citizens whose loyalty *was* questioned by the administrative authorities; the detention of the Issei, loyal or otherwise; and the detention of all persons, including admittedly loyal citizens, in the camps outside the Western Defense Command set up under Public Proclamation No. WD1.

2. The legality of the exclusion orders as of *the date of this decision.*[50]

3. The validity of the mass evacuation under Civilian Exclusion Order No. 52 and Public Proclamation No. 7.

4. The validity of Executive Order No. 9066 as so construed and applied, since the W.R.A. cited it as the source of its authority to detain loyal citizens.

5. The constitutionality of the prospective delegation of the statute of March 21, 1942, which certainly was broad enough in its terms to include the Relocation Program, irrespective of the fact that the latter was not debated when the bill was under consideration. And what of the admitted ratification by an appropriation act passed after the program had been in operation for some time?

As it was, the administration did what it could to present the Supreme Court with moot questions in the cases of both Korematsu and Endo. The mass exclusion program was terminated on December 17, 1944 — the day before the decisions in these cases were announced — to be effective January 2, 1945, by Public Proclamation No. 21 of the commanding general of the Western Defense Command; but the legal precedents created by the decisions of the Court remain, leaving a principle which, in the words of Mr. Justice Jackson, "lies about like a loaded weapon ready for the hand of any authority that can bring forward a plausible claim of an urgent need."[51]Of course, it would be naïve to ignore the ample precedents which exist in our history for both discriminating against a minority group on the basis of their race and color, and forcing a minority group to live in economic subjugation in concentration camps. We have had for a long time, and we still have, Jim Crow and the Red Man. It is significant, however, that this was the first time that such discrimination had been linked to the concept of political crime and assumed overtones that bore a remarkable resemblance as a concept to the "thought control" enforced by the Japanese police upon Japanese citizens.

With the conclusion of the mass exclusion program, individual exclusion orders continued to be issued when deemed necessary by the military, as had been done throughout the war in the case of German and Italian aliens in the Western Defense Command and all enemy aliens in the Eastern Defense Command. In a few instances where resistance was encountered, individual exclusion was accomplished through "physical and military force" by the commanding general of the Western Defense Command. His claimed right to expel by force any person from the defined military areas was rejected, however, by a district court which held that the statutory provision for criminal prosecution in the federal courts was the only permissible means of enforcing the military orders in cases of noncompliance. Admittedly, the commanding general had broad rule-making powers delegated to him by Executive Order No. 9066, and the ordinary principles of administrative law could not be applied by a court exercising judicial review; but the effect of the statute was to *limit* the discretion vested in the military by the executive order, leaving the commanding general without summary power to enforce the laws which he was empowered to make. Enforcement must therefore be in the regular courts; to hold otherwise would be to admit that "an effective means has been found for actually suspending the writ of habeas corpus without appearing to do so."[52]

To the same effect was the decision in another federal district court in a civil damage suit against General DeWitt. The plaintiff here was not a Japanese-American, but the San Diego manager of "Mankind United," an organization which was designated in the formal report of the Army's hearing board as a "religious racket." The same board decided that Wilcox, the plaintiff, was a "crackpot" but not subversive, and recommended against his exclusion; it is noteworthy, however, that in an independent action, Wilcox was convicted of sedition under a World War II statute. The War Department advised DeWitt that he could constitutionally remove Wilcox from the Western Defense Command by military force, apparently on the strength of the *Hirabayashi* decision. Although this was ultimately done, it was preceded by a long and complicated series of administrative actions; and although "due process" was denied Wilcox by the military, in the judgment of the court in this case, he certainly was not dealt with arbitrarily, and an immense amount of time, trouble, and expense was involved in getting him physically removed from California. The court ruled that General DeWitt had exceeded the scope of his authority under the act of March 21, 1942, and Executive Order No. 9066, since the proper sanction for the violation of an individual exclusion order was not recourse to military force but lay in a criminal indictment as authorized by the statute. The court also noted that such a procedure would have been infeasible as a practical solution to the problem of mass enforcement as in the case of the Japanese-Americans in 1942, although it was suitable for use where particular individuals were involved. Nominal damages of $100 were awarded.[53]

Trading with the Enemy

The constitutional power of the President to proclaim a blockade of enemy ports was upheld without exception by the courts when captures were brought in for condemnation under the authority of Lincoln's proclamation of April 27, 1861.[54] A district court held that the President had "plenary" power as Commander in Chief to proclaim and to enforce a blockade when war *de facto* existed without the necessity of a prior declaration of the war by Congress:

There can be no doubt of the right of the President to make maritime captures and submit them to judicial investigation. . . .

Some have thought that it was to be deemed enemy's country, because of the proclamation of the president. It seems to me rather that the proclamation and the blockade are to be upheld as legal and valid because the territory is that of an enemy.[55]

In the disposition of the above and other cases on appeal, the Supreme Court delivered what remains today its most direct and authoritative opinion on the power of the President to proclaim and to wage an "undeclared war." By a five to four vote, the majority held that the blockade was valid as an exercise of the President's constitutional powers; that in any event it had been authorized by prior statutory delegation of authority, and that even assuming that he had exceeded his powers — and the Court expressly held otherwise — the Bill of Indemnity of August 6, 1861, sanctioning all antecedent wartime acts of the President, cured any such defects and made his acts valid.[56]

Closely related to the question of the power of the President to declare a blockade was his authority to suspend it in particular instances by setting up a licensing system. One incidental effect of this plan was to withdraw from residents of the states under blockade the status to sue in the federal district courts,[57] but even though citizens of the confederate states were "quasi-enemies" they might sue in a court of the United States on the basis of a presidential license.[58]

A number of Supreme Court cases — significantly, perhaps, decided during the post-bellum period — strictly construed the President's power to license trading with the enemy during the Civil War. It was held that under the original act of June 13, 1861, only the President could grant or authorize a permit to pass through the blockade; and a license, issued by a special agent of the Treasury Department acting under the orders of the commanding general of the Union Army in New Orleans, but with no indication that it had been directed by the President, was declared a nullity, and no protection was granted the vessel and cargo when seized for condemnation as a prize of war.[59] The same was true of "certificates" issued by the British consul, to "protect" cotton from seizure by Union forces before it could be transported to New Orleans and exported to England, because:

The military orders set forth in the record were unwarranted and void. The President alone could license trade with the rebel territory, and when thus licensed, it could be carried on only in conformity to regulations prescribed by the Secretary of the Treasury [which had been approved by the President]. The subject was wholly beyond the sphere of the powers and duties of the military authorities.[60]

Similarly, a license to purchase cotton in rebel territory and bring it back through the military lines was invalid, since the authority of the commanding general of the Department of the Gulf extended only to permission to pass through the military lines; but even a valid presidential license could not have authorized the purchase of the cotton in this particular case, the Court added, because the grower and seller was an officer of the Confederate government, and such a sale was expressly proscribed by the Confiscation Act of July 17, 1862.[61]

In the leading case of *Hamilton v. Dillin*, however, the Court faced squarely the questions of constitutional powers which were largely assumed or ignored in the preceding decisions. In order to institute the licensing system, it had been necessary to define the area to which the regulations were applicable: this President Lincoln had done in his proclamation of July 1, 1862, declaring the states of the Confederacy to be in insurrection. The Court held that the President had been delegated the discretionary authority to do this by the act of July 13, 1861;[62] the power to license, as a form of administrative control, was expressly upheld;[63] and in any event, Congress had approved of the regulations issued and the action taken thereunder, so that they were as valid as if incorporated in the statute itself.[64] "The war power vested in the government," noted the Court, "implied all this without any specific mention of it in the Constitution."[65] However, in a later case involving a cotton speculator who possessed a presidential license (which he had attempted, without success, to use fraudulently) the Court avoided the constitutional question of the President's power to license commercial intercourse, in time of war, in the *absence* of statutory delegation of authority:

[The question is] whether, notwithstanding the repeal of the fifth section of the said act of July 13, 1861, authorizing the President, in his discretion, to license or permit commercial relations in any state or section in insurrection, he could not, in virtue of his power as commander-in-chief of the army, license trade with insurgents within the lines of Confederate military occupancy. If this question has not been distinctly concluded by the former decisions of this court, we deem it unnecessary now to consider or determine it.[66]

Oddly enough, in only one case was a direct challenge raised to the licensing system for foreign commerce set up through executive ordinances by President Wilson in World War I, and this decision did not come until after the outbreak of World War II. Acting under the Espionage Act of June 15, 1917, the President had issued several proclamations and orders, prohibiting exports from the United States without a license from the proper administrative authority, and providing for and setting up an organization to carry out and enforce the provisions of the new regulations.[67] One case involved a claim for damages against the United States on behalf of a Finnish vessel which had been detained in a United States port for 130 days because of the failure of the War Trade Board to grant a license for the export of necessary ships stores; but the Court of Claims dismissed the suit, remarking:

The United States was only carrying out and making effective the provisions of the act of congress and Executive orders enacted and issued in the lawful exercise of the power and authority possessed by the Government of the United States, and any inconvenience or loss resulting from delay incident to the exercise of such authority . . . is not damage . . . as would make the United States liable to indemnify the owner of such vessel therefor. . . .

We are of the opinion that the War Trade Board . . . had reasonable cause or ground to delay issuing licenses for ship's stores and supplies. This was a war period and the regulatory statutes, Executive orders, and the regulations were war measures, and what might be reasonable or proper cause in peacetime does not . . . establish standards for wartime requirements.[68]

A different World War I statute was the basis for the World War II system of controls, however. The Trading with the Enemy Act of October 6, 1917,[69] as amended by the Emergency Banking Act of March 9, 1933,[70] was the authority for Executive Orders No. 8389 of April 10, 1940, No. 8405 of May 10, 1940, and No. 8785 of June 14, 1941, which "froze" the assets in the United States of nationals of Norway and Denmark, Belgium and the Netherlands and Luxembourg, and all continental European states, respectively, by prohibiting all transactions in foreign exchange and transfers of credit except under a licensing system administered by the Treasury Department. Although the United States was not yet at war, Europe was, and the obvious purpose of the freezing orders was to prevent the control of monies located in the United States from falling into Nazi hands. The broad subdelegation of power by the President to the Secretary of the Treasury[71] was considered by a New York court to be indistinguishable, as a source of legal authority, from an act of Congress itself: "The executive orders have the force and effect of law and in their construction and interpretation the accepted canons of statutory construction are to be applied."[72]

The two aspects of the system of controls which appeared to be most vulnerable to legal attack were (1) the vesting in the Secretary of the Treasury the power to define for enforcement purposes the meaning of "nationals" to include corporations organized under the laws of states not subject to the freezing orders but nevertheless alleged to be under direct or indirect Axis control, and (2) the breadth of the original delegation of power to the President.

A New Jersey court dealt with the first question, citing the *Gold Clause* cases[73] as authority for its decision that the Secretary of the Treasury had properly blocked, under Section 9, subsection F, of Executive Order No. 8405, the account of LeCarbone Company, Inc. This firm was owned by French nationals, who had sold its assets to the Carbone Corporation for the apparent purpose of evading or avoiding the provisions of the executive order and Treasury regulations.[74]

The delegation issue was emphatically laid to rest by the Second Circuit Court of Appeals in a case charging criminal conspiracy, including the allegation that the defendant had made false declarations in regard to the importation of diamonds in order to avoid the licensing requirements of Executive Order No. 8405. This decision is noteworthy in offering one of the earliest of several open suggestions from federal courts to the effect that the principle of separation of powers is completely irrelevant to presidential-congressional action in the "sphere of foreign relations" in time of either war or peace:

It is true that the statute . . . in effect when the first "freezing" order of April 10, 1940, was issued, gave the Executive *unlimited discretion* during any "period of national emergency declared by" him to regulate or prohibit transactions in foreign exchange. As no standard was prescribed to guide him in the exercise of the power so delegated, the appellants urge that the test established in *Panama Refining Co.* v. *Ryan* . . . and *Schecter Poultry Corp.* v. *United States* . . . was not met. When Order No. 8405 of May 10, 1940 was issued Congress had passed the Joint Resolution of May 7, 1940, 54 Stat. 179, section 2 of which provided: "Executive Order Numbered 8389 of April 10, 1940, and the regulations and general rulings issued thereunder by the Secretary of the Treasury are hereby approved and confirmed" . . . [but] there is much persuasive force in the appellee's argument that the power exerted by the Executive with regard to property of foreign nationals in a time of proclaimed emergency falls within the sphere of foreign relations *and is thus free from the limitations imposed on delegated authority.*[75]

Related to the freezing orders were the export controls set up by Presidential Proclamation No. 2143 of July 2, 1940, issued under the authority of the National Defense Act[76] of the same date, which prohibited (among other things) the exportation of "platinum group metals" after July 5, 1940, except under license. The presidential power to determine what "military equipment and supplies" should be subject to regulation was upheld in a criminal prosecution of defendants who had attempted to smuggle platinum out of the United States to Portugal and other places.[77]

Almost identical was the ruling of a federal district court in Maryland in another criminal prosecution for smuggling platinum out of the country without a license, although the offense here took place after the enactment of the amendatory act of June 30, 1942, which had the effect of removing all limitations upon the President's power to determine the character of commodities which might be subjected to the controls while retaining the same procedural requirements. The President was also given express authority to transfer his rule-making powers under the act to any agency he saw fit, but he left them with the Board of Economic Warfare; and it was the general regulations of the board which were violated in this case. Rejecting the argument that there had been unlawful delegation of legislative power to the President, the court held: "If . . . broad authority may be delegated to the President as a necessary incident to the exercise of his constitutional authority with respect to international relations when our country is at peace, a fortiori must the same principle apply when our country is at war."[78]

Executive Bills of Attainder

During the undeclared naval war of the John Adams administration between the United States and France, Congress annually passed a non-intercourse act suspending all trade between the two countries. The *Flying Fish*, a Danish vessel having on board Danish and other neutral property, was captured on December 2, 1799, while en route from Hispaniola to St. Thomas, by the United States frigate *Boston* commanded by Captain Little. In accordance with his instructions,[79] Captain Little brought the *Flying Fish* into Boston, where she was libeled in the district court as an American vessel that had violated the non-intercourse law. In a countersuit against Captain Little by the owners of the vessel, his action was held to be tortious and damages were awarded against him; on appeal, Chief Justice Marshall, speaking for the unanimous Court, held that the President's instructions were invalid — and therefore furnished no protection to Little, who obeyed them at his peril — because the act of February 9, 1799, authorized only the seizure of vessels proceeding from the United States *to* French ports. The Supreme Court did not reach the alternative grounds that the instructions were invalid for the additional reason that they purported to authorize the seizure of vessels and cargoes covered by foreign papers while the statute was limited to property that was American as evinced by the ship's papers; neither did the Court consider the claim that even if the President's orders had been valid, Captain Little's action was still illegal, because he had brought the prize to Boston instead of "the nearest port in the United States." Marshall did, however, invite subsequent litigation by suggesting that, if Congress had not passed Section 5 specifying the conditions of capture, the presidential orders might well have been constitutional:

It is by no means clear that the President of the *United States*, whose high duty it is to "take care that the laws be faithfully executed," and who is commander in chief of the armies and navies of the *United States*, might not, without any special authority for that purpose, in the then existing state of things, have empowered the officers commanding the armed vessels of the *United States*, to seize and send into port for adjudication, *American* vessels which were forfeited by being engaged in this illicit commerce. But . . . the legislature seems to have prescribed that the manner in which this law shall be carried into execution, was to exclude a seizure of any vessel not bound *to* a *French* port.[80]

An opportunity to test the Marshall thesis was afforded by the War of 1812, and in the first suitable case to reach the Supreme Court, it was argued by counsel; but the Court sidestepped the issue at this time in an unanimous opinion delivered by Justice Story:

As to the authority of the president, we do not think it necessary to consider how far he would be entitled, in his character of commander in chief of the army and navy of the United States, independent of any statute provision, to issue instructions for the government and direction of privateers. That question would deserve grave consideration; and we should not be disposed to entertain the discussion of it, unless it became unavoidable. In the case at bar, no decision on the point is necessary; because we are all of opinion that, under the eighth section of the prize act of 1812, ch. 107, the president had full authority to issue the instruction of the 28th of August [by which the public and private vessels belonging to citizens of the United States coming from British ports to the United States laden with British merchandise were made exempt from seizure, in consequence of the supposed repeal of the British orders in council.][81]

A lower federal court had already ruled that the President could direct the seizure of enemy property without any express statutory authority, as a power he might lawfully exercise under the law of nations, when war had been declared by Congress;[82] but the next year, the Supreme Court held the direct opposite, with Justice Story now dissenting, arguing that Marshall's dictum in *Little* v. *Barreme* should be applied at least to the extent that the President, unless expressly limited by an act of Congress, was empowered to conduct war under any rule or usage recognized by international law.[83]

During the Civil War, all property located in the states in insurrection was subject to seizure upon their occupation by the Union armies. That taken under the Confiscation acts of August 6, 1861, and July 17, 1862, was forfeited; that seized under the Captured and Abandoned Property Act of March 12, 1863, was sequestered subject to return to the former owner upon his furnishing proof of his loyalty. Herein lay the crucial significance of the President's proclamations of amnesty, for acceptance of the conditional pardons they held forth[84] was a condition precedent to the recovery of their properties by the supporters of the Confederacy. Proof of loyalty without a pardon was possible for those resident within the Confederate States, but was difficult because of the legal presumption of disloyalty attaching to such residence. No cases reached the Supreme Court in which the constitutionality of these statutes or presidential action under them was successfully challenged;[85] but in one case the Court denounced in scathing terms what the majority held to have been the President's unconstitutional orders, in the absence of statutory authority, to certain of his military subordinates to confiscate the estate of General Robert E. Lee. The procedure authorized by Congress for the confiscation of rebel property was that of condemnation on the libel of the federal district attorney in one of the regular district courts. In this instance, however, the property had been seized during the war for default in the payment of direct taxes, and converted into Fort Myer and Arlington National Cemetery; and the attempts of Lee's heirs to obtain compensation for the property had been consistently frustrated. This was a five to four decision and came, it should be noted, long after the war was over; Mr. Justice Miller reached a kind of apogee of judicial passion in his statement of the self-righteous opinion of the majority of the Court:

[N]o person in this government exercises supreme executive power, or performs the public duties of a sovereign. . . .

This right [to the possession of the ancestral "homestead" of the claimant] being clearly established, we are told that the court can proceed no further, because it appears that certain military officers, acting under the orders of the President, have seized this estate, and converted one part of it into a military fort and another into a cemetery.

It is not pretended, as the case now stands, that the President had any lawful authority to do this, or that the legislative body could give him any such authority, except upon payment of just compensation. . . .

No man in this country is so high that he is above the law. No officer of the law may set that law at defiance, with impunity. All the officers of the government, from the highest to the lowest, are creatures of the law, and are bound to obey it.

Shall it be said . . . that the courts cannot give a remedy when the citizen has been deprived of his property by force, his estate seized and converted to the use of the government without lawful authority, without process of law, and without compensation, because the President has ordered it and his officers are in possession?

If such be the law of this country, it sanctions a tyranny which has no existence in the monarchies of Europe, nor in any other government which has a just claim to well regulated liberty and the protection of personal rights.

It cannot be, then, that when, in a suit between two citizens for the ownership of real estate, one of them has established his right to the possession of the property according to all the forms of judicial procedure, and by the verdict of a jury and the judgment of the court, the wrongful possessor can say successfully to the court, Stop here, I hold by order of the President, and the progress of justice must be stayed.[86]

The other "private citizen" party to this dispute was, of course, the United States of America which had, by public act of its highest executive officer, and in time of war, seized the property of a notorious traitor.[87] A patent fallacy in the reasoning of the Court is its shift from the concept of *governmental* immunity from suit, which is the point at issue in this case, to the concept of *sovereign* immunity, which is the point discussed. In his dissent, Justice Gray speaks of the Sovereign as though such a person actually existed in the United States in 1882, while the majority opinion takes great pains to repudiate this precise point in the course of its lengthy sermon on the theoretical limitations on presidential action and the necessity for holding the President subservient to the "rule of law." The only practical effect of the decision, of course, was to cause a disbursement of monies from the treasury to Lee's heirs-at-law; none of Lincoln's successors has perceptibly been inhibited in the exercise of the powers of his office by the Supreme Court's brave words. Like the *Milligan* case, the *Lee* case appears to be an aberration rather than a norm of our constitutional law. There are methods of challenging excesses of presidential authority in the courts, but until the enactment of the Federal Tort Claims Act in 1946, the right to sue the government for the tortious acts of the President and his subordinates on the theory that *he* is not the King of England — who, interestingly enough, lost his own official irresponsibility for the torts of his minions through the enactment of the Crown Proceedings Act of 1947 — was not one of them.

The slower process of judicial condemnation under a statute was replaced by summary seizure by administrative officers in World War I. As originally enacted, the Trading with the Enemy Act of October 6, 1917, authorized sequestration of the property of enemy aliens for the duration of the war emergency; but the failure of Congress to provide for the owner's recovery made the policy of sequestration, in effect, one of confiscation. The President appointed an alien property custodian, in whom power was vested by the statute summarily to vest in himself upon demand any property owned or controlled by an enemy alien; the avowed purpose was to prevent such property being withheld from the use of the United States in the prosecution of the war or to prevent its being actively used against the interests of the United States.

With a solitary exception, all the cases challenging the exercise of the alien property custodian's authority were decided after the war had ended. The exception was decided only two weeks before the Armistice, and in this case the Court of Chancery of New Jersey ruled invalid a vesting order of the custodian applicable to property held by a trustee under a will for the benefit of an alien enemy;[88] but this decision was reversed by the New Jersey Court of Errors and Appeals.[89] The lower federal courts were unanimous in upholding the various facets of the regulatory system questioned before them, including the summary nature of the transfer of title upon the formal demand of the custodian,[90] and the mandatory nature of the obligation to deliver property to the custodian upon his demand.[91] Since Congress failed to provide relief for the recovery by a German national of the value of property seized in the courts of the United States, his remedy was against his own government under the Treaty of Berlin, which provided also that the United States should assume the responsibility for the redress of claims of nationals of the United States for properties seized and confiscated by the German government.[92]

But the fundamental questions concerning the President's powers to dispose of property seized under the Trading with the Enemy Act were not settled by the Supreme Court until October 11, 1926, when an opinion was handed down in the *Chemical Foundation* case. At the close of World War I, the American chemical manufacturers who had been operating under confiscated German patents wanted such patents to remain their exclusive property. The Democratic administration, however, had set up a quasi-governmental corporation, the Chemical Foundation, to forestall a patent monopoly and to make the patents generally available to encourage the growth of an American chemical industry. President Harding subsequently directed the Department of Justice to undertake a prosecution under the antitrust laws to set aside the sale of the patents to the foundation, lodging a charge of fraud and conspiracy against "all the previously named officers and agents of the Government participating in the transaction except . . . President [Wilson], against whom the charge is withheld on the theory that he was either uninformed or misinformed as to what was going on."[93]

Wilson was in Europe at the time of the sales of the patents to the foundation. Before sailing, he issued his Executive Order No. 3016 of December 3, 1918, vesting in Frank L. Polk, the counselor of the Department of State, "all power and authority conferred upon the President by the provisions of sec. 12" of the Trading with the Enemy Act, as amended. Polk, by his orders of February 26, 1919, and April 5, 1919, authorized the alien property custodian to sell at private sale to the Chemical Foundation, without advertisement, at such places and upon such terms and conditions as the custodian might deem proper, all patents found to relate to the objects and purposes of the foundation as expressed in its charter. These orders contained a statement of the reasons for the sale and stated that it was in the public interest. Polk's orders were, therefore, the legal equivalent of such executive orders to the same effect as President Wilson himself personally might have issued had he been in the United States at the time of the sale.

As originally enacted, Section 12 made the custodian a mere conservator who was authorized to sell only to prevent waste. The amendment of March 28, 1918,[94] eliminated the restriction upon the power of sale, and authorized the custodian, acting under the direction of the President, to dispose of such properties by sale or otherwise "in like manner as though he were the absolute owner thereof."

Although the district court and circuit court of appeals had unhesitatingly upheld the constitutionality of Wilson's subdelegation to Polk and the validity of the sale by the custodian, the government still argued before the Supreme Court the illegality of the executive order of December 3, 1918, basically on the grounds that the President's power to determine the public interest — a condition precedent to the holding of a private sale as in this case — could not be subdelegated.[95] It was also charged that the form of the order was fatally defective in that it failed to allege either that Polk, to whom the power was delegated, was a public officer, or that the Woodrow Wilson who signed it was the President of the United States. The Supreme Court rejected both of these arguments and held substantially as had the district court, pointing out in addition that inept language indicating on its face improper delegation will not invalidate an order if the facts show that the intention and things done were within the valid limits.[96] The Attorney General's staff appear to be the only persons involved who took very seriously the argument that this was delegation of public power to a private person.

By 1938, action under the Trading with the Enemy Act had become accepted to such a point that a state court held it had no jurisdiction to pass upon the validity of an order of the alien property custodian, although this matter was the major point in the case:

[T]he validity of the action of the President in making the Executive Order of [August 25] 1935 and the validity of the subsequent action of the Attorney General [who was ex officio alien property custodian at this time] . . . have no place in this court. These questions are justiciable only in the federal courts. . . .

In our own state there is . . . finality in the recognition of the right of the federal government to demand and seize through the Executive Order of the President, supplemented by the demand of the Custodian, the property of enemies or those defined to be enemies by the federal statutes.[97]

It is worthy of incidental note that during World War I enemy property was seized other than under the Trading with the Enemy Act. For instance, by a joint resolution of May 12, 1917, Congress authorized the President to take over for the United States the immediate possession of and title to any vessel within its jurisdiction which at the time of coming therein was owned by any corporation, citizen, or subject of an enemy nation. By executive order of June 30, 1917, the President decreed that the vessel *Neckar* was enemy property, and ordered the United States Shipping Board to take possession. The owner denied the legality of the seizure under international law, but the Supreme Court ruled:

In the absence of convention every government may pursue what policy it thinks best concerning seizure and confiscation of enemy ships in its harbors when war occurs . . . a Joint Resolution of Congress whose language is very plain and refers only to enemy vessels . . . authorized the President to take "possession and title," and, obeying, he took them. We do not doubt the right of any independent nation so to do without violating any uniform or commonly accepted rule of international law. . . . Certainly all courts within the United States must recognize the legality of the seizure.[98]

Apart from the summary nature of the President's powers under the Trading with the Enemy Act is his authority conclusively to determine enemy status for the purpose of seizing property under the act. Since this power of determination was also summary in its nature, thus forestalling the possibility of proof of non-enemy character as a defense to enforcement proceedings,[99] Section 9 of the act[100] authorized suit for repossession of any property, or the interest therein or value thereof, which had been seized from a person who was not in fact — that is, not in the judgment of the courts — an enemy alien. Both the conclusiveness of the presidential determination of enemy status for seizure purposes and the adequacy of the statutory plan for judicial review were upheld by the Supreme Court shortly after the end of the war. In the one case, Justice Holmes delivered the unanimous opinion of the court that the determination of the alien property custodian that certain property was liable to seizure as that of an alien enemy must, whether right or wrong, be deemed conclusive in a possessory action brought by that officer to obtain immediate possession;[101] and again by a unanimous Court, a stockholder's suit to prevent disposition of the capital stock of a New Jersey subsidiary of a German corporation, on the basis that the President could not subdelegate his statutory power of determination to the custodian, was flatly dismissed:

It . . . is as if the words relied on had been "which the President, acting through the Alien Property Custodian, shall determine after investigation" is enemy owned, etc. In short, a personal determination by the President is not required; he may act through the Custodian, and a determination by the latter is in effect the act of the President.[102]

With the advent of World War II, the President's powers under the World War I statute were reactivated, and the office of alien property custodian was set up once again.[103] Just as it became necessary, even before our formal entrance into World War II, for the President to "freeze" the commercial credit and domestic bank accounts of non-enemy countries under the domination of the Axis, so also was it necessary for the custodian to vest in himself title to property that belonged to nominally "friendly" aliens and foreign nationals, who were administratively defined, for enforcement purposes, as "enemy nationals." In 1941, Congress amended Section 5(b) to give the President express statutory authority to seize the property of friendly aliens, when necessary to carry out the purposes of the statute, and no one succeeded in raising the question of this delegation as a constitutional issue until over two years after hostilities had ceased. Then the Silesian-American Corporation, a debtor in reorganization under the Bankruptcy Act, appealed from an order of a bankruptcy court in answer to its petition for instructions whether to comply with a demand made upon it by the alien property custodian to turn over shares in the debtor. These shares stood in the name of a Swiss corporation, and the certificates were held by certain Swiss banks as pledges. Finding that, although they were "owned" by the Swiss corporation, the corporation held them for the benefit of a German corporation, thus making them the property of a "national of a designated enemy country," the custodian issued his vesting order on November 17, 1942, stating "that to the extent that . . . such nationals are persons not within a designated enemy country the national interest . . . requires that such persons be treated as nationals of the aforesaid designated enemy country."

The circuit court of appeals and the Supreme Court upheld the statutory delegation, presidential subdelegation, and custodial implementation of this power as against the claims that "unrestricted discretion," admittedly given to the President by the act, constituted an unconstitutional delegation of legislative power. The courts also denied that Executive Order No. 9095 was so vague and indefinite that it violated due process; and that the Constitution forbade the taking of the property of friendly aliens without just compensation.[104] In the latter respect, both courts admitted the premise, but indulged in the pious presumption that Congress would, contrary to all existing evidence and practice,[105] provide for the just compensation required by the Fifth Amendment.[106] On the same day, however, the Court also decided that the effect of classifying a friendly alien as an "enemy national" for the purpose of summarily seizing his property was *not* automatically to give him the same classification under Section 9; for if this were true, such friendly aliens would not only be denied compensation for the taking of their property in the public interest; they would also then be denied any opportunity to claim or repossess it after hostilities (or the necessity for retention of possession by the custodian) had ended:

It was notorious that Germany and her allies had developed numerous techniques for concealing enemy ownership or control of property which was ostensibly friendly or neutral. They had through numerous devices, including the corporation, acquired indirect control or ownership in industries in this country for the purposes of economic warfare. Sec. 5 (b) was amended on the heels of the declaration of war to cope with that problem. Congress by that amendment granted the President the power to vest in an agency designated by him "any property or interest of any foreign country or national thereof." The property of all foreign interests was placed within reach of the vesting power, not to appropriate friendly or neutral assets but to reach enemy interests which masqueraded under those innocent fronts.

Thus the President acquired new "flexible powers" . . . to deal effectively with property interests which had either an open or concealed enemy taint.

While the scope of the President's power was broadened, there was no amendment restricting the scope of section 9(a). As we have noted, section 9(a) granted "any person not an enemy or ally of enemy" claiming an interest in property seized, the right to reclaim it.[107]

Since this decision, there have been no serious challenges to presidential authority in this area. Unlike the earlier cases which conceptualized the seizure of alien enemy property as a presidential function, however, more recent decisions look upon the matter as an administrative process, thus enabling the courts to apply the administrative law doctrine of "jurisdictional fact" and to reverse the custodian's determination of alien enemy status in a few instances where the equity of the case seemed clearly incompatible with the bureaucratic finding.[108]

Notes

[1] *In re* Lockington, Brightley's Reports, N.P., 269 (Pa., 1813).

[2] Lockington v. Smith, 15 Fed. Cas. 758, 760 (1817), No. 8,448.

[3] *Ex parte* Graber, 247 F. 882 (N.D.Ala.S.D., 1918).

[4] It should be recalled that due process is not necessarily judicial process.

[5] Minotto v. Bradley, 252 F. 600 (N.D.Ill., 1918).

[6] *Ex parte* Fronklin, 253 F. 984 (N.D.Miss., 1918). A World War II case which purported to follow expressly the three preceding decisions agreed that the courts had no

power to review the Attorney General's finding that the restraint of a petitioner was necessary as a measure of public safety, and that the only question open to the courts was that of whether he *was* an alien enemy within the terms of the proclamation and statute. In this instance, the court found that an Austrian Jew who came to the United States before the *Anschluss* was stateless, and not an alien enemy; he was therefore ordered released. United States *ex rel* Schwarzkopf v. Uhl, 137 F. 2d 898 (2 C.C.A., 1943). Accord: United States *ex rel* DeCicco v. Longo, 46 F. Supp. 170, 172 (D.Conn., 1942).

[7] "Alien enemies have no rights, no privileges, unless by the king's special favor, during time of war." 1 Blackstone 372.

[8] DeLacey v. United States, 249 F. 625 (9 C.C.A., 1918).

[9] *Ex parte* Risse, 257 F. 102 (S.D.N.Y., 1919). Cf. United States *ex rel* Zdhunic v. Uhl, 46 F. Supp. 688 (S.D.N.Y., 1942).

[10] *Ex parte* Gilroy, 257 F. 110, 112 (S.D.N.Y., 1919). The latter point was subsequently rejected by the Supreme Court; see the discussion of *Ludecke v. Watkins, infra.*

[11] "It should be noted that despite the holding of the World War I cases that no hearing was required, the President, during World War II, did provide for hearings for arrested alien enemies. In January, 1942, the Attorney General established alien hearing boards, 10 U.S. Law Week, 1942, page 2456. These boards, composed of from three to six civilian members, served without compensation, heard the alien's evidence, and made recommendations which were not binding on the Attorney General. The 'hearing has been provided, not as a matter of right, but in order to permit them to present facts in their behalf,' according to the instructions issued to the hearing boards, Department of Justice Supplemental Instructions to Alien Enemy Hearing Boards, January 7, 8, 1942." United States *ex rel* Schlueter v. Watkins, 67 F. Supp. 556, 565 (S.D.N.Y., 1946).

[12] United States *ex rel* Zdhunic v. Uhl, 46 F. Supp. 688, 690 (S.D.N.Y., 1942).

[13] United States v. Heine, 149 F. 2d 485 (2 C.C.A., 1945), c.d. 325 U.S. 885 (1945). Cf. United States v. Barra, 149 F. 2d 489 (2 C.C.A., 1945).

[14] 10 *Fed. Reg.* 12189.

[15] Citizens Protective League v. Byrnes, 64 F. Supp. 233 (D.Ct.D.C., 1946).

[16] Citizens Protective League v. Clark, 155 F. 2d 290, 294 (1946), c.d. 329 U.S. 787 (1946). Accord: United States *ex rel* Schlueter v. Watkins, 158 F. 2d 853 (2 C.C.A., 1946); United States *ex rel* Hack v. Clark, 159 F. 2d 552 (7 C.C.A., 1947); and United States *ex rel* Hoehn v. Shaughnessy, 175 F. 2d 116 (2 C.C.A., 1949), c.d. 338 U.S. 872 (1949).

[17] The effect of this decision was, of course, to require equivalent administrative procedure on the part of both the Secretary of State and the Attorney General and to ignore the foreign policy implications of Proclamation No. 2662. It is probable that the President's power would have been much broader if his proclamation had been based only on his constitutional authority and the international resolution and no reference had been made to the statute; compare Missouri v. Holland, 252 U.S. 416 (1920).

[18] United States *ex rel* Von Heymann v. Watkins, 159 F. 2d 650 (2 C.C.A., January 17, 1947). The government did not choose to appeal this decision to the Supreme Court.

[19] United States *ex rel* Dorfler v. Watkins, 171 F. 2d 431 (2 C.C.A., December 23, 1948), c.d. 337 U.S. 914; followed by United States *ex rel* Jaegeler v. Carusi, 187 F. 2d 912 (3 C.A., 1951). These practices resulted, in time, in a case where a man was held by the Immigration and Naturalization Service in what appeared to be protective custody for life. This national of an Iron Curtain country had been a resident of the United States for a quarter of a century. He was denied re-entry after a trip abroad on the grounds that he was a security risk; he was denied an administrative hearing; no other country would admit him either. By a 5–4 vote, the Supreme Court upheld his continued internment by executive fiat. Shaughnessy v. United States *ex rel* Mezei, 345 U.S. 206 (1953).

[20] *Ex parte* Zenzo Arakawa, 79 F. Supp. 468, 470–471 (E.D.Pa., 1947). Accord: Citizens Protective League v. Clark, 155 F. 2d, 290, 295 (C.A.D.C. 1946) and United States *ex rel* Jaegeler v. Carusi, 72 F. Supp. 805, 806 (E.D.Pa., 1947). This legal fiction was

destined to be perpetuated for another five years with respect to Japan, and almost as long in the case of Germany. The President's proclamation of October 24, 1951, confirming the congressional joint resolution of October 19, 1951, announced that the state of war which had existed between the United States and Germany since December 11, 1941, was terminated as of the date of the resolution. Therefore, the Supreme Court vacated the judgments of the lower courts and directed the release of a German enemy alien petitioner, because of this intervening joint resolution which terminated the Attorney General's statutory power to deport him. United States *ex rel* Jaegeler v. Carusi, 342 U.S. 347 (January 28, 1952). The Attorney General had acted in this case under Presidential Proclamation No. 2655; presumably, both this proclamation and No. 2662 remained in full effect with respect to Japanese nationals pending the ratification of the peace treaty with Japan. The Senate did not consent to the ratification of the treaty of peace with Japan until March 20, 1952; and the termination of war between the United States and Japan was announced as being effective April 28, 1952, in the President's Proclamation No. 2974 of that same date.

[21] 333 U.S. 138 (1948).

[22] Ludecke v. Watkins, 335 U.S. 160, 167, 170, 171-173 (1948). In his dissenting opinion, Justice Black argued that, since the Wilson administration had assumed that the President's powers under this statute had lapsed with the Armistice and had induced Congress to adopt legislation expressly authorizing the deportation of interned alien enemies but only after a fair hearing and with the right of judicial review of the Attorney General's decision, the same interpretation should have been made and the same course pursued by the Truman administration.

Subsequent attempts to get the Supreme Court and the lower courts to reconsider the issues of due process and restoration of peace were uniformly unsuccessful: United States *ex rel* Dorfler v. Watkins, 171 F. 2d 431 (2 C.C.A., December 23, 1948), c.d. 337 U.S. 914 (1949); United States *ex rel* Bejeuhr v. Shaughnessy, 177 F. 2d 436 (2 C.A., 1949), c.d. 338 U.S. 948 (1950).

[23] See Morton Grodzins, *Americans Betrayed* (Chicago: University of Chicago Press, 1949).

[24] The relocation centers were not, of course, called "concentration camps" by the government. Compare the Soviet attitude toward the naming of "corrective-labor (I.T.L.) camps": David J. Dallin, "The Slave Empire within the Soviet Empire," *New York Times Magazine*, pp. 36, 38 (October 14, 1951). See also the Associated Press dispatch under the dateline of December 31, 1951, reporting an announcement of the Attorney General that work had "begun on three detention camps to hold more than 3,000 potential spies and saboteurs in the event of war or similar national emergency." The statutory basis for this "full-scale plan for the detention of subversive elements of the population" was the Internal Security (McCarran) Act of 1950 (P.L. 831, 81st Cong., 2d sess.), Title II, which was directed at Communists and fellow travelers.

[25] 7 *Fed. Reg.* 1407 (February 19, 1942).

[26] 56 *Stat.* 173, 18 U.S.C.A. sec. 97a.

[27] A full account is given in Grodzins, *op. cit.*, and Alexander Leighton, *The Governing of Men* (Princeton, N.J.: Princeton University Press, 1945).

[28] This information was denied on the ground that the facts which warranted the order against her were confidential.

[29] Schueller v. Drum, 51 F. Supp. 383 (E.D.Pa., 1943).

[30] Ebel v. Drum, 52 F. Supp. 189 (D.Mass., 1943).

[31] Von Knorr v. Miles, 60 F. Supp. 962 (D.Mass., 1945).

[32] Von Knorr v. Griswold, 156 F. 2d 287 (1946); but see Alexewicz v. General Analine and Film Corp., 43 N.Y.S. 2d 713 (1943), upholding the dismissal from employment by presidential authority, of an American citizen who had been working for a corporation designated as a "foreign national."

[33] Alexander v. DeWitt, 141 F. 2d 573 (1944).

[34] *Ex parte* Ventura, 44 F. Supp. 520, 523 (W.D.Wash.N.D., 1942).

[25] The alleged violation of due process inherent in the discriminatory classification of the military orders.

[36] *Ex parte* Kanai, 46 F. Supp. 286 (1942).

[37] I.e., "No person shall . . . be deprived of life, liberty, or property without due process of law." Constitution of the United States, Amendment V.

[38] United States v. Gordon K. Hirabayashi, 46 F. Supp. 657, 661, 662 (W.D.Wash.-N.D., 1942). Italics supplied.

[39] United States v. Minoru Yasui, 48 F. Supp. 40, 54 (D.Ore., 1942).

[40] Hirabayashi v. United States, 320 U.S. 81 (1943); Yasui v. United States, 320 U.S. 115 (1943).

[41] Korematsu v. United States, 140 F. 2d 289, 291, 292, 293, 295 (1943). Italics in the original.

[42] Korematsu v. United States, 323 U.S. 214, 219 (1944). It is an interesting excursion into the realm of judicial politics and ethics to compare the high degree of separability discovered by the Court in the "separate steps" of the amazing plethora of administrative subdelegation of power, transferral of power, assumption of power, duplication of authority, and intermixture of civil with military control that characterized the complex and integrated evacuation program, with the "inseparability" attributed to the Guffey-Snyder Coal Act and the administrative programs authorized by it in the case of Carter v. Carter Coal Co., 298 U.S. 238 (1936).

[43] "To find that the Constitution does not forbid the military measures now complained of does not carry with it approval of that which Congress and the Executive did. That is their business, not ours." 323 U.S. 214, 224–225.

[44] 7 *Fed. Reg.* 4498.

[45] *Ibid.*, 8346.

[46] *Ibid.*, 6593.

[47] *Ibid.*, 7656.

[48] 9 *Fed. Reg.* 154.

[49] *Ex parte* Endo, 323 U.S. 283, 297 (1944).

[50] Compare the position taken by the Court in Duncan v. Kahanamoku, 327 U.S. 304 (1946).

[51] Korematsu v. United States, 323 U.S. 214, 246 (1944).

[52] Ochikubo v. Bonesteel, 60 F. Supp. 916, 926 (S.D.Cal.C.D., 1945).

[53] Wilcox v. Emmons, 67 F. Supp. 339, 355 (S.D.Cal.C.D., 1946). This decision was not appealed. In an earlier action, Wilcox had attempted unsuccessfully to enjoin his exclusion from the Western Defense Command; see Wilcox v. DeWitt, 71 F. Supp. 704 (S.D.Cal.S.D., 1943), dismissed on stipulation of counsel for parties, in 144 F. 2d 353 (9 C.C.A., 1944). See also a connected case, United States v. Bell, 48 F. Supp. 986 (1943), reversed on grounds not material here, 159 F. 2d 247 (9 C.C.A., 1947).

[54] 12 *Stat.* 1259.

[55] *The Amy Warwick*, 1 Fed. Cas. 799, 804, 805 (D.Mass., 1862), No. 341. In *The Aigburth*, 21 Fed. Cas. 462 (1861), No. 12,352, Judge Betts, sitting in district court in New York City, held that the President's power to declare the blockade was authorized not only by the Constitution but also that it was a valid blockade under the rules of international law. See also Hunter v. United States, 2 Wall. 135 (1865).

[56] The Prize Cases, 2 Black 635, 666, 668, 671 (1863). See Rossiter, *op. cit.*, pp. 65–77, for a more extended discussion of the background of this case. Justice Nelson dissented on the ground that the President could not exercise his "war powers" until war was declared, and that the Constitution clearly vested that decision in Congress; but see James Grafton Rogers, *World Policing and the Constitution* (Boston: World Peace Foundation, 1945), especially Chapter IV.

[57] Currie v. The *Josiah Harthorn*, 6 Fed. Cas. 987 (S.D.N.Y.), No. 3491a. This was an admiralty case, arising from a maritime accident which took place before the war began; but since one of the parties was a resident of Richmond, Virginia, the suit was dismissed.

[58] United States v. One Hundred Barrels of Cement, 27 Fed. Cas. 292 (E.D.Mo., 1862), No. 15,945. The goods here were forfeited, however, because the license had been obtained by fraud and had been used fraudulently.

[59] *The Sea Lion*, 5 Wall. 630, 647 (1867).

[60] Coppell v. Hall, 7 Wall. 542, 556 (1869).

[61] McKee v. United States, 8 Wall. 163 (1869). Nor was the government bound by a contract entered into by a Treasury agent at Norfolk, Virginia, to purchase cotton located within the Confederate lines; for although the act of 1861 was amended by Section 8 of the act of July 2, 1864, to permit the issuance of licenses by Treasury agents, Congress had not conferred power on such agents to license trading within the military lines of the enemy. United States v. Lane, 8 Wall. 185 (1869).

[62] 21 Wall. 73, 95 (1875).

[63] *Ibid.*, 90, 93.

[64] *Ibid.*, 96–97.

[65] *Ibid.*, 87.

[66] Walker's Executors v. United States, 106 U.S. 413, 421 (1882).

[67] Including (1) the executive order of June 22, 1917, creating an Exports Council with advisory powers; (2) the proclamation of July 9, 1917, as amended on August 27, 1917, and February 14, 1918, making the Secretary of Commerce the licensing authority, and delegating rule-making powers to him and listing the items subject to controls; (3) the executive order of August 21, 1917, creating an Exports Administration Board which succeeded to the licensing powers of the Secretary of Commerce; and (4) the executive order of October 12, 1917, creating the War Trade Board which succeeded to the powers of the Exports Administration Board.

[68] J. A. Zachariassen & Co. v. United States, 94 Ct. Cl. 315, 341, 343 (1941), c.d. 315 U.S. 815 (1942).

[69] 40 *Stat.* 411.

[70] 48 *Stat.* 1. This amendment gave the President authority to exercise his statutory powers "through any agency that he may delegate." In practice, fiscal controls were administered by the Secretary of the Treasury, and all other control of alien property was under the jurisdiction of the alien property custodian during World War II.

[71] Section 1 of the basic executive order provided: "All of the following transactions are prohibited, except as specifically authorized by the Secretary of the Treasury by means of regulations, rulings, instructions, licenses, or otherwise"; and Section 8 stated that any violation of the provisions of the executive order, including the administrative legislation and other action subsequently adopted pursuant thereto, was made a penal offense punishable by fine or imprisonment or both by Section 5(b) of the Trading with the Enemy Act, as amended.

[72] Brown v. J. P. Morgan & Co., 31 N.Y.S. 2d 323, 333 (1941).

[73] Norman v. Baltimore and Ohio Railroad Company, 294 U.S. 240 (1935); Nortz v. United States, 294 U.S. 317 (1935); and Perry v. United States, 294 U.S. 330 (1935).

[74] Carbone Corp. v. First National Bank of Jersey City, 21 A. 2d 366, 369 (1941). Cf. Draeger Shipping Co. v. Crowley, 55 F. Supp. 906 (S.D.N.Y., 1944).

[75] United States v. Von Clemm, 136 F. 2d 968, 970 (1943), c.d. 320 U.S. 769 (1943). Italics supplied. In Hartman v. Federal Reserve Bank of Philadelphia, 55 F. Supp. 801 (E.D.Pa., 1944), the validity of Executive Order No. 8389 was upheld on the ground that any question of constitutionality had been "conclusively" eliminated by congressional ratification in the joint resolution of May 7, 1940, and the act of December 18, 1941.

[76] 54 *Stat.* 714.

[77] United States v. Rosenberg, 47 F. Supp. 406, 408 (E.D.N.Y., 1942); affirmed by the Second Circuit Court of Appeals, which had decided the *Von Clemm* case, on the alternative grounds that the delegation was justified either as a defense measure under the war power or because it was within the "sphere of foreign relations," 150 F. 2d 788, 790, 794 (1945). Judge Chase concurred, relying only on the second ground and arguing

The Fifth Column

that it was unnecessary to consider the first, since "It is enough that the delegation concerned the conduct of the foreign affairs of this country."

[78] United States v. Bareno, 50 F. Supp. 520, 525 (D.Md., 1943). In addition to platinum, practically all synthetic textiles, including rayon dresses, had been subjected to the export controls. An attempt to smuggle such material across the border into Mexico near El Paso was frustrated and the seized goods condemned, the district court ruling that the various presidential proclamations and orders involved were valid and "well within the bounds of the Act." United States v. 251 Ladies Dresses, 53 F. Supp. 772 (S.D.Tex., Brownsville D., 1943).

[79] From President Adams, dated March 12, 1799: "it is the command of the president *that you consider particularly the fifth section as part of your instructions.* . . . You are not only to do all that in you lies to prevent all intercourse, whether direct or circuitous, between the ports of the *United States* and those of *France* and her dependencies, in cases where the vessels or cargoes are *apparently, as well as really, American,* and protected by *American* papers only; but you are to be vigilant that vessels or cargoes really *American, but covered by Danish or other foreign papers* and bound to *or from French* ports, do not escape you." A copy of the act of February 9, 1799, which was in effect at the time, was enclosed. Section 5 of that act read: "That it shall be lawful for the President of the *United States* to give instructions to the commanders of the public armed ships of the *United States,* to stop and examine any ship or vessel *of the United States* on the high seas, which there may be *reason to suspect* . . . if, upon examination, it shall appear that such ship or vessel is bound or sailing *to* any port or place *within the territory of the French republic* . . . it shall be the duty of the commander of such public armed vessel, to seize every such ship or vessel engaged in such illicit commerce, and send the same to the nearest port in the *United States.*" See Little v. Barreme, 2 Cranch 170, 171 (1804).

[80] *Ibid.,* 177–178.

[81] *The Thomas Gibbons,* 8 Cranch 421, 427–428 (1814).

[82] *The Emulous,* 8 Fed. Cas. 697 (C.Ct.Mass., 1813), No. 4479. This decision was not appealed.

[83] Brown v. United States, 8 Cranch 110 (1814).

[84] Excepting that of December 25, 1868; but by this time, statutes of limitations and vested interests of third parties barred recovery of many former owners and their heirs who had not chosen or been able to accept the conditions of the earlier proclamations.

[85] See, for instance, "The Confiscation Cases," 20 Wall. 92 (1874).

[86] United States v. Lee, 106 U.S. 196, 206, 219–221 (1882).

[87] "Treason against the United States, shall consist only in levying War against them, or in adhering to their Enemies, giving them Aid and Comfort." Constitution of the United States, Article III, 3 (1).

[88] Keppelmann v. Keppelmann, 105 A. 140, 142 (1918).

[89] Keppelmann *et al.* v. Palmer, Alien Property Custodian, 108 A. 432 (1919).

[90] Kohn v. Jacob & Josef Kohn, 264 F. 253, 255 (S.D.N.Y., 1920). Accord: Garvan v. Marconi Telegraph Co. of America, 275 F. 486, 488 (D.N.J., 1921); and *In re* Miller, 281 F. 764, 772, 774 (2 C.C.A., 1922), appeal dismissed in Schaefer v. Miller, 262 U.S. 760 (1923).

[91] *In re* Garvan, 270 F. 1002, 1003 (E.D.N.Y., 1921).

[92] Munich Reinsurance Co. v. First Reinsurance Co. of Hartford, 300 F. 345 (D.Conn., 1924); affirmed in 6 F.2d 742 (2 C.C.A., 1925).

[93] The same theory of presidential ignorance was indulged in Harding's own behalf in cases arising from the Teapot Dome scandal, which reached the Supreme Court at about the same time as the Chemical Foundation case. See Chapter 3, *supra.*

[94] Section 12, as amended, provided: "The alien property custodian . . . acting under the supervision and direction of the President, and under such rules and regulations as the President shall prescribe, shall have power to manage such property and to do any act or things in respect thereof or to make any disposition thereof or of any part there-

of, by sale or otherwise . . . : *Provided*, That any property sold under this Act, except when sold to the United States, shall be sold only to American citizens . . . at public sale which shall be where the property or a major portion thereof is situated, *unless the President stating the reasons therefore, in the public interest shall otherwise determine."* Italics supplied.

[95] It is noteworthy that on this point, Judge Buffington of the Third Circuit Court of Appeals differed from his colleagues, remarking in his separate opinion: "It was the President who was to determine, and his determination involved his ascertainment of public necessity and his statement of the reasons thereto moving him. In my judgment this personal presidential trust could not be delegated, and the delegation of it to Mr. Polk was not in accordance with the statute, and therefore was without warrant of law. But the President's subsequent approval and ratification of what was done under the delegation [by his executive order of February 13, 1920] constituted such personal action by the President as validates the sale. I therefore concur in the conclusion reached." United States v. Chemical Foundation, 5 F. 2d 191, 214 (3 C.C.A., 1925).

[96] United States v. Chemical Foundation, 272 U.S. 1 (1926). The "inept language" was the use of the word "vest" instead of "delegate." The Court held that the President could not possibly divest himself of responsibility that had been vested in him by statute; but he could delegate to another his duties, requiring that they be performed subject to his direction and control.

[97] *In re* Sielcken's Estate, 3 N.Y.S. 2d 793, 797 (Surrogate's Court, New York County) (1938).

[98] Littlejohn & Co. v. United States, 270 U.S. 215, 226–227 (1926).

[99] Section 7 made the seizure lawful even though the determination that it was enemy owned was clearly erroneous. Becker Steel Co. of America v. Cummings, 296 U.S. 74, 79 (1935).

[100] As materially amended by the act of June 5, 1920, 41 *Stat.* 977.

[101] Central Union Trust Co. v. Garvan, 254 U.S. 554 (1921).

[102] Stoehr v. Wallace, 255 U.S. 239, 245 (1921). Both this case and the preceding one were expressly reaffirmed and followed by the Supreme Court in McGrath v. Manufacturer's Trust Co., 338 U.S. 241 (November 7, 1949).

[103] See Executive Orders No. 9095 and No. 9193. The President's custodial functions respecting seized enemy property had been exercised by the Attorney General ex officio during most of the preceding two decades.

[104] Silesian-American Corp. v. Markham, 156 F. 2d 793 (2 C.C.A., 1946); affirmed by Silesian-American Corp. v. Clark, 332 U.S. 469 (1947). The office of the custodian had been abolished during the interim before the Supreme Court gave its decision, and just as happened after World War I, his duties were transferred to the Attorney General, who was substituted for the wartime custodian as the defendent there. See Executive Order No. 9788, 1 C.F.R. 1946 Supp. 169.

[105] Congress made no special provision after World War I. Suit under Section 9 for the return of the property or the proceeds thereof remained the exclusive remedy for non-enemy aliens.

[106] "We must assume that the United States will meet its obligations under the Constitution." 332 U.S. 469, 480 (1947).

[107] Clark v. Uebersee Finanz-Korp., 332 U.S. 480, 484–486 (1947). It was also necessary, in some instances, to extend the power of definition even more broadly, to include citizens of the United States within the concept of "alien enemy"; see Draeger Shipping Co. v. Crowley, 55 F. Supp. 906, 912 (S.D.N.Y., 1944); and *In re* Viscomi's Estate, 60 N.Y.S. 2d 897 (1946).

[108] Josephberg v. Markham, 152 F. 2d 644 (3 C.C.A., 1945); Kotohira Jinsha v. McGrath, 90 F. Supp. 892 (1950); Kaku Nagano v. McGrath, 187 F. 2d 759 (1951), affirmed *per curiam* by an equally divided Court (Clark not participating), 342 U.S. 916 (1952); and Guessefeldt v. McGrath, 342 U.S. 308 (1952).

8

The Seizure Power and Emergency Regulation

Temporary Seizure by the President

In addition to its power to confiscate the property of enemy aliens in time of war, the national government in time of emergency may rigidly control the use of its citizens' property. The powers of the President in this regard have become increasingly important during the last forty years, largely because of the demands that the prosecution of major foreign wars, and their aftermath, have made upon the nation's entire economy. This movement began during World War I, when President Wilson, acting under statutory powers, seized in the name of the government various transportation utilities including all railroads in the United States and the terminals in seaports for ocean-going vessels, and such communications facilities as the telephone and telegraph lines and the commercial cables.

Under authority of the National Defense Act of August 29, 1916, the President issued his proclamation of December 26, 1917, taking possession of the railroads and creating the office of director general of railroads, to which he appointed the Secretary of the Treasury, William G. McAdoo.[1] Shortly thereafter, Congress adopted the Federal Control Act of March 21, 1918, Section 10 of which authorized the President to set rates during the period of federal control pending a final determination by the Interstate Commerce Commission, and specifically ratified his proclamation of December 26. The proclamation, in turn, had stated that "any orders, general or special, hereafter made by said Director, shall have paramount authority and be obeyed as such." The director proceeded to exercise his subdelegated rule-making powers extensively to prevent the federal and state judiciary from being used to harass either the operating companies or the government during the period of federal control.[2]

Numerous cases decided in the state and lower federal courts dealt with the validity of the orders of the director general, the majority of those decided by the federal courts upholding their validity while the majority of those decided by state courts denied the constitutionality of this exercise of his rule-making powers. Relatively few cases were concerned with the question of the constitutionality of the President's proclamation under which all action by the director general was taken, but those decided after the statute of March 21, 1918, had been adopted all upheld this subdelegation on the ground that Congress had ratified the President's action.[3] The other most controversial aspect of federal control related to the President's interim rate-making powers. The director general's order of May 25, 1918, had set rate schedules for both intrastate and interstate commerce, and the North Dakota State Utilities Commission secured a peremptory writ of mandamus from the state supreme court commanding the director general to authorize only the lower rates previously approved by the Utilities Commission for intrastate hauls in North Dakota rather than those set by his general order. However, this decision was reversed by the Supreme Court, thereby upholding the power of the President to determine, through the director general, all rate schedules for railroads for the duration of the war emergency.[4]

By his proclamation of July 22, 1918, promulgated under authority of the joint resolution of July 16, 1918, the President also assumed possession and control over the operation of all telegraph and telephone systems in the United States. He directed the Postmaster General to assume control as of August 1, 1918, and to set a rate schedule. An order of the South Dakota Supreme Court enjoining the operating companies in the state from putting into effect the higher schedule of rates for intrastate telephone service established by the Postmaster General was reversed by the Supreme Court in accordance with its own decision of that same day in the intrastate railroad rate case,[5] on the basis that the joint resolution was constitutional, the acts of the Postmaster General under that delegation were the same in legal effect as though performed by the President himself, and the judiciary had no power to review the wisdom or necessity of the determination of the particular rate schedule here involved.[6] The Court followed its precedent again in a case which held that a railroad company was not liable for a tort committed while its properties were under federal control;[7] but since the Postmaster General had issued no order comparable to the director general's General Order No. 50 (which directed that suits be filed against him rather than the operating companies), neither the government (which was, of course, immune from suit for tort unless it specifically granted permission to sue) nor the telegraph company — under the rule of the *Missouri Pacific* case — was liable.[8]

Acting under the same joint resolution, the President took over, on the eve of the Armistice, the commercial cable systems by his proclamation of November 2, 1918. As in the case of the telephone and telegraph lines, he acted through the Postmaster General. A federal district court, facing squarely the constitutional issue implicit in this action, held that the companies that owned the cables were in no position to challenge the taking of their property because the Chief Executive's discretion was immune from challenge; but since the cables were returned to their owners while the Supreme Court held the case under advisement, that Court dismissed the petition on the ground that the President's action in relinquishing governmental operation and control (and turning over to the company the revenues it had collected) had made the controversy moot.[9]

With the exception of the three weeks of federal control of the railroads during the winter of 1943–1944 and the isolated instances of individual seizure under the National Defense Act of 1916, most seizures of industrial and commercial properties during World War II were made by the President under Section 3 of the War Labor Disputes (Smith-Connally) Act of 1943, which amended Section 9 of the Selective Service Training Act of 1940.[10] The theory underlying this statute was that the President could take possession of any plant engaged in war production that was threatened by a strike which might "unduly impede or delay" the "war effort," and direct the management of the enterprise until such time as the labor dispute was settled. Very few cases challenging such presidential seizure were decided by the courts, and none reached the Supreme Court until after hostilities had ceased.

In the first to arise, an attempt was made to enjoin Carroll Badeau, a colonel in the United States Army, from putting into effect a War Labor Board order directing certain wage readjustments, and from seizing, retaining possession of, or operating any of the properties of the Ken-Rad Corporation, which were engaged exclusively in war production. Colonel Badeau had assumed possession in the name of the United States and managed the properties in accordance with the President's order of April 13, 1944. Ken-Rad argued that, since the President's order directing the seizure of the plants was based on the fear of threatened strikes resulting from the refusal of Ken-Rad to comply with an allegedly invalid order of the War Labor Board, therefore the President's order was likewise invalid. The federal district court, however, held that the question of the validity of the War Labor Board order was irrelevant:

The record fails to disclose any grounds upon which the court could find that the President, in issuing the order, acted arbitrarily or without cause. He was not bound by the findings of the War Labor Board. Even though they might have been based upon erroneous procedure or wrongful construction of facts, the President may have had other facts upon which he determined his course . . . it is my judgment that section 9 does not confine the President to any one field of information but that he may make his own independent investigation and, subject to the determination by the courts that his action was not arbitrary, may act to prevent a cessation of operations of any plant or business or other agency which might be utilized to contribute to the war effort.

I further conclude that without an act of the Congress there was sufficient authority by the terms of the Constitution itself to justify the action of the President in this case . . . when war has been declared and is actually existing, his functions as Commander in Chief become of the highest importance and his operations in that connection are *entirely beyond the control of the legislature*. There devolves upon him, by virtue of his office, a solemn responsibility *to preserve the nation* and it is my judgment that there is specifically granted to him authority to utilize all resources of the country to that end.[11]

Since the constitutionality of government operation of the railroads under presidential direction had been clearly established by the World War I cases, and the scope of presidential statutory authority was greater during World War II — to say nothing of the growth in judicial recognition of an enlarged scope of direct constitutional presidential powers during the intervening period — only one district court decision appears to deal with the constitutionality of presidential action in this regard. The plaintiff railroad in this case had been taken over by the Office of Defense Transportation pursuant to Executive Order No. 9108, March 21, 1942, and subsequently the Secretary of War on December 27, 1943, had taken possession of it along with all the other rail common carriers in the continental United States, in accordance with the President's Executive Order No. 9142 of the same date. The possession and control was continued by the Secretary of War until January 18, 1944, when the Secretary, acting under Executive Order No. 9142, determined that continued possession, operation, and control by the United States of the carriers taken under *that order* were no longer necessary to prevent interruption of transportation or service. The plaintiff's properties were then turned back to the possession of the former federal manager under the Office of Defense Transportation. The railroad argued that the effect of the Secretary of War's determination was to terminate federal control under Executive Order No. 9108 as well, although that order stated that "operation of plaintiff's property should be continued only until *the President* determined that such temporary possession and operation was no longer required for successful prosecution of the war"; and the court agreed with this line of reasoning.

Holding that only the ratification of Congress had saved Wilson's action in ordering federal operation during World War I under the Secretary of the Treasury instead of the Secretary of War, who was the agent specified in the basic 1916 statute, the court also ventured the dictum that President Roosevelt's Executive Order No. 9108, directing that possession of this railroad be taken by the director of defense transportation, would likewise have been invalid if based solely on the 1916 statute. The court considered that Roosevelt's action was saved, however, by the broad powers of reorganization granted to the President in the First War Powers Act. Although the director of defense transportation would certainly be as much the alter ego and agent of the President as the World War I director general of railroads had been held to be by the courts, and his resumption of control must certainly be accepted as an expression of the presidential judgment that continued possession and control by the government was essential to the continued prosecution of the war, this federal judge undertook to substitute his own judgment for that of the President by declaring that Executive Order No. 9108 had been automatically revoked by Executive Order No. 9142, and that the purported exercise of control and possession by the government subsequent to January 18, 1944, was invalid.[12]

Without any question, however, the most vigorous and determined challenge to the President's seizure powers was that of Montgomery Ward. Ward was aided, in its first direct legal thrust, by that self-avowed champion of the cause of labor[13] and late ornament of the bench of the District Court of the District of Columbia, Judge T. Alan Goldsborough, who denied both Montgomery Ward's motion for a preliminary injunction to restrain the board from exceeding the scope of its authority and the board's motion to dismiss.[14] Since the *Employers Group* opinion had been announced only two weeks before Goldsborough's decision and he had refused to follow it, the court of appeals reversed and dismissed the petition on the authority of that decision,[15] and certiorari was denied by the Supreme Court.[16]

Six weeks later President Roosevelt issued Executive Order No. 9508, directing the Secretary of War to take possession of and to operate the plants and facilities of the company. Formal occupation took place the following day; it was front page news at the time that Sewell Avery, the chairman of the board, had to be carried bodily out of his Chicago office by military personnel in order for occupation to be symbolically consummated. The government then sought a declaratory judgment in the Chicago federal district court to get explicit judicial confirmation of the validity of Executive Order No. 9508, but that court decided that Montgomery Ward was engaged in retail selling and distribution, not *production*. Since the War Labor Disputes Act applied only to war production, and the President had no direct constitutional authority to seize the corporation on the state of facts then existing, his executive order was unconstitutional.[17] In a split decision, the Seventh Circuit Court of Appeals reversed, holding that the definition of "production" in the Fair Labor Standards Act (which, of course, included the activities of Montgomery Ward) was controlling in the definition of the same word in the War Labor Disputes Act; and that they would uphold the inclusion of Ward within the latter act even "without the aid of the definition found in the Fair Labor

Standards Act." The majority also indicated that they would be willing if necessary — and they did not find it necessary in this case since there was ample statutory authority — to uphold the seizure of Ward on the basis of the absence of judicial power to review the President's determination.[18] The Supreme Court then vacated the judgment of the circuit court of appeals and remanded the case to the district court with directions to dismiss as moot; the President had returned Ward's properties before the Supreme Court reached the case on its docket.[19] This, it might be noted, was not the first time[20] that the Supreme Court dismissed as moot a case in which a lower federal court had written a judgment that was exceptionally generous in its tolerance of the scope of the President's constitutional powers to convert private property to public uses in time of war.

The Supreme Court did affirm the existence of such power in the President, although it did not find it necessary to separate his constitutional power from his statutory powers to the same effect, in the celebrated *United Mine Workers* case, in which the contempt fines meted out to John L. Lewis and his union by Judge Goldsborough were scaled down to $700,000 in the case of the latter.[21] No question of the conclusiveness of the President's determination of the necessity for taking over the mines or of his power to seize them was directly raised before the Supreme Court, since it was concerned with the illegality of the union's strike in the face of the district court's injunction after seizure and governmental operation and control under the Secretary of the Interior had begun. The Court stated, *as facts*, however:

In October, 1946, the United States was in possession of, and operating, the major portion of the country's bituminous coal mines. (1) The United States had taken possession of the mines pursuant to Executive Order 9728 of May 21, 1946, 11 FR 5593, in which the President, after determining that labor disturbances were interrupting the production of bituminous coal necessary for the operation of the national economy during the transition from war to peace, directed the Secretary of the Interior to take possession of and operate the mines and to negotiate with representatives of the miners concerning the terms and conditions of employment.

The President's action was taken *under the Constitution, as President of the United States and Commander in Chief of the Army and Navy,* and by virtue of the authority conferred upon him by the War Labor Disputes Act.[22]

Shortly after the Korean War broke out, labor disputes threatened to disrupt the transportation of men and supplies vitally needed to support the military action and national defense. By his executive orders of July 8 and August 25, 1950, President Truman seized and undertook to operate a substantial number of the nation's railroads. The recent *United Mine Workers* decision of the Supreme Court made it clear that the President's orders — if valid — could be enforced by the equity powers of the federal district courts, with contempt of court convictions as the ultimate sanction. As in the earlier instances of railroad seizure, the President invoked his statutory powers under the National Defense Act of August 29, 1916. In one instance where the strike was already underway and the union had refused to order the men back to work, claiming that the President's attempt to act under wartime powers was unconstitutional, the trial court granted the government's motion for an injunction, ruling that World War II *de jure* continued in the absence of peace treaties with Germany and Japan.[23] This court also took judicial notice of the Korean War; and although the solitary judicial precedent arising from World War II[24] was noted, it was distinguished as immaterial to the facts of this case. Citing the *Chemical Foundation* and *United Mine Workers* cases, the court ruled that "The Executive Order herein, or the basis of fact on which it rests, cannot be reviewed judicially."[25] In a later but similar case, the union argued that the seizure was a mere token act and nothing but a sham; their members, it was claimed, were not really government employees. But an injunction issued,[26] and as was becoming customary, the issue was moot by the time the Supreme Court was ready to decide it.[27]

These apparent trends in the development of a number of related strands of case law governing presidential power to assume temporary control and possession of private property were thrown into substantial confusion by the Supreme Court's 1952 decision in the *Steel* case.[28] The principal question at issue was the scope of the independent constitutional power of the Chief Executive to intervene by temporarily seizing control of plants and facilities in order to forestall a strike in a basic industry which would have very serious implications for national defense. Although the seizure order was promulgated at a time when the threat of war with the U.S.S.R. seemed grave, and a threefold national emergency was in existence,[29] the government chose to waive part of this defense[30] and the majority of the Supreme Court considered the case as though Normalcy were Here Again.[31]

This assumption served to eliminate the presidential status as Commander in Chief as an available source of constitutional power, which in turn opened the door for the interjection of the theory of separation of powers as the determinative criterion and constitutional principle guiding the Court's decision. The consensus of the majority was that the investiture of executive power in the President combined with the "faithful execution" clause gave him no authority of a "legislative" nature, and that the national power of eminent domain was a "legislative" power.[32] Congressional intent was inferred from a perusal of the texts of the Taft-Hartley Act of 1947, the Selective Service Act of 1948, and the Defense Production Act of 1950.[33] Since the Taft-Hartley Act made no provision for presidential seizure as a sanction to induce settlement of labor-management disputes, and the other two acts delegated seizure powers for more limited purposes[34] and contained procedural prerequisites with which the Secretary of Commerce had not, of course, complied,[35] the Court construed the absence of statutory delegation of power, to seize the steel industry to prevent a nationwide strike, to imply disapproval by Congress of the exercise of such seizure power by the President.

The dissenting opinion argued that the silence of Congress implied neither consent nor dissent, and that the President had chosen to exercise the alternative — to Taft-Hartley — procedure authorized by the Defense Production Act of 1950 by referring the steel dispute to the Wage Stabilization Board. Only after he had exhausted his powers under that statute did he resort to seizure, and in this regard, his position was no different from that of choosing the alternative course of seizure after exhausting his powers under the Taft-Hartley Act. The constitutional basis for the exercise of such authority by the President was found by the dissenting justices to lie in the unbroken executive practice and decisions of the Supreme Court extending back through a period of ninety years.[36] This national emergency was not of the sort contemplated by the Taft-Hartley Act, but was in the nature of an international crisis affecting our relationship with our allies in the North Atlantic Treaty Organization and elsewhere, so that the President's powers as the "Sole Organ of the Nation" in the conduct of foreign affairs and as Commander in Chief very properly assumed pre-eminence. In such areas, the opinion pointed out, there was substantial overlapping of congressional and presidential powers, and the President's independent authority was more than adequate to justify his action. Especially was this so in view of the fact that here, far from acting contrary to the will of Congress, the President was carrying out his constitutional obligation to see that many laws of the Congress dealing with the defense emergency and our treaty commitments were carried into effect.

The decision, however, was clear: Executive Order No. 10340 was unconstitutional; it violated the basic principle of separation of powers, because the President had attempted to usurp a legislative power. The case had immense political implications and attracted wide public attention; and it illustrates the Supreme Court functioning at the highest political level. Obviously, the Court did not rely upon precedent — either judicial or executive — in reaching its conclusion.[37]

One subsequent case has concerned presidential action to settle a labor dispute which, while not involving executive seizure, nevertheless is closely related to the problems of the *Youngstown* case. This one grew out of a labor dispute in a plant which manufactured fissionable materials for the Atomic Energy Commission; a strike would immediately and seriously have delayed the production of equipment and fissionable material essential to the making of atomic weapons for national defense. By his Executive Order No. 10233 of December 29, 1951 (as in the *Youngstown* case), the President had referred the dispute to the Wage Stabilization Board. By consent of the parties, the W.S.B. delayed action on this case while it tried to settle the steel industry disputes; but the W.S.B. lost its jurisdiction, before coming to a decision, because of the 1952 amendments to the Defense Production Act of 1950. And, in the meantime, the Supreme Court decided *Youngstown*. When the union called a strike in August, the President invoked the Taft-Hartley procedure; and in December, as one of his final official acts, President Truman issued his Executive Order No. 10417, creating a board of inquiry to investigate the dispute. He also directed the Attorney General to seek an injunction to restrain either the company or the union from interrupting production in any way. Although the union challenged the constitutionality of both the Taft-Hartley Act and the President's executive orders, the trial court upheld both without hesitation.[38]

Seizure Power and Emergency Regulation

The clear implication of the *Youngstown* decision was that a similar result would have been reached in the steel industry dispute, if the President had chosen in that case to rely upon the Taft-Hartley procedure instead of his wartime power of executive seizure. The question remains whether the President does not still have such a choice among alternative procedures. Certainly the Supreme Court would uphold his selection if he acted under circumstances which the Court would accept as time of war, and the *Youngstown* case is the only instance in our entire history when the Supreme Court has failed to follow the leadership of the Commander in Chief in such a matter. Like so many other of the great "blows for civil liberty" which the Court has struck, it is altogether likely that the future will find the *Youngstown* decision being confined to its very special facts, something to be reprinted in casebooks for the enlightenment of students of constitutional law but not a precedent which the Court is obliged to take seriously in a moment of national crisis.

The Executive Power of Eminent Domain

A broader power than the power to take possession and operate private industrial and commercial properties for temporary wartime use, after which they are returned to their former owners, is the power to condemn and convert private property permanently (at least insofar as the former owner is concerned) under the power of eminent domain. In either case, of course, there is an obligation on the part of the government to make proper compensation to the owner,[39] although payment may be deferred until after the return of peace, and the requirements of the Fifth Amendment are satisfied by the owner's right to sue on implied contract.

Apparently the exercise of this power by the President raised no questions in the courts until the advent of World War I. After President Wilson had suspended all wartime orders relating to the control of fuel, and the Fuel Administration was inactivated, a nationwide coal strike was threatened. On October 30, 1919, the President issued an executive order, under the Lever Act, revoking and annulling the "orders of January 31, 1919 and February 20, 1919, to the extent necessary to restore all of the said rules, regulations, orders, and proclamations therein suspended" concerning the fixing or regulating of prices, and the rule-making power respecting the production and sale of coal delegated to the fuel administrator. Under the authority of the Overman Act of May 20, 1918, the fuel administrator re-delegated to the director general of railroads authority to divert shipments of coal and to regulate the use of coal by railroads under his control. An executive order of November 5 and an order of the fuel administrator of November 12 excepted from the price-fixing regulations contracts made before October 30; finally on March 19, 1920, the President again suspended all regulations governing the use of fuel.

A group of cases in which this exercise of wartime powers after the Armistice was challenged were decided by both the state and federal courts several years later. The Supreme Court of Pennsylvania held that the Lever Act could not be a basis for this action because it had delegated authority to the President to apportion and divert commodities and to fix prices only in time of war: consequently the executive order of October 30, 1919, was invalid.[40] On appeal, however, the United States Supreme Court returned to the basis of decision of the trial court: that this was a case of taking private property under eminent domain, and that just compensation — the difference between the market price and the price paid by the government in this instance — must be paid. The prices fixed by the fuel administrator were considered to be an administrative valuation of private property taken for public use; but since "just compensation" was considered a judicial question, the administrative determination was binding on neither the private owner nor the courts.[41]

Notwithstanding this intervening decision of the United States Supreme Court, the Supreme Court of Massachusetts returned, the following year, to the rationale of the Pennsylvania court. In this suit for the recovery of the value of thirteen carloads of coal consigned to the Hood Rubber Company and converted by the director general of railroads while the shipment was in transit on the Pennsylvania Railroad, the state court held that the Lever Act conferred on the President certain powers to regulate the prices and distribution of coal as a war measure only. Therefore his executive orders of October 30 and November 5 and 12, 1919, not in any way connected with the war and purporting to reinstate a suspended prior order of the fuel administrator in order to regulate contracts for the sale of coal in anticipation of a strike, were beyond the President's statutory powers and invalid.[42] In the light of the action of the Supreme Court of the United States in the *Davis* case the year before, the failure of the Solicitor General to appeal this case for the government is explicable only in terms of the desire of the Coolidge administration to make what political capital it could out of the unconstitutional and lawless actions (according to the Massachusetts court) of the Wilson administration. This inference, in any event, was apparently drawn a few years later in a similar case by a Supreme Court justice who was himself a Republican and a former chief justice of the Massachusetts Supreme Court.

Here the War Department had placed an obligatory order with a power company, but instead of taking delivery of the electricity for direct governmental use, it had given directions to the power company indicating to whom and in what amounts it should make power available. One of these orders had the effect of cutting off from the petitioner, as a non-essential user, all the power to which it was entitled under its contract with the power company. Could the government then refuse to pay just compensation equivalent to the petitioner's direct overhead expenses for the period from February 7 to November 30, 1918, during which the company had been denied access to power? Mr. Justice Holmes, speaking for the Court, held that it could not, and pointedly remarked:

The Government has urged . . . that it does not appear that the action of the Secretary was authorized by Congress. [The government at this time (1931) was Republican; at the time of the requisition (1917), it was Democratic.] We shall give scant consideration to such a repudiation of responsibility. The Secretary of War, in the name of the President, with the power of the country behind him, in critical time of war, requisitioned what was needed and got it. Nobody doubts, we presume, that if any technical defect of authority had been pointed out it would have been remedied at once.[43]

Land was also taken for direct use of the armed forces during World War I, but no constitutional questions of importance were raised about the legislation which authorized this. The act of July 1, 1918, for example, empowered the President to take for the United States immediate possession of and title to land for which appropriations were made, and to pay just compensation therefor as he should determine. If the compensation so determined should be unsatisfactory to the owner, he was to be paid 75 per cent of the amount the President had fixed and he was entitled to sue the United States to recover such further sum, in addition to the amount already received, as a court should decide would constitute just compensation. Title vested immediately in the United States upon the issuance of a presidential proclamation taking possession.[44]

Much more controversial, however, was the attempt to use such wartime powers during the early period of the New Deal, and perhaps the most spectacular act of President Franklin D. Roosevelt was the declaration of the bank holiday almost immediately upon assuming his office. He acted under Section 5 (b) of the Trading with the Enemy Act of October 6, 1917, which authorized the President to "investigate, regulate, or prohibit, or otherwise, any transactions in foreign exchange, export or earmarkings of gold or silver coin or bullion or currency . . . between the United States and any foreign country," presumably in time of war to aid in the successful prosecution of that war. The President's executive order of March 6, 1933, proclaimed the bank holiday; the order of the Secretary of the Treasury of the same date, approved by the President, directed the Treasurer of the United States to make payments in gold only under license issued by the Secretary of the Treasury. Then on March 9, 1933, Congress passed the Emergency Banking Act, Section 2 of which amended the Trading with the Enemy Act and ratified all orders issued by the President or the Secretary of the Treasury since March 4, 1933, under the authority of that act.[45] This statute also delegated authority to the President, during any period of national emergency so proclaimed by him, to investigate, regulate, or prohibit, by licensing or otherwise, any transaction in foreign exchange, transfers of credit between or payments by banking institutions as defined by the President, and export, hoarding, melting, or earmarking of gold or silver coin or bullion or currency, by any person within the United States or any place subject to the jurisdiction thereof. Willful violation of the act or regulations thereunder was made punishable by fine or imprisonment or both.

Acting under these powers, the President issued on the following day his executive order of March 10, 1933, authorizing the banks to reopen under certain conditions, and banning the export of gold except under license of the Secretary of the Treasury. By executive order of April 5, 1933, hoarding was forbidden, and all gold was required to be exchanged at banks for legal tender by May 1, 1933. An executive order of April 20, 1933, amended the order of March 10 regarding the export of gold and exchange transactions. Additional executive orders of August 28, August 29, October 25, 1933, and January 2 and 15, 1934, made further changes in the regulations on the hoarding, sale, or export of, and exchange transactions in gold. The President also approved orders of the Secretary of the Treasury of December 28, 1933, and January 15, 1934, requiring the delivery of all gold to the United States Treasury.

The reason for requiring all gold to be turned in to the Treasury (which was almost completely accomplished before devaluation took place), and for permitting private ownership or possession of gold only under Treasury license, was to forestall the tremendous and unwarranted profits that otherwise would have accrued as a windfall to anyone who possessed gold bullion at the time. Instead, the "profits" of devaluation accrued almost exclusively to the Treasury itself. Those who had possessed or owned gold that had to be turned in to the Treasury in exchange for "legal tender" nevertheless argued that their property, namely the gold, had been taken by the government for public purposes, and that they were therefore entitled to the "just compensation"—presumably, the value of the gold in the inflated dollars of post-devaluation—guaranteed by the Fifth Amendment.

The federal district court in New York City ruled in the *Campbell* case that the Emergency Banking Act was valid, but that the President and his Secretary of the Treasury were independent recipients of the powers delegated by it. The President could act "in personam" by investigating, requiring reports from, and directing the prosecution of individuals who owned or possessed gold, but the power to requisition *the gold itself* belonged exclusively to the Secretary of the Treasury. Therefore, Section 5 of Executive Order No. 6260 of August 28, 1933, which provided for "what is, in effect, the requisition of gold bullion, either as incidental to a prohibition against the hoarding thereof or as a means of insuring the enforcement of such prohibition" was invalid, because the President had usurped a statutory authority of the Secretary of the Treasury.[46] Nor was this all; the judge determined that the executive order was invalid for the additional reason that it made no provision for the payment of "just compensation" for the requisitioned gold (although certainly this result would have been the same whether the administrative rule-making took the form of executive order or Treasury regulation).[47]

A similar decision was reached by the federal district court for

Massachusetts, which sustained in part a demurrer to an indictment involving another gold hoarder, expressly following the decision in the *Campbell* case and on the ground that Section 5 of Executive Order No. 6260 violated the Fifth Amendment:

[T]o condemn as criminal all who failed to yield up valuable property rights, lawfully acquired, without providing for just compensation, is not only requisition, but unlawful requisition . . . the right to prohibit hoarding of gold would not extend to confiscation of private property, assuming, as we all may, that such property is affected with a public interest.[48]

Shortly thereafter, the Supreme Court upheld the validity of the joint resolution of June 5, 1933, as well as the Emergency Banking Act, but did not pass upon the validity of the presidential or administrative sections concerning the regulation of gold.[49] Several years later, however, the question of the President's power to direct the Secretary of the Treasury in the performance of duties expressly vested in the latter by statute was raised again. By then, the situation had become historical, and the Court upheld the validity of Executive Order No. 6102, April 5, 1933, and the regulations of the Secretary of the Treasury dated April 29, 1933 — at least in part, however, on the ground that the Secretary had ratified the President's action![50]

The advent of World War II reopened some questions turning on the scope of presidential powers of eminent domain, although conflict was centered around a few instances in which property was under trustees and courts of bankruptcy and there was unquestionably adequate statutory authority for the Chief Executive's action. The First and Second War Powers acts provided that when the President, acting through such department, agency, board, or officer as he should appoint, determined that any property was needed for the defense of the United States, and that such need was immediate and would not admit of delay or resort to any other source of supply, and that all other means of obtaining the use of such property for the defense of the United States upon fair and reasonable terms had been exhausted, he should requisition the property.[51]

One of the lower federal courts resisted what apparently was felt to be an attempted encroachment of the Chief Executive upon the administrative functions of the judiciary with respect to the disposition of the assets of bankrupts; but just as in the previously noted cases of conflict between the alien property custodian and courts functioning as the trustees of alien enemy incompetents, individual judges could hardly be presumed to be better judges of the necessity for requisitioning civilian property in time of war than the agencies of the national government responsible for civilian and military production and supply. Such was the rationale of the appellate courts and most of the district courts, which held that the presidential determination (i.e., the determination of the administrative subordinates to whom he had subdelegated his power) of the necessity to requisition any given property was not reviewable in the courts;[52] that the extraordinary method of injunction was not an appropriate means for challenging such broad discretion;[53] that the statutes did not require that determination and payment of compensation be made before the requisition;[54] and, in at least one case, that the President possessed independent constitutional powers to seize property essential to national defense in time of war.[55]

Emergency Regulation of Private Enterprise

It is almost a quarter of a century from the first inauguration of F.D.R. to the end of Eisenhower's first term; and twenty-one of these twenty-four years marked periods of national emergency. The fundamental legal theory under which the New Deal attacked the crisis of the economic depression in 1933 was that this domestic emergency warranted the use of wartime powers by the national government; and although this experiment terminated in the spring of 1935, the outbreak of World War II in Europe brought successive declarations by the President of a limited national emergency on September 8, 1939, and of an unlimited national emergency on May 27, 1941. The President relinquished many of his emergency powers by his Proclamation No. 2714 of December 31, 1946, but his legal authority to act under permanent wartime legislation never lapsed because a peace treaty with Japan had not yet been signed when the undeclared Korean War broke out on June 25, 1950; and less than six months later, the President again announced by his Proclamation No. 2914 of December 16, 1950, the existence of a national emergency (without specifying whether it was "limited" or "unlimited").[56]

A whole generation of American children, some of them already in college, is growing up having never lived under any conditions other than those of a greater or lesser degree of national emergency and international crisis. It is the particular responsibility and function of the

President himself to proclaim, with or without a precedent declaration of war *de jure* by the Congress, the existence of such an emergency, with the result that he himself decides when conditions warrant his exercise of the extraordinary constitutional and statutory powers which then center around the person and office of our Commander in Chief.[57] The distinction between the legal powers of the Presidency in time of war and of peace has never been the clear-cut line that has been popularly assumed to exist; such a dichotomy appears today to be not merely obsolescent but almost anachronic. As a federal district judge put the matter over a decade ago:

It is to be noted with emphasis that the matter of a national emergency is, and always has been, left to the judgment of the President. This has been expressly and repeatedly confirmed in many statutes giving the President varied powers whenever in his judgment a National Emergency exists. . . .

In these statutes . . . the following phrases are used synonymously, "During the existence of war or of a national emergency"; "During time of war or during any other period of national emergency"; "In time of war or threatened war"; "In time of war or when the President shall so direct."

The various Acts of Congress authorizing the President to take action in the event of a National Emergency show that congress throughout the years made little or no distinction between a State of National Emergency and a State of War.[58]

It is certainly true that such statutory language can be found covering not only the century and a half spanned by the Alien Enemy Act of 1798 and the Defense Production Act of 1950, both of which are obvious examples, but preceding and following these benchmarks as well.[59] It is not unnatural that owners of private property who sought to resist this expansion of control by the national government have turned to the courts, particularly since modern emergency regulation relies so heavily on executive rather than on statutory law as its basis. It is noteworthy also that the techniques of control — price-fixing, rationing, allocating materials, and making public contracts — are the same as those which, under slightly different labels, are characteristic of "peacetime" public utility regulation.

Although in times past, as will be seen, the courts have interposed their authority to stay the hand of the Executive, that appears now to be a matter of legal history; limitations on the regulatory powers of the national government over private property must be found in political processes, not in the judicial process. The implications of this metamorphosis, recent and rapid as it has been, are great, and one of the clearest ways to see this development is by tracing the evolution of the role of the President in this regard as seen through the eyes of the courts.

During World War I, for instance, the government appropriated all the wool clip of 1918 as a form of rationing in order to ensure an adequate supply for the armed forces' use, with the understanding that if all was not actually used by the government, it would be allocated to manufacturers as the government might direct. The original statutory authority for this action was the National Defense Act of June 3, 1916, a peacetime statute enacted in anticipation of the subsequent war emergency, which created what was in effect a war cabinet — the Council of National Defense — and empowered the President to place compulsory orders for necessary material and established penalties for noncompliance with such orders. The power to take possession and control of manufacturing plants, with just compensation, was the President's ultimate sanction under the act. The council was delegated rule-making powers over subordinate government agencies by the statute, including the power to create new agencies; and it accordingly created, among others, the War Industries Board as an advisory agency. The President gave the board greater prestige by establishing it as an independent agency under the chairmanship of Bernard Baruch by his executive order of May 29, 1918, and the board became Wilson's personal agency to which he subdelegated extensive powers. The Armistice came less than six months later, however, and the War Industries Board was dissolved by executive order of December 31, 1918; its functions with respect to the regulation of wool were then transferred to the Bureau of Markets of the Department of Agriculture.

The wool division of the board issued rules and regulations which set up a licensing system to control the sale of the wool clip from growers through middlemen to those manufacturers holding government contracts to whom deliveries of wool were authorized. Documentary licenses were not distributed until the program was well under way, but the agency assumed that compliance with part of the regulations bound those under the program to the rest. All dealers were required by the regulations to turn over to the government profits in excess of those allowed, and it was planned that the government would distribute such funds among the wool growers to compensate them for the fixed prices they received.[60] Most of the cases arose as suits by the government to recover excess profits illegally retained by dealers in violation of the regulations and of the terms of some of their licenses, although some cases arose as suits to recover from the government excess profits paid upon demand. Much of the confusion manifested in the judicial opinions may be traced directly to the looseness of the delineation, application, and enforcement of the licensing system. In general, the courts preserved the *status quo* at the time of suit, because, on the one hand, the monies paid into the treasury were not recoverable, while on the other, the government never succeeded in recovering more than nominal damages.

Two unresolved contradictory lines of decision emerged, with five cases upholding the price-fixing scheme under the war power[61] and an equal number holding it to have been invalid;[62] but none of these cases was ever appealed to the Supreme Court.[63] The opinion of a district court typifies the point of view of the judges who upheld this system of presidential price control:

The regulations for the control of the wool clip of 1918 had their origin in the necessities of war. In time of war, by virtue of the Constitution and usually by standing statutory enactments of Congress, comprehensive powers reside in the President of the United States as commander-in-chief of the army and navy. . . . The President of necessity is required to act largely through heads of departments and subordinates, and it was not required that the defendant's license should have been immediately issued or signed by the President. . . . The regulations governing the wool clip of 1918 and the permit issued to the defendant were, however, acts of the President, although prepared and executed by his chosen agents. . . .

[W]hether [the President] and his subordinates acted beyond his [Constitutional and statutory] power is, however, immaterial in the light of subsequent legislation. It is clear that Congress could by appropriate legislation have conferred on him the authority to control the wool clip and to make such a contract as is here in question.[64]

However, the Fourth Circuit Court of Appeals held that the board's requirement that wool dealers surrender excess profits to the government, being in the nature of a penalty for profiteering, was invalid because beyond the powers of the board; and although the court avoided a specific ruling that the executive order of May 29, 1918, was unconstitutional, it clearly stated that the President had neither constitutional nor statutory power to authorize such regulations:

The President, as Commander-in-Chief of the Army and the Navy, doubtless had the constitutional power in war time, in cases of immediate and pressing exigency, to appropriate private property to public uses; the government being bound to make just compensation therefor. . . .

The President was [also] given certain powers to fix prices of various commodities, of which it does not appear that in the spring of 1918 wool was one. . . .

The War Industries Board was by the President directed to act as the "eye" of all the supply departments. He did not attempt to authorize it to legislate on such far-reaching questions as the proper place of middlemen in industry, and the limitation of the maximum profits of traders, and he could not have done so, if he would.[65]

The First Circuit Court of Appeals came to a similar conclusion but by a different route, anticipating decisions on the legal status and powers of the War Labor Board in World War II:

In March, 1918, the President, with or without authority, removed the War Industries Board from its subordination to the Council of National Defense, which he confirmed by executive order in May, 1918, apparently under the Overman Act of May 20, 1918 (40 Stat. 556), and made it an administrative agency directly responsible to him. . . . [In terms of the authority delegated to it by Congress and the President] it could suggest and recommend, but could not order. The power to compel obedience was vested in a higher authority [i.e., the President]. . . .

Without some legislative or executive order that prohibited the doing of any wool business without a permit, any license or permit issued by the Wool Division or any conditions imposed by it upon which such permit could be exercised had no validity or binding force . . . nor does it appear from the statutes and executive orders that the President ever gave his agents, if such they were, any authority to adopt such regulations.[66]

The other principal instance of direct price-fixing during World War I which raised challenges to the authority of the President involved coal. Under authority of Section 25 of the Lever Act of August 10, 1917,[67] the President issued an emergency price regulation on August 23, 1917, fixing the gross margin to be charged by coal jobbers pending investigation by the Federal Trade Commission. A district court rejected the argument that the failure on the part of Congress to provide for review by the courts brought the statute into conflict with the Fifth Amendment:

It is true that the act afforded no opportunity for judicial review of the reasonableness of the prices fixed by the President, and this had been determined, under ordinary circumstances . . . to be want of due process of law. . . . But due process of law is not to be tested by form of procedure merely . . . and varies with the subject-matter and necessities of the situation.

Public danger warrants the substitution of executive process for judicial process. . . . During the war . . . extended investigations . . . necessary to judicial review of the economic orders . . . [were] impracticable and impossible; and, under the circumstances then existing, the fixing of prices in public industries necessary for the prosecution of the war, by the President, under the authority of the act of Congress, was not the deprivation of due process of law.[68]

The Sixth Circuit Court of Appeals affirmed, rejecting the contention that the statute required the President to fix prices so that the plaintiffs would be allowed "cost plus" even though his order caused them financial loss, because this "overlooks the summary nature of the power conferred upon the President, to meet the emergency by making temporary orders which should, so far as possible, save the immediate situation until the commission should have time and opportunity, through its slower processes, to make more complete investigations of conditions and remedies."[69] Although the Supreme Court reversed the lower courts on the grounds that the order should not be interpreted to have retroactive effect and to apply to coal purchased before the adoption of the Lever Act, thus avoiding any discussion of the constitutional questions they had considered, it in effect upheld the validity of the President's order as applied prospectively.[70]

The Supreme Court also upheld, and this time directly, Executive Orders No. 2686-A of August 23, 1917, and No. 2743-A of October 27, 1917, which also fixed the prices of bituminous coal under the Lever Act. The contract between the parties to this case had stipulated higher prices for coal than those permitted by the executive orders, and the plaintiff, who had received the price fixed by the government, sued to collect the difference, alleging the unconstitutionality of both the statute and the executive orders. The Pennsylvania Supreme Court held that prices fixed by the President that did not allow a reasonable return constituted a denial of due process, and the determination of reasonableness was, of course, a judicial question; but the burden of proof that a presidential order was unreasonable fell on the plaintiff who, in this case, failed to establish his case.[71] The Supreme Court affirmed, adding that since the executive orders were a war measure, there was a strong presumption of their validity.[72]

Direct consumer rationing was not usually resorted to during World War I, reliance being placed instead upon the allocation of raw materials and manufactured and processed commodities. The first step toward the adoption of the Eighteenth Amendment was, in fact, the wartime prohibition program, based on the Lever Act, which authorized the President to forbid or to regulate the use of foods for the production of malt liquors for beverage purposes, and directly prohibited the use of food for "intoxicating beverages." The actual cessation of beer manufacture was accomplished by a series of presidential proclamations, one of which, that of December 6, 1917, forbade the production of all malt liquor with a greater alcohol content than 2.75 per cent; another, of September 6, 1918, and effective the following December 1, directly prohibited the production of all malt liquor; while a third, of January 30, 1919, permitted the manufacture of nonintoxicating beverages; and a fourth, of March 4, 1919, amended the proclamation of September 16, 1918, so as to prohibit only the production of intoxicating malt liquors for beverage purposes. The Supreme Court construed all these proclamations, but no question of the President's power to issue them was raised.[73]

An earlier precedent was created by the Supreme Court's upholding the President's power to modify private contracts,[74] although the contract in this case was quasi-governmental, since it involved a ward of the government, and the President's power was proprietary and therefore different from such power as he subsequently exercised governing contracts between private citizens. Although the Court made no point of this at the time, the basis of his authority was in delegation by a treaty rather than by a statute; and although the question has never been directly decided by the Court, it is almost certain that, whatever may be the limitations on the scope of statutory delegation, the permissible scope of delegation by treaty is so broad as to be immune from judicial review. If the treaty itself was otherwise constitutional (and none has ever been held to the contrary by the Supreme Court), it is inconceivable that it could be considered unconstitutional because of a delegation of power to the President that offended "some invisible radiation"[75] from the Constitution such as the principle of separation of powers.

There were actually two quite different kinds of presidential action with respect to contracts during World War I. In the first, he directed the placing of compulsory war contracts, or otherwise interfered with the execution of private contracts; in the second, which loomed as much the larger issue during and after World War II, he canceled or modified the terms of existing government contracts. No direct challenge appears to have been made to the placing of compulsory contracts, although formal orders were required on occasion;[76] but two cases were decided by New York courts in which presidential orders were subjected to collateral attack in suits for breach of contract between private citizens, where the defendants pleaded that government contracts had prevented them from carrying out their civil contracts. The trial court in the first case denied that the President had any constitutional power to place compulsory war contracts or otherwise to interfere with the execution of private contracts, except under martial law:

[T]he argument . . . is that the acts and contracts of governmental department heads are presumed to be by authority of the President, and, where the executive acts, no statute is necessary, authority being in the Constitution; article 2, section 2, making the President commander in chief of the army and navy. The decisions cited . . . support the proposition of presumptive authority, but not the defendant's theory of executive power, which is in law much narrower than the theory assumes. . . .

The rule thus is that while the President, when acting as commander in chief, has all the powers recognized by the usages of war, but when he does not act by martial law he is governed by the acts of Congress, and executive orders, not authorized thereby, will be no warrant of power, or cover of protection. The present case is not a question of martial law. . . . I conclude, therefore, that in the performance of contracts with the government, even for military supplies, precedence over civilian contracts does not necessarily inhere, nor may be imported or imposed otherwise than as provided by act of Congress.[77]

Although there was little question of the desirability of having these textile mills produce cloth for uniforms rather than tuxedos in the autumn of 1917, it was also true that the more profitable government contracts were sometimes eagerly sought by manufacturers who welcomed this legal loophole whereby they could drop less lucrative civil contracts. The rule suggested by the trial court in the above *Millbrook* case,[78] however, would have been difficult and often unfair to have applied in practice, because of the highly informal nature of the negotiations in many bona fide cases, where the authorization might have been the unrecorded nod of a staff officer in Washington or in a field office, with official confirmation coming months later after work on civil contracts had long been suspended and delivery on the part of the government contract already completed.[79] As the appellate division of the Supreme Court in New York held:

[C]ounsel for the respondent contends that no facts showing the right of the government thus, in effect, to commandeer the yarn are pleaded. It is not necessary to plead the acts of Congress or the proclamations of the President. If the President was authorized to do the things it is, in effect, alleged he caused to be done through said board, it was sufficient to allege that he thus caused them to be done.

Under [the acts of June 3, 1916, and August 10, 1917], he [the President] could have seized and operated plants for the manufacture of yarn, and all the yarn in the country or that came into the country, and . . . he could through a government agency duly created . . . control its use.[80]

It was the other aspect of the power, the cancellation of public contracts, that was upheld by the Supreme Court at this time. President Wilson had subdelegated his statutory power "to modify, suspend, cancel, or requisition any existing or future contract for the building, production, or purchase of ships or material . . . through such agency or agencies as he shall determine from time to time" to the Secretary of the Navy, among others, in an executive order dated August 21, 1917. A suit was begun in the Court of Claims to contest the cancellation of a Navy Department contract for gun mounts, and on appeal, Justice Sutherland, speaking for the Supreme Court, remarked:

We do not mean to deny the power of Congress, in time of war, to authorize the President to modify private contracts (leaving the parties free, as between themselves, to accept or not), nor do we suggest that Congress has not done so by the present statute . . . [which] was intended . . . (1) To enable the President, during the emergency to utilize his powers over contracts to stimulate production to the utmost; and then, (2) upon the passing of the emergency, to enable him to utilize these same powers to stop that production as quickly as possible . . . we conclude, he was authorized to cancel the Government's own contracts such as the one here involved, upon making just compensation to the parties concerned.[81]

Nevertheless, summary cancellation by the personal order of the President was held to be unconstitutional for want of procedural due process, because the contractor was given neither notice, an opportunity to be heard, nor any reason for the action taken. This was an unnumbered executive order dated June 14, 1921:

The White House

By virtue of the power vested in me, I hereby declare void, the contract of September 24, 1920, and the two contracts of December 9, 1920, between the Director of Sales of the War Department and the U. S. Harness Co.

(signed) Warren G. Harding

To implement this order, the Secretary of War issued a directive under which a Lieutenant Colonel Graham, accompanied by soldiers, removed by military force from the plaintiff company certain government property which had been placed in their possession for remanufacture under the terms of the contracts. A state court'granted an injunction against the government officers concerned and the case was then removed to the federal district court for the northern district of West Virginia, which ruled that Harding's executive order was unconstitutional and contrary to the Fifth Amendment:

Is that order a usurpation of that power which is reposed under our government only in the judicial branch, and never constitutional in the executive branch?

Is the citizen to be denied his right of intervention and protection from the judiciary *solely* because the President has signed a paper that would strike down the *claimed* vested legal property right of a citizen?

Can contracts *alleged* to have been legally entered into between citizens and duly authorized representatives of the government be declared void by the President without resort to the judiciary and an opportunity being given those *claiming vested rights* thereunder to be heard?

I do not think so.[82]

The theory that an emergency justifies the Executive to regulate private property was extended to cover the determination of positive standards and conditions to govern private production and competition in 1933. Since the New Deal represented not only an accretion of power in the national government but also a vastly increased concentration of power in the hands of the executive branch, it is somewhat surprising that the standard interpretation of the major New Deal cases is preoccupied with the question of what Congress could and could not do. The National Recovery Administration was a gigantic experiment in presidential legislation, because each of the codes was legally promulgated by an executive order of the President. Until the President approved, a code remained inert and lifeless, a mere recommendation; and his authority was by no means limited to a veto: he could modify, delete, append to, or substitute a new and different code for the one presented for his approval. During the two years of their existence, these codes were laws of the United States throughout the greater part of the country, with violators subject to fine, imprisonment, or both under the terms of the enabling act.

An extensive literature in the contemporary law journals and in many subsequently published works deals with two of the major constitutional issues to which the Court addressed itself: (1) Did Congress delegate "legislative power" to the President? and (2) Did Congress exceed the scope of its power under the interstate commerce clause in attempting to authorize the regulation of production and manufacturing? That familiar ground will not be retraversed here.[83] In retrospect, however, we can reassess the significance of these decisions[84] by noting that the interpretation given the commerce clause in the *Schecter* case was repudiated by a new majority of the Court two years later and has not been returned to; and the *"Hot Oil"* and *"Sick Chicken"* cases remain today isolated and unique as the only instances in which the Supreme Court has ever discovered an unconstitutional delegation of power — *legislative or otherwise* — to the President. Although the executive orders of the President were declared illegal in both cases because they were based on an unconstitutional statute, the Court announced that there were independent grounds for declaring unconstitutional the presidential regulations involved in the *Panama* case. The delegating statute provided no rational standards in terms of which the courts could measure presidential compliance, and the President had failed to make (like a hearing examiner in a case of administrative adjudication) formal findings indicating his compliance with these nonexistent standards. But whatever may have been the conceptual confusion and political inspiration of these decisions, it is clear that they no longer state the understanding of the American judiciary of the constitutional power of Congress and the President to cooperate in authorizing and establishing programs of economic regulation in time of national emergency.

THE COMMANDER IN CHIEF

The authority exercised by the President over the economy during World War II was both more extensive and intensive than in either World War I or the New Deal experiment, but there were relatively few direct challenges to the rule-making power of the Commander in Chief; as in Great Britain, judicial attack was focused on administrative orders and regulations that carried out subdelegated executive powers. Rationing was the twin of price control during World War II, and the President exercised his powers through the same administrative channels as for price control. The major pattern of subdelegation was from the act of June 28, 1940, as amended by the act of May 31, 1941, through Executive Order No. 8629, creating the Office of Production Management; Executive Order No. 8734, creating the Office of Price Administration, as amended by Executive Order No. 8875; Executive Order No. 9024, creating the War Production Board, and Executive Order No. 9040, transferring the powers of O.P.M. to the W.P.B. on January 24, 1942; and Directive No. 1 of the W.P.B., which redelegated to O.P.A. the President's power to ration.[85]

The constitutionality of the relevant executive orders was neither challenged nor directly passed upon by the Supreme Court in the first case to reach it, although Justice Douglas did assume throughout his opinion that the orders of the administrator, acting under subdelegated presidential authority, were equivalent to executive orders of the President, and that the chain of subdelegation was valid.[86] Notwithstanding this decision of the Supreme Court, a West Virginia district court subsequently decided that the President had no power to order conservation of food on the part of bakers by prohibiting the practice of reclaiming unsold goods which encouraged retailers to accept more than they could sell, thereby creating a surplus of stale products. This judge came to the astounding conclusion that the prohibition of such patently wasteful practices bore no reasonable relationship to the wartime conservation of food, which was one of the fundamental objectives of the rationing program:

The Ashley Bread Company was charged with violating a regulation contained in a food distribution order promulgated by the War Food Administration under authority of the Second War Powers Act of 1942 . . . the primary and fundamental ground of the demurrer is that the regulation, violation of which is charged, is not a valid exercise of the powers granted to the President by the Second War Powers Act, 56 Stat. 176, in that the prohibition contained in paragraph (g) bears no reasonable relationship to the power granted to the President to allocate materials and facilities.

Defendant does not dispute the authority of the War Food Administrator to establish and promulgate any regulation which the President himself was authorized to make. . . . [I]s the regulation whose validity is assailed . . . within the scope of the administrative power so granted to the President [?]

[D]ue consideration of [the] broad principle of interpretation [that the means used be such as are reasonably necessary or appropriate to achieve the sought for result] does not require the court to abdicate its judicial function of discriminating between a proper exercise of the granted power and an attempted exercise of the power which goes beyond the bonds of the grant. . . .

I am not unmindful that courts must be extremely cautious in dealing with the exercise of power by the executive departments in time of war, when it is necessary that such powers be given their broadest possible scope; but Congress and not the Executive is the source of the power; and whenever a regulation which is clearly beyond the authority of the appropriate administrative officer to establish and promulgate is sought to be enforced by an executive department, the court would be remiss in its duty if it failed to hold such a regulation invalid when properly challenged.[87]

However, in a similar prosecution of a black market operator in meat, who used and possessed counterfeit ration stamps, the Ninth Circuit Court of Appeals came to a contrary, and undoubtedly the correct, conclusion.[88]

Direct administrative control of both wholesale and retail prices throughout the United States by an agency under the immediate legal direction of the President was used for the first time during World War II. In only two cases, however, does it appear that direct challenges to the role and authority of the President were raised. The first of these was decided by the Sixth Circuit Court of Appeals and was not appealed to the Supreme Court. Although it affirmed the conviction of a Nashville policeman who had been a scalper in the sale of retread tires, without rationing certificates, at 400 per cent of O.P.A. retail prices, it denied the existence of any constitutional power in the President to establish a system of national civilian price control and rationing. Instead, this court adopted the rationale of Cardozo's dissent in the *Hot Oil* case, and decided that the statute set up sufficiently clear standards to stay within the limits of delegation, and that the President had in turn indicated his compliance with these standards:

Appellant's principal attack is based upon the proposition that Title III, Section 2(a) of the Second War Powers Act of 1942 and the Revised Tire Rationing Regulations as amended, and Section 4(a) of the Emergency Price Control Act of 1942 and Revised Price Schedule No. 66, are unconstitutional because the statutes delegate pure legislative power to the President. . . .

[T]he principal war power of the President arises as Commander-in-Chief of the Army and Navy and does not include any war power legislative in its nature . . . the power to establish shortage rationing, and the power to fix prices upon the entire range of civilian goods is neither expressly nor impliedly included in any war power of the President.

[Under the Second War Powers Act] the President is authorized to allocate, that is to ration, critical materials and facilities only when he is "satisfied that the fulfillment of requirements for the defense of the United States will result in a shortage." While the President is not required in so many words to make findings, he is given sweeping powers of investigation in the enforcement and administration of the statute . . . and in light of this provision we read the word "satisfied" as being equivalent to and including the word "finds." The same word, "satisfied," was used in the statute which was upheld against a similar contention in *Field* v. *Clark.* . . . When the President is satisfied that a shortage exists, it becomes his duty to ration or allocate. But it is not the President who declares that priorities shall exist and allocations of materials and facilities be made; it is the Congress. Moreover additional standards under which the President must act are declared in the Second War Powers Act. It is true that these standards are not detailed at great length, but they are substantial. They require that when the President is satisfied that the shortage exists, allocations must be made upon conditions and to the extent that the President shall deem necessary or appropriate (1) in the public interest, and (2) to promote the national defense.

Since the President cannot order the allocations except as he deems it necessary or appropriate in the public interest and for the common defense, which are drastic limitations, we think that no illegal delegation of legislative power exists, and the Act is valid. . . .

Nor does the wide discretion confided in the President in the Second War Powers Act of 1942 invalidate the statute [citing again *Field v. Clark* and earlier cases cited therein.][89]

But the cases cited by the court such as *Field v. Clark* have very little to do with the wartime delegation of vast discretionary powers to the President. The peacetime delegation of authority to the President to make tariff reductions was much more narrowly and specifically defined, and was in the field of foreign relations where the Supreme Court had in strong terms upheld the independent constitutional authority of the President in the *Curtiss-Wright* case; while in this case, the court upheld as standards abstractions as broad as the implied constitutional limitations upon the spending power of Congress. Nevertheless, when the same question reached the Supreme Court, the role of the President was completely ignored, and the case was discussed as though it were exclusively a matter of statutory delegation directly to the price administrator. Here is another instance of the Court's characteristic avoidance of any direct conflict with the Commander in Chief. With the issues thus defined, the Court in what is considered to be the leading case found the statutes to be constitutional.[90]

Only a single federal district judge appears to have come face to face with the constitutional issues directly presented by all these cases, and in this case, the question was complicated by the interjection of a claimed right flowing directly from the local option clause of the Twenty-First Amendment.[91] Although this was a novel approach, it was unquestionably true that presidential liquor price control during World War II must have been valid if presidential prohibition of the manufacture or sale of beer was constitutional, as it appeared to be, during World War I. Furthermore, decisions of the Supreme Court upholding presidential regulation of intrastate rail and telephone rates during World War I would seem to have afforded ample precedent;[92] but the court reasoned directly from the scope of the constitutional powers of the Commander in Chief:

In our opinion the Twenty-first Amendment did not clothe the State's right to control the sale of liquor with any higher degree than it had over the sale of other commodities within the State. Therefore when the President chooses to exercise his war powers the State has no particular priority over liquor regulation within its borders. . . .

The position of the President of the United States, the Commander-in-Chief, acting through act of Congress, in thus controlling the liquor industry, this court believes is justified and within his war powers and such can be legally a regulation of the Office of Price Administration.[93]

As in World War I, presidential control over contracts assumed two principal forms during World War II: the first related to the effect of presidential orders and regulations upon private contracts, and the second to his power directly to modify or cancel a private contract. Thus, the Supreme Court of Wyoming took judicial notice of the presidential proclamations prohibiting the export of scrap iron and steel without a license,[94] and held that since the proclamations made the possession of a government license a prerequisite to engaging in the business of exporting iron and steel, a contract to perform such trade without a license was illegal and unenforceable.[95] In considerable contrast to at least the practice during the postwar period, moreover, it was held that the President's rule-making powers extended to the proscription of "five percenters," and that an executive order, which required every war contract to warrant that the contractor had not employed anyone to solicit the contract for a fee unless the person so employed was regularly retained by the contractor for securing business, was valid. Furthermore, such an executive order was a law and source of public policy, and therefore the violation of it rendered any contract illegal and unenforceable: "Executive Order 9001, promulgated by the President pursuant to the authority delegated to him by Congress, *has the effect of a statute and is 'part of the law of the land.'* "[96]

Executive Order 9001 also delegated discretionary authority to the War Department, the Navy Department, and the Maritime Commission to modify existing contracts, without consideration, when this would facilitate prosecution of the war, and the administrative practice was to give consideration to appropriate relief in hardship cases (i.e., those in which the contractor was deprived of a "fair profit") involving lump-sum contractors. Executive Order 9116, March 30, 1942, extended the provisions of Executive Order 9001 to include the National Housing Administration, which apparently did not follow the practice of the service departments in hardship cases. A contractor with the N.H.A. who claimed to fall in that category subsequently sued the government in the Court of Claims to recover his increased labor costs resulting from the curtailment of the workweek in the Akron, Ohio, area by executive order and administrative regulation of the War Manpower Commission. The court dismissed his claim, however, holding that any additional costs resulting from the executive order were speculative, and not a definite, fixed, and directly applicable legal charge, and that since the power of the N.H.A. under the other executive order was discretionary, the lack of definite proof in the record made it inadvisable for the court to rule upon the validity of the general practice of the agency in such cases:

The Government's demurrer is based upon the proposition that the acts of the Government which are alleged to have harmed the plaintiff are acts done by the Government in its sovereign capacity, rather than in its capacity as a contractor. . . .

We think that the Government's defense is valid. The President's Executive Order No. 9301 relating to the work week was applied by the War Manpower Commission to some 150 areas within the United States. We suppose that so many areas, of which Akron was one, would include all of the areas of industrial importance in the country. There was, then, no lack of generality in its application. *It was law for those parts of the country where such law was needed or useful.* The plaintiff and no doubt many others who had contracts with governments or private enterprises were harmed by it. Persons are frequently subjected to increased costs by regulatory laws. But, under the doctrine asserted here by the Government, and now apparently well settled, the Government is not liable for such harms.[97]

Certainly, a comparison of the World War II cases with those of World War I indicates a significant shift in judicial attitudes toward expansion in the exercise of national powers of emergency regulation, and the emergence of the Commander in Chief as the "organ of the government" most suitable for the direction and exercise of such emergency power. Viewed from the perspective of two decades, the New Deal decisions have not functioned in any way effectively to limit the delegation of emergency powers to the President, or to induce more specific standards of congressional guidance. Probably the basic factors underlying the truncated development of judicial review in this area are traceable to the tremendous growth during the interim in judicial recognition of the scope of the constitutional authority of the President in matters touching national defense and foreign relations. In time of perpetual crisis, Clausewitz' dictum becomes particularly relevant, and practically everything in both public and private life may fall under the penumbra of war and foreign policy. Whether the state of war is hot or cold, the emergency remains. Thus more and more questions relating to the exercise of presidential power become political in nature, and therefore beyond the scope of judicial review.

Notes

[1] The statute, however, authorized the President to take possession through the agency of the Secretary of *War*. Partly because of this, and partly because the court thought that the President could not subdelegate his statutory powers unless specifically authorized to do so, a federal district court held the proclamation to be unconstitutional, declaring that "such papers [presidential proclamations] cannot have any effect as laws, in the absence of express constitutional or congressional authorization." Muir v. Louis-

ville and Nashville Railroad Co., 247 F. 888, 895 (W.D.Ky., 1918). This decision preceded the enactment of the act of March 21, 1918.

[2] Especially General Order No. 18, April 9, 1918, directing suits against carriers under federal control to be initiated in the judicial district where the cause of action arose; No. 18A, April 18, 1918, extending this to include the place of residence of the plaintiff as an alternative; No. 26, May 23, 1918, suspending the trial of certain suits for the duration of federal control; No. 50, October 28, 1918, requiring most actions against the railroads to be brought against the director general rather than the operating companies themselves; and No. 50A, extending the substitution of the director general as defendant to all then pending suits. These orders were in effect affirmed and continued by Section 206 of the Transportation Act of 1920, which permitted suits or causes of action that had arisen during the period of federal control to be brought in state or federal courts against an agent designated by the President, subject to the state or federal statutes of limitation. See Davis v. Dantzler Lumber Co., 261 U.S. 280 (1923), upholding the authority of the President and the Congress thus to displace any conflicting procedures authorized by state law for the attachment of railroad property.

[3] "Any order issued by Mr. McAdoo as Director General must be considered as the order of the President," Rhodes v. Tatum, 206 S.W. 114, 118 (Texas, 1918); Dahn v. McAdoo, 256 F. 549 (N.D. Iowa, E.D. at Dubuque, 1919); "the orders of the Director General were in the sense of the act of 1918, the orders of the President," Mardis v. Hines, 267 F. 171, 173 (8 C.C.A., 1920).

[4] Northern Pacific Railroad Co. v. North Dakota ex rel William Langer, 250 U.S. 135 (1919).

[5] Idem.

[6] Dakota Central Telephone Co. v. South Dakota ex rel Payne, 250 U.S. 163, 184 (1919). To substantially the same effect were Kansas v. Burleson, 250 U.S. 188 (1919), dismissing a bill to enjoin the Postmaster General from enforcing a schedule of intrastate telephone rates, since this was in effect a suit against the government, not one to prevent an officer from exceeding the scope of his lawful authority; and Burleson v. Dempcy, 250 U.S. 191 (1919), reversing the decision of a state court which had issued a permanent injunction against the Postmaster General restraining him from charging rates higher than those set by the state utilities commission. Accord: MacLeod v. New England Telephone and Telegraph Co., 250 U.S. 195 (1919).

[7] Missouri Pacific Railroad Company v. Ault, 256 U.S. 554 (1921).

[8] Western Union Telegraph Co. v. Poston, 256 U.S. 662 (1921). The Court suggested that the only possibility for recovery of damages would be by suit on implied contract under the Tucker Act.

In addition to assuming control over the railroads under the 1916 statute, the President also took over certain harbor facilities; and the lessee of Pier No. 7 of Bush Terminal in New York Harbor, which had been requisitioned on December 31, 1917, by the Secretary of War by direction of the President, was held entitled to sue on implied contract in the Court of Claims for an amount additional to that allowed by the War Department which would represent, in the judgment of the court, just compensation for the period until May 14, 1919, when government control and possession terminated. Phelps v. United States, 274 U.S. 341, 343 (1927).

[9] Commercial Cable Co. v. Burleson, 255 F. 99 (S.D.N.Y., 1919); 250 U.S. 360 (1919).

[10] See Appendix II to Mr. Justice Frankfurter's concurring opinion in Youngstown Sheet and Tube Co. v. Sawyer, 343 U.S. 579, 620–628 (1952), for a complete list and analysis of all such presidential seizures.

[11] Ken-Rad Tube & Lamp Corp. v. Badeau, 55 F. Supp. 193, 197–198 (W.D.Ky., Owensboro D., 1944). At about the same time, the Court of Appeals of the District of Columbia ruled that War Labor Board orders were unreviewable, in part because there was no statutory procedure for judicial review, and in part on the theory that they were unenforceable, and merely a form of administrative advice to the President. The fact that the director of economic stabilization was authorized by Executive Order No.

Seizure Power and Emergency Regulation

9370, August 16, 1943, upon notification by the board that one of its orders was not being obeyed, to direct withdrawals of priorities and government contracts in order to coerce compliance was considered to be irrelevant; equally so was the possibility that the President might seize the plants and facilities of the petitioner in this case, since this was an attempt to annul and enjoin the board's order before the director or the President had yet acted. Employers Group of Motor Freight Carriers, Inc. v. N.W.L.B., 143 F. 2d 145 (1944).

The majority of the Supreme Court in the *Youngstown* case, discussed below, appear to have directly overruled the *Ken-Rad* decision on the point of the President's status as Commander in Chief as a source of constitutional power for such seizure, although it is noteworthy that the *Youngstown* decision did not come at a time and under circumstances that the Court considered to be those of wartime.

[12] Toledo, Peoria & Western Railroad v. Stover, 60 F. Supp. 587, 589 (S.D.Ill.N.D., 1945). The government did not appeal this decision.

[13] United States v. United Mine Workers of America, 70 F. Supp. 42, 52 (D.Ct.D.C., 1946).

[14] Montgomery Ward & Co. v. N.W.L.B., 56 F. Supp. 502 (D.Ct.D.C., 1944).

[15] N.W.L.B. v. Montgomery Ward & Co., 144 F. 2d (C.A.D.C.) 528 (1944).

[16] 323 U.S. 774 (November 13, 1944).

[17] United States v. Montgomery Ward & Co., 58 F. Supp. 408, 415–416 (N.D.Ill.E.D., 1945). The court incidentally noted that in a sufficiently great emergency, "the power resides in the President, as a function of his military office, to do the things necessary to preserve *the Government* [sic]." Italics supplied.

[18] United States v. Montgomery Ward & Co., 150 F. 2d 369, 381–382 (1945).

[19] Montgomery Ward & Co. v. United States, 326 U.S. 690 (1945).

[20] See Commercial Cable Co. v. Burleson, 250 U.S. 360 (1919), *supra.*

[21] The trial court remained compassionate, in spite of some apparent evidence to the contrary, as evinced by his reference to the miners whose officers and organization he was holding in contempt of his court: "Father, forgive them, for they know not what they do." See United States v. United Mine Workers of America, 70 F. Supp. 42, 52 (D.Ct.D.C., 1946).

[22] United States v. United Mine Workers of America, 330 U.S. 258, 262 (1947). Italics supplied. However, the government was liable to pay the difference in the increased wages of miners resulting from a W.L.B. order which was put into effect during the period of government operation following presidential seizure on May 1, 1943, in order to avert a threatened nationwide strike. Again, the constitutionality of presidential seizure was assumed by the whole Court, but the matter was not discussed. United States v. Pewee Coal Co., 341 U.S. 114 (1951).

[23] United States v. Switchmens Union of North America, 97 F. Supp. 97 (W.D.N.Y., 1950). No appeal was taken. Nor did action under the war power necessarily stop after a peace treaty with Germany was signed: Ladue and Co. v. Brownell, 220 F. 2d 468 (7 C.A., 1955), certiorari denied, 350 U.S. 823 (October 10, 1955).

A related question was raised in a recent case. Foreign Assets Control Regulations were issued by the Secretary of the Treasury on December 17, 1950, under World War II Executive Order No. 9193, dated July 6, 1942. The President, in turn, acted on the authority of the World War I Trading with the Enemy Act of 1917. The defendants in this case argued that the Secretary of the Treasury's authority under the executive order lapsed with the end of World War II; and that the President should have issued a new executive order on this subject for the Korean War in order to authorize the Secretary to make new regulations. The court thought that there might be some merit in this proposition in the abstract, but decided that the World War II emergency had not in fact terminated until April 26, 1952 (the date of the peace treaty with Japan); and in the meantime, of course, the President had declared the Korean emergency by his Proclamation No. 2914 of December 16, 1950 — the day *before* the new regulations were issued. At the time the peace treaty with Japan was promulgated, the President had issued his Executive Order No. 10348, reasserting the Korean emergency and continuing in effect the executive delegations previously made under Executive Order No. 9989 of August 20, 1948, for the duration of the Korean emergency. So the regulations were valid. China Daily News v. United States, 224 F. 2d 670, 672 (2 C.A., July 5, 1955), certiorari denied, 350 U.S. 885 (November 7, 1955).

[24] Toledo, Peoria, & Western Railroad v. Stover, 60 F. Supp. 587 (S.D.Ill.N.D., 1945).

[25] 97 F. Supp. 97, 102.

[26] United States v. Brotherhood of Locomotive, Firemen and Enginemen, 104 F. Supp. 741 (N.D. Ohio E.D., 1952).

[27] Brotherhood of Locomotive, Firemen and Enginemen v. United States, 343 U.S. 971 (1952).

[28] Youngstown Sheet and Tube Co. v. Charles Sawyer, 343 U.S. 579 (1952). The opinion of the Court (in which Frankfurter, Douglas, Jackson, and Burton expressly joined) was delivered by Black. Separate concurring opinions were written by Frankfurter, Douglas, Jackson, Burton, and Clark. Vinson, Reed, and Minton dissented in an opinion delivered by the chief justice.

[29] Executive Order No. 10340, the authority for the seizure order, and Secretary Sawyer's seizure order, were both dated April 8, 1952. At this time: (1) the end of war de jure with Japan did not officially come until three weeks later on April 28, 1952; (2) the war de facto in Korea, which began on June 25, 1950, was still very much in progress; (3) the national emergency proclaimed by the President on December 16, 1950, was still in effect.

[30] Justification, on the basis that World War II de jure was legally in effect when the executive order was issued, was waived. See the concurring opinion of Justice Frankfurter, 343 U.S. 579, 613 (1952); and see the Brief for Plaintiff Companies, Petitioners in No. 744 and Respondents in No. 745 (In the Supreme Court of the United States, October Term, 1951), p. 59.

[31] As the dissenting opinion pointed out, the majority opinions did not contravene the presidential declaration of a national emergency; they simply ignored its existence and considered the circumstances, relied upon by the government as justification for the seizure, to be irrelevant as a matter of law. See Chief Justice Vinson's opinion, 343 U.S. 579, 709 (1952).

[32] The ambivalence in the use of the word "legislative" in these two differing contexts is obvious. The President's executive order, according to the opinion of the Court delivered by Mr. Justice Black, was "legislative" in terms of its form and function (ibid., 588); but the power of seizure was "legislative" because it was an implied constitutional power of the Congress. Justice Black clearly intimated that there was no question that Congress might have explicitly authorized or directed the President to seize the steel industry (idem.). It should be noted that this is an opposite use of the principle of separation of powers from that given it by the Court in the spring of 1935: then it meant that Congress couldn't delegate to the President its "legislative power"; now, seventeen years later, it meant that Congress had to delegate its legislative power to the President before he could act constitutionally.

[33] In the case of Justice Frankfurter, it involved consideration of the legislative history of these statutes.

[34] In the case of the Selective Service Act of 1948, the purpose was to permit the acquisition of material and facilities that were otherwise unobtainable and that were needed for defense production; and in the case of the Defense Production Act of 1950, the purpose was to compel delivery on government defense production contracts.

[35] There was no pretense on the part of the government that its authority or action was in any way based on the seizure sections of these statutes.

[36] Dissenting opinion, 343 U.S. 579, 683, 700, 710 (1952).

[37] For a further discussion of the background and significance of this decision, see Edward S. Corwin, "The Steel Seizure Case: A Judicial Brick without Straw," Columbia Law Review, 53: 53–66 (January 1953); John P. Roche, "Executive Power and

Seizure Power and Emergency Regulation

Domestic Emergency: The Quest for Prerogative," *Western Political Quarterly*, 5: 592–618 (December 1952); and Glendon A. Schubert, Jr., "The Steel Case: Presidential Responsibility and Judicial Irresponsibility," *Western Political Quarterly*, 6: 61–77 (March 1953).

[38] United States v. American Locomotive Co., 109 F. Supp. 78 (W.D.N.Y., December 29, 1952); affirmed *sub. nom.* United States v. United Steelworkers of America, 202 F. 2d 132 (1953); certiorari denied, United Steelworkers of America v. United States, 344 U.S. 915 (1953).

[39] In zones of actual combat, the executive seizure power can extend to the taking for military purposes without compensation; but there have been no such areas in the continental United States since the Civil War and there seem to be no cases dealing with such confiscation in American territories during World War II, or at least none which raise an issue of presidential power. See, however, United States v. Caltex (Philippines) Inc., 344 U.S. 149 (1952).

[40] Newton v. Davis, Director General of Railroads, 126 A. 192 (1924).

[41] Davis v. Newton Coal Co., 267 U.S. 292 (1925).

[42] Hood Rubber Co. v. Davis, Director General of Railroads, 151 N.E. 119, 121 (1926). Cf. the circumstances of the presidential action in the *Steel Seizure* case, *supra*.

[43] International Paper Company v. United States, 282 U.S. 399, 406 (1931).

[44] 40 *Stat.* 724, 738, and 1874. See United States v. McIntosh, 2 F. Supp. 244 (E.D. Va., 1932), affirmed in 70 F. 2d 507 (4 C.C.A., 1934), and c.d. 293 U.S. 586 (1934).

[45] "The actions, regulations, rules, licenses, orders and proclamations heretofore *or hereafter* taken, promulgated, made, or issued by the President of the United States or the Secretary of the Treasury since March 4, 1933, pursuant to the authority conferred by subdivision (b) of section 5 of the Act of October 6, 1917, as amended, are hereby approved and confirmed." 48 *Stat.* 1. Italics supplied. Although the British Parliament has from time to time used statutory language indicating that orders in council or ministerial orders made under a particular statute would be considered to have the same force and effect as if incorporated within the body of the statute itself, this technique of lawmaking is exceptional even in Britain; and the *prior ratification* of executive and administrative legislation authorized by the quoted language of the Emergency Banking Act raises serious and dubious questions under the American system. Since the apparent intent of prior ratification as a technique is to frustrate any possibility of judicial review in terms of statutory standards, a double hurdle would appear to be posed under the principle of separation of powers: abdication of legislative power, and encroachment upon judicial power. If this statutory language had been challenged during the subsequent ten months before Congress made doubly sure by providing retroactive ratification, it might well have been held unconstitutional on either or both of the indicated grounds.

[46] United States v. Campbell, 5 F. Supp. 156, 177 (November 16, 1933). But the Secretary of the Treasury's rule-making powers were specifically conditioned upon presidential approval. Whether his regulation took the form of a Treasury regulation or that of an executive order, it would (at least, at this time) have been drafted by and carried into execution by the Secretary of the Treasury, and the regulation in either case would have been approved by the President.

[47] *Ibid.*, 175 (1933). The Supreme Court disposed of the case without consideration, dismissing the government's appeal on motion of the Solicitor General: United States v. Campbell, 291 U.S. 686 (1934).

[48] United States v. Driscoll, 9 F. Supp. 454, 456 (1935). The government did not appeal.

[49] The "Gold Clause Cases": Norman v. Baltimore and Ohio Railroad Co., 294 U.S. 240 (1935); Nortz v. United States, 294 U.S. 317 (1935); Perry v. United States, 294 U.S. 330 (1935).

[50] British-American Tobacco Co. v. Federal Reserve Bank of New York, 104 F. 2d 652, 654 (2 C.C.A., 1939).

[51] Acts of October 16, 1941 and March 27, 1942, 50 U.S.C.A. Appendix s. 721.

[52] In re Spier Aircraft Co., 49 F. Supp. 896 (D.N.J., 1943), affirmed in 137 F. 2d 736, 739 (3 C.C.A., 1943), and c.d. 321 U.S. 770 (1944); Alpirn v. Huffman, 49 F. Supp. 337, 342, 343 (D.Neb., Omaha D., 1943); In re Inland Waterways, 49 F. Supp. 675, 677 (D.Minn., 5 D., 1943); and In re Mississippi Valley Iron Co., 58 F. Supp. 222, 226 (E.D.Mo.E.D., 1944), affirmed on rehearing, 61 F. Supp. 347, 350 (E.D.Mo.E.D., 1945).

[53] In re Spier Aircraft Co., 137 F. 2d 736, 738 (3 C.C.A., 1943); Alpirn v. Huffman, 49 F. Supp. 337, 341 (D.Neb., Omaha D., 1943).

[54] In re Spier Aircraft Co., 137 F. 2d 736, 740 (3 C.C.A., 1943); In re Inland Waterways, 49 F. Supp. 675, 678 (D.Minn., 5 D., 1943).

[55] Alpirn v. Huffman, 49 F. Supp. 337, 340 (D.Neb., Omaha D., 1943): "[Q]uite independently of any congressional grant of authority, the power of requisition in emergencies incident to war has been held to rest in the President as a function of his military office." Compare the language used in In re Inland Waterways, 49 F. Supp. 675, 678 (D.Minn., 5 D., 1943).

[56] On April 28, 1952, President Truman signed his Proclamation No. 2974, terminating the national emergency proclaimed by President Roosevelt on September 8, 1939, and the unlimited national emergency that Roosevelt had proclaimed on May 27, 1941, in view of the fact that the war with Japan officially had ended. A saving clause declared that Proclamation No. 2974 was not to be construed in any way to affect the new and independent national emergency proclaimed by President Truman on December 16, 1950, by his Proclamation No. 2914. 66 Stat. c. 31–32.

[57] It is also the President's function to decide when the emergency is over: Werner v. United States, 119 F. Supp. 894 (S.D.Cal.C.D., 1954).

[58] Brown v. Bernstein, 49 F. Supp. 728, 731–732 (M.D.Pa., 1943).

[59] For a list of approximately a hundred "Statutes Which by Their Terms Grant Powers That May Be Exercised by the Executive in Emergency or State of War," see the appendix to the letter from the Attorney General of the United States to the President of the Senate, October 4, 1939, reprinted in Executive Powers under National Emergency, Senate Document No. 133, 76th Cong., 2d Sess. The statutes listed include, however, delegations to department heads (presumably subject to the President's direction) as well as delegations to the President himself. For more recent examples see Public Law 921 (81st Cong., 2d Sess.), approved January 12, 1951, substituting the words "national defense" for "prosecution of the war" wherever the latter appear in Section 201 of the First War Powers Act of 1941, and reactivating Title II thereof for the period of the national emergency proclaimed by the President on December 16, 1950; between April 14, 1952, and June 30, 1953, there were adopted several Emergency Powers Continuation acts (66 Stat. 54, 330 and 67 Stat. 18, 131), after which Congress continued various wartime acts on an individual rather than a general basis. See also the Internal Security (McCarran) Act, passed over the President's veto on September 22, 1950, Public Law 831 (81st Cong., 2d Sess.), Sec. 102: "DECLARATION OF 'INTERNAL SECURITY EMERGENCY,'" authorizing the President to declare an "Internal Security Emergency" in the event of invasion, a formal declaration of war, or insurrection within the United States in aid of a foreign enemy.

[60] The parallel to the pricing system of the first Agricultural Adjustment Act of 1933, declared unconstitutional in United States v. Butler, 297 U.S. 1 (1936), is obvious.

[61] United States v. Powers, 274 F. 131 (W.D.Mich.S.D., 1921); United States v. Smith (Smith I), 285 F. 751 (D.Mass., 1922); United States v. Gordin, 287 F. 565 (S.D. Ohio W.D., 1922); United States v. Schmidt (Schmidt II), 2 F. 2d 290 (E.D.Mich.S.D., 1924); and United States v. Kraus, 33 F. 2d 406 (7 C.C.A., 1929).

[62] United States v. Schmidt (Schmidt I), 291 F. 382 (E.D.Mich.S.D., 1923); United States v. McFarland, 15 F. 2d 823 (4 C.C.A., 1926); United States v. Avery, 30 F.2d 728 (N.D.N.Y., 1927); United States v. Smith (Smith II), 32 F. 2d 901 (D.Mass., 1929); United States v. Smith, 39 F. 2d 851 (1 C.C.A., 1930).

[63] Certiorari was granted in the McFarland case, 273 U.S. 688, but was subsequently

revoked, 275 U.S. 485, on the ground that the petition did not accurately state the basis of the government's appeal. See, however, Lichter v. United States, 334 U.S. 742, 755–60 (especially ftn. 3, 755), 765, and 782, upholding the constitutionality of the Renegotiation Act which authorized recovery by the United States of "excessive profits" from subcontractors, and accepting for its thesis the almost complete fusion of presidential and congressional sources of authority for such purposes.

[64] United States v. Gordin, 287 F. 565, 568 (S.D. Ohio W.D., 1922).

[65] United States v. McFarland, 15 F. 2d 823, 826, 831 (4 C.C.A., 1926).

[66] United States v. Smith, 39 F. 2d 851, 855, 857, 858 (1 C.C.A., 1930).

[67] Variously known as the Food Control Act and the Food Conservation Act, 40 *Stat.* 276.

[68] United States v. Ford, and United States v. M. Addy Co., 265 F. 424, 425 (S.D. Ohio W.D., 1920).

[69] 281 F. 298, 302 (1922).

[70] Addy v. United States, and Ford v. United States, 264 U.S. 239, 244–246 (1924).

[71] Highland v. Russell Car and Snow Plow Co., 135 A. 759, 761 (1927).

[72] Highland v. Russell Car and Snow Plow Co., 279 U.S. 253 (1929).

[73] United States v. Standard Brewery, 251 U.S. 210 (1920). The case turned on the "factual" question of whether 0.5 per cent beer was intoxicating.

[74] Starr v. Campbell, 208 U.S. 527 (1908).

[75] Mr. Justice Holmes in Missouri v. Holland, 252 U.S. 416, 434 (1920).

[76] Such as the following:

"To the Millbrook Woolen Mills, Inc., 215 Fourth Avenue, New York, N.Y.

"Gentlemen: The President of the United States, by virtue of and pursuant to the authority vested in him, and by reason of the existing emergency requiring such action for the national security and defense, does hereby requisition for public use connected with common defense, and hereby places an order with you for the following necessary supplies:

"(a) All cloth in your possession now ready for delivery to the United States government.

"(b) All cloth now in process of manufacture by you for the United States government, the same to be completed to conform to the requirements of your contract.

"You are further directed to utilize all machinery under your control exclusively in the production of cloth contracted for the use of the government, and, as required by section 120 of the act of June 3, 1916 (39 Stat. 213), you are hereby required, in filling this order, to give preference thereto over all work for parties other than the United States government, without regard to the order or date of contracting therefor.

"Kindly acknowledge receipt thereof.

"Very respectfully,

"Newton D. Baker, Secretary of War."

Mawhinney v. Millbrook Woolen Mills, 172 N.Y.S. 461, 463 (1918).

[77] *Ibid.*, 464–465. This statement is pure dictum, however, for the President's action in this case was clearly based on authority under the National Defense Act, as stipulated in Secretary Baker's order cited in the preceding footnote. In any event, the New York Court of Appeals reversed on the ground of overriding public policy in time of war, 231 N.Y. 290 (1921).

[78] That a government contract was "voluntary" in nature until confirmed by a specific formal written order from the President personally, or at least from his agent, the Secretary of War.

[79] This is emphasized in the Court of Appeals opinion in the *Millbrook* case, 231 N.Y. 290, 298–299 (1921).

[80] Crown Embroidery Works v. Gordon, 180 N.Y.S. 158, 161 (1920).

[81] Russell Motor Car Co. v. United States, 261 U.S. 514, 520, 522 (1923). Italics in the original.

[82] United States Harness Co. v. Graham, 288 F. 929, 934 (1921). "That power" to which the court refers in the first paragraph quoted is apparently "summary power." The government did not choose to appeal this decision. Italics in the original.

[83] See my discussion of congressional delegation of power to the President in "The Executive Rule-Making Power: Hart and Comer Revisited," *Journal of Public Law* 4:376–382 (1955), and references cited therein.

[84] Panama Refining Co. v. Ryan, 293 U.S. 388 (1935), and Schechter v. United States, 295 U.S. 495 (1935) are the "leading cases."

[85] For extended discussion of the subsequent administrative development through the Office of War Mobilization and the Office of War Mobilization and Reconversion, see Herman Miles Somers, *Presidential Agency* (Cambridge, Mass.: Harvard University Press, 1950); for an excellent discussion of the legal aspects, see Nathan Grundstein, "Presidential Subdelegation of Administrative Authority in Wartime," *George Washington Law Review*, 16: 301–341, 478–507 (April, June 1948).

[86] L. P. Steuart & Bro. v. Bowles, 322 U.S. 398, 404 (1944).

[87] United States v. Ashley Bread Co., 59 F. Supp. 671, 672–674 (S.D.W.Va., November 27, 1944). The government did not choose to appeal this decision.

[88] Ruggiero v. United States, 156 F. 2d 976, 977 (9 C.C.A., 1946).

[89] O'Neal v. United States, 140 F. 2d 908, 911–913 (6 C.C.A., 1944).

[90] Yakus v. United States, 321 U.S. 414 (1944). Issues of executive power were also ignored in the rent control cases, which likewise approached this form of price control as though the statutes had delegated authority directly to administrative officers. See Kittrell v. Hatter, 243 Ala. 472 (1942), and following the *Yakus* decision, Bowles v. Willingham, 321 U.S. 503 (1944).

[91] Constitution of the United States, Amendment XXI, 2: "The transportation or importation into any State, Territory, or possession of the United States for delivery or use therein of intoxicating liquors, in violation of the laws thereof, is hereby prohibited."

[92] Northern Pacific Railway Co. v. North Dakota, 250 U.S. 135 (1919), and Dakota Central Telephone Co. v. South Dakota *ex rel* Payne, 250 U.S. 163 (1919).

[93] Brown v. Jatros, 55 F. Supp. 542, 544 (E.D.Mich.S.D., 1944).

[94] Under the act of July 2, 1940, 54 *Stat.* 712: Presidential Proclamations No. 2413 of July 2, 1940, No. 2449 of December 10, 1940, and No. 2456 of February 4, 1941.

[95] Takahashi v. Pepper Tank and Contracting Co., 131 P. 2d 339 (1942). The court pointed out that the English cases categorize this power as "the doctrine of frustration of enterprise."

[96] Bradley v. American Radiator and Standard Sanitary Corp., 6 F.R.D. 37, 41 (S.D.N.Y., 1946). Italics supplied.

[97] Clemmer Construction Co. v. United States, 71 F. Supp. 917 (1947). Italics supplied.

IV

The Chief Magistrate:
"Under the Law"?

"With all its defects, delays, and inconveniences, men have discovered no technique for long preserving free government except that the Executive be under the law, and that the law be made by parliamentary deliberations." Mr. Justice Jackson, concurring in Youngstown Sheet and Tube v. Sawyer, 343 U.S. 579, 655 (1952)

"Executive orders have the force and effect of law and in their construction and interpretation the accepted canons of statutory construction are to be applied." Brown v. J. P. Morgan and Co., 31 N.Y.S. 2d 323; 177 Misc. 626, 635 (1941)

"There are certain limitations placed upon powers of courts beyond which a court cannot go, and these involve the discretionary powers of the Executive Department." Nordmann v. Woodring, 28 F. Supp. 573, 575 (W.D.Okla., 1939)

Legal Sources of Presidential Power

The Implied Powers of the Executive Branch

SHORTLY after his appointment to the Supreme Court, Mr. Justice Joseph Story, sitting in circuit court, just *prior* to the declaration of the War of 1812, stated with his usual clarity: "I take it to be an incontestable principle, that the president has no common law prerogative to interdict commercial intercourse with any nation; or revive any act, whose operation has expired. His authority for this purpose must be derived from some positive law." [1] Interestingly enough, Justice Story changed his mind within a year following the outbreak of the war,[2] and was led to dissent in strong terms from a decision of his brethren on the Supreme Court which agreed with his own views as stated above. At this time he argued that:

[T]he executive authority, to whom the execution of the war is confided, is bound to carry it into effect. He has a discretion vested in him, as to the manner and extent; but he cannot lawfully transcend the rules of warfare established among civilized nations. He cannot lawfully exercise powers or authorize proceedings which the civilized world repudiates and disclaims. The sovereignty, as to declaring war and limiting its effects, rests with the legislature. *The sovereignty, as to its execution, rests with the president. If the legislature do not limit the nature of the war, all regulations and rights of general war attach upon it.* . . . The modern usage of nations is resorted to merely as a limitation of this discretion, not as conferring the authority to exercise it. The sovereignty to exercise it is supposed already to exist in the president, by the very terms of the constitution.[3]

It is notable that with the possible exception of the recent *Steel Seizure* case, decided June 2, 1952, the decisions of the courts denying implied powers to the President have been repudiated at a later time by decisions of the Supreme Court which have validated, in the most outspoken terms, the particular presidential action that was at issue. Thus, for *Lorimier v. Lewis,* we have *United States v. Midwest Oil Co.;*[4] for the *Western Union* case, we have the *Curtiss-Wright* case;[5] and in place of *Brown v. United States,* we have a number of recent decisions which assert that the President is not bound even by the rules of international law, and perhaps not by statutory law either: quite to the contrary, his proclamation may be the source of both constitutional and international law.[6]

As for the *Steel Seizure* case, the exception here may be more apparent than real. Notwithstanding Mr. Justice Black's views "for the Court," it would be highly misleading to tout this case as holding against the President's right to exercise implied ("inherent," "residual," "prerogative") constitutional powers. On the contrary, a majority of the Court explicitly affirmed their acceptance of the theory of implied presidential powers; two members of the Court expressly reserved the question;[7] and only two held against such a theory, and then only insofar as it would justify the President's action in this particular case.[8] In the words of Justice Jackson:

When the President acts in absence of either a congressional grant or denial of authority, he can only rely upon his own independent powers, but there is a zone of twilight in which he and Congress may have concurrent authority, or in which its distribution is uncertain. Therefore, congressional inertia, indifference, or quiescence may sometimes, at least as a practical matter, enable, if not invite, measures on independent presidential responsibility. In this area, any actual test of power is likely to depend on the imperatives of events and contemporary imponderables rather than on abstract theories of law.[9]

Justice Clark, like Jackson, was a former Attorney General; and although he agreed with Jackson that the executive order in this case was unconstitutional, he took pains to include in his brief opinion the following statement:

In my view — taught me not only by the decision of Chief Justice Marshall in *Little* v. *Barreme,* but also by a score of other pronouncements of distinguished members of this bench — the Constitution does grant to the President extensive authority in times of grave and imperative national emergency. In fact, to my thinking, such a grant may well be necessary to the very existence of the Constitution itself. As Lincoln aptly said, "[is] it possible to lose the nation and yet preserve the Constitution?" In describing this authority I care not whether one calls it "residual," "inherent," "moral," "implied," "aggregate," "emergency," or otherwise. I am of the conviction that those who have had the gratifying experience of being the President's lawyer have used one or more of these adjectives only with the utmost of sincerity and the highest of purpose.

I conclude that where Congress has laid down specific procedures to deal with the type of crisis confronting the President, he must follow those procedures in meeting the crisis; but that in the absence of such action by Congress, the President's independent power to act depends upon the gravity of the situation confronting the nation.[10]

The dissenting opinion of Chief Justice Vinson, joined by Justices Reed and Minton, upheld in strong terms not only the general theory of implied presidential powers, but also its application to the facts of this particular case:

[I]f the President has any power under the Constitution to meet a critical situation in the absence of express statutory authorization, there is no basis whatever for criticizing the exercise of such power in this case. . . .

[T]he Presidency was deliberately fashioned as an office of power and independence. . . .

[And] we are not called upon today to expand the Constitution to meet a new situation. For, in this case, we need only look to history and time-honored principles of constitutional law — principles that have been applied consistently by all branches of the Government throughout our history. It is those who assert the invalidity of the Executive Order who seek to amend the Constitution in this case. . . .

"[T]he President is the active agent, not of Congress, but of the Nation. As such he performs the duties which the Constitution lays upon him immediately, and as such, also, he executes the laws and regulations adopted by Congress. He is the agent of the people of the United States, deriving all his powers from them and responsible directly to them. In no sense is he the agent of Congress. He obeys and executes the laws of Congress, not because Congress is enthroned in authority over him, but because the Constitution directs him to do so." [11]

The Supreme Court first gave authoritative utterance to a theory of implied judicial powers in 1803, when it claimed the right to exercise judicial review over acts of Congress.[12] Initially the Court acted in defense of its own constitutionally defined jurisdiction, but later the Court presumed to judge the scope of the substantive powers of Congress.[13] In 1819 the Court recognized that Congress could exercise implied powers in addition to those explicitly delegated in the Constitution.[14] Commentators, including the Court itself, have inferred from these early cases broad axioms of implied judicial and legislative power. These axioms are thought to be somewhat incompatible with the principle of separation of powers, since the maximization of either axiom would lead, alternatively, to a theory of judicial supremacy or legislative supremacy. Indeed, exponents of such theories have not been wanting.[15]

That men should fear the abuse of executive power is understandable; in some modern democracies — notably France — this fear is a political disease that puts in constant jeopardy the very existence of constitutional democracy. But if the genius of the American constitutional system is a balanced polity, is it not passing strange that two of three presumptively "equal and co-ordinate branches of government" possess implicit as well as explicit powers, while the third branch has only explicit powers? In fact, of course, American Presidents always have acted beyond the scope of their explicit legal powers when this appeared necessary in the public interest, and many decisions of the Supreme Court have approved their authority to do so.[16] Yet, there has been no formulation of a general theory of implied presidential powers. What American Presidents have lacked has not been power, but a theoretical justification for their exercise of it. It would be most ironic, although not altogether unlikely, if the contrariety of opinions in the *Steel Seizure* case should turn out to be the godfather of such a child.

The Fusion of Presidential-Congressional Powers

On September 5, 1917, the Honorable Charles E. Hughes, a then recent candidate for the Presidency, a former justice of the Supreme Court, and subsequently to become the chief justice of that Court, embellished his address before the American Bar Association with the statement "The power to wage war is the power to wage war successfully." [17] This view has now been accepted as official dogma by the Supreme Court.[18] This is perfectly consistent with the unmistakable trend during the two world wars to define the war power of the national government in terms of the illimitable boundaries of military necessity.[19] Among the hundreds of relevant decisions, there appear to have been only three World War II cases in which the courts have discovered any practical limitations upon the military power. All were decided by district courts; each thought that the war power should not extend to include the arbitrary treatment of citizens of the United States, classified by the executive branch as enemy aliens, as though they were in fact enemy aliens. The government did not appeal two of the decisions,[20] probably because before such appeals could have been taken, the Supreme Court reversed that part of the trial court's decision, in the third of these cases, that was adverse to the government.[21]

The prevailing climate of opinion among the federal judiciary is well expressed in the dictum of another district court:

I further conclude that without an act of the Congress there was sufficient authority by the terms of the Constitution itself to justify the action of the President in this case . . . when war has been declared and is actually existing, his functions as Commander in Chief become of the highest importance and his operations in that connection are entirely beyond the control of the legislature. There devolves upon him, by virtue of his office, a solemn responsibility to preserve the nation and it is my judgment that there is specifically granted to him authority to utilize all resources of the country to that end. . . .

Charged with the grave responsibility of preserving a government which guarantees the *property* rights of individuals, the Chief Executive, as Commander in Chief, must not be hampered in the prosecution of the war effort.[22]

The Constitution makes no delegation of "war power," as such, to the national government. Apart from the military status of the President,[23] the Congress has the power to declare war. One very interesting aspect of the war power which emerged from the World War II cases, however, was the consistency with which the courts came to conceptualize the fusion or merging of the powers of the political branches of the national government so that either the President or the Congress might individually or conjointly exercise any power attributable to the United States as a sovereign state at war. Under this theory, agreement between the President and the Congress places any action in time of war beyond the pale of judicial review.[24]

Again, however, we must go back to the Civil War for the genesis of doctrine. In his special session message on the state of the Union on July 4, 1861, President Lincoln stated: "It is believed that nothing has been done beyond the constitutional competency of Congress." [25] At the close of the year, he added, in his first annual message on December 3, 1861: "I have been unwilling to go beyond the pressure of necessity in the unusual exercise of power." [26] The Chief Executive clearly had established the precedent; the Supreme Court provided a rationale for legalizing his action when it decided, a few years later, that:

[W]hatever view may be taken as to the precise boundaries between the legislative and executive powers in reference to the question under consideration [i.e., the declaration of war by the President by his proclamations declaring the states of the Confederacy to be in insurrection], there is no doubt that a concurrence of both affords ample foundation for any regulations on the subject. [27]

Further expansion of this doctrine occurred during World War I, when a federal district court ruled:

In time of war broad powers are conferred upon the President of the United States both by the Constitution and by standing statutory enactments of Congress. . . .
Whether such authority and power were conferred by the act of Congress, or whether it was derived from the general powers conferred upon the executive branch of the government in times of war, is quite immaterial. [28]

The merger theory did not achieve the stature of orthodoxy, however, until the advent of World War II, when the Supreme Court gave its full blessing in several major decisions. Probably the most influential of these decisions came in the middle of the war, when it was held that:

The question . . . is not one of Congressional power to delegate to the President the promulgation of the Executive Order, but whether, acting in cooperation, Congress and the Executive have constitutional authority to impose the curfew restriction. . . . The question [is] whether it is within the constitutional power of the national government, through the joint action of Congress and the Executive, to impose this restriction as an emergency war measure. [29]

The President's war power can be invoked, of course, before war *de jure* is declared, [30] and can be relied upon to support action taken long after active hostilities have ceased. [31] Entirely apart from such expansion, which in effect permits the President's war power to extend over a longer period of time than the war itself, is another recent statement of the Court. Here the Court, speaking through Mr. Justice Jackson, contemplated a *triple* merger consisting of the presidential war power, the President's normal peacetime constitutional primacy in formulating foreign policy, and the exclusive (in terms of federal relationships) power of Congress, in war or peace, over foreign commerce:

The President also possesses in his own right certain powers conferred by the Constitution on him as Commander-in-Chief and as the Nation's organ in foreign affairs. For present purposes, the order draws vitality from either or both sources. Legislative and Executive powers are pooled obviously to the end that commercial strategic and diplomatic interests of the country may be coordinated and advanced without collision or deadlock between agencies.[32]

If the war power of the President is indistinguishable from the war power of Congress, and the war power of the President will support commercial regulation in time of peace, we have indeed gone a long way in the direction of substituting political controls for what used to be accepted as the constitutional function of the Supreme Court.

The *Steel Seizure* case indicates the point beyond which the Court would not go in upholding the war power. There the Court struck down an executive order purportedly based in part on the President's constitutional powers as Commander in Chief, in a period of national emergency and preparation for the imminent possibility of war. A majority of the Court agreed that the President could not justify the seizure of the steel industry, during what the Court chose to define as a time of peace, on the basis of his military powers. Ignored were the many precedents established by other Presidents who had used troops to intervene actively and with force to settle crippling strikes;[33] the majority here found the legal fiction of presidential seizure to offend the Constitution:

The order cannot properly be sustained as an exercise of the President's military power as Commander in Chief of the Armed Forces. The Government attempts to do so by citing a number of cases upholding broad powers in military commanders engaged in day-to-day fighting in a theater of war. Such cases need not concern us here. Even though "theater of war" be an expanding concept, we cannot with faithfulness to our constitutional system hold that the Commander in Chief of the Armed Forces has the ultimate power as such to take possession of private property in order to keep labor disputes from stopping production. This is a job for the Nation's lawmakers, not for its military authorities.[34]

Nothing in this decision, however, detracts from what has been suggested concerning the *conjuncture* of executive and legislative policy. It was precisely because the Supreme Court viewed the circumstances as presenting direct conflict between the President and the Congress that the Court felt that a choice had to be made between their respective authorities. The opinions all made it perfectly clear, however, that presidential seizure would have been upheld unanimously by the Court *if* the President had enjoyed the support — or even the neutrality — of Congress. As Mr. Justice Jackson, this time in a concurring opinion, put the matter:

When the President acts pursuant to an express or implied authorization of Congress, his authority is at its maximum, for it includes all that he possesses in his own right plus all that Congress can delegate. In these circumstances, and in these only, may he be said (for what it may be worth) to personify the federal sovereignty. If his act is held unconstitutional under these circumstances, it usually means that the Federal Government as an undivided whole lacks power.[35]

Retroactive Delegation of Congressional Power

So much has already been written on the subject of prospective delegation of power by Congress to the President that it seems justifiable to omit discussion of this facet of the sources of presidential power.[36] But what about retrospective delegation of power? No reported case holds invalid a retroactive delegation of authority to the President to do anything that was within the original competence of the Congress; and there are only three decisions by lower courts in which it has been held that statutes purporting to ratify executive action did not have such an effect, because of judicial doubts as to the constitutionality of the statutes if so construed.[37] The power of Congress to ratify not merely what it might have authorized, but also what it might itself have done, constitutes another technique whereby the theoretical separation of powers has been effectively by-passed.

The Civil War affords one of our best examples of this kind of lawmaking. It is generally conceded that many of Lincoln's proclamations issued during the first four months of his administration were without any basis of authority under the Constitution as it had been previously interpreted; but once the war was well under way, the President called Congress into special session and on the following August 6, the first of a series of bills of indemnity was enacted.[38] Such legislation was frequently enacted throughout the period preceding and following the Civil War, and the courts uniformly have upheld the power of Congress to ratify executive action and presidential legislation, either explicitly by direct reference, or implicitly as in appropriating funds to support the action taken or authorized by the Executive.[39] The fact of ratification is not evidence of the prior illegality of the action ratified, nor is it to be construed to create a presumption of the absence of legal power prior to the retroactive delegation.[40]

How specific must the language of the statute be in order to bring about the desired ratification? The answer to this question depends entirely upon judicial discretion, and upon where the court feels justice to lie in the particular case. Normally, the judiciary accept any sort of congressional approval, including the remarks of individual congressmen as printed in the *Congressional Record*, as constituting an adequate expression of the legislative will; but in a few instances courts have made exacting requirements of specificity in the use of "apt words" in the ratifying statutes.[41] On the other hand, ratification may be brought about by the complete silence of Congress: acquiescence in the exercise of legislative power by the President is also a form of ratification.[42] Occasionally it has been held that the failure or refusal of Congress to ratify an action of the President, after a specific request for it had been made, clearly indicated that no ratification had been intended in some other action of the Congress, such as the appropriation of funds to support the executive function;[43] but this is certainly a most tenuous form of institutional psychoanalysis.[44] The reorganization statutes pose the obverse of this question: is ratification automatically accomplished by the failure of either house (or both, depending upon the particular statute) to adopt a nullifying resolution? This constitutional question has been raised before but has not yet been decided by the Supreme Court.[45] Certainly, however, the intent of this device for maintaining a congressional check upon delegated executive legislation is that the silence of Congress, throughout the mandatory period of incubation, does mean consent and acquiescence, and is therefore a ratification by Congress of the action taken; and the absence of cases is doubtless a reflection of the certainty of what the judicial holding would be.

One curious question remains. Can Congress prospectively ratify an executive order? The Emergency Banking Act of March 9, 1933, appears to do so,[46] but none of the cases dealing with the relevant regulations and executive orders appear even to consider this point, let alone to rule upon it. Nevertheless, its implications are certainly interesting, and are by no means unknown in the United Kingdom, where Parliament has in several acts provided that regulations to be made under such a statute are to be considered as having the same effect and force as though they were included in the text of the statute itself.[47] There is, of course, no constitutional bar to the delegation of legislative power in the British system; but as a practical matter, there does not seem to be much in our own any longer, so far as that goes. As a technique of legislation, its importance lies in the fact that it removes any question of *ultra vires* and judicial divination of legislative intent from the case; the only question open to the courts is to ask whether the regulations purport to have been made under the authority of the statute. If the statute is itself constitutional, then so are all such regulations based upon it, *ipso facto*. It is a very effective, although perhaps not a very wise, means of absolutely frustrating judicial review of executive legislation based on statutory powers.

The Effect of Conflict between Executive and Congressional Legislation

What happens when the President legislates under a constitutional delegation of authority, and his order conflicts with an act of Congress? Can Congress delegate to the President the power to suspend, revive, amend, or repeal a specific statute in whole or in part? Such questions are by no means novel; they are the counterpart to the ones contested over by the Stuarts, the Parliament, and the judges during the first half of the seventeenth century.

The power of dispensation — the creation of legal exceptions to a rule of law whose generality remains otherwise untouched — is certainly a lesser power than the power to suspend the operation of a statute completely, either temporarily or permanently. It is not a power exercised very frequently by American Presidents, but, as a former inseparable prerogative of the Crown, it was not an unfamiliar type of executive power to the judiciary of Thomas Jefferson's administration. Jefferson apparently had expressly authorized the fitting out of a military expedition against Spain under the command of one Colonel Smith, in direct violation of the act of April 24, 1800. The expedition was abortive, however, and the President subsequently refused to assume responsibility for the fiasco, which resulted in

Smith's conviction in a criminal action. The Circuit Court for New York, which heard the case on appeal, asked:

> Who holds the power of dispensation? True, a nolle prosequi may be entered, a pardon may be granted; but these presume criminality, presume guilt, presume amenability to judicial investigation and punishment, which are very different from a power to dispense with the law. . . .
>
> The president of the United States cannot control the statute, nor dispense with its execution, and still less can he authorize a person to do what the law forbids. If he could, it would render the execution of the laws dependent on his will and pleasure; which is a doctrine that has not been set up, and will not meet with any supporters in our government.[48]

The Smith expedition was unusual. A much more serious question was raised in the post-Civil War period, when basic disunity existed in the conflict between the President and the Congress over policy toward the conquered territory of the Confederacy. One facet of this quarrel was expressed in the President's attempt to use his constitutional pardoning power to further his own plans, and his use of the executive prerogative of grace and mercy is perhaps symbolic of the wide gulf that separated Lincoln and Johnson from the Radical Republicans.

An attempt on the part of Congress to nullify the effect of an individual pardon was declared to be unconstitutional shortly after the end of hostilities.[49] A year later, the President issued his proclamation of unconditional amnesty, the effect of which was, of course, to relieve many former members of the Confederacy from the pains and penalties which Congress had placed in the way of their regaining their former properties, confiscated or sequestered following Union military occupation. When it became evident that the courts were accepting this amnesty proclamation of December 25, 1868, as legal evidence of loyalty (which was one of the conditions to the recovery of such property), Congress adopted a rider to the appropriation act of July 12, 1870. This act appropriated $100,000 for the payment of judgments which might be rendered against the United States by the Court of Claims, but it also provided that presidential pardons, whether general or special, should not be admitted in evidence. Instead, proof of loyalty in fact should be as defined in the Captured and Abandoned Property Act of 1863, as amended. The jurisdiction of the Supreme Court to hear appeals in cases from the Court of Claims was removed if such a pardon were admitted in evidence; and the Court of Claims was directed to hold the acceptance of a pardon, when offered in evidence, as conclusive of the guilt and disloyalty of the claimant unless a specific and express disclaimer of and protestation against such presumption of guilt were contained in the acceptance of the pardon itself. Nevertheless, such a case reached the Supreme Court, which decided that this section of the statute was in direct conflict with the President's proclamation, and that therefore the statute was to this extent unconstitutional as an attempted encroachment of Congress on the constitutional power of the Executive.[50] However, the Court rejected the subsequent argument that the proclamation had had the effect of repealing the Confiscation Act of 1862.[51]

It was also argued at a later time that, since the granting of amnesty was an aspect of the President's pardoning power, any attempt on the part of Congress to grant amnesty by a compulsory testimony statute was an unconstitutional violation of the constitutional separation of powers; but the Supreme Court rejected this contention, declaring that the President and Congress shared the power to grant amnesty, which could be exercised by either proclamation or statute.[52]

It has been pointed out already that President Truman's Executive Order No. 10340 was declared unconstitutional by the Supreme Court in the *Steel Seizure* case because, in the view of the majority, it was in conflict with congressional policy. Congressional intent was inferred from several post-World War II statutes including provisions for presidential seizure of industrial properties and facilities, of which the most important appeared to be the highly controversial Taft-Hartley (Labor-Management Relations) Act of 1947 (which President Truman had vetoed). "Under these circumstances," said Mr. Justice Burton, "the President's order of April 8 invaded the jurisdiction of Congress. It violated the essence of the principle of the separation of governmental powers."[53] It remained for Mr. Justice Jackson to formulate what has been widely accepted as the correct statement of the applicable constitutional principle:

When the President takes measures incompatible with the expressed or implied will of Congress, his power is at its lowest ebb, for then he can rely only upon his own constitutional powers minus any constitutional powers of Congress over the matter. Courts can sustain exclusive Presidential control in such a case only by disabling the Congress from acting upon the subject. Presidential claim to a power at once so conclusive and preclusive must be scrutinized with caution, for what is at stake is the equilibrium established by our constitutional system.[54]

There has been an increasing tendency, particularly during the past decade, for the Congress to enact "open-end" statutes, which by their own terms terminate either by presidential order or concurrent resolution of the Congress, or in the alternative, on a named date unless sooner terminated by presidential order or concurrent resolution. Obviously, this kind of legislation delegates to the President the power to repeal the basic statute, and frequently on no standard whatsoever except his own judgment. It has become standard operating practice for the President to exercise such power, sometimes with respect to individual statutes, sometimes with respect to whole blocs of them, as in the case of his Proclamation No. 2714 of December 31, 1946. The constitutionality of such delegation of presidential action does not appear to have been questioned.[55] In terms of current judicial attitudes in the matter of the delegation of legislative power to the Executive, there is no reason why the practice should be questioned.

An instructive example is provided by the recent decision of a federal district court. The owner of forty acres of land adjoining a military air base, which had been leased in 1943 to the government for a nominal annual rental, sought to regain control over his property a decade later. The lease provided for its termination six months after the expiration of the national emergency declared by President Roosevelt by his Proclamation No. 2487 of May 27, 1941. In one of his unsuccessful attempts to induce the courts to order the government to give his land back to him, the owner argued that the emergency had been terminated by Section 3 of the joint resolution of July 25, 1947.[56] Actually, this resolution does not purport to end the emergency as such, but rather to terminate certain designated statutes whose expiration dates were dependent upon the end of the "state of war" or one of the various concurrent national emergencies that the President had declared. The statute under which the land had been leased was one of those declared to have been terminated by the joint resolution. The government argued that Congress had no power to end an emergency that the President had declared — even though President Truman had signed this joint resolution — and that the emergency remained in effect until terminated by the unilateral act of the President by his Proclamation No. 2974 of April 28, 1952. At issue, potentially, was the government's liability to pay the difference between nominal and market rentals over a five-year period for lots of property all over the country. As defined by the court, the question was not one of the constitutionality of presidential power, but rather, it was a matter of congressional and judicial power:

There has been no contention that anyone other than the President may issue a Proclamation determining the existence of a national emergency. There is no suggestion that the other two branches of government, or either of them — judicial or legislative — may in any way usurp the duties of the President by declaring the existence of a national emergency. If the President is the only one who may declare a national emergency, is he alone empowered to terminate it? [57]

Not only was this judge's answer a thundering "Yes"; he went further, and defined "political" action in such a way as to exclude the decisions of legislative majorities! Politics, too, was part of the executive prerogative:

It seems to this court the determination that a national emergency existed is a matter of political judgment, and determination that the national emergency no longer exists is also a matter of political discernment, which judges have "neither technical competence nor official responsibility" to decide. If this case is a matter which has been given exclusively to the executive branch of the government and the judicial branch has no official responsibility therein, it would also seem to this court that the legislative branch has no right to determine matters of political judgment. [58]

There remains, however, the constitutional question of the use of the concurrent resolution, which the President does not sign, as a device to terminate statutes. This does not appear to have been challenged before the courts, [59] although President Roosevelt considered this device to be clearly unconstitutional. [60] There would appear to be no greater objection to this than to the presidential order for the same purpose. If statutes can be "repealed" by the unilateral act of the President, it is certainly arguable that powers delegated under them should be subject to revocation by the unilateral act of the Congress. [61]

A more difficult problem is presented by the concurrent resolution or the resolution of a single house [62] which purports to limit the President in the exercise of his own constitutional powers, such as the command of the armed forces, the decision to maintain diplomatic representation at the Vatican, or the divulgence of his personal diplomatic conversations with the Prime Minister of Great Britain. The intent

Legal Sources of Presidential Power

and effect of such maneuvering is almost entirely political; but if such resolutions of the Congress should be contested in the courts, it is difficult to see, in view of the *Klein* case and its satellites, how the judiciary could do otherwise than to hold such legislative action unconstitutional, unless — as seems more likely — the courts are to withdraw from the field of battle, viewing such questions as these to be of a political nature.

Notes

[1] *The Orono*, 18 Fed. Cas. 830 (C.Ct.Mass., 1812), No. 10,585. Accord: Brown v. United States, 8 Cranch 110 (1814), holding that enemy property was not liable to seizure under international law in the absence of specific congressional enactment, and that a declaration of war was not such an enactment.
See also Lorimier v. Lewis, 39 Am.D. 461, 462 (1843), holding that the power to lease lead mines in the public lands was "not a branch of prerogative"; and United States v. Western Union Tg. Co., 272 F. 311, 313 (S.D.N.Y., 1921): "If the President has the original power sought to be exercised, it must be found expressly, or by implication, in the Constitution. It is not sufficient to say that he must have it because the United States is a sovereign nation and must be deemed to have all customary national powers."

[2] See *The Emulous*, 8 Fed. Cas. 697 (C.Ct.Mass., 1813), No. 4479.

[3] Brown v. United States, 8 Cranch 110, 153–154 (1814). Italics supplied. This theory that the President has inherent power to exercise belligerent rights except when he is expressly restrained by statutory or international law is embraced in a number of subsequent cases: United States v. Reiter, 27 Fed. Cas. 768 (Prov.Ct. State of La., 1865), No. 16,146; United States v. Heinszen, 206 U.S. 370, 378 (1907); and United States v. Pennsylvania Central Coal Co., 256 F. 703 (W.D.Pa., 1918). Perhaps the baldest statement is that of the trial court in Commercial Cable Co. v. Burleson, 255 F. 99, 103 (S.D.N.Y., 1919), holding that "Without the co-operation of Congress the President is substantially without means to exercise his prerogative. If he must justify before courts any occasion he may have to accept their assistance, government becomes in the final analysis not one of laws, but of courts."

[4] 236 U.S. 459 (1915). See also Shaw v. Work, 9 F. 2d 1014 (C.A.D.C., 1925); and *Ex parte* Grossman, 267 U.S. 87 (1925).

[5] 299 U.S. 304 (1936).

[6] *Ex parte* Quirin, 317 U.S. 1 (1942); *In re* Yamashita, 327 U.S. 1, 12–13 (1946); Homma v. Patterson, 327 U.S. 759 (1946) Hirota v. MacArthur, 338 U.S. 197, 207–208 (1949); Johnson v. Eisentrager, 339 U.S. 763, 787–789 (1950).

[7] Justice Frankfurter, 343 U.S. 579, 597 (1952), and Justice Burton, *ibid.*, p. 659.

[8] Justice Black, *ibid.*, pp. 584, 587–588 and Justice Douglas, *ibid.*, pp. 631, 633.

[9] *Ibid.*, p. 637.

[10] *Ibid.*, p. 662.

[11] *Ibid.*, pp. 680, 682, 683, 690–691.

[12] Marbury v. Madison, 1 Cranch 137 (1803).

[13] Dred Scott v. Sanford, 19 Howard 393 (1857).

[14] McCulloch v. Maryland, 4 Wheaton 316 (1819).

[15] Robert H. Jackson, *The Struggle for Judicial Supremacy* (New York: Knopf. 1941); Charles Grove Haines, *The American Doctrine of Judicial Supremacy* (Berkeley: University of California Press, 1914); Woodrow Wilson, *Congressional Government* (Boston: Houghton, Mifflin, 1885).

[16] Among these: *In re* Neagle, 135 U.S. 1 (1890); United States v. Midwest Oil Co.,

236 U.S. 459 (1915); Myers v. United States, 272 U.S. 52 (1925); United States v. Curtiss-Wright Export Corp., 299 U.S. 304 (1936).

[17] 42 A.B.A. Rep. 232, 238 (1917). He concluded on the bellicose note: "we have a *fighting* constitution." *Ibid.*, p. 248. (Italics in the original.)

[18] Lichter v. United States, 334 U.S. 742, 780–782 (1948); see also Hirabayashi v. United States, 320 U.S. 81, 93 (1943).

[19] The trend began during the Civil War. At that time the Supreme Court held, concerning the government of occupied territory by the military, that "In such cases the laws of war take the place of the Constitution and laws of the United States as applied in time of peace." New Orleans v. N.Y. Mail S. S. Co., 20 Wall. 387, 394 (1874).

[20] Ebel v. Drum, 52 F. Supp. 189 (D.Mass., 1943); Schueller v. Drum, 51 F. Supp. 383 (E.D.Pa., 1943).

[21] United States v. Yasui, 48 F. Supp. 40 (D.Ore., 1942), reversed in 320 U.S. 115 (1943).

[22] Ken-Rad Tube and Lamp Corp. v. Badeau, 55 F. Supp. 193, 197–198 (W.D.Ky., Owensboro D., 1944). Italics supplied. With respect to the latter point, compare the Supreme Court's subsequent statement: "In total war it is necessary that a civilian make sacrifices of his property and profits with at least the same fortitude as that with which a drafted soldier makes his traditional sacrifices of comfort, security, and life itself." Lichter v. United States, 334 U.S. 742, 754 (1948).

Among other broad statements of the scope of the presidential war power, see particularly Brown v. Bernstein, 49 F. Supp. 728, 733 (M.D.Pa., 1943); and United States v. Montgomery Ward & Co., 58 F. Supp. 408, 415 (N.D.Ill.E.D., 1945).

[23] The word "military" is used advisedly, with full awareness that the President, during time of war, remains a civilian for federal income tax purposes.

[24] Therefore, it was futile to ask the courts to invalidate acts of Congress which delegated vast discretionary powers to the President in time of war. The courts could hardly be expected to hold that Congress had unconstitutionally delegated "legislative power" if the President had equal claims to the constitutional investiture of the war power; the "national police power" is at root political and not legal power, and it belongs to both President and Congress. Some of the World War II cases which accepted this thesis, with varying degrees of sophistication and sympathy, include United States v. Tire Center, 50 F. Supp. 404, 406 (D.Del., 1943); United States v. Bareno, 50 F. Supp. 520, 525 (D.Md., 1943); LaPorte v. Bitker, 55 F. Supp. 882 (E.D.Wis., 1944); Walter Brown & Sons v. Bowles, 58 F. Supp. 323, 324 (D.Ct.D.C., 1944); Yakus v. United States, 321 U.S. 414 (1944); Bowles v. Willingham, 321 U.S. 503 (1944); Kramer v. United States, 147 F. 2d 756, 759 (6 C.C.A., 1945); Silesian-American Corp. v. Markham, 156 F. 2d 793, 796 (2 C.C.A., 1946), affirmed in Silesian-American Corp. v. Clark, 332 U.S. 469 (1947); Woods v. Miller, 333 U.S. 138, 144–145 (1948); Lichter v. United States, 334 U.S. 742, 778–787 (1948).

[25] Richardson, *op. cit.*, VI, 24. Compare, however, the modern statement of a federal district court which goes even further: "When Congress is *in session*, but when the emergency is so great that the national safety would be imperiled before Congress could act, the power resides in the President, as a function of his military office, to do the things necessary to preserve the Government, but which it would not be lawful for him to do except for the emergency." United States v. Montgomery Ward & Co., 58 F. Supp. 408, 415 (N.D.Ill.E.D., 1945). Italics supplied. Lincoln's justification was, of course, that he had to act beyond his admitted powers because Congress was *not* in session.

[26] Richardson, *op. cit.*, VI, 50.

[27] Hamilton v. Dillin, 21 Wall. 73, 88 (1875). Compare Wilson v. Shaw, 204 U.S. 24, 32 (1907).

[28] United States v. Powers, 274 F. 131, 132–133 (W.D.Mich.S.D., 1921). See also United States v. Western Union Tg. Co., 272 F. 311, 318 (S.D.N.Y., 1921), reversed on stipulation of the parties, 260 U.S. 754 (memorandum opinion, 1922).

Legal Sources of Presidential Power

[29] Hirabayashi v. United States, 320 U.S. 81, 91–92 (1943). Accord: *Ex parte* Quirin, 317 U.S. 1, 29 (1942); Weightman v. United States, 142 F. 2d 188, 191 (1 C.C.A., 1944); Lichter v. United States, 334 U.S. 742, 755–760, 765, 782 (1948); Hirota v. MacArthur, 338 U.S. 197, 207–208 (1949).

[30] "Nor can it be considered necessary that the United States must be at war in order that Congress and the Executive possess the constitutional sanction to prepare for it." United States v. Chester, 144 F. 2d 415, 419 (3 C.C.A., 1944). Accord: United States v. City of Philadelphia, 56 F. Supp. 862, 865 (E.D.Pa., 1944); and Silesian-American Corp. v. Clark, 332 U.S. 469, 475 (1947).

[31] "The cessation of hostilities does not necessarily end the war power. . . . Whatever may be the reach of that power, it is plainly adequate to deal with problems of law enforcement which arise during the period of hostilities but do not cease with them." Fleming v. Mohawk W. & Lumber Co., 331 U.S. 111, 116 (1947). See also Woods v. Miller, 333 U.S. 138, 140–143 (1948); Ludecke v. Watkins, 335 U.S. 160, 167–169 (1948). Note also the assumption of the Court in United States v. United Mine Workers of America, 330 U.S. 258, 262 (1947). Not even the termination of war *de jure* ends the war power, according to Ladue and Co. v. Brownell, 220 F. 2d 468 (7 C.A., 1955), c.d. 350 U.S. 823 (October 10, 1955).

[32] Chicago & Southern Airlines v. Waterman S.S. Co., 333 U.S. 103, 109–110 (1948). Relying upon the *Chicago & Southern Airlines* decision as authority, the Court has extended the application of this principle. Again, in Mr. Justice Jackson's words: "It is pertinent to observe that *any* policy towards aliens is vitally and intricately interwoven with contemporaneous policies in regard to the conduct of foreign relations, the war power, and the maintenance of a republican form of government. Such matters are so exclusively entrusted to the political branches of government as to be largely immune from judicial inquiry or interference." Harisiades v. Shaughnessy, 342 U.S. 580, 588–589 (1952). Italics supplied. The specific question in this case was whether the Attorney General could constitutionally order the deportation of a legally resident alien, who had dropped his membership in the Communist party before the enactment of the Alien Registration Act of 1940.

[33] I.e., *In re* Debs, 158 U.S. 564, 582 (1895).

[34] Youngstown Sheet and Tube v. Sawyer, 343 U.S. 579, 587 (1952).

[35] *Ibid.*, pp. 635–637.

[36] See, for example, Glendon A. Schubert, Jr., "The Executive Rule-Making Power: Hart and Comer Revisited," *Journal of Public Law*, 4:376–382 (1955).

[37] McCall v. McDowell, 15 Fed. Cas. 1235 (C.Ct.Cal., 1867), No. 8673; United States v. McFarland, 15 F. 2d 823, 833 (4 C.C.A., 1926); and United States v. Smith, 32 F. 2d 901, 902 (D.Mass., 1929).

[38] "[A]ll the acts, proclamations, and orders of the President of the United States after the fourth of March, eighteen hundred and sixty-one, respecting the army and navy of the United States, and calling out or relating to the militia or volunteers from the States, are hereby approved and in all respects legalized and made valid, to the same intent and with the same effect as if they had been issued and done under the previous express authority and direction of the Congress." 12 *Stat.* 326. See also Section 4 of the act of March 3, 1863, 12 *Stat.* 820, and Section 1 of the act of May 11, 1866, 14 *Stat.* 46. The constitutionality of these statutes was upheld in United States v. Hosmer, 9 Wall. 432, 434 (1870), and Hamilton v. Dillin, 21 Wall. 73, 96 (1875). Note also the remarks of Justice Douglas, concurring in Youngstown Sheet and Tube v. Charles Sawyer, 343 U.S. 579, 631 (1952).

[39] A partial list of cases upholding the validity of ratifying statutes and the Presidential orders thus "legalized" includes: *The Orono*, 18 Fed. Cas. 830 (C.Ct.Mass., 1812), No. 10,585; *The Thomas Gibbons*, 8 Cranch 421 (1814); *The Amy Warwick*, 1 Fed. Cas. 799 (D.Mass., 1862), No. 341; The Prize Cases, 2 Black 635 (1862); United States v. Anderson, 9 Wall. 56 (1870); United States v. Leathers, 26 Fed. Cas. 897 (D.Nev., 1879), No. 16,581; *In re* Wilson, 140 U.S. 575, 576 (1891); Wilson v. Shaw, 204 U.S. 24,

32 (1907); Santiago v. Nogueras, 214 U.S. 260, 266 (1909); United States v. Pelican, 232 U.S. 442 (1914); Rhodes v. Tatum, 206 S.W. 114, 117 (Ct. of Civ. Ap. of Tex., 1918); Santa Rita Oil v. Board of Equalization, 54 P. 2d 117 (S.Ct.Mont., 1936); Norman v. B. & Ohio R. R. Co., 294 U.S. 240 (1935); Swayne v. Hoyt, 300 U.S. 297 (1937); United States v. W. Va. Power Co., 91 F. 2d 611, 614 (4 C.C.A., 1937); United States v. Query, 37 F. Supp. 972, 976 (E.D.S.C. Columbia D., 1941); Hirabayashi v. United States, 320 U.S. 1, 8 (1943); Schueller v. Drum, 51 F. Supp. 383, 386 (E.D.Pa., 1943); United States v. Von Clemm, 136 F. 2d 968, 970 (2 C.C.A., 1943); Hartmann v. Federal Reserve Bank of Philadelphia, 55 F. Supp. 801, 804 (E.D.Pa., 1944); Von Knorr v. Miles, 60 F. Supp. 962, 969 (D.Mass., 1945); California Lima Bean Growers Ass'n. v. Bowles, 150 F. 2d 964, 967 (Emer.C.A., 1945); Troy Laundry Co. v. Wirtz, 155 F. 2d 53, 56 (9 C.C.A., 1946); Porter v. American Distilling Co., 71 F. Supp. 483 (S.D.N.Y., 1947); Fleming v. Mohawk W. & Lumber Co., 331 U.S. 111, 118 (1947); Ludecke v. Watkins, 335 U.S. 160, 173 ftn. 19 (1948).

[40] *The Hiawatha*, 12 Fed. Cas. 95 (S.D.N.Y., 1861), No. 6,451; United States v. Midwest Oil Co., 236 U.S. 459 (1915).

[41] See the discussion of the presidential tariff in the Philippines, Chapter 5, and that of the Wool Clip of 1918, Chapter 8, both *supra*.

[42] United States v. Hodges, 218 F. 87, 88 (D.Mont., 1914); United States v. Midwest Oil Co., 236 U.S. 459 (1915); Norwegian Nitrogen Products Co. v. United States, 288 U.S. 294 (1933).

[43] United States v. Smith, 39 F. 2d 851, 858 (1 C.C.A., 1930).

[44] A recent example is afforded by Mr. Justice Frankfurter's opinion for the majority in Guessefeldt v. McGrath, 342 U.S. 308 (1952); as Chief Justice Vinson commented in his caustic dissenting opinion: "the Court rewrites Section 39 so that the Trading with the Enemy Act of 1917, as amended, will conform more closely to its own notions of statutory symmetry. . . . Statutory revision by this Court is not consistent with our judicial function of enforcing statutory law as written by the legislature." *Ibid.*, 321–322.

[45] It was considered to have been mooted by the specific ratification by the Merchant Marine Act of 1936 of the executive order involved in Isbrandtsen-Moller Co. v. United States, 300 U.S. 139 (1937). See also United States v. Paramount Publix Co., 73 F. 2d 103 (C.C.P.A., 1934).

[46] "The actions, regulations, rules, licenses, orders, and proclamations heretofore *or hereafter* taken, promulgated, made or issued by the President of the United States or the Secretary of the Treasury since March 4, 1933, pursuant to the authority conferred by subdivision (b) of section 5 of the Act of October 6, 1917, as amended, are hereby approved and confirmed." 48 *Stat.* 1. Italics supplied.

[47] Sir Cecil T. Carr, *Concerning English Administrative Law* (New York: Columbia University Press, 1941), pp. 47–48.

[48] United States v. Smith, 27 Fed. Cas. 1192, 1230 (C.Ct.N.Y., 1806), No. 16,342. In fact, however, the President does have the power to dispense in the sense that he may direct non-enforcement of the laws, in particular instances as well as generally. The history of anti-trust law enforcement is certainly instructive on this point.

[49] "It is not within the constitutional power of Congress thus to inflict punishment beyond the reach of executive clemency." *Ex parte* Garland, 4 Wall. 333, 381 (1867).

[50] United States v. Klein, 13 Wall. 128 (1871). See also Armstrong v. United States, 13 Wall. 154 (1872); Pargoud v. United States, 13 Wall. 156 (1872); Knote v. United States, 10 Ct. Cl. 397, 407 (1874), affirmed in 95 U.S. 149 (1877); and note the argument, not reached by the Court in its decision, in United States v. Lovett, 328 U.S. 303 (1946), which also related to an unconstitutional rider to an appropriation act, intended in this case to interfere with the President's power of removal. Cf. Cole v. Young, 226 F. 2d 337, 340 (C.A.D.C., July 28, 1955), discussed in Chapter 2, *supra*.

It was later decided, however, that the rule of the *Klein* case was not applicable when the statute of limitations had elapsed and it was necessary for Congress to pass a special jurisdictional act in order that the Court of Claims might entertain a suit. In such a case, Congress might waive the immunity of the government from suit on such conditions as it might choose, including the demand of proof of loyalty in fact, for which the innocence in law established by the amnesty proclamation could not be substituted. Austin v. United States, 155 U.S. 417 (1894).

[51] "To this we cannot assent. No power was ever vested in the President to repeal an Act of Congress." United States v. Clarke, 20 Wall. 92, 112–113 (1874).

[52] Brown v. Walker, 161 U.S. 591 (1896).

[53] Youngstown Sheet and Tube v. Sawyer, 343 U.S. 579, 660 (1952).

[54] *Ibid.*, pp. 637–638.

[55] Compare, however, *Opinion of Justices*, 52 N.E. 2d 974, 977 (S.Jud.Ct. of Mass., 1944).

[56] 61 *Stat.* 449, 451.

[57] Werner v. United States, 119 F. Supp. 894, 896 (S.D.Calif.C.D., 1954).

[58] *Idem*, following Ludecke v. Watkins, 335 U.S. 160 (1948) and United States *ex rel* Knauff v. Shaughnessy, 338 U.S. 537 (1950), both discussed in Chapter 7, *supra*. No appeal was taken from the district court's decision.

[59] Robert W. Ginnane, "The Control of Federal Administration by Congressional Resolution and Committees," *Harvard Law Review*, 66:569 (1953).

[60] Robert H. Jackson, "A Presidential Legal Opinion," *Harvard Law Review*, 66: 1353 (1953).

[61] Cf. the argument advanced by Bernard Schwartz, "Legislative Control of Administrative Rules and Regulations; I. The American Experience," *New York University Law Review*, 30:1031, 1043 (May 1955).

[62] An example would be S. Res. 99, 82d Cong., 1st Sess. (April 4, 1951), stating that the President should obtain "Congressional approval" before sending additional troops abroad in implementation of Article 3 of the North Atlantic Treaty. But see *Powers of the President to Send the Armed Forces Outside the United States,* Senate Committee Print, Committee on Foreign Relations and Committee on Armed Services, 82d Cong., 1st Sess. (February 28, 1951).

Due Process in Presidential Lawmaking

The Format of Presidential Legislation

UNTIL fairly recently, distinctions between the form of executive orders and the form of presidential proclamations were imprecise and fluid. In general, proclamations usually contain a preamble and a formal reference to the source of the President's authority, with the name of the President who issued it; the first person is usually used, and the Secretary of State countersigns and affixes the seal of the United States. Executive orders, on the other hand, do not usually include a preamble, may or may not refer to the authority under which they are issued, are generally written in the third person, and bear no countersignature of the head of an executive department. During the nineteenth century, many executive orders were not signed by the President, but were issued "by the direction of the President" and signed by department heads. The courts have not infrequently referred to executive orders as "proclamations," and vice versa; and administrative orders bearing no indication of express authorization by the President often have been referred to as "executive orders" by the judiciary.

Even the Federal Register Act of 1935 fails to distinguish between executive orders and proclamations in making requirements for their promulgation. As a consequence, such distinctions as do exist are the result of executive orders[1] and administrative practice[2] rather than of standards set outside of the executive branch by either the legisla-

Due Process in Presidential Lawmaking

ture or the judiciary. As far as the courts are concerned, not only may a statute that authorizes presidential action by "proclamation" or by "executive order" be satisfied by any document signed by the President, but even administrative orders issued with only his presumed approval satisfy the statutory requirements; there does not appear to be a single reported case to the contrary. The leading case on this point was decided by the Supreme Court over seventy years ago, when it announced:

It is true, in that section [8 of the act of 1841] only a reservation by a law of Congress or the proclamation of the President are specially spoken of, but it must have been the intention to include in this all lawful reservation. . . .

[The case of Wilcox v. Jackson] is conclusive on this, unless the word "proclamation," as used in the present statute, has a signification so different from "order" in the other as to raise a material distinction between the two cases. We see no such intention on the part of Congress. A proclamation by the President, reserving lands from sale, is his official public announcement of an order to that effect. No particular form of such an announcement is necessary. It is sufficient if it has such publicity as accomplishes the end to be attained.[3]

This doctrine was pushed to its logical conclusion a year later in the opinion of a federal district court, which held:

No set form of words or phrases is necessary to set aside a reservation. The sovereign is not parting with the title, but only setting it apart to be used for a specific public purpose. It is enough if there are sufficient words to indicate the purpose of the power that can act to show that in the given case it intended to act.[4]

The only circumstance which has evoked anything even resembling judicial dissent over the form, or rather lack of form, that an executive ordinance may take concerned a matter of interpretation bordering on the ridiculous. Did President Wilson's statement in his State of the Union message of November 11, 1918, to the effect that the war was "at an end," constitute an official "proclamation" of the conclusion of the war within the meaning of various wartime statutes which expired upon the return of peace? One federal district court did decide that the President's announcement was a "Proclamation,"[5] but the Supreme Court soon came to a contrary conclusion in a different case.[6] There was, in any event, neither evidence nor other indication that the President had ever intended that such legal effect should be attributed to his speech on the first Armistice Day.

Perhaps mention should also be made of the recent observation of Justice Black, speaking for the majority in the *Steel Seizure* case. Expressing pained surprise at his discovery of the state of affairs described below, Justice Black noted, with reference to Executive Order No. 10340 of April 8, 1952:

The preamble of the order itself, like that of many statutes, sets out reasons why the President believes certain policies should be adopted, proclaims these policies as rules of conduct to be followed, and again, like a statute, authorizes a government official to promulgate additional rules and regulations consistent with the policy proclaimed and needed to carry that policy into execution.[7]

The Court in no way undertook to rule upon the question of the legality of the form of the executive order, however. The quoted sentence was part of the Court's argument that the basis of seizure *should* have been a statute rather than an executive order; in the opinion of the Court, it was the lack of constitutional power in the President, and not the format of his executive order, that made it invalid.

Must the President Cite the Sources of His Authority?

Although the practice of including in executive regulations specific reference to their constitutional and statutory authority is undoubtedly desirable from the point of view of both effective administration and fairness to the affected public,[8] there is no judicial requirement to this effect. Conversely, the tendency of the draftsmen of executive orders and presidential proclamations to include, in an excess of caution, the phrase "as President of the United States, and otherwise" after listing specific sources of authority in the preamble of an executive ordinance, adds nothing to the validity of the order and contributes nothing to its defense in the courts because it is completely unnecessary.[9] If the President has other authority known to be relevant to the ordinance, it should be cited explicitly in the order itself. However, if such authority is brought to light only at a later time, perhaps through the research of government counsel (or sometimes, counsel for private litigants), and after a challenge to its validity has been raised in the courts, it may still be pleaded in justification. If such authority is brought to its attention by other means, including the court's own independent research, the court nevertheless will take judicial notice of such evidence without its being specially pleaded.[10] In the words of a federal district judge in a recent case:

Due Process in Presidential Lawmaking

Plaintiff raises the question that Executive Order No. 9108 . . . was invalid under the First War Powers Act because (a) there is contained in the order no reference to any particular statute under which the President acted. . . .

It may be that language of the exactitude stated to be essential to the validity of the action of the President, was not employed in the wording of Executive Order No. 9108, but the language shows that the President was exercising the power granted to him by statutory authority. It was not necessary that any precise form be employed for meticulous precision was not required. . . . It is not necessary in Executive Orders that the President identically refer to a statutory provision under which he exercises a power. It is sufficient, if he actually has such power, and exercises it according to some existing statute.[11]

The courts have never invalidated a presidential order where authority has in fact existed because of a mere defect in form; in fact, it is almost certain that they would also consider inconsequential a mistaken reference to the wrong statute as a source of authority.

When Does Presidential Legislation Take Effect?

The rule of the common law was that the purpose of proclamations was to give publicity to already existing law: to warn violators to desist from criminal acts.[12] It is generally true that before the Civil War, proclamations of the President were used most usually for hortatory and ceremonial purposes;[13] but there has been an increasing tendency since that time for proclamations to serve as vehicles for direct substantive lawmaking.[14]

The question of precisely *when* a presidential proclamation goes into effect did not arise until after the Civil War. It related then to the effective date of a proclamation of President Johnson of June 24, 1865, which lifted, for all the former states of the Confederacy west of the Mississippi River, the restrictions upon commercial intercourse imposed by President Lincoln's earlier wartime proclamations. A similar proclamation affecting the area under military occupation east of the Mississippi already had been issued on June 13, 1865.

Under the licensing system authorized by an act of July 2, 1864, agents of the Treasury Department had been directed to purchase cotton in areas under the military control of the Union armies, deducting 25 per cent of the value of the cotton as a tax. On June 26, 1865, an agent purchased from one Lapeyre cotton imported from west of the Mississippi. The tax was paid without protest because it was impossible for either the Treasury agent or Lapeyre to know of the existence of the President's proclamation of June 24, since it was publicly promulgated for the first time anywhere in the newspapers published on June 27. Lapeyre subsequently sued to recover the amount of the tax, and when the Court of Claims dismissed his petition, he appealed to the Supreme Court. The only question raised by the appeal was whether the signature of the President, together with the affixing of the seal of the United States in the Department of State, constituted such a publication or promulgation of the proclamation as to give it binding legal effect. The Court noted the silence of Congress on this point — a silence which remained unbroken for the next sixty-two years — and announced that it would apply the same rule to proclamations that held for statutes: "they had a valid existence on the day of their date, and to permit no inquiry upon the subject." Conceding publication to be necessary, the officer upon whom rests the duty of making it "should be conclusively presumed to have promptly and properly discharged that duty."[15]

It is obvious that the underlying basis of the Court's difficulties lay in the unrecognized change in the nature of the proclamation as a legal device. When proclamations were not used to make law, but to publicize it, the question of the *Lapeyre* case could not arise; now that proclamations were being used to make law, some other means of publicizing *them*, or some agreement upon a legal fiction, would have to be resorted to. A few years later, the Court was faced with a series of eight cases raising the same question as in Lapeyre's case about the proclamation of June 13, 1865, which applied to territory east of the Mississippi. The significant difference was that in five of these, the tax had been paid on that very day, so that it now became necessary to determine the precise time of day when the proclamation went into effect. Further expansion of the legal fiction accepted in the *Lapeyre* decision was the most logical and the easiest solution, and the Court embraced it in a unanimous decision:

In our opinion, this case is governed by the decision in *United States* v. *Lapeyre* (17 Wall. 191), which, although not concurred in by all the justices then composing the court, is accepted as conclusive upon the question involved.

Under the ruling in that case, the proclamation took effect as of the *beginning* of June 13, 1865, and, therefore, covers all the transactions of that day to which it is applicable.[16]

The *Norton* decision was announced on January 28, 1878. On December 23, 1878, the same Court, again by unanimous decision, "distinguished" the *Lapeyre* case, ignored completely its own precedent of the same year, the *Norton* case, and accepted the principle suggested by Justice Hunt in his dissenting opinion in the *Lapeyre* case.[17] Speaking for the whole Court this time, Justice Hunt held that a revenue act approved by the President on the afternoon of March 3, 1875, would be "ex post facto" in effect if applied to a collection made on the morning of the same day.[18] This decision apparently accepted the principle that the law would, when substantial justice made it necessary, take cognizance of fractions of a day, and established a precedent that would presumably be followed in the case of presidential proclamations.[19] The general rule which emerges, therefore, is that proclamations are promulgated by the signature of the President and the affixing of the seal of the United States, and they take effect at the beginning of the day of their date unless substantial justice necessitates inquiry as to the exact time when these acts were performed. The nature of "substantial justice" remained, of course, a question for the courts to determine independently in each case as it might arise.

In subsequent decisions, the Court of Claims has ruled that President McKinley's executive order of July 12, 1898, proclaiming a tariff for the Philippines, did not go into effect until the order had actually been received and promulgated *in Manila;*[20] but the same court later held that President Harding's proclamation of May 6, 1921, which provided for the suspension of certain port duties on and after the date of the proclamation itself, was conclusive on this point; and the date of the promulgation of the proclamation must be accepted as the "controlling date as to the suspension and discontinuance of the imposition of the taxes."[21]

This process of judicial rule-making governing promulgation and the effective date of presidential orders culminated in the bizarre *"Hot Oil"* case, when neither the trial court, the local prosecutor, nor the defendant knew of the existence of an executive order revoking an earlier executive order defining the criminal offense with which the defendants were charged.[22] The next session of the Congress enacted the Federal Register Act, Section 7 of which provided:

No document required under Section 5 (a) to be published in the Federal Register shall be valid as against any person who has not had actual knowledge thereof until the duplicate originals or certified copies of the document shall have been filed with the Division and a copy made available for public inspection as provided in Section 2; and, unless otherwise specifically provided by statute, such filing of any document, required or authorized to be published under Section 5, shall, except in cases where notice by publication is insufficient in law, be sufficient to give notice of the contents of such document to any person subject thereto or affected thereby. The publication in the Federal Register of any document shall create a rebuttable presumption (a) that it was duly issued, prescribed, or promulgated; (b) that it was duly filed with the Division and made available for public inspection at the day and hour stated in the principle notation; (c) that the copy contained in the Federal Register is a true copy of the original; and (d) that all requirements of this Act and the regulations prescribed hereunder relative to such document have been complied with.[23]

It has since been held that an executive order which was not of general applicability did not have to be published in the Federal Register in order to become effective, providing that the party concerned was given direct notice, since this was consistent with both the intent and the language of the statute.[24]

Judicial Notice of Executive Law

Both federal and state courts take judicial notice of the proclamations and executive orders of the President. The writer has collected over fifty cases explicitly holding to this effect, and he has found none that deny such an obligation on the part of the courts. The state cases range from a decision of the Supreme Court of Tennessee in September 1869 [25] to a decision of the Supreme Court for New York County on February 19, 1947,[26] and the federal cases range over an even longer period; it would probably serve no useful purpose to list them all. The statement of the Supreme Court of the United States is typical: "[A] public proclamation of the President . . . has the force of public law . . . of which all courts and officers must take notice, whether especially called to their attention or not."[27]

The courts also judicially notice executive agreements,[28] and the advisory formal reports of administrative agencies, such as the Tariff Commission, upon which presidential legislation is based.[29] One early case, which is of dubious standing today, decided that there was "no rule of law or practice requiring this, or any other court, to take notice of the various orders issued by a miiltary commander in the exercise of the authority conferred upon him."[30] It is certainly inconceivable, however, that a court today would refuse to take judicial notice of such military orders as the public proclamations issued by General DeWitt during World War II, or the directives of General MacArthur for the governance of Japan during the early postwar period, or those of his counterpart in the United States zone of Western Germany. The reason for this, which was equally true in the Civil War case, is that such military orders are, in a constitutional sense, a subdelegated form of presidential legislation.

Executive Orders: Laws of the United States?

Is executive legislation part of the "supreme Law of the Land"? Is it even law?

Two strands of judicial opinion conflict on this point, but since the series of cases that hold in the negative are truncated at the close of World War I, while those which affirm the status of presidential orders as public laws have multiplied rapidly since that same time, there is no question of what is the modern and prevailing attitude of the courts.

It is understandable that judges imbued with Blackstonian principles and with the memory of what Lord Chief Justice Coke said to James I of England still fresh in their minds should look unfavorably upon the intrusion of executive legislation as a recognized branch of law.[31] At an earlier time, Parliament had fought a comparable struggle to achieve judicial recognition of statutes as a source of law, but that seemingly had been forgotten by the American judiciary during the nineteenth century. It was presumed that the Constitution had substituted a new and overruling principle: "laws" were made by either constituent or legislative assemblies and emerged as constitutions and statutes; the judges did not make laws, although they did interpret them; and the Executive did not make laws, it was his job to enforce laws. Even as recently as 1925, Professor James Hart could write that the customary and, by implication, the proper function for a presidential proclamation was to notify the public concerning existing (i.e., statutory) law, but not to create new law.[32] As for managerial regulations, they were considered to be enforceable through the President's power of removal, but not by judicial process.[33]

The classic but — for the Supreme Court — latter-day statement of this point of view is found in a case that related to the binding effect of Treasury regulations, which were considered to be a form of presidential order:

Regulations prescribed by the President and by the heads of departments, under authority granted by Congress, may be regulations prescribed by law, so as lawfully to support acts done under them and in accordance with them, and may thus have, in a proper sense, the force of law; but it does not follow that a thing required by them is a thing so required by law as to make the neglect to do the thing a criminal offence in a citizen, where a statute does not distinctly make the neglect in question a criminal offence.[34]

The final rear-guard action was not fought for another quarter of a century, however. The facts, practice, and congressional intent in this case are all so clearly contrary to the judicial rationale that the decision, read today, has the appearance of a guileless anachronism. The Selective Service Act of May 18, 1917, explicitly authorized the issuance of presidential regulations to govern the process of registration, and it also specifically defined the penalty for violations of such regulations.[35] Nevertheless, the Sixth Circuit Court of Appeals held that President Wilson's proclamation of May 18, 1917, was designed to give notice of and to explain the statute, but not to have the force of law itself:

It was not intended that the proclamation should itself be law, but that it should give notice of the provisions of a most important statute which Congress had just enacted, and which required prompt enforcement. It is sufficient, therefore, to say that its purpose was not to add to the law, nor to make regulations, but to give to the public the most prompt and the widest possible notice of certain provisions of a new law . . . the obvious purpose of the provision in this statute requiring the issuing of a proclamation by the President . . . was thereby to give notice of the provisions of the act . . . and the act provides that the proclamation thus made shall carry with it a presumption of notice.[36]

But the act had specifically authorized "registration in accordance with regulations to be prescribed by the President"; Wilson's proclamation not only gave notice of the duty to register but also indicated the time and places of registration; and Sugar was indicted for having failed to register at such a place and time. How could a proclamation be more a law than under such circumstances?[37]

There are many cases upholding presidential orders as a source of

Due Process in Presidential Lawmaking

law binding on both citizens and courts,[38] but the recent utterances of a state court and a lower federal court indicate the revolution that has taken place in the general pattern of judicial thinking on this matter. A New York court said: "The executive orders have the force and effect of law and in their construction and interpretation the accepted canons of statutory construction are to be applied." [39] And the federal court, speaking of an executive order regulating the provisions of war contracts, held: "Executive Order 9001, promulgated by the President pursuant to the authority delegated to him by Congress, has the effect of a statute and is 'part of the law of the land'." [40]

In fact, the issue has become settled to the extent that the emphasis is now on a lower level of legislative authority. The binding effect of presidential legislation generally is assumed, and the critical question now has become whether administrative legislation, based on statutory and executive law, will support criminal prosecutions in the courts,[41] and whether it is law to the extent that it can be challenged by private groups who incur civil disabilities and discrimination as the result of the policy decisions implicit in the administrative orders[42] or legislation.

There would seem to be little question of the judicial rule today: executive legislation is law. It can collect money from those who would be liable under a statute; it can cause people to be put in jail; it can cause some people to be shot. Any theory that cannot accommodate these facts has, on this ground alone, outlived its usefulness.

Notes

[1] See Executive Order No. 7298 (February 18, 1936), Sections 3, 7; superseded by Executive Order No. 10006 (October 11, 1948), 44 U.S.C.A. sec. 305.

[2] For further and more detailed discussion of the forms of executive legislation, see James Hart, *op. cit.*, pp. 315–319; *Report of the President's Committee on Administrative Management* (Washington, D.C.: G.P.O., 1937), No. V, Part I: James Hart, "The Exercise of Rule-Making Power," pp. 320, 337–339; and Work Projects Administration Historical Records Survey, *Presidential Executive Orders: List* (New York: Hastings House, 1944), I, Introduction, especially pp. v–vi, viii–ix.

[3] Wolsey v. Chapman, 101 U.S. 755, 769–770 (1880). See also Wilcox v. Jackson, 13 Peters 498, 513 (1839), and Lockington v. Smith, 15 Fed. Cas. 758, 761 (C.Ct.Pa., 1817), No. 8,448: "As to the necessity of a seal, to give validity to the orders of the president, it is I think a sufficient answer, that there is no law or usage which requires it."

[4] United States v. Payne, 8 F. 883, 888 (W.D.Ark., 1881).

[5] United States v. Hicks, 256 F. 707, 710 (W.D.Ky., 1919).

[6] Hamilton v. Kentucky Distilleries & W. Co., 251 U.S. 146, 167 (1919). Nevertheless, the first division of the Alaska District Court chose to follow the *Hicks* case rather

than the Supreme Court in a decision made the following year, United States v. Switzer, 6 Alaska 223 (1920).

[7] Youngstown Sheet and Tube Co. v. Charles Sawyer, 343 U.S. 579, 588 (1952).

[8] See Sir Cecil T. Carr, *Concerning English Administrative Law* (New York: Columbia University Press, 1941), p. 51.

[9] Compare, however, footnote 20 of the majority opinion and the footnote to the dissenting opinion in Cole v. Young, 351 U.S. 536, 557, 568 (1956).

[10] As the Supreme Court pointed out in such a case, "it was not necessary that the statute should be expressly referred to. It was public law of which everyone was bound to take notice." Russell Motor Car Co. v. United States, 261 U.S. 514, 523 (1923).

[11] Toledo, P. & W. R. R. v. Stover, 60 F. Supp. 587, 595–596 (S.D.Ill.N.D., 1945).

[12] "[I]t was resolved . . . that the King by his proclamation cannot create any offence which was not an offence before, for then he may alter the law of the land by his proclamation in a high point; for if he may create an offence where none is, upon that ensues fine and imprisonment; also the law of England is divided into three parts: common law, statute law, and custom; but the King's proclamation is none of them. . . .

"But the King for the prevention of offences may by proclamation admonish his subjects that they keep the laws, and do not offend them; upon punishment to be inflicted by the law." Lord Chief Justice Coke, in The Case of Proclamations, 12 Coke's Rep. 74; 77 E.R. 1352, 1354 (1610).

[13] For examples of this, see any of the early volumes of Richardson, *op. cit.*, *passim*.

[14] Thus, Jefferson's proclamation commanding Burr's army to disperse, mentioned in Chapter 11, below, in the discussion of the Burr trials, should be compared with Franklin Roosevelt's proclamation which was the basis for the criminal prosecution of the Curtiss-Wright Export Corporation; see 299 U.S. 304 (1936).

[15] Lapeyre v. United States, 17 Wall. 191, 200 (1873). This was a decision that divided the Court, with four justices joining in the majority opinion, one concurring, and four others dissenting. Justice Hunt, in his dissenting opinion, argued: "We are not called upon to decide what would amount to a sufficient publication, or in what manner the required notice may be given. We are simply to decide whether, upon the facts before us, a legal publication of the proclamation had been made on the 24th day of June, 1865 . . . its effect is presumptively of the day of its date . . . when justice requires it . . . [but] until [the President] gave life to his proclamation, by some public or official notice of its existence, it was inchoate merely. The last act had not been performed." *Ibid.*, 206, 204, 205.

[16] United States v. Norton, 97 U.S. 164, 170 (1878). Italics supplied. Note that the Court was still applying the same rule for proclamations which applied in the case of statutes.

[17] See ftn. 15, *supra*.

[18] Burgess v. Salmon, 97 U.S. 381 (1878).

[19] There does not appear to have been any subsequent reported case in which the applicability of the principle to proclamations or executive orders was ever explicitly decided.

[20] Ho Tung & Co. v. United States, 42 Ct. Cl. 213, 225 (1907). The Secretary of War's order of October 13, 1898, directed that the executive order was not to go into effect until November 10, 1898, but the court's decision would still appear to be directly contrary to the latest ruling of the Supreme Court in the *Lapeyre* and *Norton* cases, which do not seem to have been considered by the Court of Claims.

[21] Standard Oil Co. v. United States, 2 F. Supp. 922, 927, 928 (Ct.Cl., 1933).

[22] See Panama Refining Co. v. Ryan, 293 U.S. 388, 412 (1935), and Louis Jaffe, "An Essay on Delegation of Legislative Power," *Columbia Law Review*, 47:359, 561 (1947).

[23] 49 *Stat.* 502, July 26, 1935. See also Section 5(a) of the statute and Executive Orders No. 7298 and 10006 issued thereunder, which provide that constructive public notice (i.e., effective promulgation) may be accomplished by actual publication in the

Due Process in Presidential Lawmaking

Federal Register *or* by the filing of an original and/or certified copies of an order with the Division of Federal Register, where it is stamped with the date and hour it became available for public inspection.

Executive orders and presidential proclamations are, of course, subject to the provisions of Sections 5(a) and 7, but there has been very little relevant litigation with respect to executive legislation under the statute. See, however, United States v. Krepper, 159 F. 2d 958, 964 (3 C.C.A., 1946), certiorari denied 330 U.S. 824 (1947), and State *ex rel* Kaser v. Leonard. 102 P. 2d 197, 199, 202, 206 (S.Ct.Ore., 1940). See also Frank C. Newman, "Government and Ignorance — A Progress Report on Publication of Federal Regulations," *Harvard Law Review*, 63:929–956 (1950).

[24] Toledo, P. & W. R. R. v. Stover, 60 F. Supp. 587 (S.D.Ill.N.D., 1945). Compare: Alger-Rau, Inc. v. United States, 75 F. Supp. 246, 247 (Ct.Cl., 1948).

[25] Sutton v. Tiller, 98 Am.D. 471, 472; 6 Cold. 593 (1869).

[26] Larsen v. McCann, 188 Misc. 752, 756; 68 N.Y.S. 2d 352 (1947).

[27] Jenkins v. Collard, 145 U.S. 546, 561 (1892). Section 7 of the Federal Register Act of 1935 also provided that "The contents of the Federal Register shall be judicially noticed"; so there would now be relatively few instances in which a court would have discretion to exercise with respect to the notice of presidential legislation, in any event.

[28] Vowinckel v. First Federal Trust Co., 10 F. 2d 19 (9 C.C.A., 1926); United States v. Belmont, 301 U.S. 324, 330 (1937).

[29] United States v. Best & Co., 86 F. 2d 23 (C.C.P.A., 1936).

[30] Burke v. Miltenberger, 19 Wall. 519, 526 (1873).

[31] The memory would appear to be still within the recollection of American judges. Mr. Justice Jackson wound up his concurring opinion in *Youngstown Sheet and Tube v. Sawyer* by returning to the early years of the seventeenth century as the most suitable point of departure for a proper orientation to resolve the question of whether President Truman could seize steel mills. His concluding footnote reads: "We follow the judicial tradition instituted on a memorable Sunday in 1612, when King James took offense at the independence of his judges and, in rage, declared: 'Then I am to be *under* the law — which it is treason to affirm.' [etc.]" 343 U.S. 579, 655, ftn. 27 (1952). Unlike his Stuart predecessors-at-law, it is noteworthy that Mr. Truman had publicly promised to comply with any decision the Supreme Court might make (as well as to carry out any statutory mandate that might be forthcoming). Mr. Truman kept his promise. James I claimed to rule by divine right; Harry Truman claimed to rule by popular right. In this regard, see particularly the dissenting opinion of Chief Justice Vinson, *ibid.*, 701, 703.

[32] *Op. cit.*, 316.

[33] See, however, Kutcher v. Gray, 199 F. 2d 783 (C.A.D.C., 1952), and Peters v. Hobby, 349 U.S. 331 (1955), Chapter 2, *supra*.

[34] United States v. Eaton, 144 U.S. 677, 688 (1892). See also *The Mary and Susan*, 1 Wheat. 46 (1816); Kurtz v. Moffitt, 115 U.S. 487 (1885); Muir v. Louisville & N. Ry. Co., 247 F. 888 (W.D.Ky., 1918).

[35] Section 5 provided: "Any person who shall wilfully fail or refuse to present himself for registration or to submit thereto as herein provided [i.e., in the presidential regulations subsequently formulated], shall be guilty of a misdemeanor and shall, upon conviction in the district court of the United States having jurisdiction thereof, be punished by imprisonment for not more than one year, and shall thereupon be duly registered."

[36] Sugar v. United States, 252 F. 74, 77–78 (1918), certiorari denied, 248 U.S. 578 (1918). The Supreme Court's action here, if any significance is to be attributed to it, should be compared with its subsequent position in the *Curtiss-Wright* case, where the trial court had ruled that the President's proclamation of November 24, 1935, revoking his former embargo proclamation but specifically preserving criminal liability for acts committed during the period when the embargo was in effect, was void and without legal effect. At this later time, the Supreme Court reversed in sweeping terms.

[37] Another interesting comparison may be made with a decision of the Dauphin County (Pennsylvania) Court of Common Pleas, which was also concerned with the binding effect of presidential draft regulations, including Army Order 99 which had set up the plan for selecting, drawing, and enforcing the attendance of the militia from the respective states. This judge ruled: "I am clearly of the opinion that the order was valid, and must have the force of an Act of Congress." Commonwealth *ex rel* Wendt v. Andress, 2 Pitts. R. 402, 404 (1863).

[38] A partial list includes Albridge v. Williams, 3 Howard 9 (1845); United States v. Freeman, 3 Howard 556 (1845); Armstrong v. United States, 13 Wall. 154 (1872); *Ex parte* Reed, 100 U.S. 13 (1879); Jenkins v. Collard, 145 U.S. 546, 560 (1892); Peters v. United States, 33 P. 1031, 2 Okla. 116 (1893); Stansbury v. United States, 37 P. 1083, 2 Okla. 151 (1894); Dempsey v. United States, 44 P. 382, 2 Okla. 151 (1894); Lincoln v. United States, 49 Ct. Cl. 300 (1914); Givens v. Zerbst, 255 U.S. 11, 18 (1921); United States *ex rel* Johanson v. Phelps, 14 F. 2d 679, 681 (D.Vt., 1926); Campbell v. Chase National Bank of City of New York, 5 F. Supp. 156, 173 (S.D.N.Y., 1933); Baldrich v. Barbour, 90 F. 2d 867, 871 (1 C.C.A., 1937); Foster v. United States, 26 C.C.P.A. (Customs) 59, 62 (1938); Nordmann v. Woodring, 28 F. Supp. 573, 576 (W.D. Okla., 1939); United States v. Query, 37 F. Supp. 972 (E.D.S.C., Columbia D., 1941); United States v. Pink, 315 U.S. 203 (1942); Wyman v. Pan-American Airways, 43 N.Y.S. 2d 420 (1943); Conn v. United States, 68 F. Supp. 966, 972 (Ct.Cl., 1946); Mitchell v. Flinkote Co., 185 F. 2d 1008, 1011 (2 C.C.A., 1951).

[39] Brown v. J. P. Morgan & Co., 31 N.Y.S. 2d 323; 177 Misc. 626, 635 (1941).

[40] Bradley v. American Rad. & San. Co., 6 F.R.D. 37, 41 (S.D.N.Y., 1946).

[41] Ruggerio v. United States, 156 F. 2d 976, 977 (9 C.C.A., 1946).

[42] Joint Anti-Fascist Refugee Committee v. McGrath, 341 U.S. 123 (1951).

The Scope of Judicial Review of Presidential Action

Judicial Self-Abnegation

THE DUTY OF COURTS TO UPHOLD PRESIDENTIAL ACTION

IN TERMS of the theory of separation of powers, the relationship between the judicial branch and the executive is no different from the judges' relationship to the legislature: it is, in the language of John Marshall, the "delicate" function of the courts not "to intermeddle with the prerogatives of the executive," but on the other hand, and again, in either case, "It is emphatically the province and duty of the judicial department to say what the law is." [1] Generally the courts indulge these presumptions, and consider themselves limited to the same extent, in deciding questions about the constitutionality of executive legislation, as they do in the case of statutes. In the only case in which the Supreme Court has been exclusively concerned with the interpretation of the effects of a presidential proclamation, the Court stated a broad rule of construction that has never been explicitly contravened: that the same rule of presumption should be applied to proclamations of the President as is applied to statutes; that is, in this instance, that they became valid on the day that the President signed them. [2]

In numerous cases the courts have affirmed the principle that the judiciary must render a valid construction of an executive ordinance if that is at all possible. In one such case, the Court ruled that an executive order should not be interpreted to have retroactive effect, but should be conclusively presumed to apply only prospectively, thus avoiding the constitutional questions discussed and decided by the lower courts in this case;[3] and in another case decided about the same time, the Court said that "if two constructions are possible, and one of them would render the order useless and the other give it validity, the latter is to be adopted."[4] Two more recent decisions of lower federal courts go even further in the direction of judicial indulgence of executive acts, one on the ground that constitutional questions ought to be reserved for the decision of appellate courts,[5] and the other on the basis of the narrower scope of property rights in time of war: "[I]t is doubtful that courts ought to be overzealous to search Acts of Congress, executive proclamations and regulations where only property is involved, to find more or less technical grounds from which to declare the regulations invalid or inoperative in cases before them."[6]

The Supreme Court seems to have accepted a contrary principle in the decision of the "*Hot Oil*" case,[7] apparently on the theory that the Court's responsibilities in reviewing executive action based on statutory delegation of authority differed from those it held when the action was based on constitutional authority. It must be remembered, however, that that decision is something of a judicial sport, occupying a unique and isolated enclave within the applicable body of law.

THE LEGAL EFFECT OF EXECUTIVE INTERPRETATION

A closely related question concerns the effect given to executive construction of executive powers, whether the source of delegation is constitutional or statutory. Among the many decisions that are in agreement on this point, three recent cases may be cited as typical. In the first, the court stated that the judiciary must entertain an allegation that an executive order is unconstitutional with "cautious skepticism," because it is then dealing "with considered results reached by [a member] of [a] coordinate [branch] of the government, sworn, as courts are, to sustain and defend the Constitution."[8] In the second, the court referred to "The President of the United States, [and] the heads of the various departments of the United States, to whose opinions the courts always give great weight";[9] and to the same effect is a recent decision of the Supreme Court, which held:

Section 1 of the First War Powers Act does not explicitly provide for creation of a new agency which consolidates the functions and power previously exercised by one or more other agencies. But the Act has been repeatedly construed by the President to confer such authority. Such construction by the Chief Executive, being both contemporaneous and consistent, is entitled to great weight.[10]

No general rule can be stated concerning the amount of evidence necessary to sustain — or to contravene — the initial presumption in favor of the validity of presidential action. The mere fact that a presumption of validity exists shifts the burden of proof to one who seeks to challenge the legality of executive legislation,[11] but in at least one decision (subsequently overruled by the Supreme Court), a "legislative" court required the government to prove not only substantial but the weight of evidence to overcome the allegation of unconstitutionality of a complainant.[12] Although the burden of proof that an executive order is unconstitutional is shifted to one who seeks to assail it, the precise degree of proof he must provide seems to be a function of several variables, including the nature of the substantive power exercised, whether an emergency exists, the nature of the right claimed, and the court.

THE PRESUMPTION THAT THE PRESIDENT ACTS LEGALLY

The courts will always presume that the President has complied with the statutory conditions that authorize him to take action or limit his power to act. Over a century ago, the Supreme Court formulated the rule that is still followed today. A statute adopted in 1832 provided that a second patent might properly be issued if the error causing the original patent to be invalid had arisen by inadvertency, accident, or mistake and without any fraudulent or deceptive intention. The plaintiff in error objected to the admission of such a second patent as evidence in the trial of this case on the ground that it did not contain any recital that the statutory prerequisites had been complied with, and that "without such special recitals . . . the second patent is a mere nullity, and inoperative." Speaking for an unanimous Court, Justice Story rejected this suggestion:

The patent was issued under the great seal of the United States, and is signed by the President, and countersigned by the Secretary of State. It is a presumption of law, that all public officers, and especially such high functionaries, perform their proper official duties, until the contrary is proved. . . . [W]here . . . an act is to be done, or patent granted upon evidence and proofs to be laid before a public officer, upon which he is to decide, the fact that he has done the act, or granted the patent, is prima facie evidence that the proofs have been

317

regularly made, and were satisfactory. No other tribunal is at liberty to re-examine or controvert the sufficiency of such proofs . . . when the law has made such officer the proper judge of their sufficiency and competency. . . . It is not, then, necessary for the patent to contain any recitals that the prerequisites to the grant of it have been duly complied with, for the law makes the presumption.[13]

A number of more recent cases are all to the same effect. Thus, a court held that, in fixing price margins for coal jobbers under the World War I Lever Act by his emergency regulation of August 23, 1917, "it should be conclusively presumed that the President gave the subject all the investigation and consideration which the emergency permitted." [14] And a few years later, the Supreme Court added that "The President will be presumed to have known the material facts and to have acted in the light of them" in issuing his executive order of February 13, 1920.[15] There is also a presumption that when an administrative officer acts in the name of the President, the President has authorized him to do so;[16] and the same presumption holds true for the administrative officer and his own subordinates.[17]

THE PRESIDENT'S PERSONAL AND OFFICIAL IMMUNITY FROM JUDICIAL ORDERS

It is accepted as a political and legal fact today that the President of the United States is immune from prospective control by the judiciary. The principal reason for this is the President's power of direction over the Department of Justice and other national police agencies, and his position as Commander in Chief of the armed forces: therefore, he cannot be forced to accept service of legal process. Certainly, no positive law grants him this immunity, nor does it necessarily follow from his legal or political status. Neither was it the understanding or intent of many of the principal participants in the Philadelphia Convention that he alone, of all the one hundred and sixty million people of the United States today, should enjoy personal immunities appertaining elsewhere in the Western state system only to reigning monarchs like the Queen of the United Kingdom. In fact, the express understanding of most of the delegates to the Philadelphia Convention was that, in approving the plan for a republic, they were not creating in the Presidency a monarchical office; Hamilton had offered them that alternative, and they had rejected it. Therefore, the principle of presidential immunity from judicial process is not a constitutional rule, but a judicial one, based primarily upon the decisions of judges who were brought face to face with the brute fact that they could not coerce the President. It was Lincoln, more than any other President, who made the judges familiar with this "ultimate constitutional fact." There was no such rule of presidential immunity in 1860.

The *Burr* case, which has already been discussed in another context, perhaps best illustrates this point. President Jefferson had issued an exhortatory proclamation on November 27, 1805, commanding Aaron Burr's followers to disperse in peace on pain of sharing his criminal liability; Burr himself was subsequently apprehended and brought back to Virginia to stand trial for his frustrated venture.[18] When Burr, who argued much of his own defense, asked for official papers in the President's possession to be introduced in evidence, Chief Justice Marshall ruled that a subpoena *duces tecum* could issue to the President of the United States directing him to appear in court as a witness and to bring with him any paper sought by the defendant to which the latter had a right to avail himself. Furthermore, added Marshall, the accused was entitled to the subpoena as of course; and if affairs of state prevented the President from attending,[19] he could so state in his return to the writ, and it would then be up to the sound discretion of the Court to keep the President from being harassed by motions such as this.[20] But Marshall also held that the subpoena *duces tecum* would issue where it did not affirmatively appear that letters and executive orders in the hands of the President, which might be material to the defense of the accused, did contain any matter that would be imprudent to disclose. The fact that such letters and orders contained matter not essential to the defense (or state secrets) which ought not to be disclosed would appear upon the return to the writ. Concerning the issuance of judicial process to compel the President to appear before the court and testify in person, Chief Justice Marshall ruled:

[I]t is not known ever to have been doubted, but that the chief magistrate of a state might be served with a supoena *ad testificandum*. If, in any court of the United States, it has ever been decided, that a supoena cannot issue to the President, that decision is unknown to this court.[21]

On the other hand, President Jefferson ignored the subpoena *duces tecum*; the originals of the papers Burr sought as evidence were never introduced as evidence in the trial; and although the President offered "voluntarily to furnish such information as in his judgment is proper," he thus denied both explicitly and implicitly his amenability to the process of the Circuit Court for Virginia or any other court of the United States.

Four years previous to his decision in the *Burr* case, Marshall had ruled, in *Marbury v. Madison*,[22] that a writ of mandamus might issue against the heads of the executive departments to compel their performance of purely ministerial acts not involving judgment or discretion, but this case has been generally construed as holding in effect that courts have no jurisdiction to compel the President by mandamus to perform even a purely ministerial act incidental to his office.[23] There has never been an attempt to mandamus the President personally to perform a ministerial act, if indeed it can be said that any of his duties are ministerial; and it is certain beyond dispute that this unbroken practice of over a century and a half would afford a conclusive answer to any latter-day attempt to induce a court to mandamus the Chief Executive.

Neither will an injunction lie against the President. The leading and only case arose as a bill filed by the state of Mississippi to enjoin President Johnson from executing or in any manner carrying out the Reconstruction acts of March 2 and March 23, 1867, on the grounds of their alleged unconstitutionality. The Supreme Court decided that the President's duty to see that the laws are faithfully executed was "in no just sense ministerial" but was "purely executive and political. An attempt on the part of the judicial department of the government to enforce the performance of such duties by the President might be justly characterized, in the language of Chief Justice Marshall, as 'an absurd and excessive extravagance.'" Noting also that the very fact that this was the first time the question had arisen was in itself an indication that the judiciary had no such power, the Court stated:

[W]e are fully satisfied that this court has no jurisdiction of a bill to enjoin the President in the performance of his official duties; and that no such bill ought to be received by us. . . . A bill praying an injunction against the execution of an act of Congress by the incumbent of the presidential office cannot be received, whether it describes him as President or as a citizen of a State. . . .

The Congress is the legislative department of the government; the President is the executive department. Neither can be restrained in its action by the judicial department; though the acts of both, when performed, are, in proper cases, subject to its cognizance.[24]

The Scope of Judicial Review

As in the case of mandamus, the President's personal immunity from injunctive process does not extend to his subordinates, whether they act under presidential subdelegation or direct statutory delegation of power.[25]

Although there appear to be only lower court cases bearing on the point, it probably can be assumed that the scope of judicial review of prospective presidential action under the Federal Declaratory Judgment Act is no greater than that in the case of injunction.[26]

The President's immunity from subpoena and the prospective control of the courts does not mean, of course, that he may not voluntarily submit to the jurisdiction of the courts, either personally or in his official capacity. In order to implement the enforcement of certain statutes,[27] it is necessary for suit to be brought in the name of the President rather than in the name of the United States. So far, "the President" has won all the cases arising under the Connally Act,[28] and has lost both of those brought in his name under the other statutes.[29] But the fact that the President may be held amenable to the judicial process in his official character,[30] notwithstanding the patent disparity between the fact and the fiction in these cases, creates a juristic precedent which cannot be completely ignored.[31]

Executive Discretion

POLITICAL QUESTIONS

Although the courts cannot interfere with or review the exercise of executive discretion, this is not quite the same thing as to say that the exercise of executive *power* cannot be reviewed by the courts. The doctrine of executive discretion is rather a means of distinguishing the kinds of executive decision-making that are not subject to review. Of these latter, the most absolute form that presidential power can take is that which the courts designate as political. Repeatedly, the courts have said that they have neither the competence nor the inclination to interfere with executive action that raises what are essentially "political questions." Therefore, any indication of expansion in the scope of the concept of political questions furnishes a rough sort of index to the trend toward executive and administrative finality. Particularly is this so when the political questions come to include action that was considered, at an earlier time, to be subject to judicial control.

It is also significant that the concept of the political question limits judicial review of legislation. In fact, it would appear in the light of many recent decisions of the courts that conjoint action of the President and Congress has a peculiar efficacy to generate questions of an inherently political nature.[32] The expanding power of judicial review of statutes in American courts during the past century has not, however, led to any increase in judicial review of formal acts of the Chief Executive. It has tended to bring about equivalent standards and criteria for the review of both congressional and presidential legislative acts. But in spite of this equivalence at the level of the formal, top, and external relationships of the executive and legislative branches, there is a considerable difference in the exercise of judicial review of the antecedent processes of the legislative and executive branches. Judicial review of administrative procedure remains a central and large problem area of American administrative law; but comparable administrative procedure in the Congress and its committees, where it is traditionally referred to as "legislative" procedure, comes within the doctrine of political questions and, at least in the case of the national government, is not reviewable in the courts.[33] Nevertheless, antecedent administrative procedure culminating in formal presidential action is thus sanctified and becomes, like all personal actions of the President himself, political in nature.

The judicial definition of the political acts of the President includes the acquisition and divestiture of foreign territory by presidential proclamation,[34] the recognition of both foreign[35] and our own state governments,[36] the power to declare and to terminate national emergencies,[37] the power to declare martial law[38] and to call out the militia,[39] and the power to take care that the laws were faithfully executed in the reconstructed states of the Confederacy.[40] Both the payment of awards certified by an international claims commission[41] and questions relating directly to the creation and determinations of such a commission[42] are political matters; likewise, presidential action to carry out international obligations under an executive agreement[43] or a treaty[44] was political to the extent that the conflicting acts of neither a foreign government nor one of our states could create a justiciable right in a federal court. One district court decision goes so far as to declare that in the case of a conflict between the President and a state, the question of presidential compliance with congressional standards, in a statute delegating and limiting his authority to act, is likewise political in nature.[45] Thus, in such important areas of constitutional law as international and federal-state relations, there has been a pronounced trend in recent decisions of the Court to consider presidential action as political. And, of course, the exercise of practically any facet of the presidential war power is a political act in the highest degree.

EXECUTIVE ACTION TO FRUSTRATE JUDICIAL REVIEW

The President may take direct and affirmative action to frustrate or interfere with the judicial process. He can declare martial law, suspend the privilege of the writ of habeas corpus, transfer prisoners out of the territorial jurisdiction of particular district courts, change the venue of trials in particular cases, seize property in the custody of courts under bankruptcy proceedings, and revoke or amend his orders *pendente lite*.

The most absolute form of his power to frustrate the courts lies in the executive declaration of martial law with the consequent substitution of provost courts and military commissions for the civil courts. Limited martial law may be retained during a period when over-all military control is deemed necessary but the danger of hostile military action has passed. In such circumstances, civil courts may co-exist with military tribunals, although with curtailed and modified jurisdiction, and subject to the whiphand of the military commander as in Hawaii during World War II when General Richardson ordered the summary military arrest and confinement of any civil judge who assumed jurisdiction over certain proscribed categories of cases normally within the scope of the civil rather than the military courts.[46]

The fundamental weakness of the judiciary in the face of naked executive power has been painfully demonstrated to the courts in a number of instances. The most celebrated example was undoubtedly President Lincoln's defiance of Chief Justice Taney shortly after the outbreak of the Civil War,[47] but this was by no means the only such instance. When Judge Betts ordered the appearance before him in federal district court in New York City of Purcell McQuillon, who was held in custody by the military authorities at Fort Lafayette, Lieutenant Colonel Burke refused to obey the writ of habeas corpus on the basis of the direct orders of Lieutenant General Scott; and Judge Betts then directed the federal marshal not to execute the writ, since the military authorities declined to obey it as a matter of right and the civil power was not sufficient to command its enforcement.[48] In another fracas of the same period, Judge Merrick of the Circuit Court for the District of Columbia issued a writ of habeas corpus to the provost marshal of the District on October 19, 1861. General Porter, who was the provost marshal, threatened with military arrest the lawyer who served the writ upon him, and did in fact subsequently arrest and imprison the process server. As for Judge Merrick, General Porter attempted to intimidate him by stationing an armed military guard in front of his home, so the judge remained indoors but reported the circumstances in which he found himself to his brethren on the Circuit Court. On October 22, 1861, the remaining two members of that court directed that a show-cause order be served on General Porter. President Lincoln personally ordered the court's deputy marshal not to serve the judicial order, however, and the President also ordered the suspension of the writ of habeas corpus for prisoners of members of the armed forces stationed in the District. At this point the judges gave up, but not without delivering, a week later, an opinion which states about all there is to be said about this kind of executive-judicial conflict:

The existing condition of the country makes it plain that [the deputy marshal] is powerless against the vast military force of the executive, subject to his will and order as commander-in-chief of the army and navy of the United States . . . the case presented is without a parallel in the judicial history of the United States, and involves the free action and efficiency of the judges of this court. The president, charged by the constitution to take care that the laws be executed, has seen fit to arrest the process of this court, and to forbid the deputy marshal to execute it. . . . The issue ought to be and is with the president, and we have no physical power to enforce the lawful process of this court on his military subordinates against the president's prohibition.

We have exhausted every practical remedy to uphold the lawful authority of this court.[49]

In another example of the judicial spirit of an earlier age, an attempt by the national government to transfer jurisdiction over the accused in a piracy case from a South Carolina federal district court to one in Georgia was denied by the South Carolina court as an attempt at presidential interference with the exercise of judicial power.[50] During World War II, however, the Supreme Court of Oregon asserted the President's power to direct a change in venue of suits against railroads during World War II, even in the absence of direct federal control such as was resorted to during World War I.[51]

Vesting orders of the alien property custodian, also issued during World War II, raised the question of the President's power to seize property under the jurisdiction of both federal and state courts, but the handful of cases directly bearing on this point are rather inconclusive of the issue. The abundant statutory authority of the President would seem to be clear with respect to judicial administration of the property of nonresident citizen incompetents[52] and bankruptcy proceedings, although in the latter instance the question was expressly reserved by one federal district court[53] and was avoided by others.[54]

Perhaps the most obvious way in which the Executive can act to defeat judicial review is simply to revoke an order being primarily challenged before the courts. The issue, in such a case, is ethical rather than legal, however. In the celebrated *"Hot Oil"* case, for instance, the President issued an executive order on September 13, 1933, modifying (apparently in anticipation of a possibly adverse decision of the lower federal courts) the very provisions of the petroleum production code at issue in a criminal case then being tried. He later reinstated the identical sections after a favorable decision was obtained from the circuit court of appeals; and although both the majority opinion and the dissenting opinion of Justice Cardozo criticize the haphazard administrative procedure followed, the executive orders were not considered to be invalid for this reason.[55]

NONFEASANCE

With very few exceptions, the courts have been powerless to force the President to take any particular action, even under circumstances where his legal obligation to do so appears to be clear. This is true irrespective of whether the source of his authority is constitutional or statutory. The basis for the policy underlying this rule lies in the inability of the courts to enforce presidential compliance with judicial orders, but the semantics of judicial rationalization reject the discretionary-ministerial dichotomy (insofar as the President is concerned) so that *all* his acts, no matter how they are defined, become in effect discretionary. For administrative reasons alone, it would be impossible for the judiciary to intercede in the exercise of presidential judgment under the faithful execution clause to determine, for instance, the priority of prosecutions under Section 2 of the Clayton Act, or to decide whether or not prosecution should be undertaken. To attempt this would destroy the power of the courts to exercise the judicial function; the courts would become assimilated by the administrative process, like the barbarians who have in times past "conquered" China, only to disappear in its vast human sea.[56] Some authorities speak of presidential obligation under "constitutional morality,"[57] but this patently is a "higher law" concept whose content will be supplied only by the value system of the moralizer. It may well be that the most moral thing the President can do at a given time is to confound the Congress by failing to exercise powers delegated to him by statute, or by directing his subordinates to fail to carry out their statutory responsibilities (although in this latter instance, there is a greater possibility that the courts may intervene and order the administrator to act). The "faithful execution" clause provides no solution for presidential decision-making under circumstances where there is conflict among statutory policies, or between statutory policy and his own direct constitutional responsibilities. The Supreme Court's decision in the *Steel Seizure* case is not an exception to this principle, because the Court's majority did not recognize the existence of such conflict in that case. It bears reiteration that the Constitution is predicated on a theory of conflict, not on one of cooperation; and the only Supreme Arbiter consonant with the premises of responsible government is the people of the United States themselves. In the interim between elections, it may well be the President who, for the making of certain decisions, is best qualified to function as the tribune of all the people.

In one early case an evenly divided Supreme Court upheld the power of the lower federal courts to act independently and directly to carry out the provisions of the Extradition Treaty of 1842 with Great Britain, in the absence of a presidential warrant of arrest, upon the proper request of the British consul for the apprehension of a fugitive from justice in Ireland; but all the justices agreed that presidential action was necessary before deportation could take place.[58] The essence of the Court's holding was that the President had discretionary power to refuse to comply with a request for extradition under the treaty; while the judiciary had the right to pass upon the "legal" sufficiency of the request. Where a statute authorized the President to restore to the public domain lands from an Executive Order Indian

Reservation, such public lands were not open to entry and settlement until the President chose to exercise his statutory powers by issuing a proclamation;[59] and no rate changes under the flexible tariff can take place until the President has made affirmative findings of fact and issued his proclamation announcing the changes.[60]

Even more emphatic is a decision of the Court of Claims. Section 4228 of the Revised Statutes authorized the President to issue a proclamation suspending the collection of certain impost duties for vessels of any state that did not impose discriminatory lightage duties upon vessels of American registry. The statute also declared that the date on which the President was notified that discrimination did not exist, or had ceased to exist, was to serve as the date on which penalty duties collected by the United States were to be suspended. The determination of what constituted "satisfactory proof" of non-discrimination was held to be entirely within the discretion of the President; therefore, the fact that his proclamation did not issue until some two years after Poland and Danzig had, as a matter of undisputed fact, ceased to discriminate against American vessels and the President had been so notified, could not be judicially questioned. Moreover, the proclamation need not have retroactive effect: the date on which satisfactory proof was furnished to the President and the penalty duties were suspended was the date on which his proclamation was promulgated.[61]

EXECUTIVE POWER TO WITHHOLD INFORMATION

Although no cases have as yet arisen in the courts to challenge the presidential claim of constitutional authority in this matter, a frictional issue during the past several years has centered around the power of the Chief Executive to withhold, and to order his administrative subordinates to withhold, official information from congressional investigating committees and, as in President Truman's security information Executive Order No. 10290 of September 25, 1951, from the general public. It is logical to assume, moreover, that if the President can deny similar information to the courts of law, his power to deny the Congress and the press is on unimpeachable grounds. With respect to the judiciary, there are precedents which go back to the early days of the republic.

The earliest case involved three of the most dynamic and pre-eminent figures of our entire history as a nation: Thomas Jefferson, John

Marshall, and Aaron Burr. One was our third President; another was our fourth and perhaps our greatest chief justice; and the third was a former Vice President, Jefferson's rival for the Presidency, the man who had killed Alexander Hamilton in a duel, and who aspired to become dictator of a rival empire in the West. In the course of his trials for treason and misdemeanor for his leading role in the latter adventure, Burr sought to introduce as evidence for his defense a letter written to President Jefferson by his co-conspirator, General Wilkinson. This letter had led directly to the counteraction that broke up his expedition, and was without question relevant, material, and from Burr's point of view indispensable to his ability to defend himself. Accordingly, Chief Justice Marshall, presiding over the Circuit Court for Virginia, issued a subpoena *duces tecum* on June 13, 1807, ordering President Jefferson to appear before the court and bring the letter with him so that the court might examine it. The President made no direct reply, but sent General Wilkinson's letter to United States Attorney Hay, "accompanied by a communication from the President authorizing the attorney to use his discretion in the case."

On the following September 4, Marshall ruled in one of the numerous opinions in this case that "If there be a paper in the possession of the executive, which is not of an official nature, he must stand, as respects that paper, in nearly the same situation with any other individual who possesses a paper which might be required by the defense." He then went on to hold, however, that the President might withhold the papers requested in the subpoena providing that he stated that he did so because of the secret nature of their contents:

The president may himself state the particular reasons which may have induced him to withhold a paper, and the court would unquestionably allow their full force to those reasons. . . . But on objections being made by the president to the production of a paper, the court could not proceed further in the case without such an affidavit as would clearly show the paper to be essential to the justice of the case. . . .

In no case of this kind would a court be required to proceed against the president as against an ordinary individual. . . . In this case, however, the president has assigned no reason whatsoever for withholding the paper called for. The propriety of withholding it must be decided by himself, not by another for him. Of the weight of the reasons for and against producing it, he is himself the judge. It is their operation on his mind, not on the mind of others, which must be respected by the court. . . . It does not even appear to the court that the president does object to the production of any part of this letter.[62]

The chief justice did have an indirect sanction that he could bring to bear. Although he had no way of forcibly gaining possession of the letter, he could, since this was a criminal trial, have granted a continuance to the defense until such time as his ruling was respected by the Executive. Therefore, Hay requested and received permission from the court on September 5 to send to Monticello for further instructions from the President; and on September 9, the United States attorney presented a certificate from the President, annexed to a *copy* of General Wilkinson's letter, with such parts deleted as Jefferson thought should not be made public. Thus, the court never did view or gain possession of the original letter, but only a certified copy of such parts of it as the President saw fit to divulge.

In a more recent period, similar questions have been raised in a number of different substantive areas. It should be noted that the complex institutionalization of the administrative process during the intervening century has tended to make many of these latter cases presidential decisions in form only, and administrative decisions in fact; and in other instances, what used to be a presidential decision has now become an administrative decision in both form and fact. The same considerations that were persuasive in the eyes of the court when the President acted, however, are now considered to be equally pressing when one of his principal executive assistants acts in his place. Thus, it was held that where the President had ordered in his proclamation of April 6, 1917, the arrest by the United States marshals of dangerous alien enemies, he could not be required to disclose the basis on which he (i.e., the Department of Justice) had directed the issuance of arrest warrants.[63] Another lower federal court decided, concerning presidential (i.e., Post Office Department) seizure and operation of telephone, telegraph, and cable facilities during World War I:

[T]hat he should be compelled at the suit of an individual to disclose and justify the reasons for his act is beyond possibility. . . . If he must justify before courts any occasion he may have to accept their assistance, government becomes in the final analysis not one of laws, but of courts.[64]

A number of cases arising under the flexible tariff acts are also concerned with information and records security. The first attempt to get behind a report of the Tariff Commission, which was by statute an essential factor in the decision of the President, was mooted by presidential action on the report before the case had reached the court.[65] Four years later, however, this same point — the power of the commission to withhold information concerning the trade secrets of a witness before it — was specifically upheld.[66] The Court of Customs and Patent Appeals also denied a subsequent request by an importer to have the members of the commission haled before the court so that his attorney might interrogate them about any additional information beyond their formal written report that they may have given directly to the President.[67] The logical extreme of these demands to penetrate the formal hearing process was a request to have the direct testimony of the President himself taken concerning the facts upon which he based his judgment; but this, of course, was denied too.[68]

A recent decision of the Supreme Court considers the constitutional question of the *Burr* case in modern institutional context. Instead of the President, it is now the agent in charge of the Federal Bureau of Investigation field office in Chicago who refuses to comply with the subpoena *duces tecum* of a federal district court. The Court approved the recalcitrance of this presidential alter ego (once removed):

We granted certiorari . . . to determine the validity of the Department of Justice Order No. 3229. Among the questions duly presented by the petition for certiorari was whether it is permissible for the Attorney General to make a conclusive determination not to produce records and whether his subordinates in accordance with the order may lawfully decline to produce them in response to a subpoena *duces tecum*.

We find it unnecessary, however, to consider the ultimate reach of the authority of the Attorney General to refuse to produce at a court's order the government papers in his possession, for the case as we understand it raises no question as to the power of the Attorney General himself to make such a refusal. The Attorney General was not before the trial court. It is true that his subordinate, Mr. McSwain, acted in accordance with the Attorney General's instructions and a department order. But we limit our examination to what this record shows, to wit, a refusal by a subordinate of the Department of Justice to submit papers to the court in response to its subpoena *duces tecum* on the ground that the subordinate is prohibited from making such submission by his superior through Order No. 3229. . . .

We think that Order No. 3229 is valid and that Mr. McSwain in this case properly refused to produce these papers. . . .

[I]t was appropriate for the Attorney General, pursuant to the authority given him . . . to prescribe regulations not inconsistent with law for "the custody, use, and preservation of the records, paper, and property appertaining to" the Department of Justice, to promulgate Order No. 3229. . . .

The constitutionality of the Attorney General's exercise of a determinative power as to whether or on what conditions or subject to what disadvantages to the Government he may refuse to produce government papers under his charge must await a factual situation that requires a ruling. We think Order No. 3229 is consistent with law.[69]

In his concurring opinion, Mr. Justice Frankfurter returned directly, although not expressly, to the rationale of the *Burr* opinion, as he declared his understanding to be that the majority decision and opinion should *not* be construed to imply that the Attorney General could not be reached by legal process to appear before an appropriate court to argue the extent to which he might claim privilege from testimonial compulsion.[70] Frankfurter also added that this question lay "near the judicial horizon." The horizon has kept its distance during the last several years, however.

STATUTORY MANDATES AND PRESIDENTIAL COMPLIANCE

To what extent is the President's formal statement that he has complied with the standards established in statutes delegating conditional powers to him considered by the courts to be irrebutable? A consideration of several fairly recent cases may help to indicate the position customarily taken by the courts in this matter. During World War I, for instance, President Wilson instituted, by his proclamations of October 8, 1917, and January 18, 1918, a licensing and rationing system for the domestic use of sugar. The President had stated in the proclamations that sugar was a "necessity" within the meaning of the Lever Act, under which he acted. A circuit court of appeals upheld the President's determination, noting:

Section 1 of the act . . . expressly authorized the President to make such regulations and to issue such orders as are essential effectively to carry out the provisions of the act. . . . [These proclamations] were public acts, and we think it was unnecessary for the prosecution to introduce additional proof that sugar was a necessary.[71]

Neither could the presidential determination that the private sale of certain seized enemy property for less than its market value was in the public interest be probed by the judicial process:

The power to dispose of the property in suit as though he were the absolute owner thereof having been granted to the Custodian, acting under the supervision and direction of the President, the courts may not nullify the sale because the terms and conditions thereof were otherwise than in the judgment of the courts they should have been. . . . Courts do not know the "state of the Union," and, as I apprehend, are not equipped to ascertain it. Those to whose keeping the public interest, so far as it is intermixed with enemy property, has been confided by Congress, must be the sole judges of what the public interest requires. . . .

The statement of the reasons actuating the President does not make his act any the less an act of discretion. Moreover, the judicial power to determine whether the reasons assigned are supported by the facts extends to any and all reasons or to none. It is conceded that the President may not be brought into court to substantiate his reasons. . . . The statute does not limit the Executive in the assignment of reasons to such as may be supported by legal evidence or by facts available to the public.[72]

This rationale of the *Chemical Foundation* case "and the broad interpretation therein given as to the powers vested in the President" was pushed to its logical limits a few years later by another federal district judge, who announced:

Furthermore, in my judgment full power is given to the President by the act to determine whether or not a private sale is in the public interest. The statutory requirement is that he state his reasons for a private as against a public sale; he is not required to state the reasons for his determination that such a sale is in the public interest. In any event, however, his determination that for any reason satisfactory to him the specific private sale is in the public interest must suffice. Congress could, and in my opinion did, vest the Commander-in-Chief with this power free from any judicial control. Because he must state his reasons, a failure to state any reason would render the order invalid; but the reasons stated by him are beyond judicial investigation. Therefore difficult as it may be to appreciate why a private sale to Kropff was in the public interest, the fact that the President stated that it was so must suffice. If then a private sale to Kropff was in the public interest, the reasons given, therefore, "to more effectually secure to and vest title in Kropff," must likewise suffice even though they are not detailed or apparent as are those stated for the sales to the Chemical Foundation.[73]

A similar question was raised in an Indian claim case, raising questions of legal rights under a long-since-executed treaty of January 14, 1846. The Indians had ceded most of their lands, with the express condition that if the President were subsequently satisfied, after a survey had been made, that the remaining lands reserved to the Indians did not contain sufficient timber for their needs, he should select for them another tract containing adequate timber elsewhere in the public lands. Acting upon the respective recommendations of an Indian agent in the field, the superintendent of Indian affairs, and the Secretary of War, the President resettled the tribe temporarily on Council Grove Reservation; in 1873, they were moved again, and this time permanently, to the Indian Territory. Council Grove Reservation was smaller than the insufficiently wooded treaty reservation in Kansas, and although the Indians had been compensated for the Council Grove lands, their heirs-at-law sued, generations later, for the difference in value between the original treaty reservation and the new, alleging: "(2) No proper investigation was made to determine the sufficiency of timber, and no finding made by the President. (3) As a matter of fact there was ample timber." The Court of Claims, however, ruled that the word "satisfied" was to be construed, as in *Field v. Clark,* to mean "found as a fact," and decided:

The approval by the President of the report of the Indian agent . . . that there was not a sufficiency of timber on the lands, conclusively establishes the fact that the President was "satisfied" that there was not a sufficiency of timber. That ended the matter, and the court cannot go behind his action and inquire as to whether in fact there was, or was not, a sufficiency of timber for the use of the plaintiff on the unceded lands. . . . The same rule applies to the question as to whether or not the Council Grove Reservation was a "suitable country" within the requirements of article 5 [of the treaty]. . . . The report was approved by the President, who, under the treaty, was to determine the suitability of the lieu reservation. This action by the President is conclusive as to the question of the suitability of the Council Grove Reservation, and is not subject to review by the court.[74]

One of the points argued in the *Curtiss-Wright* case was "that the Joint Resolution never became effective because the President failed to find essential jurisdictional facts." In his proclamation, President Roosevelt had stated:

I have found that the prohibition of the sale of arms and munitions of war in the United States to those countries now engaged in armed conflict in the Chaco may contribute to the reestablishment of peace between those countries, and that I have consulted with the governments of other American Republics and have been assured of the co-operation of such governments as I have deemed necessary as contemplated by the said joint resolution.[75]

The basis of the defendant's argument was that since the proclamation and the joint resolution were both signed on the same day, it would have been physically impossible for the President to have undertaken the consultation required by the resolution, as he claimed to have done. It is, however, difficult to see how the court could have looked behind this formal statement of compliance and gained access to the secret and pre-eminently political negotiations that must have comprised whatever "evidence" was the basis for the President's decision. In any event, this had been an administration bill, and the President may well have undertaken such negotiations while it was under congressional consideration, or even before it was introduced. Certainly this was the position of the trial court which, although of the opinion that for other reasons this proclamation was unconstitutional, ruled on this point:

[T]his recital of what has been done precludes inquiry on the subject by the court. The joint resolution does not require that the Proclamation shall recite the processes conducted by the Executive, which might lead to its issuance. The mere statement that the prescribed things have been done by the President which the Joint Resolution said were requisite to the issuance of the Proclamation, is conclusive for present purposes. . . .

[T]he President was not instructed as to the exact measure or manifestation of co-operation which he was expected to secure from other nations. An assurance of co-operation implies a meeting of the minds, and thus of itself constitutes the essential element of the specified requirement. It does not lie with this court to apply a more precise test.[76]

In the very recent decision in *Cole v. Young*, however, a majority of the Supreme Court did find that President Eisenhower had failed to comply with the standards of the Summary Suspension Act of August 26, 1950. Since the Court was of the opinion that Congress had intended a narrow scope to be given to the phrase "national security," Executive Order No. 10450 was illegal in that it purported to extend the provisions of the statute to positions in the classified civil service that had no direct relationship to "national security" (as defined by the Court). The executive order was, therefore, in direct conflict with the

Veterans Preference Act, since the President had attempted to authorize the administrative discharge of veterans without preserving their statutory right of appeal to the Civil Service Commission. "The basis for our decision," stated the Court, "is simply that the standard prescribed by the Executive Order and applied by the Secretary [of Health, Education, and Welfare] is not in conformity with the Act." To this sentence was appended a footnote which reads: "When the President expressly confines his action to the limits of statutory authority, the validity of the action must be determined solely by the congressional limitations which the President sought to respect, whatever might be the result were the President ever to assert his independent power against that of Congress." [77]

This decision marks a sharp break with the Court's previous practice in this regard, and the fair inference is that the present Supreme Court may be disposed to add the weight of the judiciary to that of the government lawyers and congressional committees who have been in the past so largely responsible for the enforcement of statutory standards affecting the President.

THE CONCLUSIVENESS OF PRESIDENTIAL FACT-FINDING

Most statutes which delegate determinative powers to the President do not require that he make formal findings or statements of compliance before he acts. As we have seen, the effect of creating statutory standards conditional to his action usually is to strengthen, rather than to weaken, the position of the President, because the courts accept his formal declaration as conclusive proof that he has in fact complied with the statutory standards. Conversely, statutes that create vague or imprecise standards, or require no special procedural standards at all, may have the effect of making the President's action more vulnerable to judicial re-examination, *because the courts in this instance have to invent and apply their own standards*, and are thus enabled to consider and weigh the actual evidence in justification of the President's determinations. This suggestion is in direct contradiction to orthodox "theorizing" on the subject, which appears to be based upon deductive logic instead of upon an examination of what the courts actually do.

This does not mean that the courts will usually undertake to substitute their judgment for that of the Chief Executive. On the contrary, the judiciary will in most instances hold that presidential fact-finding is conclusive, even when founded on mistake and error or an excess or abuse of discretion. But there are a few cases in which judgments are presidential only in legal fiction, and are patently administrative in fact, where the courts have overturned the "presidential" determinations.

The general rule was established in an early decision by Justice Story in the Circuit Court for Massachusetts:

It has been contended by the attorney for the United States, that this proclamation [of April 19, 1809] being founded on a mistake of fact [Erskine's promise that the British Orders-in-Council, directing the interdiction of American commerce with France, would be revoked as of a certain date], had no legal effect, and was merely void. Whether it was so founded in mistake, is not for the court to determine. It does not belong to the court to superintend the acts of the executive, nor to decide on circumstances left to his sole discretion. So far as applies to courts of justice, the president's proclamation, being founded on law, is to be considered as duly and properly issued, and of course as completely suspending the act of 1st March, 1809, as to Great Britain and her dependencies. . . . [When authority under positive law for presidential action] is once found to exist, the court have nothing to do with the manner and circumstances under which it is exercised.[78]

Even where the President's decision is purely formal, and ratifies the routine administrative process of an executive agency, it is binding upon both his administrative subordinates and private citizens, particularly those who are parties to what are in effect contracts with the government. This point was illustrated in one of the more literally dramatic cases concerning bureaucratic behavior, which in this instance might appropriately be termed *papierasserie* gone amok. Having found that one Bicknell had complied with all the requirements conditional to the issuance of a patent to certain lands in the Des Moines River grant, the commissioner of the General Land Office issued a patent to him, which was duly signed by the President on May 1, 1869. In accordance with standard operating procedures, the patent was recorded at the headquarters of the General Land Office in Washington, D.C., and the original was then transmitted through the agency's field office at Fort Dodge, Iowa, to Bicknell. Almost a decade later, however, the commissioner ordered the return of the patent to the Washington office of the General Land Office, and upon its having been received, he "Tore off the seals and erased the President's name from said patent, and mutilated the record thereof in the General Land-Office, all without the consent and against the protest of the grantees of said Bicknell." Needless to say, this rather primitive and decidedly summary form of license revocation or breach of contract, whichever it may have been considered to be — although it is unlikely that such conceptual niceties crossed the threshhold of the commissioner's mind at the time — did not win approval from the Supreme Court, which decided:

That this action was utterly nugatory and left the patent of 1869 to Bicknell in as full force as if no such attempt to destroy or nullify it had been made, is a necessary inference from the principle established by the court. . . . [W]hen the patent has been executed by the President and recorded in the General Land Office, all power of the Executive Department over it had ceased. . . .

It is not necessary to decide whether this patent conveyed a valid title or not. It divested the title of the United States if it had not been divested before.[79]

The principle has not always been followed, however, as in the government's disposal of a surplus steam yacht at the close of World War I. Notwithstanding the facts and evidence clearly establishing that his action was consistent with the terms of neither the statute nor the executive order on which his authority was based, the Supreme Court held that the Secretary of the Navy's acceptance of a specified bid as the highest bid was conclusive in favor of the successful bidder.[80] It was an undisputed fact in this case that a higher bid had been received, but it was alleged that this bid had been "misplaced and overlooked."

The "largess theory" of public employment, previously noted, applies in principle to other presidential determinations in which the Chief Executive acts under managerial or proprietary powers. Veterans' regulations, for instance, are like Civil Service regulations subject to formal presidential approval and review prior to promulgation; and such regulations determined, among other things, the power of the veterans' administrator to re-examine World War I war risk insurance claims and to make allowances in such cases. Section 17 of the Economy Act of March 20, 1933, made such decisions of the administrator final and not subject to review in the courts, and two circuit courts of appeals approved this executive and administrative finality.[81] The Supreme Court, however, reversed and held Section 17 to be unconstitutional because the insurance policies were contracts and entitled to the protection of the Fifth Amendment; but "gratuities" such as pension benefits and hospitalization were properly left subject to the final and conclusive determination of the President, or subordinates acting under his direction.[82]

A series of cases decided by lower federal courts and dealing with the fraudulent disposition of enemy alien properties seized during World War I are the least sympathetic to the conclusiveness of "presidential" fact-finding.[83] All these cases involved what was in fact administrative determination of citizenship, and it is highly unlikely that any President has ever heard of any of these determinations, or of the ensuing reversal of "his" decisions by the courts. The *Rodiek* case was an action by the United States to recover twenty per cent of the amount paid by the alien property custodian to the defendant's testator pursuant to a presidential order under the Trading with the Enemy Act. As an alien enemy, he was entitled to not more than eighty per cent of the proceeds of the sale, but on the basis of the mistaken — in the subsequent judgment of the courts — finding that he was a citizen, he had received the entire amount. The district judge had held "that the presidential allowance of Hackfield's claims was made under a mistake of law," and for that reason and also "because of the commencement of the proceedings in the Court of Claims," he held that presidential allowance could be reconsidered by the court. The Trading with the Enemy Act, however, appeared to make the President's determinations final and conclusive, especially Section 7(c) "and Section 12 [which] likewise pointedly treats a Presidential allowance or a judicial decree under Section 9 as alternative methods of decision of equal weight and finality." Nevertheless, the Second Circuit Court of Appeals held:

[I]t is our conclusion that whatever may be the proper construction of section 9 of the Act as to the finality of a presidential allowance which the claimant has treated as closing the controversy, the President's determination is subject to judicial review when the claimant himself seeks additional relief from the United States.[84]

In a similar and contemporaneous proceeding, the Court of Appeals for the District of Columbia also ruled that a presidential finding was not so conclusive as to preclude subsequent challenge and correction in an independent action. One Isenburg had sued to recover more than he had been paid, alleging that the custodian had sold his property for less than its fair value; and the United States filed a counterclaim for twenty per cent of the proceeds of the sale, asserting that Isenburg was an alien enemy who had received the full amount as a citizen of the United States as the result of an error on the part of the President induced by Isenburg's own fraud. Isenburg replied "that the determination by the President [that he] was an American citizen was correct, but whether correct or not, is non-reviewable by any court." Rejecting this proposition, the Court of Appeals reversed the presidential fact-finding and remarked:

The final point urged is that, even if the President was wrong in determining that Isenberg was an American citizen, the President's error is not subject here or elsewhere to challenge or correction. Counsel, to support this theory, quote from Professor Corwin's book "The President; Office and Powers," in which the author says that so far as he has been able to discover the court — presumably the Supreme Court — has never ventured to traverse a presidential finding of fact, whether it was expressed or merely implied from the order or regulation before the court. And this statement he dramatizes with a quotation from Secretary Seward to the effect that — "We elect a king for four years, and give him absolute power within certain limits, which, after all, he can interpret for himself." But with great deference to the views of Professor Corwin and Secretary Seward, we find nothing in our history which will justify a comparison of the powers of the presidential office with the royal prerogatives of a king, and we much prefer to anchor our hopes for the future safety of the Republic on that better and truer sentiment expressed by Justice Miller [in United States v. Lee, 106 U.S. 196 (1882)] that "All the officers of the government, from the highest to the lowest, are creatures of the law and are bound to obey it." But such abstract matters to one side, the identical question on this point was decided by us [in the *Société Suisse* case].[85]

The final case in this series was a suit against the attorney for both Hackfield (in the *Rodiek* case) and Isenburg, charging that he knew that Hackfield was in fact a German citizen but had nevertheless helped to draw up the papers for his claim, and further that he had bribed a vice-consul of the United States consulate in Bremen, Germany. This proceeding differed from those involving his clients, however, because this was an independent action for the recovery of attorney's fees allowed under a prior settlement, rather than a counterclaim. In the judgment of the federal district court which decided his case, however, this was a distinction without a difference:

The defendant . . . contends that the president exercised discretionary powers in allowing Hackfield's claim and that such determination is not open to surmise, re-examination, or collateral attack, but is final, conclusive and not reviewable by the courts.

The question of the conclusiveness of prior presidential allowances has been considered in several recent decisions . . . in each of these cited cases, the court ultimately based its determination that a presidential allowance might be re-opened on the ground that the claimant invited such re-examination when suit was filed for an increased allowance by the recipients. In so doing, however, the courts in each instance indicated that such re-examination by judicial review would not be foreclosed by any assumed conclusiveness even where there was not a prior re-opening by the claimant himself. . . .

"The government is never bound by the unlawful action of its own officers; nor is it estopped by the acts of its agents in entering into an agreement or arrangement to do or cause to be done what the law does not sanction or permit." . . . [I]t is a well settled rule that administrative determinations in matters relating to payment of public funds are never final . . . "in matters of account and payment [an executive determination] cannot be regarded as conclusive . . . when brought in question in a court of justice." Where fraud is charged there is cogent reason to re-open the allowance and ample authority under which may be found the power to do so.[86]

As might be expected, decisions handed down in the middle of World War II showed no disposition to reconsider judgments of the Commander in Chief. These were cases relating to the conclusiveness of presidential fact-finding, under statutory powers, precedent to the requisitioning of scarce materials needed for the prosecution of the war. The alien property cases, it should be emphasized, were decided long after the emergency to which they related had passed, and raised the quite different question of statutory rights to reimbursement where there was conclusive evidence of fraud. In the World War II cases, the precise questions were whether the Metals Reserve Corporation could take, under eminent domain, scrap iron and steel in the possession of a reluctant junkyard dealer, and an ore-handling bridge which had been tied up in litigation and was in the possession of a trustee in bankruptcy. Was it, as a matter of fact, necessary for the successful prosecution of the war for the government to take over this property? Naturally, the courts upheld the action of the Commander in Chief in robust terms:

Upon the authorities suggested and the general principle of the immunity of the executive function from frustration by the judiciary through the process of injunction, the court will not interfere with the defendants in their performance in this emergency of an executive task duly and expressly committed to the President. . . . When [the President], through appropriate channels, so determines and declares, the foundation for requisition is laid. *He may be mistaken in his conclusion but once made it is final,* and beyond both the power and inclination of this court to review or overturn.[87]

It already has been suggested that, in the *Steel Seizure* case, the majority of the Court evaded the question of the conclusiveness of President Truman's declaration, by his Proclamation No. 2914 of December 16, 1950, that a national emergency existed. Chief Justice Vinson did make the following statement in his dissenting opinion:

We also assume without deciding that the courts may go behind a President's finding of fact that an emergency exists. But there is not the slightest basis for suggesting that the President's finding in this case can be undermined.[88]

Whether such a concession of judicial authority to determine the "fact" of national emergency would have been made under circumstances such that the Court found it necessary to decide the matter; or whether this claim of judicial authority would be upheld by a majority of the Court, is very dubious. The Supreme Court has shown little predisposition to displace the President as "Sole Organ of the Nation" in the conduct of foreign affairs; and even less has the Court disclosed any ambitions to take over the functions and responsibilities of the Commander in Chief.

Notes

[1] Marbury v. Madison, 1 Cranch 137, 168, 170, 177 (1803).

[2] Lapeyre v. United States, 17 Wallace 191 (1873).

[3] M. Addy v. United States, 264 U.S. 239, 244–246 (1924).

[4] United States v. Chemical Foundation, 272 U.S. 1, 13 (1926); cf. Josephburg v. Martin, 152 F. 2d 644, 649 (2 C.C.A., 1945).

[5] Garcia v. Pan American Airways, 50 N.Y.S. 2d 250, 251 (1944).

[6] Henderson v. Smith-Douglass, Inc., 44 F. Supp. 681, 682 (E.D.Va., 1942).

[7] Panama Refining Co. v. Ryan, 293 U.S. 388, 432 (1934).

[8] Campbell v. Chase National Bank of New York, 5 F. Supp. 156, 167 (S.D.N.Y., 1933).

[9] United States v. Query, 37 F. Supp. 972, 976 (E.D.S.C., Columbia D., 1941).

[10] Fleming v. Mohawk Wrecking and Lumber Co., 331 U.S. 111, 116 (1947). Compare, however, Foley Bros., Inc. v. Filardo, 336 U.S. 281, 288–289 (1949).

[11] United States v. Gordin, 287 F. 565, 568 (S.D. Ohio W.D., 1922); Draeger Shipping Co. v. Crowley, 55 F. Supp. 906, 912 (S.D.N.Y., 1944).

[12] David L. Moss Co. v. United States, 26 C.C.P.A. (Customs) 381, 384 (1939). This

decision was, however, impliedly overruled by the Supreme Court's decision in United States v. Bush & Co., 310 U.S. 371 (1940), and was expressly overruled by the Court of Customs and Patent Appeals itself in T. M. Duche & Sons, Inc. v. United States, 36 C.C.P.A. (Customs) 19 (1948).

[13] Philadelphia & Trenton R. Co. v. Stimson, 14 Peters 448, 458 (1840). Note also the language of Mr. Justice Cardozo, dissenting in Panama Refining Co. v. Ryan, 293 U.S. 388, 444 (1935): "The President was not required either by the Constitution or by any statute to state the reasons that had induced him to exercise the granted power. It is enough that the grant of power had been made and that pursuant to that grant he had signified the will to act. The will to act being declared, the law presumes that the declaration was preceded by due inquiry and that it was rooted in sufficient grounds. Such, for a hundred years and more, has been the doctrine of this court."

[14] Ford v. United States, 281 F. 298, 302 (6 C.C.A., 1922).

[15] United States v. Chemical Foundation, 272 U.S. 1, 16 (1926). Compare, however, the presumption of the Supreme Court concerning the President's knowledge of the material facts and action taken on the basis of Harding's executive order of May 31, 1921, in the Court's contemporaneous decision in Mammoth Oil Co. v. United States, 275 U.S. 13, 31 (1927).

[16] Porter v. Coble, 246 F. 244, 249 (8 C.C.A., 1917); Seltzer v. United States, 98 Ct. Cl. 554, 562 (1943).

[17] Roxford Knitting Co. v. Moore & Tierney, 265 F. 177, 190 (2 C.C.A., 1920).

[18] There were actually two trials, one on the charge of treason, United States v. Burr, 25 Fed. Cas. 55 (C.Ct.Va., 1807), No. 14,693, and a second on the charge of misdemeanor, United States v. Burr, 25 Fed. Cas. 187 (C.Ct.Va., 1807), No. 14,694. Neither trial resulted in conviction.

[19] Jefferson was in fact enjoying one of his sojourns at Monticello at the time of the trial.

[20] Mr. Wirt, one of the attorneys for the United States, admitted the propriety of Burr's motion in open court: "The counsel for the prosecution do not deny that the general subpoena ad testificandum, may be issued to summon the president of the United States, and that he is as amenable to that process as any other citizen. If his public functions disable him from obeying the process, that would be a satisfactory excuse for his non-attendance pro hac vice; but does not go to prove his total exemption from the process. . . . The supoena, ad testificandum, is a matter of right, and the prisoner might have demanded it from the clerk without the intervention of the court." D. Robinson, Burr's Trial (Philadelphia: Hopkins & Earle, 1808), I, 136.

[21] United States v. Burr, 25 Fed. Cas. 30, 34 (C.Ct.Va., June 13, 1807), No. 14,692d.

[22] 1 Cranch 137 (1803). Compare Kendall v. Stokes, 12 Peters 524 (1838).

[23] Weeks v. United States ex rel Creary, 51 A.D.C. 195, 200 (1922).

[24] Mississippi v. Johnson, 71 U.S. 475, 499, 501, 500 (1867). See also Georgia v. Stanton, 6 Wall. 50 (1867). A latter-day David recently appeared in the form of Andrew J. Easter, who asked the Court of Appeals of the District of Columbia to enjoin the President from encouraging the passage of legislation raising the ceiling on the national debt, to compel the President to "mandate" the orderly reduction and the eventual liquidation of the national debt, and (by no means least) to enforce immediate racial desegregation. The Court of Appeals dismissed the suit for lack of jurisdiction, and the Supreme Court denied certiorari. Easter v. Eisenhower, 24 U.S. Law Week, 3282; 351 U.S. 908 (April 23, 1956).

[25] Avery v. Fox, 2 Fed. Cas. 245, 248 (C.Ct., 6 C., W.D.Mich., 1868), No. 674; Von Knorr v. Miles, 60 F. Supp. 962, 968 (D.Mass., 1945); Snyder v. Buck, 75 F. Supp. 902 (D.Ct.D.C., 1948), reversed on other grounds, 179 F. 2d 466 (C.A.D.C., 1949), and affirmed 340 U.S. 15 (1950); Youngstown Sheet & Tube v. Charles Sawyer, 343 U.S. 579 (1952). Compare, however, Alpirn v. Huffman, 49 F. Supp. 337, 342 (D.Neb., Omaha D., 1943), and Dakota Central Telephone Co. v. South Dakota ex rel Payne. 250 U.S. 163 (1919).

[26] See, for example, State of Wyoming v. Franke, 58 F. Supp. 890, 897 (D.Wyo., 1945); Schueller v. Drum, 51 F. Supp. 383 (E.D.Pa., 1943).

[27] This was true of provisions of the habeas corpus code governing deportation and extradition, and also of the Connally Act of February 22, 1935, 49 Stat. 33, s. 10; 15 U.S.C.A. s. 715i, 715j. It is also interesting to note that the latter statute was enacted as the direct result of the Supreme Court's decision in the *"Hot Oil"* case, Panama Refining Co. v. Ryan, 293 U.S. 388 (1935).

[28] President of the United States v. Artex Refining Sales Corp., 11 F. Supp. 189 (S.D.Tex., Houston D., 1935); Griswold v. The President of the United States, 82 F. 2d 922 (5 C.C.A., 1936); The President of the United States v. Skeen and The President of the United States v. Theron Oil Co., 118 F. 2d 58 (5 C.C.A., 1941).

[29] President of the U.S. *ex rel* Fedele v. Karnuth, 13 F. Supp. 904 (W.D.N.Y., 1936); and President of the U.S. *ex rel* Caputo v. Kelly, 19 F. Supp. 730 (S.D.N.Y., 1937), affirmed, 92 F. 2d 603 (2 C.C.A., 1937), certiorari denied, 303 U.S. 635 (1938), and application denied, 304 U.S. 579 (1938), affirmed on rehearing, 96 F. 2d 787 (2 C.C.A., 1938).

[30] Note also Miscellaneous Order No. 512 of the Supreme Court at the 1947 Term, Everett v. Truman, Commander in Chief of the Armed Forces of the United States, 334 U.S. 824 (May 18, 1948).

[31] It is interesting to note that the authorization for bringing judicial actions in the name of the President represents a kind of retrogression historically. In the United Kingdom, quite to the contrary of American practice, certain criminal and other actions formerly brought in the name of the Crown are now taken in the name of the Attorney General.

[32] ". . . when the Congress recites that the President may dismiss summarily executive employees whenever he deems dismissal necessary or advisable in the interest of the national security, the enactment is valid. The policies to be pursued in the matter by the Congress and by the President are for them to determine, not for us." Cole v. Young, 226 F. 2d 237, 340 (C.A.D.C., 1955). The majority of the Supreme Court reversed on the assumption that there was conflict between the policies of the President and the Congress, but the political question doctrine was emphatically reiterated in the dissenting opinion. 351 U.S. 536, 567 (1956).

[33] Christoffel v. United States, 338 U.S. 84 (1949), United States v. Rumely, 345 U.S. 41 (1953). The application of the self-incrimination clause of the Fifth Amendment to witnesses before investigating committees is a recent exception to the rule. See Quinn v. United States, 349 U.S. 155 (1955), Emspak v. United States, 349 U.S. 190 (1955), and Bart v. United States, 349 U.S. 219 (1955).

[34] Foster & Elam v. Neilson, 2 Peters 253 (1829); Jones v. United States, 137 U.S. 202 (1890); Neeley v. Henkel, 180 U.S. 109 (1901).

[35] Oetjen v. Central Leather Co., 246 U.S. 297 (1918); Wilson v. Shaw, 204 U.S. 24 (1907); United States v. Belmont, 301 U.S. 324 (1937).

[36] Luther v. Borden, 7 Howard 1 (1849).

[37] Werner v. United States, 119 F. Supp. 894 (S.D.Cal.C.D., 1954).

[38] *Ex parte* Field, 9 Fed. Cas. 1 (D.Vt., 1862), No. 4761.

[39] Luther v. Borden, 7 Howard 1, 43, 44 (1849).

[40] Georgia v. Stanton, 6 Wall. 50 (1868). Presidential Reconstruction was never challenged before the Supreme Court, but it was upheld in several state cases, and would almost certainly have been considered political by the Court if the question had arisen for decision.

[41] Frelinghuysen v. United States *ex rel* Key, 110 U.S. 63 (1884).

[42] Z & F Assets Corp. v. Hull, 114 F. 2d 464 (1940).

[43] United States v. Pink, 315 U.S. 203 (1942).

[44] Clark v. Allen, 331 U.S. 503, 514 (1947). Presidential denunciation, under statutory delegation of authority, of treaty provisions in conflict with the statute was held to raise no justiciable issue in Van der Weyde v. Ocean Transport Co., 297 U.S. 114, 117–118 (1936).

⁴⁵ State of Wyoming v. Franke, 58 F. Supp. 890 (D.Wyo., 1945).

⁴⁶ *Ex parte* Duncan, 146 F. 2d 576 (9 C.C.A., 1944).

⁴⁷ *Ex parte* Merryman, 17 Fed. Cas. 144 (C.Ct.Md., 1861), No. 9487.

⁴⁸ *Ex parte* McQuillon, 16 Fed. Cas. 347 (S.D.N.Y., 1861), No. 8924.

⁴⁹ United States v. Porter, 27 Fed. Cas. 599, 602 (C.Ct.D.C., 1861), No. 16,074a. Compare *Ex parte* Benedict, 3 Fed. Cas. 159, 171 (N.D.N.Y., 1862), No. 1292.

⁵⁰ United States v. Corrie, 25 Fed. Cas. 658, 668–669 (C.Ct.S.C., 1860), No. 14,869. See also United States v. Burr, 25 Fed. Cas. 201 (C.Ct.Va., 1807), No. 14,694a; United States *ex rel* Wampler v. Hill, 8 F. Supp. 469, 470 (M.D.Pa., 1934), affirmed, 74 F. 2d 940 (3 C.C.A., 1934), and certiorari denied, 295 U.S. 732; and Bowles v. United States, 73 F. 2d 772 (4 C.C.A., 1934).

⁵¹ Union Pacific R. R. Co. v. Utterback, 146 P. 2d 76 (1944).

⁵² Josephberg v. Markham, 152 F. 2d 644 (2 C.C.A., 1945), denied such authority to the President. So did *In re* Viscomi's Estate, 53 N.Y.S. 2d 416 (1944), which was reversed, however, in 60 N.Y.S. 2d 897 (1946). Numerous decisions of the Supreme Court appear to admit of no exceptions to the vesting power.

⁵³ *In re* Spier Aircraft Co., 49 F. Supp. 896 (D.N.J., 1943). The circuit court of appeals affirmed and upheld the vesting order without facing the issue squarely, since it found that the presidential disposition of the assets was in accordance with the order of the court, and not contrary to it, 137 F. 2d 736 (3 C.C.A., 1943), certiorari denied, 321 U.S. 770 (1944).

⁵⁴ *In re* Inland Waterways, 49 F. Supp. 675 (D.Minn. 5 D., 1943); *In re* Mississippi Valley Iron Co., 58 F. Supp. 222 (E.D.Mo.E.D., 1944).

⁵⁵ Panama Refining Co. v. Ryan, 293 U.S. 388, 412–413, 434 (1935). For inhibition of review by the amendment of an executive order, see United States *ex rel* Knauff v. Shaughnessy, 338 U.S. 537 (1950), and especially the appellant's brief.

⁵⁶ Simons v. McGuire, 204 N.Y. 253 (1912), is instructive reading on this point.

⁵⁷ "Where it is unquestionable that the delegation is meant to be mandatory, it would seem that, under the duty of law enforcement in its broadest sense, the President is bound, by constitutional morality, to carry out the legislative instructions. But the obligation is not strictly legal." James Hart, *The Ordinance Making Powers of the President of the United States* (Baltimore: Johns Hopkins, 1925), p. 177.

⁵⁸ *Re* Kaine, 14 Howard 103 (1852).

⁵⁹ McFadden v. Mountain View Mining and Milling Co., 97 F. 670, 677 (9 C.C.A., 1899). Compare United States v. Gear, 3 Howard 120, 132 (1845), and Sisseton and Wahpeton Bands of Sioux Indians v. United States, 58 Ct. Cl. 302 (1923).

⁶⁰ "Until such proclamation has been issued, the President may not, under this statute, be coerced or controlled by the mandates of the courts." J. W. Hampton, Jr. and Co. v. United States, 14 C.C.A. 350, 369 (1927), affirmed in 276 U.S. 394 (1928).

⁶¹ Standard Oil Co. v. United States, 2 F. Supp. 922 (1933), certiorari denied, 290 U.S. 632 (1933).

⁶² United States v. Burr, 25 Fed. Cas. 187, 191–192 (1807), No. 14,694. See also *Ex parte* Bollman, 4 Cranch 75 (1807), and the Appendix, Notes (A) and (B) to volume 4 Cranch.

⁶³ Minotto v. Bradley, 252 F. 600 (N.D.Ill., 1918).

⁶⁴ Commercial Cable Co. v. Burleson, 255 F. 99, 104, 103 (S.D.N.Y., 1919), reversed on the grounds that the controversy had become moot, 250 U.S. 360 (1919).

⁶⁵ Norwegian Nitrogen Products Co. v. United States, 274 U.S. 106 (1927).

⁶⁶ Frischer & Co. v. Bakelite Corp., 39 F. 2d 247 (C.C.P.A., 1930).

⁶⁷ Union Fork & Hoe Co. v. United States, 86 F. 2d 423 (C.C.P.A., 1936).

⁶⁸ Westergaard Berg-Johnson Co. v. United States, 27 C.C.P.A. (Customs) 207 (1939). Compare Waterman S. S. Corp. v. C.A.B., 159 F. 2d 828, 830 (5 C.C.A., 1947).

⁶⁹ Touhy v. Ragen, 340 U.S. 462, 467–469 (1951).

⁷⁰ *Ibid.*, 472–473. Compare with the decision of the Supreme Court in Joint Anti-Fascist Refugee Committee v. McGrath, 341 U.S. 123 (1951), ruling that the Attorney

The Scope of Judicial Review

General must at least argue in justification of the evidence — whether or not and to what extent that must be introduced into the record of the trial is not indicated — on the basis of which he had designated organizations as subversive under the President's loyalty executive order. This issue remains undecided after the lapse of five years; see Joint Anti-Fascist Refugee Committee v. McGrath, 104 F. Supp. 567 (1952); Joint Anti-Fascist Refugee Committee v. Brownell, 215 F. 2d 870 (1954); and National Lawyers Guild v. Brownell, 225 F. 2d 552 (C.A.D.C., 1955), c.d. 351 U.S. 927 (May 7, 1956). The right to withhold secret evidence from both a dismissed employee and the courts was a central issue in the removal cases arising under the loyalty order, but the lower court upheld the executive and the Supreme Court divided equally, without opinion, on this point; see Bailey v. Richardson, 341 U.S. 918 (1951).

In oral argument before the Court in the *Knauff* case, Chief Justice Vinson defined the issue squarely when he demanded of Mr. Monahan, the attorney for the Justice Department, if *he* knew the reason why Mrs. Knauff had been adjudged a security risk. When Monahan admitted that he did, the chief justice said that in other words, the government claimed the right to keep this evidence secret from the Supreme Court itself, and the Court was therefore being asked to uphold the refusal to admit this woman on the basis of such secret evidence, and to accept the judgment of the Justice Department as to both the reliability and sufficiency of the evidence. Monahan agreed, and the Court subsequently upheld him by its decision.

[71] Merritt v. United States, 264 F. 870, 873 (9 C.C.A., 1920). It is true that this decision was reversed in a memorandum opinion of the Supreme Court, 255 U.S. 579 (1921), but this was done on confession of error by the Solicitor General and not on the merits of the above issue. There are a number of decisions which did not accept the conclusiveness of formal presidential determinations under the Lever Act, but they dealt with different questions under other sections of the statute, such as Section 5 which made presidential determination of "reasonable prices" only prima-facie evidence and expressly permitted judicial review on the matter of "reasonableness" in defense to criminal prosecutions for violations. Oglesby Grocery Co. v. United States, 255 U.S. 108 (1921).

[72] United States v. Chemical Foundation, 294 F. 300, 329, 331 (D.Del., 1924), affirmed 272 U.S. 1 (1926).

[73] Mulhens & Kropff v. F. Mulhens, Inc., 38 F. 2d 287, 294 (S.D.N.Y., 1929). The Second Circuit Court of Appeals affirmed that part of the decision of the trial court quoted above, 43 F. 2d 937, 939 (1930); and certiorari was denied by the Supreme Court, 282 U.S. 881 (1930).

[74] Kansas or Kaw Tribe of Indians v. United States, 80 Ct. Cl. 264, 313 (1934).

[75] Presidential Proclamation No. 2087, May 28, 1934, 48 *Stat.* 1744.

[76] United States v. Curtiss-Wright Export Corp., 14 F. Supp. 230, 235–236 (S.D.N.Y., 1936); reversed on other grounds by the Supreme Court, which also held: "There is no suggestion that the resolution is fatally uncertain or indefinite; and a finding which follows its language, as this finding does, cannot well be challenged as insufficient." 299 U.S. 304, 331 (1936). Cf. T. M. Duche & Sons, Inc. v. United States, 36 C.C.P.A. (Customs) 19, 25 (1948).

[77] Cole v. Young, 351 U.S. 536, 557 ftn. 20 (June 11, 1956).

[78] *The Orono*, 18 Fed. Cas. 830 (1812), No. 10,585. Compare the conclusiveness of fact-finding by the President by the director of Selective Service, who acted under an express subdelegation of presidential authority: United States v. Bussoz, 218 F. 2d 683, 686–687 (9 C.A., 1955), certiorari denied, 350 U.S. 824 (1955).

[79] Bicknell v. Comstock, 113 U.S. 149, 151 (1885). The similarity of the logic to that of Marshall in *Marbury v. Madison*, insofar as that case relates to the effect of the presidential signature on a commission to the vesting of title to an office, is apparent.

[80] Levinson v. United States, 258 U.S. 198 (1922).

[81] Lynch v. United States, 67 F. 2d 490 (5 C.C.A., 1933); Wilner v. United States, 68 F. 2d 442 (7 C.C.A., 1934).

[82] Lynch v. United States, 292 U.S. 571 (1934).

[83] Cummings v. *Société Suisse pour Valeurs de Metaux*, 85 F. 2d 287, 289 (C.A.D.C., 1936); United States v. Rodiek, 117 F. 2d 588 (2 C.C.A., 1941); Isenberg v. Biddle, 125 F. 2d 741 (C.A.D.C., 1941); United States v. Silliman, 65 F. Supp. 665 (D.N.J., 1946).

[84] United States v. Rodiek, 117 F. 2d 588, 590–593 (2 C.C.A., 1941), affirmed *per curiam* by an equally divided court, 315 U.S. 783 (1942), with Chief Justice Stone, Murphy, and Jackson not participating because each had formerly been the alien property custodian ex officio.

[85] Isenberg v. Biddle, 125 F. 2d 741, 743, 745 (C.A.D.C., 1941). In Cummings v. *Société Suisse pour Valeurs de Metaux*, 85 F. 2d 287 (C.A.D.C., 1936), the court had upheld the power of the President to direct by executive order that the Attorney General institute a suit in counterclaim against *Société Suisse*, which had been fraudulently paid over $3,000,000 with the collusion of the former alien property custodian, who had already been convicted for his part in the transaction.

[86] United States v. Silliman, 65 F. Supp. 665, 673–674 (D.N.J., 1946). Accord: Johnston v. United States, 175 F. 2d 612 (4 C.A., 1949). There are also the dicta of two earlier cases decided by the Court of Customs and Patent Appeals, stating that although a mistake in fact on the part of the Tariff Commission would not affect the validity of the President's proclamation based (in part) thereon, a mistake on his own part would invalidate the proclamation: Foster v. United States, 20 C.C.P.A. (Customs) 15, 25 (1932), and United States v. Sears, Roebuck & Co., 20 C.C.P.A. (Customs) 295, 304 (1932).

[87] Alpirn v. Huffman, 49 F. Supp. 337, 342–343 (D.Neb., Omaha D., 1943). Italics supplied. Compare *In re* Mississippi Valley Iron Co., 58 F. Supp. 222, 226 (E.D.Mo. E.D., 1944): "The findings by the President of the United States incident to requisitioning property necessary for the conduct of the war are conclusive and the court cannot question the basis of such findings"; affirmed on rehearing, 61 F. Supp. 347, 350 (E.D.Mo.E.D., 1945). See also *In re* Inland Waterways, 49 F. Supp. 675, 677 (D. Minn., 5 D., 1943); *In re* Spier Aircraft Corp., 49 F. Supp. 896 (D.N.J., 1943); and R. J. Tresolini, "Eminent Domain and the Requisition of Property during Emergencies," *Western Political Quarterly*, 7:570–587 (December 1954).

[88] Youngstown Sheet and Tube v. Sawyer, 343 U.S. 579, 678 (1952).

12

Recapitulation

It should be perfectly obvious by now that the most significant aspect of judicial review of presidential orders is its ineffectiveness. If the courts are the most important bulwark of freedom and liberty in the United States, then we have every right to view with alarm the future security of the republic. And yet, the courts have an indispensable role to perform in ensuring that our government will afford in the future, as it already has ensured in such substantial measure in the past, a maximum of freedom under law, and that balance between the rights of the few and the many, of the individual and society, which has constituted the central problem of all liberal political philosophers. How is this seeming paradox to be explained?

First and most fundamentally, we should give up the myth that the judiciary either can or should resolve the critical questions of public policy that each generation must face anew. It is both unreasonable and antidemocratic for us to expect the judges to fulfill such a function. This is merely a way of saying that the elected representatives of the people — the President and the Congress — must decide the great questions of constitutional law.[1] Obviously, this places a premium upon the efficacy of political processes, including the enormously expanding job of administering the manifold functions of modern government.

Deciding constitutional questions is a means of making law: law is the formal statement of public policy. If the courts are not to, and

normally do not, attempt to second-guess the President on fundamental issues of public policy, what is left for them to do?

Much. There remains, for instance, the obligation of incumbent officials to comply with requirements and limitations imposed by the
laws that they themselves, and their predecessors, have made. It is in
this sense that "the Rule of Law" assumes its largest significance, and
it is here that the courts are peculiarly well adapted to function and
act. In truth, there is much evidence to suggest that this is precisely
what is happening in the United States today. The day of *Railroad Retirement Bd. v. Alton R. R. Co.*[2] is gone, and there are doubtless few
who have regrets at its passing; the characteristic case of today is
Peters v. Hobby.[3] For the courts to return to their historic role in
Anglo-Saxon polities of enforcing, for citizen and official alike, the
requirements of existing law is a large enough task. Our concern, therefore, should be with the extent to which the judiciary have fulfilled
this responsibility, rather than with their inevitable failure to discharge the impossible function of substituting their judgment for that
of the President in time of crisis. To speak of the federal judiciary
alone, it simply is not true that in this sense and at such a time, three
hundred heads are better than one.

Measured in terms of such criteria, what is the record of eight
generations and eight hundred cases, in which constitutional questions
concerning the exercise of presidential power have been raised before
the courts?

When the President acts, literally, as Commander in Chief, his constitutional authority is on unimpeachable grounds. He may raise
armies and send them where he wills. In addition to regular members
of the armed forces, his authority extends (or has extended historically) to militiamen, volunteers, draftees, and conscientious objectors.
Although a civilian Court of Military Appeals recently has been created near the apex of the system of military courts, the President continues to function as the highest reviewing authority and the agency
of final determination. There are a number of Civil War cases which
hold to the contrary, but the preponderance of judicial opinion has upheld and the unquestionable practice has been that the President can
declare martial law when in his judgment the exigencies of military
necessity make this step imperative; and at such a time and in such
places, civilians generally are subject to the jurisdiction of military

courts. The vanquished enemy, whether his role was that of professional soldier or politician, may be tried for "unlawful belligerency" or "crimes against humanity" before military commissions authorized by the President alone, or in cooperation with the governments of other states. The civilian residents of territory occupied by the military forces of the United States, as well as the American-citizen entourage of our occupying forces, are subject to the jurisdiction of special military government courts whose constitution lies, again, in the authority and powers of the President. None of these various types of military courts dispensing military justice is subject to the supervision and review of the regular federal judiciary; as to them, the President himself is the Supreme Court.

Alien enemies — a classification which includes, for various purposes, many citizens of the United States, both naturalized and natural-born — are subject to what amounts in practice to almost absolute presidential control, and he may deal with them in ways which unquestionably are contrary to the normal requirements of both permanent statutory law and the Bill of Rights, as these are usually interpreted. The alien enemy may be interned, either in a regular jail with common criminals, or in a special concentration camp specially constructed for thousands like himself. If not incarcerated, he may be placed under surveillance, licensed, restricted in his movement, and required to report periodically like a parolee. His property may be summarily confiscated by the government, and returned to him, if at all, only as an act of grace years after the hostilities have ended. As soon as conditions permit, he may be deported to his country of nationality, although he must, if Congress has granted him such a privilege, be given an opportunity to leave voluntarily for any country of his choice which is willing to admit him. Indeed, the alien who is classified as a "security risk," even though he is not an "alien enemy" in the legal sense, may be interned for what is in effect life imprisonment.[4] The regulatory authority in all these actions is the President; and it is he who in substantial measure makes the laws which determine the obligations of the alien enemy.

The President also legislates to license, prohibit, and otherwise to control the carrying on of commerce with the enemy in time of either civil or international war, whether it be war *de facto* or war *de jure*. Vessels and persons who violate his regulations may be seized; and in the case of property, may be confiscated, while in the case of persons, may be indicted on criminal charges. Where in his judgment this is necessary, the property of any person within the jurisdiction of the United States, enemy or friend, alien or citizen, may be seized for either the temporary or permanent use of the government. In the case of alien friends and citizens, there is an obligation on the part of the government to pay just compensation for this use, but the presidential power of acquisition is untrammeled and the mechanics of payment are, in practice, left up to the discretion and judgment of the President and Congress.

There are no apparent legal limitations upon the power of the President to proclaim the existence of a national emergency. Certainly, the courts will not substitute their judgment of the state of the Union for that of the Chief Executive.[5] He may then claim the right to exercise, throughout the duration of his self-proclaimed emergency, extraordinary powers which would not be considered available for his use in time of "normalcy." Increasingly, Congress has adopted permanent legislation which is automatically invoked and revivified upon a presidential declaration of a national emergency. This state of emergency has no necessary relationship to the existence of war *de jure*. It may be occasioned by domestic crisis, as in the spring of 1933, or it may either precede the outbreak of war *de jure* (as during the period 1939–1941) or extend beyond the end of war *de jure* (as in the case of the continuing extension of the emergency declared by President Truman in December 1950 beyond the date of the ratification of the peace treaty with Japan on April 28, 1952). The whole period of the Civil War was that of a presidentially declared emergency, although there was no war *de jure*. On the other hand, the United States was at war *de jure* throughout the decade extending from December 7, 1941, until April 28, 1952, and there was also the presidentially declared national emergency which includes this same period.

During the period of such a national emergency, the President may exercise such abnormal powers over private property as that of fixing prices for producers, manufacturers, wholesalers, retailers, and consumers; he may allocate raw materials and ration the consumption of finished goods; under his direction, public contracts may be made, modified, and broken, and rights under private contracts may be altered to the extent that they conflict with the requirements of the

Recapitulation

public contracting power. The President does all these things in the right of his constitutional status and authority as the Commander in Chief, although his constitutional powers are usually reinforced by almost unlimited delegation of statutory powers.

As the Chief of State, his power is, if anything, even more absolute and beyond the scope of challenge in the courts, because in this area, he does not share constitutional power as an equal of the Congress, as he does in the case of the war power of the national government. In the realm of foreign relations, he is either the primary or else the exclusive organ of governmental power. He is, in the words of the Supreme Court, the *sole* organ of the nation. It is he who recognizes, or refuses to recognize, the governments of foreign states. He may make agreements with them which have the same binding force and effect as treaties. He may extend the national *imperium* over new lands which are acquired through discovery, conquest, or — as in the case of the tidelands — as the result of his own assertion of title. His supplementary regulations may contribute substantially to the national policy governing immigration and admission to the United States. Similarly, he may act to place an embargo upon or to license trade by residents of the United States with foreign countries. Since the power to regulate foreign commerce is vested by the Constitution in the Congress in unequivocal terms, the President's action in this area is usually undertaken on the basis of statutory delegation of authority, but his own independent constitutional power is such that there are no apparent limitations on the power of Congress to transfer to him the power to legislate for the regulation of such foreign commerce. He may also be delegated by statute considerable discretion over the regulation of trade on the part of residents of foreign states with the United States; and his action in this respect has never been successfully challenged in the courts. His decision, in such specific areas of this field as the changing of tariff duties or the licensing of foreign air transportation, may be guided by an administrative fact-finding agency, but based upon other and secret information that reaches him through diplomatic, military, or other non-public channels. For this reason, his judgment in such matters is final.

As the Chief Administrator, his legal authority over the personnel and properties which constitute the executive branch of the government of the United States is limited, as a matter of administrative necessity, by statutory law, regulations of his own making, and the rule-making powers of his subordinates; but only to a very modest extent is he controlled by the power of the courts. His power of removal over his military and civil subordinates has been, throughout most of our history, practically unassailable. This was demonstrated anew in the most recently frictional aspect of this, administrative removals authorized by his own executive order on grounds of disloyalty.[6] His power of administrative direction over his subordinates cannot be challenged by them in the courts, nor has it yet been successfully forestalled before the courts by those outside the government who are indirectly affected by his power to thus control the activities of his subordinates. He may issue regulations, orders, directives, and instructions; he may transfer statutory responsibilities from one official to another; he may change the organizational status and composition of administrative agencies; and his subordinates may present their advice to him — which he of necessity is bound to follow in most instances — and all this without creating justiciable rights of a substantial enough nature for the judiciary to review his judgment.

Furthermore, the courts have since an early period recognized that he must be able to subdelegate his powers, and particularly his statutory powers, if he is to exercise more than a fraction of them, so his authority to act through his subordinates, irrespective of the language used in statutory acts of delegation to him, has been consistently recognized in hundreds of cases. This assumes importance from another point of view in that, when such a subordinate acts for him, in the eyes of the judiciary, it is still in law *the President* who has acted; consequently, the effect of this legal fiction is to expand the scope of executive discretion and judicial non-reviewability into impredictable depths of the administrative hierarchy where these doctrines are inapposite and should be inapplicable. If it is true that he is the Commander in *Chief*, it cannot follow, as the courts have in effect held, that every commander of a military district is in law the Commander in Chief too; if he is the "*Sole* Organ of the Nation," then certainly neither the Secretary of State nor the Attorney General, nor both of them together, can also be the Sole Organ at the same time; and if he is the *Chief* Administrator, or the "Chief Executive" to use the more common phrase, then neither the director of the Office of Price Stabilization, the Secretary of the Interior, nor a bureau chief in some other

Recapitulation

agency can also be the Chief Executive. For many purposes, however, they are such in the eyes of the judiciary.

In times past, the President has exercised considerable discretion over the disposition and uses to which the public lands have been put. In the absence of statutory authority, Presidents for more than a century made reservations of the public lands for military purposes, to conserve our natural resources, and for the resettlement of the aboriginal Americans, as well as for such other purposes as lighthouse reservations and bird sanctuaries. This is largely a closed chapter today save for the continuing activities of that recondite specialist, the Indian claims lawyer. Nevertheless, the subject is important to us because of the great liberality with which the courts have characteristically viewed the exercise of presidential authority in this area, creating precedents which are available, and which have been used, to justify an equally broad range of presidential discretion in other areas of substantive activity.

The sources of the President's power are various and in the view of the Supreme Court today it makes little difference whether they are clearly distinguished for purposes of justifying any particular order which is challenged. In quantitative terms, statutes are certainly the most important source, and there are today no apparent limitations upon the power of Congress to make such delegations of authority to the President, either prospectively or retroactively. Whatever the war power is, it is defined by the courts as being largely equivalent to military necessity; and it is constitutionally invested in the President fully as much as in the Congress. At least in some times and with respect to certain subjects, the Supreme Court and other courts have recognized the right of the President to act affirmatively in the public interest, even where there is no apparent authority for his action in either statute or the Constitution. This writer finds it most accurate and most useful to speak of this as the President's implied powers. Whatever they are to be called, they are a part of the panoply of authority of the presidential office. Statutes may occasionally be held unconstitutional where they conflict with or encroach upon the exclusive constitutional authority of the executive, just as presidential orders may occasionally be found unconstitutional where they conflict with valid acts of the Congress within the scope of its own exclusive constitutional authority.

Judicially determined standards of form and procedure for executive legislation are practically nonexistent. There is no necessary form for executive orders or proclamations other than that required by statute and executive order. The President probably should, but does not have to, refer to the source of his authority in his orders and regulations of general effect. He can amend or revoke his own ordinances and those of his predecessors. Statutory and executive law now determines when executive legislation goes into effect. The courts will take judicial notice of his ordinances, and are required by statute to notice the great bulk of them which are printed in the Federal Register. A proclamation or executive order is public law, just as are statutes.

When we turn to the mechanics of the exercise of judicial review, the full extent of the freedom of presidential action from judicial control becomes inescapably apparent. The courts will not review executive discretion: therefore, they will not intervene in presidential decisions of political questions; they must occasionally submit to superior force, or the threat of it, if the President chooses to take direct action to frustrate the judicial process; they cannot compel him to act no matter what the nature or certainty of his obligation may be; they cannot compel him to divulge official information that he chooses to withhold; his formal statement that he has complied with statutory conditions to his action is accepted as binding; and with rare exceptions involving subordinates acting in his name, his findings of "facts" are accepted as conclusive and are not open to judicial re-examination.

It is the duty of the courts to uphold the constitutionality of the President's action, and they must give great weight to his own interpretation and construction of the scope of his own powers. Those who seek to challenge the President's action must assume the burden of proof, and the courts will always assume that the President has complied with the requirements of law. The Chief Executive has not been and apparently cannot be forced to appear personally before any court; he is officially and personally immune from judicial process and prospective judicial control. The courts can neither force him to do anything, nor prevent him from doing anything he may decide to do, although they may, of course, decide (and on rare instances they have decided) that action he had already taken was unconstitutional.

It is also interesting to note the level at which judicial restraint takes place, to the extent that it does. There appears to be an inverse relationship between the status of a court in the hierarchy of courts in the United States (and therefore its own sense of responsibility), and its willingness to subject presidential action to judicial control. The President has been frankly dealt with in several decisions of the Customs Court, as though he were just another misguided administrative officer, bumbling along as one inevitably must who has not enjoyed the advantages of formal legal training; but there is usually a more respectful tone in opinions of the Supreme Court which refer to the Chief Executive. It is also observable that occasionally, in its enthusiasm to give adequate recognition to the President as the embodiment of executive power when the United States is at war, a court will string out all of his available titles in large capitals,[7] giving the impression of being somewhat frustrated at not being able to add: "Defender of the Faith" and "Emperor of the Territories beyond the Seas"!

The most impressive fact that an examination of Appendix A in this volume reveals is that there have been so very few cases in which presidential orders have been held unconstitutional. Only fourteen cases, throughout our entire national history, were so decided by the United States Supreme Court, the remaining two thirds of the cases have been decided by lower courts, either state or federal.[8] Three of the cases related to President Madison's Embargo Proclamation of August 9, 1809; and another seven — including all these cases that were decided during the decade of the Civil War — related to various orders of President Lincoln suspending the privilege of the writ of habeas corpus for prisoners of the military. This accounts for almost a third of the total of the cases. It is readily apparent that most of these cases relate to the exercise of what were, at the time, extraordinary presidential powers during periods of emergency. It is even more apparent that these cases involve only an infinitesimal fragment of the totality of presidential regulations, orders, and directives during the past century and two thirds; consider that, of the vast outpouring of direct presidential lawmaking during World War II,[9] only *one* case holds adversely to the constitutionality of executive action. The momentous impact of this solitary decision was to permit a few West Virginia bakers to waste flour by reclaiming stale bread from their retail outlets. Finally, only two of these decisions have had the effect of preventing the President from carrying out any important element of his administration's program at the time, and none has appeared to inhibit any subsequent President from exercising the same power at a later time. One of these two exceptions was the *Steel Seizure* case which, supercharged with political implications in a presidential election year, resulted directly and immediately in a disastrous strike which the President successfully had forestalled for over four months. The other was *Cole v. Young*, which admittedly portends important limitations on the President's power to authorize the discharge of civil servants without due process of law.

In conclusion then, it may be said that the differential nature of judicial tolerance respecting executive legislation is of considerable practical importance:

1. Emergency ordinances and those of extraterritorial effect are already almost beyond the pale of judicial review; but presidential action of domestic impact and not keyed to emergency powers — an area which is beginning to resemble, to borrow a mathematical concept, a disappearing function — may, under suitable conditions, be subjected to judicial review.

2. It is almost impossible to prevent the President from taking any given action through recourse to judicial process, even though the effect of his action may be to moot what might otherwise have been a justiciable controversy; but there are, subject to limitations already noted, means whereby it is possible to challenge the validity of his action after it has been taken.

3. The courts have been consistently more zealous in denying to the President any power summarily to seize property in time of war or other emergency, except under statutory delegation of authority, than they have been with respect to his summary powers over persons. This can be explained in various ways, but the fundamental reason probably is that the Anglo-Saxon legal order has always prized rights of property above personal rights. The Supreme Court of the United States is not certain whether the President, when he acts to raise an army, to detain citizens and aliens in protective custody, to declare martial law and to suspend the writ of habeas corpus, to determine standards of loyalty and disloyalty toward the United States, and to try and punish enemy aliens by a summary administrative process for crimes that are defined in no statute, does so under his prerogative powers as Chief of State, his constitutional powers as Commander in Chief, or his executive powers as the constitutional agent of Congress

Recapitulation

in faithfully executing the laws. All that the Court is sure of is that these powers are inherent in sovereignty and must therefore reside in the political branches of the national government. There has been no such confusion in the courts concerning the President's emergency powers over property. Such powers reside in the Congress; and where the President acts, he acts as the legislative agent of Congress.[10]

4. Finally, inasmuch as subdelegated presidential powers may be further subdelegated and redelegated, it would seem consonant with the premise of executive responsibility in a democratic polity for the courts to recognize an integrated pattern of administrative regulation when it is presented to them, and to hold responsible those who are in a position to command and direct. If this leads to the seeming dead-end of presidential immunity from judicial process, all is not necessarily lost. Marbury did not get his commission as justice of the peace for the District of Columbia, but few would say that the adjudication of his rights has left no mark upon the subsequent development of our system of government.

Notes

[1] It is arguable that the Supreme Court is the only decision-making organ of the national government that could have laid down a policy of desegregation. But apart from the question whether the Supreme Court can make its decision stick, there is another query: would the *School Segregation* cases of 1954 have been necessary if there had been no *Plessy v. Ferguson* in 1896? And what have been the social, economic, and political costs of sixty years of unequal protection of the races, authorized by judicial fiat of the Supreme Court?

[2] 295 U.S. 330 (1935); cf. United States v. Lowden, 308 U.S. 225 (1939).

[3] 349 U.S. 331 (1955). There is no question here of the *power* of the President to enact an executive order requiring the removal from federal employment of persons whose loyalty is suspect. The constitutional issue relates to the procedures governing the making of determinations of disloyalty, and to the way those procedures adversely affect persons and groups not themselves within the substantive scope of the order. But see Cole v. Young, 351 U.S. 536 (1956), in which the Supreme Court, at the very next term of court, found that President Eisenhower's "security order" version of the loyalty executive order was in conflict with the statutory standards limiting his delegating powers, and hence was *ultra vires*.

[4] Shaughnessy v. United States *ex rel* Mezei, 345 U.S. 206 (1953).

[5] The Supreme Court did not differ with the President's declaration that a national emergency existed at the time he "seized" the steel industry in April 1952; the majority of the Court simply ignored this element of the case. In any event, that opinion of the Court is *sui genesis*. See Glendon A. Schubert, Jr., "The Steel Case: Presidential Responsibility and Judicial Irresponsibility," *Western Political Quarterly*, 6:61, 73 (1953).

[6] Although *Cole v. Young* is a seeming exception, it should be noted that the Supreme Court tried to sublimate the President's role as much as possible, and to place the onus of illegality on the shoulders of former Secretary Oveta Culp Hobby. "While

the validity of this extension of the Act depends upon questions which are in many respects common to those determining the validity of the Secretary's exercise of the authority thereby extended to her, we will restrict our consideration to the latter issue and assume, for purposes of this decision, that the Act has validly been extended [by the President] to apply to the Department of Health, Education, and Welfare." 351 U.S. 536, 542 (1956).

It is fascinating to contrast the way in which both the Supreme Court and the press used President Truman as a whipping boy in the *Steel Seizure* case, while in *Cole v. Young* both Court and newspapers have handled President Eisenhower so that he appears to the audience in the role of the ghost of Banquo: only the dissenting justices can discern the spectral figure which is ensconced in the driver's seat at the White House.

[7] "The President of the United States, Chief Executive, Commander in Chief of the Army and Navy. . . ." The President sometimes does this himself in the preamble to proclamations and executive orders, particularly when the precise basis of authority for the action he is taking is a matter of some doubt. An example of this is found in the final proclamation of full amnesty for supporters of the Confederacy on Christmas Day, 1868, which begins: "I, Andrew Johnson, President of the United States, by virtue of the power and authority in me vested by the Constitution *and in the name of the sovereign people of the United States*, do hereby proclaim and declare. . . ." Richardson, *op. cit.*, VI, 708. Italics supplied.

[8] Compare Wilfred C. Gilbert, *Provisions of Federal Law Held Unconstitutional by the Supreme Court of the United States* (Washington, D.C.: GPO, 1936). Gilbert lists 76 cases in which the Supreme Court *alone* has held statutes, in whole or in part, to be unconstitutional. There appear to have been 4 more since his compilation — Tot v. United States, 319 U.S. 463 (1943); United States v. Lovett, 328 U.S. 303 (1946); United States v. Cardiff, 344 U.S. 174 (1952); Toth v. Quarles, 350 U.S. 11 (1955) — or a total of 80; while in this list of *ultra vires* and unconstitutional presidential orders, only 14 of the cases were decided by the Supreme Court.

[9] It was during this same period that it became more and more customary for executive orders to take on the detailed format and complex internal structural organization of statutes.

[10] Youngstown Sheet and Tube Co. v. Sawyer (the *Steel Seizure* case), 343 U.S. 579 (1952). An example of this also is found in the judicial distinction between compensation due for loss or damage to property and loss or damage to "life, liberty, and health" — 75 per cent of the original definition of Locke — in cases coming up after a war. The former are a question of the constitutional obligations of a government which has toyed with vested rights; the latter are but the bounties or gratuities of a generous government in which the recipient has no rights. As a circuit court of appeals said in United States v. McFarland, 15 F. 2d 823, 827 (4 C.C.A., 1926): "The overwhelming majority of the wool growers and of those who undertook to voice their wishes [during World War I] were patriotic citizens and reasonable men. They wanted to help the government in its [sic] hour of difficulty, provided that they were not called upon to do more than they thought was their share." What was the share of the war dead and the war maimed?

Appendixes, Table of Cases, and Subject Guide

APPENDIX A. CASES HOLDING PRESIDENTIAL DECISIONS UNCONSTITUTIONAL *

Title of Case	Presidential Order Declared Invalid	Function of Order	Basis of Decision	Court
1. Little v. Bareme, 2 Cranch 170 (1804)	Written Instructions, March 12, 1799, to Navy Officer	Directing seizure of vessels trading with French ports	Conflict with statute	U.S. S. Ct.
2. Gilchrist v. Collector, 10 Fed. Cas. 355 (1808), No. 5420	Written Instructions, May 6, 1808, Issued as Circular Letter of Treasury	Directing detention of vessels seeking clearance for coastwise commerce	Conflict with statute	U.S. C. Ct., So. Car.
3. The Orono, 18 Fed. Cas. 830 (1812), No. 10,585	Proclamation, August 9, 1809	Reviving interdiction of commerce established by lapsed Embargo Acts	Separation of powers theory	U.S. C. Ct., Mass.
4. President's Proclamation Declared Illegal, 19 Fed. Cas. 1289 (1812), No. 11,391	Proclamation, August 9, 1809	Reviving interdiction of commerce established by lapsed Embargo Acts	Separation of powers theory	U.S. C. Ct., No. Car.
5. The Wasp, 29 Fed. Cas. 368 (1812), No. 17,249	Proclamation, August 9, 1809	Reviving interdiction of commerce established by lapsed Embargo Acts	Separation of powers theory	U.S. C. Ct., Mass.
6. Gelston v. Hoyt, 3 Wheat. 246 (1818)	Orders, July 6, 1810	Directing civilian officials to seize ship to prevent violation of Neutrality Act	Conflict with statute	U.S. S. Ct.
7. Lorimier v. Lewis, 39 Am.D. 461; 1 Morris (Iowa) 253 (1843)	License	Leasing rights to work lead mines in public lands	Separation of powers theory	Terr. of Iowa. S. Ct.
8. Jecker v. Montgomery, 13 How. 498 (1851)	Written Orders to Senior Naval Officer in California	Authorizing local military prize courts during Mexican War	Art. III, U.S. Constitution	U.S. S. Ct.

* This list does not include lower court decisions holding presidential orders unconstitutional but reversed upon appeal; it includes only cases in which final determinations on the issue of constitutionality of such orders have been made. Unless otherwise indicated, appeal was not taken to a higher court, including the Supreme Court of the United States. Where it is indicated that an appeal was taken, the higher court did not reach and decide upon the merits of the constitutional issue.

Title of Case	Presidential Order Declared Invalid	Function of Order	Basis of Decision	Court
9. *Ex parte* Merryman, 17 Fed. Cas. 144 (1861), No. 9487	Unnumbered Executive Order, April 27, 1861	Authorizing military officers to suspend privilege of writ of habeas corpus	Art. I, s. 9 (2) U.S. Constitution	Chief Justice, U.S. S. Ct.
10. *Ex parte* Benedict, 3 Fed. Cas. 159 (1862), No. 1292	War Department General Order, August 8, 1862	Suspending privilege of writ of habeas corpus for draft evaders and persons arrested for disloyalty	Art. I, s. 9 (2) U.S. Constitution	U.S. D. Ct., No. Dist. of N.Y.
11. Jones v. Seward, 40 Barbour 563 (1863)	Proclamation, September 24, 1862	Suspending privilege of writ of habeas corpus for draft evaders and persons arrested for disloyalty	Art. I, s. 9 (2) U.S. Constitution	State of N.Y., S. Ct.
12. *In re* Kemp, 16 Wis. 382 (1863)	Proclamation, September 24, 1862	Suspending privilege of writ of habeas corpus for draft evaders and persons arrested for disloyalty	Art. I, s. 9 (2) U.S. Constitution	State of Wis., S. Ct.
13. Griffin v. Wilcox, 21 Ind. 370 (1863)	Proclamation, September 15, 1863	Suspending privilege of writ of habeas corpus for all prisoners of the armed forces	Amendments V and X, U.S. Constitution	State of Ind., S. Ct.
14. *Ex parte* Milligan, 4 Wall. 2 (1866)	Proclamation, September 15, 1863	Suspending privilege of writ of habeas corpus for all prisoners of the armed forces	Separation of powers theory and conflict with statute	U.S. S. Ct.
15. McCall v. McDowell, 15 Fed. Cas. 1235 (1867) No. 8673	Proclamation, September 24, 1862	Suspending privilege of writ of habeas corpus for draft evaders and persons arrested for disloyalty	Art. I, s. 9 (2) U.S. Constitution	U.S. D. Ct., Dist. of Calif.
16. McElrath v. United States, 102 U.S. 426 (1880)	Order of Secretary of Navy, July 10, 1873	Revoking order dismissing Marine officer and accepting his resignation	Conflict with statute	U.S. S. Ct.
17. Blake v. United States, 103 U.S. 227 (1881)	Unnumbered Executive Order, September 28, 1878	Revoking acceptance of resignation of Army officer and re-appointing him	Conflict with statute	U.S. S. Ct.

APPENDIX A — continued

Title of Case	Presidential Order Declared Invalid	Function of Order	Basis of Decision	Court
18. United States v. Lee, 106 U.S. 196 (1882)	Instructions to the War Department	Directing seizure of estate of General Robert E. Lee for non-payment of taxes	Amendment V, U.S. Constitution	U.S. S. Ct.
19. Spalding v. Chandler, 160 U.S. 394 (1896)	Executive Order, April 3, 1847	Reserving for military and other purposes lands included within treaty Indian reservation	Conflict with treaty	U.S. S. Ct.
20. Muir v. Louisville and Nashville R.R. Co., 247 F. 888 (1918)	Proclamation, December 26, 1917	Seizing all railroads in U.S. and appointing Secretary of Treasury as director general	Separation of powers theory and conflict with statute	U.S. D. Ct., W. Dist. of Ky.
21. In re Schuster, 182 N.Y.S. 357 (1920)	Executive Order, November 26, 1918	Permitting certain enemy aliens to apply for naturalization	Separation of powers theory and conflict with statute	State of N.Y., S. Ct. for Kings County
22. United States v. Western Union Tg. Co., 272 F. 311 (1921); aff'd 272 F. 893 (1921); 260 U.S. 754 (1922)	Orders to Secretary of Navy, and Revoking License for Cable in Foreign Commerce	Directing Secretary of Navy to prevent landing of oceanic cable on U.S. soil; offering conditional license	Separation of powers theory and conflict with statute	U.S. S. Ct. of Dist. Col., reversed by S. Ct. on consent of parties
23. U.S. Harness Co. v. Graham, 288 F. 929 (1921)	Unnumbered Executive Order, June 14, 1921	Declaring void a public contract between plaintiff and War Department	Amendment V, U.S. Constitution	U.S. D. Ct., Dist. of W. Va.
24. Hood Rubber Co. v. Davis, 151 N.E. 119 (1926)	Unnumbered Executive Orders, October 30 and November 5, 1919	Authorizing fuel administrator to control distribution and fix prices of coal	Conflict with statute	State of Mass., S. Ct.
25. Johnson v. Keating ex rel Tarantino, 17 F. 2d 50 (1926)	Executive Order No. 4125, January 12, 1925	Requiring visas on passports of immigrant aliens	Conflict with statute	U.S. 1 C.C.A.

APPENDIX A — continued

Title of Case	Presidential Order Declared Invalid	Function of Order	Basis of Decision	Court
26. United States ex rel. Swyston v. McCandless, 24 F. 2d 211 (1928); 33 F. 2d 882 (1929)	Proclamation and Executive Order, August 8, 1918	Directing that certain aliens be deported	Conflict with statute	U.S. D. Ct., E. Dist., of Pa.; 3 C.C.A.
27. United States v. Pan-American Petroleum Co., 55 F. 2d 753 (1932); 287 U.S. 612	Executive Order, May 31, 1921	Transferring statutory duties of Secretary of Navy to Secretary of Interior	Conflict with statute	U.S. 9 C.C.A., c.d. by S. Ct.
28. United States v. Campbell, 5 F. Supp. 156 (1933), and 291 U.S. 686 (1934)	Executive Order No. 6260 of August 28, 1933	Prohibiting the ownership or possession of gold bullion	Amendment V, U.S. Constitution	U.S. D. Ct., S.D. N.Y.; appeal dismissed by S. Ct.
29. United States v. Driscoll. 9 F. Supp. 454 (1935)	Executive Order No. 6260 of August 28, 1933	Prohibiting the ownership or possession of gold bullion	Amendment V, U.S. Constitution	U.S. D. Ct., Dist. of Mass.
30. Panama Refining Co. v. Ryan, 293 U.S. 388 (1935)	Executive Orders, July 11, 1933, and July 14, 1933	Prohibiting interstate transportation of oil in excess of state quotas; delegating authority to Secretary of Interior	Separation of powers theory and conflict with statute	U.S. S. Ct.
31. Zeiss v. United States, 23 C.C.P.A. (Customs) 7 (1935)	Presidential Proclamation No. 2020, December 14, 1932	Raising tariff duties on optical instruments suitable for use by the armed services	Conflict with statute	C.C.P.A.
32. Schechter v. United States, 295 U.S. 495 (1935)	Executive Order No. 6675-A, April 13. 1934	Approving N.R.A. Code for Live Poultry Industry, metropolitan New York area	Separation of powers theory and Art. I, s. 8 (3), U.S. Constitution	U.S. S. Ct.

APPENDIX A — continued

Title of Case	Presidential Order Declared Invalid	Function of Order	Basis of Decision	Court
33. Valentine v. United States ex rel Neidecker. 299 U.S. 5 (1936)	Preliminary Extradition Warrant Issued by U.S. Commissioner in New York City	To return to France U.S. citizens wanted as fugitives from French justice	Conflict with Constitution and treaty	U.S. S. Ct.
34. United States v. Ashley Bread Co., 59 F. Supp. 671 (1944)	Regulations Issued by War Food Administration	Prohibiting bakers from reclaiming unsold goods from retailers	Separation of powers theory and conflict with statute	U.S. D. Ct., Dist. of W. Va.
35. United States ex rel Von Heymann v. Watkins, 159 F. 2d 650 (1947)	Proclamation No. 2662, September 8, 1945	Implementing agreements for hemispheric defense, and ordering Secretary of State to deport dangerous interned enemy aliens	Conflict with statute	U.S. 2 C.C.A.
36. United States ex rel Hirshberg v. Cooke, 336 U.S. 210 (1949)	Navy Regulation, *Navy Courts and Boards*, Sec. 334	Extending court-martial jurisdiction beyond term of enlistment in which offense occurred	Conflict with statute	U.S. S. Ct.
37. Youngstown Sheet and Tube Co. v. Charles Sawyer, 343 U.S. 579 (1952)	Executive Order No. 10340, April 8, 1952 (17 Fed. Reg. 3139)	Authorizing and directing Secretary of Commerce to take possession of and operate the plants and facilities of certain steel companies	Separation of powers theory and conflict with statute	U.S. S. Ct.
38. Cole v. Young, 351 U.S. 536 (1956)	Executive Order No. 10450, April 27, 1953 (18 Fed. Reg. 2489)	Extending the provisions of the Security Act of August 26, 1950, to apply to all civilian employees of the national government	*Ultra vires* enabling statute	U.S. S. Ct.

365

APPENDIX B. DISTRIBUTION OF CASES IN APPENDIX A ACCORDING TO SUBJECT

Chapter	Subject	Number of Cases	
		All Courts	United States Supreme Court
2	Public Personnel	5	3
3	Public Domain	2	1
4	Foreign Relations	9	2
5	Executive Tariff	1	0
6	Military Rule	9	3
7	Fifth Column	3	2
8	Economic Regulation	9	3

APPENDIX C. DISTRIBUTION OF CASES IN APPENDIX A CHRONOLOGICALLY BY DECADES

Emergency*	Decade	Number of Cases	Emergency*	Decade	Number of Cases
	1791–1800	0	Civil War	1881–1890	2
War of 1812	1801–1810	2		1891–1900	1
War of 1812	1811–1820	4		1901–1910	0
	1821–1830	0	World War I	1911–1920	2
	1831–1840	0	World War I	1921–1930	5
	1841–1850	1	Depression	1931–1940	7
Mexican War	1851–1860	1	World War II	1941–1950	3
Civil War	1861–1870	7	Korean War	1950–1956	2
Civil War	1871–1880	1			

* "Emergency" refers to the time relevant to the events of the cases. Of these 38 cases, in only 7 were neither the law nor the facts, nor both, directly related to the existence of an emergency. These 7 non-emergency cases include: Lorimier v. Lewis, 39 Am.D. 461 (1843); Blake v. United States, 103 U.S. 227 (1881); Spalding v. Chandler, 160 U.S. 394 (1896); United States v. Western Union Tg. Co., 272 F. 311 (1921); United States v. Pan-American Petroleum Co., 55 F. 2d 753 (1932); Zeiss v. United States, 23 C.C.P.A. (Customs) 7 (1935); Valentine v. United States *ex rel* Neidecker, 299 U.S. 5 (1936).

Table of Cases

367

Table of Cases

Table of Cases

371

Table of Cases

THE PRESIDENCY IN THE COURTS

McIntosh v. United States, 2 F. Supp. 244 (E.D.Va., 1932); 70 F. 2d 507 (4 C.C.A., 1934); 293 U.S. 586 (1934), *277n44*

McKee v. United States, 8 Wall. 163 (1869), *221, 238n61*

MacLeod v. New England Telephone and Telegraph Co., 250 U.S. 195 (1919), *274n6*

MacLeod v. United States, 229 U.S. 416 (1913), *165n28*

McQuillon, *ex parte*, 16 Fed. Cas. 347 (S.D.N.Y., 1861), No. 8924, *323–324, 344n48*

Madsen v. Kinsella, 93 F. Supp. 319 (S.D.W.Va., 1950); 188 F. 2d 272 (4 C.A., 1951); 343 U.S. 341 (1952), *45, 63n98, 198–199, 201n37, 203n85, 203n86*

Mammoth Oil Co. v. United States, 275 U.S. 13 (1927), *42–43, 63n89, 342n15*

Marbury v. Madison, 1 Cranch 137 (1803), *8, 36–37, 40, 61n66, 147, 188, 202n58, 285, 297n12, 315, 320, 341n1, 342n22, 345n79, 357*

Mardis v. Hines, 267 F. 171 (8 C.C.A., 1920), *242, 274n3*

Maret, The, 145 F. 2d 431 (3 C.C.A, 1944), *102, 130n5*

Martin v. Mott, 12 Wheat. 19 (1827), *173, 176, 199n2*

Mary and Susan, The, 1 Wheat. 46 (1816), *313n34*

Mason v. United States, 260 U.S. 545 (1923), *80–81, 96n38, 97n61*

Mawhinney v. Millbrook Woolen Mills, 172 N.Y.S. 461 (1918); 231 N.Y. 290 (1921), *264–265, 279n76, 279n77, 279n79*

Mechanics & Traders' Bank v. Union Bank of New Orleans, 25 La.Ann. 387 (1873); 89 U.S. 276 (1875), *193, 203n70*

Merritt v. United States, 264 F. 870 (9 C.C.A., 1920), *331, 345n71*

Merryman, *ex parte*, 17 Fed. Cas. 144 (C.Ct.Md., 1861), No. 9487, *9n3, 185, 186, 201n49, 323, 344n47, 362*

Miller, *in re*, 281 F. 764 (2 C.C.A., 1922), *239n90*

Milligan, *ex parte*, 4 Wall. 2 (1866), *185, 188–189, 190, 201n47, 202n54, 202n61, 202n62, 212, 214, 228, 362*

Minotto v. Bradley, 252 F. 600 (N.D.Ill., 1918), *205, 234n5, 329, 344n63*

Mississippi v. Johnson, 71 U.S. 475 (1867), *320, 342n24*

Mississippi Valley Iron Co., *in re*, 58 F. Supp. 222 (E.D.Mo.E.D., 1944); 61 F. Supp. 347 (E.D.Mo.E.D., 1945), *257, 278n52, 325, 344n54, 346n87*

Missouri v. Holland, 252 U.S. 416 (1920), *83, 96n42, 103, 131n11, 235n17, 263–264, 279n75*

Missouri Pacific Railroad Company v. Ault, 256 U.S. 554 (1921), *243, 274n7*

Mitchell v. Flinkote Co., 185 F. 2d 1008 (2 C.A., 1951), *314n38*

Montgomery Ward & Co. v. N.W.L.B., 56 F. Supp. 502 (D.Ct.D.C., 1944), *246, 275n14*. *See also* National War Labor Board v. United States

Montgomery Ward & Co. v. United States, 326 U.S. 690 (1945), *247, 275n19*

Moore v. United States, 157 F. 2d 760 (1946); 330 U.S. 827 (1947), *98n71*

Morgan v. T.V.A., 115 F. 2d 990 (6 C.C.A., 1940), *10n14, 58n19*

Morgan v. United States, 298 U.S. 468 (1936); 304 U.S. 1 (1938), *65n118, 65n120, 153, 167n54, 169n81*

Morris v. Hitchcock, 194 U.S. 384 (1904), *63n105*

Moss & Co. v. United States, 26 C.C.P.A. (Customs) 381 (1939), *159–160, 161, 162, 168n72, 168n73, 168n74, 169n76, 169n77, 317, 341n12*

Muir v. Louisville and Nashville Railroad Co., 247 F. 888 (W.D.Ky., 1918), *273n1, 313n34, 363*

Mulhens & Kropf v. F. Mulhens, Inc., 38 F. 2d 287 (S.D.N.Y., 1929); 43 F. 2d 937 (2 C.C.A., 1930); 282 U.S. 881 (1930), *332, 345n73*

Mullan v. United States, 140 U.S. 240 (1891), *57n7, 179–180, 200n27*

Mullan v. United States, 212 U.S. 516 (1909), *179–180, 200n27*

Munich Reinsurance Co. v. First Reinsurance Co. of Hartford, 300 F. 345 (D.Conn., 1924); 6 F. 2d (2 C.C.A., 1925), *229, 239n92*

Myers v. United States, 272 U.S. 52 (1926), *19, 58n18, 106, 131n18, 286, 297n16*

National Airlines v. C.A.A., 24 United States Law Week 3192 (C.A.D.C., 1955); 350 U.S. 948 (1956), *134n50*

Table of Cases

375

Table of Cases

Table of Cases

379

THE PRESIDENCY IN THE COURTS

96n31, 96n32, 96n33, 96n35, 96n38, 96n39, 97n56, 97n61, 284, 286, 291, 297n4, 297n16, 300n40, 300n42

United States v. Mill and Mine Supply Co., 30 C.C.P.A. (Customs) 128 (1942), *164n10*

United States v. Minoru Yasui, 48 F. Supp. 40 (D.Ore., 1942), *214, 237n39, 286–287, 298n21. See also* Yasui v. United States.

United States v. Montgomery Ward & Co., 58 F. Supp. 408 (N.D.Ill.E.D., 1945); 150 F. 2d 369 (1945), *246–247, 275n17, 275n18, 298n22, 298n25. See also* Montgomery Ward & Co. v. United States

United States v. Moore, 62 F. Supp. 660 (W.D.Wash.S.D., 1945); 330 U.S. 827 (1947), *93, 97n60, 98n71*

United States v. Morrison, 240 U.S. 192 (1916), *80, 96n37*

United States v. Norton, 97 U.S. 164 (1878), *306–307, 312n16, 312n20*

United States v. One Hundred Barrels of Cement, 27 Fed. Cas. 292 (E.D.Mo., 1862), No. 15,945, *101, 130n1, 221, 238n58*

United States v. Page, 137 U.S. 673 (1891), *189–190, 200n27*

United States v. Pan-American Petroleum Co., 6 F. 2d 43 (S.D.Cal.N.D., 1925); 45 F. 2d 821 (S.D.Cal.C.D., 1930); 55 F. 2d 753 (1932); 287 U.S. 612 (1932), *40–42, 62n81, 62n82, 62n83, 62n84, 364, 366*

United States v. Paramount Publix Corp., 73 F. 2d 103 (C.C.P.A., 1934), *46, 63n101, 300n45*

United States v. Payne, 8 F. 883 (W.D.Ark., 1881), *303, 311n4*

United States v. Peach Mountain Coal Mining Co., 161 F. 2d 476 (2 C.C.A., 1947), *55, 65n121*

United States v. Pelican, 232 U.S. 442 (1914), *97n58, 299n39*

United States v. Pennsylvania Central Coal Co., 256 F. 703 (W.D.Pa., 1918), *297n3*

United States v. Perko, 108 F. Supp. 315 (D.Minn., 1952), *83–84, 97n47, 97n48. See also* Perko v. United States

United States v. Pewee Coal Co., 341 U.S. 114 (1951), *275n22*

United States v. Pink, Superintendent of Insurance of the State of New York, 315 U.S. 203 (1942), *104–105, 106, 107, 131n13, 314n38, 322, 343n43*

United States v. Porter, 27 Fed. Cas. 599 (C.Ct.D.C., 1861), No. 16,074a, *324, 344n49*

United States v. Powers, 274 F. 131 (W.D.Mich.S.D., 1921), *260, 278n61, 288, 298n28*

United States v. Query, 37 F. Supp. 972 (E.D.S.C., 1941), *299n39, 314n38, 316, 341n9*

United States v. Reiter, 27 Fed. Cas. 768 (1865), No. 16,146, *193, 203n70, 297n3*

United States v. Rodiek, 117 F. 2d 588 (2 C.C.A., 1941); 315 U.S. 783 (1942), *338, 339, 346n83, 346n84*

United States v. Rosenberg, 47 F. Supp. 406 (E.D.N.Y., 1942); 150 F. 2d 788 (1945), *224–225, 238n77*

United States v. Rumely, 345 U.S. 41 (1953), *322, 343n33*

United States v. S. Leon & Co., 20 C.C.P.A. (Customs) 49 (1932); 287 U.S. 628 (1932), *148, 149–150, 166n34, 167n45*

United States v. San Geronimo Development Co., 154 F. 2d 78 (1946); 329 U.S. 718 (1946), *71–72, 95n15*

United States v. Schmidt (Schmidt I), 291 F. 382 (E.D.Mich.S.D., 1923), *260, 278n62*

United States v. Schmidt (Schmidt II), 2 F. 2d 290 (E.D.Mich.S.D., 1924), *260, 278n61*

United States v. Sears, Roebuck & Co., 20 C.C.P.A. (Customs) 295 (1932), *157, 168n67, 346n86. See also* Sears, Roebuck & Co. v. United States

United States v. Silliman, 65 F. Supp. 665 (D.N.J., 1946), *338, 339–340, 346n83, 346n86*

United States v. Smith, 27 Fed. Cas. 1192 (C.Ct.N.Y., 1806), No. 16,342, *292–293, 300n48*

United States v. Smith (Smith I), 285 F. 751 (D.Mass., 1922), *260, 278n61*

United States v. Smith (Smith II), 32 F. 2d 901 (D.Mass., 1929); 39 F. 2d 851 (1 C.C.A., 1930), *10n9, 260, 261, 278n62, 279n66, 290, 291, 299n37, 300n43*

United States v. Sonnenschein, 1 C.M.R. 64 (1951), *201n40*

United States v. Standard Brewery, 251 U.S. 210 (1920), *263, 279n73*

380

Table of Cases

Table of Cases

Subject Guide

Congressional power of administrative direction, in general, *see* Presidential powers—
"Faithful execution"; Separation of powers—Conflict between the constitutional powers of the President and Congress
—Delegation of power by Congress to the President: in general, 6–7, 353; in the loyalty-
security program, 29–30; by acquiescence, 77–79, 150; to regulate foreign commerce,
112, 116, 224, 225, 351; in tariff legislation, 137; of "judicial" power, 155; to raise
armies, 173, 176, 177–178; to suspend the writ of habeas corpus in the Civil War,
202n56; to control enemy aliens, 204–205; by treaty, 263, 333; held unconstitutional
by the Supreme Court, 267, 276n32; in wartime, 270–271, 278n59; effect of fusion with
constitutional delegation to the President, 290; retroactive delegation, 290–292; to
repeal statutes, 295; mentioned, 66, 233
—Effect of formal presidential statement of compliance with statutory standards: in general, 331–335, 354; held conclusive, 112, 148, 269–270, 345n76; held inconclusive, 149;
implications for judicial review, 267; held unnecessary because compliance must be
presumed, 317–318. *See also* Judicial review: Presumption that the President acts
legally
—*Ultra vires* presidential action: in general, 8; President Eisenhower's Security Order,
32, 334–335, 357n3; President Harding and Teapot Dome, 40–42; executive order Indian reservation, 86–87; under a treaty, 86, 123–124; in licensing of domestic corporation in foreign commerce, 114; in regulating immigration, 125; President Madison's
embargo proclamation, 132n26; flexible tariff proclamation, 157–158; in extension of
military jurisdiction over former servicemen, 181; President Lincoln's imposition of
martial law in the North, 189; President John Adams' instructions to the United
States Navy, 225–226; President Lincoln's order to seize the estate of Robert E. Lee,
227–228; presidential seizure orders, 246, 249–251; postwar price-fixing of coal, 252;
World War II rationing order, 268–269; World War I nationalization of railroads,
273n1; compared with judicial review of acts of Congress, 355, 358n8
Constitutional rights
—Of aliens: upheld in emigration case, 126–127; denied in exclusion proceedings, 129–
130, 136n89, 235n19; enemy aliens subject to jurisdiction of the President rather than
the courts, 189–191, 197, 209–210, 349; denied to enemy aliens, 206–207, 208, 214, 349
—Of American citizens in wartime, 211–220, 240n107, 287, 349, 358n10. *See also* Presidential powers—Suspension of the writ of habeas corpus
—Of American Indians, 84–85, 91, 97n51

Subject Guide

—Of civil servants, 23–24, 356, 357n3
—Of civilians accompanying the armed forces, 198–199, 201n37
—Of entrepreneurs: and executive order airspace reservation, 84; and summary enforcement of neutrality law, 111; and the executive power of eminent domain, 251; and President Truman's steel seizure order, 251; and President Franklin Roosevelt's gold seizure orders, 255–256; and the wool clip of *1918*, 260–261; of government contractors, 266; sacrifices necessary in wartime, 273, 298n22, 316, 358n10; sacrifices of personal rights necessary to preserve property rights, 287
—Of military personnel, 18, 176–179
Federalism and the supremacy of presidential legislation over state law: the Litvinov Assignment, 103–105; the *Curtiss-Wright* opinion, 113; suspension of the writ of habeas corpus, 202n56; in state courts, 223, 231; intrastate utility rates in wartime, 242–243; wartime liquor control, 271; as a political question, 323
Judicial decisions, *obiter dicta* in opinions: in general, 8; John Marshall's "obiter dissertation," 8, 36; treated by Supreme Court as controlling precedent, 104; on constitutional power of the President to acquire national territory, 119; on inherent presidential power to exclude aliens, 123; on immigration regulation, 135n76; on statutory delegation of legislative power to the President, 138–139; on military tariffs, 141; on presidential reliance on non-record information in flexible tariff making, 150; on military power over enemy aliens, 214; on presidential licensing of contraband, 221; on presidential power to declare national emergency, 341
—Precedent value of: lower court decisions in the absence of Supreme Court decisions, 8–9; state court decisions, 69–70; Supreme Court decisions, 80, 106, 118, 157, 169n77, 194, 242–243, 251; foreign relations and war power cases considered controlling for domestic peacetime questions, 81; *Luther v. Borden* and Lincoln's theory of presidential dictatorship, 174; cases involving enemy spies and enemy aliens considered controlling for constitutional rights of American citizens, 178, 189, 198, 218–220; peacetime customs cases the basis for judicial approval of selective draft legislation, 177, 199n17; the *Milligan* case, 190, 214; *Jecker v. Montgomery*, 192; disregard of Supreme Court decisions by lower courts, 212, 252, 271, 311n6, 312n20, 344n52; domestic peacetime cases considered controlling for foreign relations and wartime questions, 224, 248, 270–271, 289, 353; the *Lee* case, 228; disregard of own precedents by Supreme Court, 250, 307; the *Schechter* and *Hot Oil* cases, 267, 273; cases unsympathetic to presidential power subsequently overruled, 284; the *Steel Seizure* case, 286, 357n5
—Significance of lower court decisions: in relation to Supreme Court decisions, 8–9, 179, 286–287, 317, 343n40, 354–355; specialization in loyalty cases of District of Columbia courts, 23; territorial court, 95n18; administrative (i.e., legislative) court review as an alternative to review by "Article III" courts, 117; policy making by administrative (legislative) courts, 156–163 *passim*; in Civil War draft cases, 187; in regulation of wool clip of *1918*, 260
Judicial enforcement of presidential decisions, *ultra vires* administrative orders: in general, 348; the Attorney General's list of subversive organizations, 26–27; the Loyalty Review Board's order "mandating" removals, 28–29; the Loyalty Review Board's post-audit procedure, 29–30; orders excluding American citizens from "military areas," 212
—Removal power of the President as an alternative to judicial review, 309
Judicial review: in general, 354; basis for, 8, 10n10, 322; duty of courts to uphold presidential action, 209–210, 315–316; congressional frustration of, 292
—Effect of executive construction of presidential powers: in general, 316–317; disregarded by the Supreme Court, 122; in determining constitutionality of legislation, 177, 209; as authoritative interpretation of the Constitution, 193, 209, 287–288; as a binding precedent for future presidential action under a statute, 236n22; in the *Steel Seizure* case, 249, 250, 289
—Effectiveness of: in general, 9, 33–34, 347, 355–356; in time of national crisis, 4; in preventing the delegation of "legislative power," 6–7; in the face of presidential defiance.

Subject Guide

War II, 271–273, 350–351; nullification of land patent, 337; and gratuities to veterans, 338

—Pardoning power, 227, 293–294, 300n49

—Price fixing (rate making), 242, 251–252, 258–263, 269, 350

—Removal power: in general, 13, 352; over military officers, 14–18; in relationship to appointment power, 17, 19, 24, 39; over civil political appointees, 19, 58n19; over civil servants, 19, 58n20

—Reservation of public lands: in aid of proposed legislation, 73–81, 86–87; in aid of proposed treaty, 91

—"Rule making" power: in general, 34–36, 61n58; the modern doctrine, 54; in the regulation of immigration, 124; in tariff making, 137–138; in the Civil War draft, 176; procedural rules of military law, 183; and establishment of a system of government for occupied territories, 193

—Seizure of private property: in general, 350; of enemies, 227, 229, 232, 297n1; under court jurisdiction, 229, 233, 256–257, 325, 340; temporary seizure of property of citizens, 241–251, 275n22; in the *Steel Seizure* case, 248–251; the executive power of eminent domain, 251–257, 278n55, 340–341; compared to summary power over persons, 356; mentioned, 52

—Summary detention in protective custody: life internment sanctioned by the Supreme Court, 136n89, 235n19; of enemy aliens, 205, 208, 209–211, 349; internment of federal judges threatened, 323, 324; compared to summary power over property, 356

—Suspension of the writ of habeas corpus: by Lincoln during the Civil War, 185–189, 202n56, 202n57; for German saboteurs in World War II, 190; for "war criminals" in World War II, 195, 200n33; and the Japanese-Americans in World War II, 219; to frustrate judicial review, 323, 324

—War power: in general, 348–349; and enemy aliens, 56, 190–191, 202n65, 205, 208, 209–210; and the military tariff, 141, 144; and the *Steel Seizure* case, 172, 251, 289; and Dorr's Rebellion, 174; in the early months of the Civil War, 174–175; military jurisdiction over former servicemen, 181–182; and military jurisdiction over civilians, 186–189, 197–199, 211–220; and prize courts in the Mexican War, 191–192; and the provisional court in Louisiana during the Civil War, 192–193; and war crimes tribunals, 196–197; extension beyond the period of hostilities, 208–209, 252, 257–258, 275n23, 288, 299n31, 350; and the theory of constitutional dictatorship, 220–221, 244, 275n17, 284–285, 287–288, 298n19, 298n25; during war *de facto*, 220–222, 237n56, 257–258, 288, 289; as basis for peacetime economic regulation, 254, 257, 266; as basis for wartime economic regulation, 270, 271, 273, 278n55, 350–351; as a political question, 286–287, 322, 323; assumption of before declaration of war, 299n30; relied upon to frustrate judicial review, 323–325

Separation of functions: the internal or external effect of presidential decisions, 35–36; discretionary and ministerial, 37, 39, 320

—Judicial and administrative: and presidential removal of military personnel, 14, 17–18, 57n8; and loyalty hearings, 23; and the naturalization of enemy aliens, 53–54; and the validity of patents, 153, 167n55

—Judicial and legislative: and the regulation of the merchant marine, 47; and intermediate orders, 48; and presidential subdelegation, 51; and the naturalization of enemy aliens, 53–54; and congressional action, 65n118; in the regulation of immigration, 124; in flexible tariff making, 162; and the *Hot Oil* case, 267

Separation of powers, in general: inferred from the Constitution of the United States, 3; defined, 9n1; and implied presidential powers, 249–250, 286; and prospective legislative ratification, 277n45; and overlap in presidential and congressional power, 294–295, 296; and judicial legislation, 300n44; and executive "law," 309; and overlap in presidential and judicial power, 315, 320, 322, 326, 327

—Conflict between the constitutional powers of the President and the Congress: in general, 284, 292–297, 353, 357; and the removal power, 13, 58n20, 59n23; and the loyalty-security program, 31–33; and withdrawal of public lands from entry, 78–80; conflict between executive agreements and statutes, 105, 107; in raising armies, 179;

Subject Guide

Secretary of the Treasury, 277n45; effect of on judicial review, 322, 357; field agents of the F.B.I., 330; mentioned, 268

—Sub-subdelegation, 55–56, 252, 268, 318, 357

Supreme Court, and public policy making: in general, 347, 357n1; in the *School Segregation* cases, 9n2; the *School Segregation* decision compared with the *Steel Seizure* decision, 33; in the *Midwest Oil* case, 80; in the *Curtiss-Wright* case, 112–113; judicial politics in the *Insular Cases*, 143, 165n21; private law premises for the solution of public law questions, 166n30; and statutory separability, 237n42; in the *Steel Seizure* case, 250, 356; in the *Schechter* and *Hot Oil* cases, 267; the *Steel Seizure* case compared with *Cole v. Young*, 357n6

—And avoidance of conflict with the President: the loyalty-security program, 28, 357n6; procedural tools of convenience, 39–40; in the Teapot Dome scandal, 42–43; in wartime, 44, 177, 179, 188, 189, 271; during consideration of the Bricker Amendment, 107; in the Japanese-American cases, 214–219, 237n42; in World War II emergency regulation of the economy, 280n90, 340–341; "construction" of executive order to avoid constitutional question, 315–316

—And political review of Supreme Court decisions: in the tidelands oil controversy, 121; in the case of Ellen Knauff, 130; and the executive tariff in the Philippines, 144–145

DATE DUE